To Professor Bruce Cumings

with best wishes,

sincerely,

Harold Demos

1994. 11

20th Century Korea

N·A·N·A·M·Communications
나·남·커·뮤·니·케·이·션·스

20th Century Korea

By Harold Hakwon Sunoo, Ph. D.

Distinguished Professor-Emeritus
Central Methodist College

NANAM Publishing House

Seoul, Korea
1994

20TH CENTURY KOREA

NANAM Publishing House
1625-11, Suhchodong, Suhchogu, 137-070
Seoul, Korea

NANAM International Publications
1817 Highridge Dr.
Columbia, MO. 65203
U.S.A

Printed in the Republic of Korea.
ISBN 89-300-6015-3

About the Author

Harold Hakwon Sunoo, a native of Korea, is professor emeritus of Political Science and History at Central Methodist College,Fayette, Missouri. He received his education in Korea, Japan, the United States, and Europe, with a Ph.D. from King Charles University, Prague. He was Visiting Professor at the City University of New York, Charles University, and also taught at University of California, Berkeley; Washington, Seattle; Yonsei, Seoul. He published seventeen books in English, French, Japanese as well as in Korean. Currently he is actively involved in peace movement and Korean unification movement. Married to Sonia, an ethnic researcher, have two grown sons and four grandchildren in California.

PREFACE

This book is a compilation of selected chapters from previously published works at different periods during my teaching career except the last two chapters on North Korea. Chapter 1 to 7 was originally published under the title of: *A Political History of Modern Korea*, by Kunkook University Press in Seoul; Chapter 8 to 13 is from *America's Dilemma in Asia: The Case of South Korea*, Nelson-Hall Publishing Company of Chicago; Chapters 14 to 17 is from *South Korean Economy*, published by Heritage Research House of Virginia Beach; Chapter 20 is from *Peace and Unification of North and South Korea*, published by One Korea Movement, USA.

As the 20th century enters its final years, it calls out increasingly for careful review and new interpretation of the history of Korea. By the beginning of the century, Korea was already a victim of modern imperialism. She became the first colony of Japanese imperialism, then, the country had been divided into North and South by the United States and the Soviet Union at the end of the World War II.

As a result of a century long domination by the foreign powers, the Korean people has suffered immensely. The people's struggle against foreign domination became a natural way of life during the century. The people struggled not only for political democracy, but economic democracy as well. Today, regardless of the fact that we have the technology to create a better world in which no one will lack food, clothing and shelter, millions still live in poverty and are mercilessly exploited by the powerful wealthy few including foreign investors in South Korea.

I perceive that history is not just the story of rulers and elites, but common people including farmers, workers, teachers, and students who have led the struggle against the corrupted military regimes in the country. The book is dedicated to those courageous patriotic young students in South Korea.

This volume is the result of suggestions and inspirations following class discussions with U.C.L.A.'s Korean-American students in "US-Korea Relations." Credit is due to those students.

CONTENTS

....

INTRODUCTION

Nationalism has become the most powerful factor in world politics today, particularly among the underdeveloped nations. There has been no parallel to this amazing political-social phenomenon that has influenced the entire world within such a short span of time--two centuries. Nationalism has brought many paradoxical consequences: order and revolution, unity and disunity, and loyalty and enmity to name a few. The ideology of nationalism has affected all of mankind.

Korea is no exception. Nationalism, in Korea however, is not monolithic ideology. It possesses a polycentric character like any other ideology. This however does not deny the universal characteristic components of nationalism its historical roots. It is suggested here that the multitudes of nationalism be observed and studied with caution for the concept has different shades of meaning to people in different parts and periods of the world. Nationalism to Europeans, for example, was to strive to unite all peoples who spoke a common language and who shared like historical and cultural backgrounds. But nationalism for Asians and Africans today involves creating a state independent of foreign domination. These are two very different situations. Because such different attitudes on nationalism exist between Europeans and Asians, the meaning of freedom is also interpreted in different ways. Freedom for the Europeans and the Americans is individual self-sufficiency; free man means free citizenship. Freedom for the Europeans and the Americans is individual and personal for them. Freedom for the Asians, on the other hand, is an independence which is not subject to foreign domination either directly or indirectly. Freedom is social and national for them.

Because of this unique concept of nationalism, it has become a successful political instrument in many underdeveloped nations in spite of many different languages and cultural backgrounds. Nationalism in the underdeveloped countries is not a movement to unite all people speaking a particular language as it has been in Europe. Although there are thirty spoken languages in Indonesia, there is no apparent movement to adopt a single language. What is desired is a single independent government free from alien influence.

Korean nationalism developed under unique circumstances. The idea of nationalism had its genesis among a small group of aristocratic intellectuals who had a chance to observe the development of Japan. It is understandable that the young pioneers wanting to modernize Korea in the manner witnessed in Japan tried to influence the court. They were soon confronted with the old guard, however whose interest was to preserve its cultural tide with the declining Manchu Empire. The young pioneers then became displaced persons in their own society due to conflict with the old establishment. The growth of nationalism suffered in its infant stage as the old guard continued to dominate the government in Korea. While the old guard still dominated the Korean government, and refused to modify its stubborn feudalistic attitude, a change took place on the Far Eastern scene.

At a time when the whole advanced world seemed to be moving toward liberalism and democracy, Japan as the most advanced nation in Asia, had crushed liberal opposition at home and began her expansion program, starting with Korea, and ending with the Pacific War. Japanese imperialism was a product of malignant nationalism which patterned itself after Bismarck's Prussian nationalism. It contained racism, militarism, wars, and the rest of the characteristics of Bismarck's and other European and American imperialism of the nineteenth century. The convenient phrase of Rudyard Kipling's ''white man's burden'' of ruling and civilizing backward peoples was adequate enough for the Japanese to adopt such slogans as ''Asia for the Asians'' and ''Asian co-prosperity'' and ''Asians, unite!'' All these slogans were as convenient as Hitler's Aryan myth or Nietsche's superman theory.

A liberal attitude of nationalism changed to an imperialistic nationalism after 1871 when every nation in Europe except Great Britain undertook to copy the German military system, including universal conscription. Anxious to modernize her nation, the leaders of Meiji government in Tokyo, too, copied the German military system. Generals and admirals became national heros just as the members of the Samurai class had been in the past. The were popular and influential, and Japan became a modernized armed camp. The Japanese Empire was to be built by these military leaders who inherited the spirit of the ancient Samurai with new technical knowledge and discipline which they learned from the Europeans. The combination of the ''blood and iron'' methods of Bismarck and the discipline and tradition of the Samurai were more than sufficient to build a military autocracy on the island empire.

The victorious results of both the Sino-Japanese War (1894-5) and the Russo-Japanese War (1904-5) established Japan as a world power. The British support of Japan during the Russo-Japanese War through the Anglo-Japanese Alliance, and the United States' tacit recognition of Japanese supremacy in Korea through the secret agreement of Taft-Katsura, gave Japan free rein in that country.

Making Japan a world power was a convenient way to check Russian aggression in the Far East. The British Empire wanted to set up a "balance of-power system" in Asia just as it had done in Europe, but, a balance of power system requires flexibility and balancing. The Japanese Empire was neither flexible nor balanced as future events were to show.

The European and American powers left Japan a free hand when she annexed Korea. It was the very first step of her continental expansion program in Asia. The imperialistic world powers justified the Japanese aggression. This was an age of imperialism. Justification of imperialism is one thing, but this justification does not weigh well with those being oppressed. Without realizing the futility of their protests in light of the Western powers' silent nod to the imperialistic policy of Japan, the Korean people raised their voices against the Japanese aggression from it's inception in "the land of the morning calm."

In this important era of the nation, many responsible government officials became corrupt while holding strategic positions in the government. Instead of helping, foreign powers took advantage of her and patriots such as So Jai-pil, and Yun Chi-ho were condemned as national traitors. Thus, any real progressive movement was brought to a stop for a long time.

After the government had become weak and inefficient due to the corruption of high ranking officials, the door swung wide open for foreign powers to move in. Had such foreign powers not intervened in Korea's internal affairs, Korea might well have taken her own measures in setting aright her chaotic condition and might have been able to participate much earlier in the world community, without having to suffer through the bitter experiences of subjugation. This would, however, not have been a natural course of history under world conditions at that time.

Since 1864, the experiences of Korea with outsiders had not been happy ones. Hence, the Koreans felt that the best way of keeping out of trouble was not to associate with outsiders. However, Korea's desire to hold to an isolation policy was not applicable when the Western powers knocked at her door.

The time came for transfer from an old age to a new, and to bring renewed life to a nation waiting for a change. Korea was to change from a feudalistic system to a modern industrialized society; from an old Confucian tradition to a new enlightened civilization introduced by Christian missionaries. Most significant in modern Korean history was a period of great activity of popular movements against the ultra-conservative groups. The outstanding movements were the Progressive Movement of 1884, the Tonghak Rebellion of 1886, and the Independent Club Movement under the leadership of So Jai-pil and Yun Chin-ho in 1894.

It was also a time of many patriotic movements. The "Righteous Soldiers' Movement" of 1905 is one good example. These patriotic movements and the progressive reform movements, failed to attract the masses, and remained rather feudalistic and aristocratic in nature rather than nationalistic. However this did not hold true for the leaders themselves. If we consider nationalism as a nation-wide awakening and a dominant factor which influences a popular movement in a nation-state, there is difficulty finding genuine nationalism in Korea even at the time of the annexation in 1910. Korean nationalism first emerged in 1919, nine years after the annexation by Japan, as a product of national self-recognition as well as a rebuke of imperialistic exploitation. The imperialistic exploitation was not a cardinal factor, but it helped to enhance national self-recognition. The cardinal factor was found within the people themselves.

The story of Korea is a story of freedom. It is a story of a small nation of people resolutely and courageously fighting for independence. Korea is especially significant as a lucid example where today the two major ideologies of democracy and communism are engaged in such an intense duel for life among a common people. Its outcome will be significant to many millions in Asia where the major battle of ideology is in process.

The development of nationalism has become an important integrated part of modern Korean history which may be traced in the historical events of Korea's relationship with foreign powers and the people's reactions against Japanese imperialism and other foreign domination.

How long can the dictatorial regimes suppress the people's aspiration to build a democratic society? How long will the U.S. government support such dictatorial regimes against the will of the American people? Why are the economists of South Korea concerned about the present economic dilemma? (The Dong-A Daily, January 16,1987) Can the Chun Doo-Hwan regime solve the existing socio-economic dilemma? Such historical perspectives help explain South Korea's student demonstrations. These are some of the serious questions that are dealt with in this book.

The fundamental problem of the present political dilemma in South Korea has to do with her export-oriented economic system which is completely dependent upon foreign countries, particularly Japan and the United States. More than 52% of the total trade is with Japan and the United States. She is a highly dependent state with respect to both raw materials, including fuel for industry, and modern technology. Matters are further complicated by the constant economic strain in the Korean-Japanese relations.

The economic modernization plan began in 1962, and achieved an average annual growth rate of 9% by 1979. In the 1980s, under the Chun Doo-

Hwan regime, however, she registered a minus growth rate, and is trying to overcome the hardship. As a whole, the growth is a remarkable achievement. Nonetheless, as an export-oriented economy, South Korea is totally dependent on others for her raw materials, plants, machinery, technology, and capital. Such an economic system constantly faces difficulty especially in the wake of the international oil crisis in 1973.

South Korea as an export-oriented nation faced the urgent task of developing advanced technology-intensive industries while continuing its efforts to upgrade her present products. In order to upgrade her present products and develop high-tech intensive industries, e.g., heavy and chemical industries, she borrowed more capital from foreign countries, now amounting to about $52.7 billion including $6 billion in loans by Korean businessmen abroad, according to the Ministry of Economic Planning in Seoul.

How great is $52.7 billion in terms of the South Korean economy? It is about 50% of the annual GNP, and three times that of the 1986 national budget of the Republic of Korea. Foreign debts doubled during the six years of President Chun's administration. Furthermore, foreign debts have been increasing not only in the amount, but at the same time unfavorable short-term loans have increased. During the 1970s, short-term loans were about 10% of the total foreign loans, but they have now increased to about 36% at the present time.

Why are we concerned about the increasing amount of the foreign debts? Can South Korea's economy pay back the loans? Is there any danger of an economic bankruptcy there?

The main purpose of borrowing foreign capital in developing countries is to develop new industries, expand existing industrial facilities, and to try to modernize in general. How about the situation in South Korea? Ever since 1982, she has spent 95.2% of the foreign loans to pay back the existing loans, and only 4.8% has been invested for production purposes. Under the circumstances, the government proposed to: 1. increase national capital through a saving program; 2. encourage direct foreign investments; 3. increase exports. These are the present government programs to solve the urgent problems of the foreign debts. In response to the government promotion for direct foreign investments in South Korea, Japan increased hers to $21.6 billion by 1986. At the present time, about 14% of the total investments in the country is considered Korean investments as against 86% of foreign investments. In view of the present policy, even 14% will shrink in due time.

It is evident that South Korea must earn foreign currencies in order to pay back her $ 52.7 billion foreign debt. One way to earn foreign currencies is to maintain a favorable trade balance. The nation's trade system, however, is not structured to favor her trade balance.

International trade is the life line of her economy since 70% of the GNP depends on it. The total economy has developed with a concept of an export-oriented economy. About 80% of her industries concentrates on the manufacture of goods for export, and 60% of her energy is spent for this purpose. Only 6% of total bank loans is for agricultural development; the rest of the commercial loans is for export purposes. Above all, about three-fourths of these export-oriented economic activities are dominated by foreign enterprises.

What has resulted after 25 years of the export-oriented economy in South Korea? First of all, South Korea's unusual trade relationship with Japan is the heart of the present dilemma in South Korea. Her economy cannot survive without Japan's support. More trade with Japan, more trade deficits against South Korea, yet more than half of Korea's trade is with Japan.

As a matter of fact, Japanese companies are moving into South Korea to take advantage of the Korean government's promotion, and at the same time, export to the United States with "made in Korea" labels in order to avoid the American protests. For instance, the automobile and electronics industries are already moving into South Korea to manufacture these goods to export to the world market. The engine and other important components of "Hyundai" automobiles, which are produced and exported to the United States, are made by Japanese Mitsubishi which also manufactures "Nissan" automobiles. *(The Dong-A Daily News,* January 17, 1987)

Today, South Korea imports about $ 8 billion worth of goods, raw materials, and semi-manufactured commodities from Japan each year, and the trade deficit amounted to $ 4.5 billion in 1986 alone against South Korea. The situation is getting worse each year.

Can South Korea rectify such an unfavorable trade relationship with Japan? It is unlikely that it can happen in the near future because most of the Korean plants, machinery and their parts are imported from Japan. Furthermore, Japan has also been supplying her technology to South Korea. Unfortunately, however, those technologies from Japan are not advanced technologies, but ten or twenty years behind the times. Under such conditions, South Korea will never be able to compete with Japanese goods in the world market, especially since more than one hundred items of advanced technologies in Japan may not be exported to South Korea. Also consider the price differences.

For instance, it costs $370.00 per metric ton of steel at Pohang Steel Company in South Korea while Japan produces it at $290.00 per M.T. How can Pohang Steel compete with Japanese steel in the market?

During the year of 1986, there were about two thousand student demonstrations against the Chun Doo-Hwan regime, and approximately five million police were mobilized to suppress them according to the official announcement. Among the demonstrations, the October Sit-ins at Kunkook University in Seoul were the most serious. Ten thousand police aided by the army was mobilized to control the situation.

These episodes have exposed a tendency that has long been at work in the Chun Doo-Hwan regime: iron-handed control of any anti-regime movements which endanger the military dictatorship. In this climate it has become traditional to ignore not only existing democratic voices but also the rules and regulations the regimes made themselves. They have made a mockery of the public political system, negated legislative participation in national policy-making deliberations and modern political institutions. As a result the Chun regime has created the worse political situation since the liberation of Korea in 1945.

To commemorate the sixth anniversary of the Kwangju Uprising and to mourn the death of Lee Dong-Su, the student who committed self-immolation in protest against the military dictatorship of South Korea, more than 3,000 students of Seoul National University on May 22, 1986 gathered on the campus grounds, according to an Associated Press report from Seoul. AP also reported the news with a sensational picture of Lee jumping in flames from the fourth floor of a university building.

After the rally, the students had a sit-in, chanting "Down with the Military Dictatorship; Down with U.S. and Japanese Imperialism; Withdrawal of the U.S. Forces," etc. On the same day, more than 8,000 students from 21 universities and colleges across South Korea staged demonstrations, shouting anti-Chun regime and anti-U.S. government's Korea policy. Meantime, 40 male and female students occupied the U.S. Information and Cultural Center in Pusan. They barricaded themselves inside the library on the first floor and held a sit-in strike shouting "Let's Remember the Kwangju Uprising; Down with the Military Dictatorship. "

On May 20,1986, 8,000 students from 27 universities and colleges held demonstrations throughout the country according to the *Dong-A Daily News,* May 22, 1986. The police report also stated that Rev. Moon Ik-Hwan lectured to an audience of 2,000 Seoul National University students on the subject of "A Historical Meaning of the Kwangju Uprising." The lecture was interrupted by the incident of Lee Dong-Su's suicide at the scene.

Why do young college students like Lee Dong-Su, Kim Se-Jin, and others pour gasoline over their bodies and burn themselves in protest? So many students have volunteered to sacrifice their bodies in protest, that there is a "waiting list" of 49 students according to the *Dong-A Daily News,* May

27,1986.

Anti-Chun regime and anti-American slogans have increased steadily since the Kwangju Uprising in May 1980. The students are convinced that the U.S. is guilty of involvement in the Kwangju Uprising in which no less than 2,000 citizens were killed. When the 73 college students occupied the U.S. Information and Cultural Center in Seoul on May 25,1985 and demanded that the U.S. officials apologize for the Kwangju Incident, the U.S. official refused. More than 2,000 Catholics and students, including the family members of the victims, held memorial services for the victims in the uprising on May 16, 1986 at a Roman Catholic Cathedral in Kwangju. Following the service, the crowd started a demonstration and their numbers immediately increased to more than 5,000. They shouted "Down with Chun Doo-Hwan; the U.S. must apologize"; similar demonstrations took place across the country. Rallies, demonstrations, and sit-ins were held by thousands of students at 17 universities and colleges on May 1, and at 24 institutions on May 2, 33 universities and colleges with 10,000 students participating on May 14,1986. The signature campaign for constitutional amendments, which started in February 1985, has expanded rapidly throughout the country with mass meetings of hundreds of thousands in Pusan, Kwangju, Taegu, Taejon, Chongju, Inchun, and Masan. Most recently, *The New York Times* reported that the meeting at Inchun on May 3,1986 was the most vocal one. The official spokesman of the ruling party declared that the Inchun Incident was instigated by communist-oriented students and workers. There were more than 5,000 participants at the May 3rd Inchun demonstrations according to media reports. Were they inspired by the communist oriented students? Is Communism the cause of the unrest in South Korea?

The New York Times reported on January 21,1987 that South Korean police had tortured to death a student, Park Chong-Chul. The incident is "the tip of iceberg" of widespread, institutionalized torture of political offenders.

This book stresses economic development, because South Korea has been widely claimed to be a model "economic miracle" in the Third World. How true is it? Did the export oriented economy succeed in South Korea? What are the results? Who benefits by such a system?

Today, top ten financial groups (Jaebul) own and control 43% of the national assets, and fifty financial groups 80.5%. All these Korean financial groups are closely associated with the foreign financial groups.

There is a very close correlation between the present social upheavals and the export-oriented economy in South Korea. I will attempt to analyze these relationships in the volume.

What are the results of all these phenomena for the economy of South

Korea? First, the city capitalists, who are under the influence of foreign capitalists, became the makers of national policies. All 50 or more Korean top corporations borrowed money from Japan and are dominated by the Japanese money. Consequently, the National economic policy favors Japanese investments in Korea. For instance, "Masan Free Export Zone" became, in effect, a Japanese "colony." Not only do the Japanese businessmen pay no tax to the Korean government, but they receive discount rates on electricity and water, their land can be purchased in lots, and abundant labor whose wages are no more than one-fifth of the Japanese wages are guaranteed by the Korean government. According to careful observers, industrial development like the "Masan Free Export Zone" benefits no Korean at all. Second, the policy makers have completely neglected the agricultural economy. The Korean government has not invested sufficiently in land improvement, crop rotation, the expansion of the farm markets, improved transportation of farm products, the use of scientific and technological implements, introduction of adequate farm machinery, and financial aids to the farmers. In other words, its agricultural development did not balance the industrial development. As a result, the consumer powers of the majority population remain unchanged at the lowest level and the industrial commodities seek markets abroad, bypassing their potential customers at home. In markets abroad, the commodities have been dumped at tremendous loss in order to meet the quota demanded by the government. As a result of such national economic policy, there is a shortage of food and ever increasing trade deficits. To meet the crisis, the Korean government increases foreign debts. The balance-of-payment deficit averaged one billion dollars per year or 12.8% of the average GNP since 1968.

More specially, the irresponsibilities of the decision makers and the support of the foreign powers resulted in several serious socio-economic conditions. First of all, the South Korean economy is completely dominated by foreign capital. There is not one Korean company which is free from foreign domination. All the major Korean firms were built either with foreign loans or joint investments with foreign capitalists. Therefore, the growth of Korean industries depends totally on foreign capital. There has been no opportunity for normal capitalistic competitive growth in the Korean economy in contrast to advanced capitalistic societies.

Secondly, the marriage between the dictatorial Park regime and the growing monopolists in South Korea is unique. The government has absolute power to make or break any firm or company at any time it chooses to do so. Companies such as the Daewoo and the Korean Air Line became economic giants over a short period of time with President Park's blessings. As a matter of fact, none of these economic giants could have been prosperous without

President Park's personal support. President Park created these economic giants for his own political purposes, but ironically, these economic giants which are dominated by foreign capital have had dominating influences upon the regime.

Third, the medium-sized Korean business firms are squeezed out by the foreign-dominated companies, and there is the ever increasing unemployment on the farms, as well as in the cities, in spite of new factories that are built.

Fourth is the ever-growing illicit activities and corruption. The inevitable situation is that economic growth cannot be obtained through the normal competitive system, but through rigid control, conspiracy, and the bribery system. The Tongsun Park bribery scandal is a good example. The circumstance in South Korea is not conducive for honest businessmen there. Conspiracy and corruption are the way of life among these economic animals and politicians who are closely associated with the regime.

Fifth, wages of the Korean workers have remained at the bottom of all Asian countries at a starvation level. For example, the average female worker in Masan Free Trade Zone earned $29.19 per month, according to Labor Standard Bureau of the Republic of Korea. Generally speaking, the average Korean worker's wage is about one fifth that of their Japanese counterparts, and one sixteenth that of American counterparts. Only 11% of the Korean industrial workers earn enough to support a family of four as reported by the Bureau of Labor Standards.

Lastly, the failure of agricultural development results in continued sufferings for the farmers comparable to Japanese colonial days.

President Park Chung Hee became an absolute ruler of the country in order to maintain these aforementioned economic situations in South Korea, and relied on American and other Western supports to remain a dictator. The Japanese conservative regime led by the Kishi and Sato brothers support the corrupt Park as the most reliable anti-communist leader and defender of their interests. Professor Sakamoto of Tokyo University, stated that the economic corruption extended to South Korea by the United States and Japan has undeniably included support for corrupt structures which serve only small privileged elites. Unquestionably, the political corruption of the Park regime is intimately allied with the economic interests of the United States and Japan.

The political corruption advanced further to a terroristic politics. An example is Kim Dae Jung's abduction in 1973. Such a terroristic approach is not an isolated incident, but applied to all those patriots who have opposed the dictatorship in South Korea.

Not only have all progressive movements, including the labor movement, been suppressed, but also the unification dialogue between North and South has been sabotaged by the dictatorial regime. Freedom of speech, press, and assembly no longer exists. Colleges, universities, and other academic institutes are infiltrated by the Korean CIA, and Korea has become a military camp. Human rights are no longer respected. Many religious leaders, scholars and students are imprisoned, tortured, and hanged. South Korea became one big concentration camp. As long as the military dictatorship, at the present time under Chun Doo-Hwan, remains in power and the foreign capitalists exploit the people, the struggle for human rights and democracy will inevitably continue.

The rich are richer, and the poor remain unchanged. Under such conditions, the dictatorial regime was installed. Corruption is relatively easy to conceal in the dictatorial regime. Nevertheless, the people became aware of the spread of corruption and feel that effective measures are not taken to punish those high officials who are involved with corruption. The prestige of government has declined, the cynical attitude of the people has spread, the moral corruption of the nation is evident. Corruption always undercuts popular faith in government to deal even-handedly. Corruption weakens the element of popular support.

Political independence has only transferred power to the dominant elite and, what is more, legitimized the political domination of the military power elite in the name of the new national political order. Besides economic difficulties, growing ecological, sociological and international problems threaten the survival of the very system they want to preserve.

The present mood in Third World countries exhibits a desperation and even a despair just below the surface. The Third World is sinking into a deep economic crisis. It has been reported at a recent UNCTAD (the United Nations Conference on Trade and Development) in Manila that Third World countries owe the West a staggering $300 billion. The debt load is so heavy that some poor countries must pay a quarter of what they earn just to stay afloat. What will be the result of all these problems? The result may be that those decisions will be made in a mood of vindictiveness and repression rather than generosity of spirit, as we are witnessing now in Iran, Nicaragua, not to mention the Southeast Asian countries.

When the U.S. parades itself around the world as an inhuman arms merchant supporting the suppression of people's movement for democracy, and a group of American scholars supports such corrupted policy with development theory, what is to be expected? The answer is clear. The scholars of the Third World countries must expose the erroneous concepts which lead them to neo-colonialistic status, and must assert their rightful claims.

1

Korea and the Foreign Powers

Korean society during the Yi dynasty was a feudalistic one. The term "feudalistic" employed here is referring to more the economics than social or political. Korean feudalism is more close with China than Japan, and is used to define an organization resting on a system of land-tenure in which there was a close personal tie between them. The underlying principles of feudalism as it appeared in this period were very old elements in Korea. The constitution of the clan, demanding on the one hand that the eldest son retain absolute power in distributing the common power to the members of the family, and on the other hand, the common duty as well as the right of all the members to participate in maintenance of the ancestral sacrifices, forms the bases upon which Korean feudalism developed. Obviously, the tradition of Confucianism has played an important role here. There were, however, much inconsistency between such theory and practice enabled feudalism to continue for a long time. Korean society now faced with two major threats: one of them was a product of it's own actions the landing of capital and grain at usury by the landlords to the peasants. The feudal system which rested on a system of land-tenure in which ownership was divided between lords and tenants had a close relationship between two groups. The other factor was the investments of commercial capital by foreign powers.

The landlords were included in the yangban or gentry class, the ruling class. Originally, all in the yangban class were landlords. This situation, however, had changed since the number in the yangban class was increased through the addition of those former public officials to the class. The yang-ban class was composed of the Tongban or the east group, and the Soban or the west group of the government, and the nine higher officers of each group. Later, any group who were able to hold these governmental positions included in the yangban class. They were the aristocrats.

According to the tradition, members of the yangban class were not permitted to engage in any commercial trade or agricultural work, although they were actually the landlords. In practice, in contrast to the China society where they had a civil service examination system, the Korean public officials were limited to those who were members of the yangban class. In the event of his engagement in anything other than ''serving the public'', a member would lose the rank of yangban. Since there were more yangbans than positions in the public office, there were still competition among the yangban for such jobs. As a result, many members of this ruling class, rather than forfeit his rank of yangban, became idle, and waited five, ten, twenty years, even a lifetime for a position in the public office. In many cases, naturally, he never achieved his aim, but had succeeded only in retaining the family in the rank of the yangban class.

The fact was that members of the yangban class were so jealous of their social position, that they preferred starvation to work. Meantime, the position or job seekers among the yangban class became so desperate that bribery was practiced to get jobs; thus bribery became common practice in this stratum. As a consequence, the two social phenomenon emerged. The first, increase of poverty among the yangban class; secondly, the corruptness of public officialdom. In 1876, the situation became so critical that the government of Korea planned a special relief for the starving families of the yangban class. According to the government officials, relief amounted to 3280 bushels of rice.[1] The poverty among the yangban class had increased while some of the wealthy yangban group practiced capital-lending at usury. Meanwhile, the corruption among the government officialdom through the bribery by the position seekers became public knowledge, and the foreign commercial capital began to move in Korea. Thus, the feudalistic society of Korea was threatened.

Under such national crisis, a serious problem of selecting a king among several potential candidates of the royal blood had to make. There were no heirs to the throne after the death of King Tsol-Jong, the twenty-fifth monarch of the Yi Dynasty.

At the palace, the elder statesmen, Cho Tu-sun, and Kim Pyonghak, led numerous discussions in regard to the selection of a proper successor to the throne. During the regime of King Tsoljong, the Kim family was a dominating power, and Kim Jwa-Kin was the most powerful man in the court. The final sanction, however, depended on the Dowager Queen Cho. The Queen Cho, wife of Mun-Jo, who died before receiving the throne, was mother of King

Hyon-Jong, and the daughter-in-law of King Sun-Jo. She was an important figure in the court, but shadowed by the Kim family. The political struggle had been engaged between Queen Cho and the Kim clan. At this politically crucial moment, Dowager Queen Cho acted swiftly. She called Yi Ho-Jun for help. Yi was the Queen's in-law through his daughter's marriage to Cho Sung-Ha, the nephew of the Queen.

At this time, Yi Ho-Jun was only a junior official under Hing-SunKun who was his in-law through his son's marriage to the latter's daughter. When Cho Sung-Ha, the Queen's nephew and her royal assistant at the palace called upon his father-in-law, Yi, for the purpose of counsel in selection of future King, Yi consulted immediately with Hing-Sun-Kun. Yi Ho-Jun said to Hing-Sun-Kun:

"Your honor, I am very sorry that you, an important royal figure, are still waiting for an opportunity to hold a leading position in the palace. At the present time, the Kim clan is ruining the country, and is exploiting the citizens with rotten politics. How can we overlook this situation! Your honor, don't you think you should come out from the long silence for the sake of the country and for the happiness of the citizens!"[2]

In reply to Yi Ho-Jun, Hing-Sun-Kun said: "Indeed, I am losing face to the public, Please instruct me if there is any good policy."

Yi Ho-Jun then informed him more in detail about the future King. Yi suggested that the second son of Hing-Sun-Kun, Yi Ja-Kwang would be the logical one to reign. Hing-Sun-Kun agreed to his suggestion, but doubted his own influence in the court. Yi Ho-Jun immediately called his son-in-law, Cho Sung-Ha and asked him the favor of suggesting Yi JaKwang as a possible candidate to the throne to Queen Cho. Cho was impressed by the eagerness of his father-in-law's suggestion, and brought the idea to Queen Cho immediately.

Next day, when there was another discussion on the problem of the throne, Queen Cho suggested Hing-Sun-Kun's second son. The elder statesmen were so much shocked that a few of them even protested the poor home background and the low official rank of Hing-Sun-Kun.[3]

Hing-Sun-Kun's family was inactive in the public life for a long time, and suffered financially. They even had to sell family treasures, such as paintings, in order to provide for necessary house-hold expenses. This condition was a disgraceful one in the view of the elder statesmen. At the palace, Queen Cho, on the other hand, believed that future King from such humble background would eliminate the influence of the Kim clan, and would enhance her own influence at public affairs.

In spite of the strong protests from the elder statesmen, Queen Cho carried through the plan, with the help of Cho Sung-Ha, and sent out envoys to Hing-Sun-Kun's place in order to arrange a welcome for the new King. Thus the twelve year old boy, the second son of Hing-Sun-Kun and the great-great-grandson of King Yong-Jo became the twenty-sixth monarch of the Yi Dynasty, by appointment of the Dowager Queen Cho.

The Dowager Queen Cho disliked the Kim clan which had monopolized the administration during the previous sixty years, so in her attempt to choose someone who could oppose the powerful Kim clan,[4] Ko-Jong was appointed in spite of his age. The dowager Queen actually had in mind that Tae-Won-Kun would become regent and he was in her good graces. For according to the crown rule, the living high ranking person of the imperial family was to appoint the successor to the throne in case of an absence of a prince; in this case, Dowager Cho was the living high ranking person in the palace and there was no prince to inherit the throne.

Theoretically, king's position in Korea was absolute and his wishes were carried out without any interference from outsiders, except his cabinet members, who helped and assisted him. The cabinet members appointed by the Kings, composed in the main, of two bodies; the Tongban or the east group, and Soban or west group. Each group consisted of nine sections which were presumably appointed by king. This, however, was not always carried through because the government was in the hands of the corrupted officers in many cases. But the young King, Kojong was not old enough to take charge of the administration, so the King's father, Tae-Won-Kun or prince parent took the position of regent, in order to help his son in 1864. This event was to prove very significant for the history of modern Korea. The King, Ko-Jong, was known as an oriental gentleman and a highly educated man, being well-versed in the Chinese classics. He had made many friends among the foreigners, especially among the Americans; but unfortunately, he was a weak-minded man as a state ruler. Mr. Sands wrote:

". . .an intelligent but untravelled man, bound hand and foot by tradition and intrigue, on the defensive against everyone, but seeking information of every kind, even the seemingly trivial, in order to enlarge his horizon and adapt that knowledge gained, to his own needs. He rarely gives an opinion, but questions always. Asking in what way certain measures might best be adapted to Korean conditions in order to obtain the best results."

"...Taught by life long experience, he is suspicious of everyone, but his confidence may always be gained through his affections and religion. He appreciates frankness, even if the subject temporarily is unpleasant; if he approves, he does not hesitate to say so; if not, he rarely shows displeasure, but dismisses the subject temporarily with a 'think it over carefully and report to me again'. Everything he does, betrays, in spite of occasional mistakes, his great desire to advance the best interests of his country. . .but he is hampered on every side by the difficulty of striking the right course in the midst of conflicting advice forced on him by each foreign legation at his capital, and by his life-long and well grounded fear of personal violence, which has necessarily affected his character. Four decades of this life has made him timid and distrustful..... All who were disinterested have formed the same opinion of him, a kindly, courteous gentleman, deeply, almost morbidly religious. . .a ruler anxious to do his duty by his people, but greatly hampered by the difficulties of all sorts which have beset him since his earliest childhood."[5]

Besides Mr. Sand's comment on the King Ko-Jong, Mr. Lowell, the former foreign secretary and counselor to the Korean special mission to the United States of America, also commented in similar note:

"His face was singularly pleasing, one of those faces that you like from the moment you first see it, and that in time you grow to love; and my after-acquaintance with him taught me that his face was truly the mirror of his character. His smile especially was winning. As I stood there with his eyes fixed upon mine, a feeling crept over me that he was really as glad to see me as his words formally expressed."[6]

So, when the sharp and intelligent administrator, Tae-Won-Kun, got in the chief executive's seat, his weak-minded son, the King, had very little chance to stand up against him. Tae-Won-Kun immediately began to reform the old traditional government and it's policies. Unlike his son, he was a courageous and an ambitious man. Dr. Hulbert wrote:

"He was a man of commanding personality and inflexible will and on the whole he was the most striking character in modern Korean history. He was variously estimated. Some have considered him the greatest statesman in Korea; others have taken him for a mere demagogue. His main characteristic was an indomitable will which took its bit in its teeth and swept towards the goal of it desire irrespective of every obstacle, whether of morals, economics, politics, or consanguinity.''[7]

There were numerous domestic reforms carried out by Tae-Won-Kun. His political change of the entire administration shocked the people and made many political enemies for him; particularly the Kim clan and others among the royal groups who held previously the dominating powers. Tae-Won-Kun, however, is the most colorful figure in recent Korean history because of the noticeable changes he made in the domestic politics. The most outstanding changes in the domestic affairs by Tae-Won-Kun are as follows: first, he changed the military regulation and the conscription system. Previously, all male Koreans had to register at the military office at the age of fifteen. They were conscripted as soldiers in the time of peace. In time of peace, and when there was no need for laborers, they had to contribute cotton or similar materials to the government as a kind of a special military tax. This system only applied to common citizens, but exempted offspring of the higher government officials. This unfair system existed for some time which indicates the existence of political maneuverings and bribery among the higher officials.

Further, the offsprings of the common people were responsible for the grain taxation which their fathers, grandfathers, great-grandfathers, and even great-great-grandfathers had been unable to pay. This system was changed by Tae-Won-Kun. He proclaimed that the conscription must apply to both the common citizens and the higher officials alike, and made a new military tax regulation of six won (Korean dollar) and sixty cents per annum on top of regular tax to be paid by every citizen including the higher officials and the royal families. Although the higher officials were strongly opposed to the new regulation, they were without immediate success in doing anything about it.

The second major change was the selection of the public officials for their individual qualifications rather than any political or social preference. He encouraged all the common citizens to participate in public offices, and shattered the traditional bureaucratic method by allowing the Sobukin or the North-Western Koreans who previously had no privilege to serve in the public office; this privilege was also extended to offsprings of the previous dynasty, Koryo.

He also gave political freedom to all parties: the No or Old, the So or the Young, and also to the South and North group.

Thirdly, Tae-Won-Kun avoided the use of all things luxurious. He prohibited the people from using silver kitchen utensils, luxurious clothing or ornate shoes, etc.[8], and since his time, simple clothes have been in use.

Forth, he adjusted the public finance and improved the currency system. He also established the public warehouse system in which the surplus grains and cotton, silver, and other mineral goods for the district and federal governments were kept in storage. By devoting special attention to the goods imported from both China and Japan, and by keeping a watch on the cunning and the troubles which existed previously, he kept the financial situation well in order.[9]

Fifth, he closed up many unnecessary Confucian institutions throughout the country; and the Buddhist temples of the Koryo Dynasty. The Confucian temples and institutions which were erected all over the nation had deemed as unnecessary because that was where the royal families and upper class people met and wasted time on social life and where they were scheming to get all the wealth into their hands. The whole system was most unproductive and noncontributive to the moral or the intellectual life of the people.

Since these groups who advocated anti-Tae Won-kun's policy, it was an excellent opportunity for Tae Won-kun to abandon his political enemies who assembled around these institutes based on the moral conspiracy of the Confucian and Buddhist.

During Tae Won-kun's administration only forty-seven such institutions remained out of the hundreds. Among the remnants were Sosu institute, the oldest one among them all, and Tosan institute of Ryoan. The common people found this reformation most welcome. Tae Won-kun emphasized patriotism and the respect for the system of the Ming Dynasty of China.

Sixth, he rebuilt the Kyongbok Palace which was originally built by the founder of the Yi Dynasty but burned to ashes during Hideyoshi's invasion in 1592. Many kings failed in their attempts to rebuild it because of its huge demand in materials as well as manpower. Tae Won-kun, however, succeeded in this grand project at the cost of seven million four thousand won from the government budget and incalculable amount of free labor from the people and also at the cost of his own political life later. The huge budget was derived from the citizen's pocket,"[10] and they began to complain of their uncompensated labor conscription besides the extra taxation for the rebuilding of this Palace. His political enemies particularly the Kim clan and the Min, represented by Queen Min who was Tae Won-kun's daughter-in-law, were bitterly opposed to this project and took this opportunity to gain the sympathy of the people.

On the whole, Tae Won-kun's achievement in the domestic affairs brought the attention to his nation. He, however, made his great mistake when he insisted upon his isolation policy.

Most of the Western authorities on Korean history believed that

TaeWon-Kun was anti-Christian from start to end; for instance, Dr. Hulbert, the former advisor to the late King Ko-Jong, says in his *The Passing of Korea*"[11] that one of the mistakes of Tae-Won-Kun's life was in supposing that he could eradicate Roman Catholicism by force; he also says that Tae Won-kun was a man of strong personality and imperious will, and however, the people may have come to hate him, they always respected him. Mrs. Isabella Bishop says in her *Korea and Her Neighbors* in regard to Tae Won-kun that he was the man who persecuted the Roman Catholic Christians so cruelly and persistently as to raise up for Korea a noble army of martyrs.[12] She further stated, "... able, rapacious, and unscrupulous, his footsteps have always been bloodstained."[13] Mr. William E. Griffis says in his *Corea: The Hermit Nation* that Tae-Won-Kun was a rabid hater of Christianity, foreigners, and progress.[14]

The prevailing social forces compelled Tae Won-kun to carry on the vogue of the day; hostility toward Christianity and foreigners. However, Tae Won-kun was much impressed by the Christian doctrine and when he held political power, he went as far as to permit missionaries to the place secretly even before they were legally permitted to the palace. As a matter of fact, his wife once asked a Roman Catholic missionary to pray to God that her son might someday become king of Korea, and her son was the king Ko-Jong. The nursemother of King Kojong, Mrs. Park(Christened. Martha) was a known Christian. In spite of all these facts he became the most cruel persecutor of the Christians in Korea. It is most natural for the Western informers to label him as a Christian-hater or a foreigner-hater if one is only aware of the facts of the cruel persecutions of the Roman Catholics. It, however, does not give us a satisfactory picture of Korea at that time if one believes that he was an anti-foreigner because he persecuted Roman Catholics. What were the causes of the Christian persecution during the Tae Won-kun period ?

In November of 1860, the Russo-China treaty was negotiated at Peking; two years later, a border dispute occurred at Saghalin Island between Russia and Japan. In March of 1864, several Russians arrived at Kyong-hing city in north-eastern Korea and asked the Korean government to open trade with her. The Russian demands were so offensive to the Koreans that it brought much uneasiness to Tae Won-kun's administration.

The border open markets in north-eastern Korea had been in existence since the end of the Koryo Dynasty and during the Yi Dynasty between the Korean and the Yo-Jin people; the latter sent their contributions, gifts to a former suzerainty. This tributary relationship was transferred to a commercial trade form when the Manchu overruled Korea. Later, the city of Hoe-Nyong also was known as an open market city soon followed with the city of Hoe-Nayong also following suit. At both cities, the main items of trade were cattle, salt, and agricultural tools for which the Koreans took in return animal skins and furs which the Manchu people offered At Hoe-Nyong, the amount of the trade was limited to 114 head of cattle, 2,600 cows, 55 pots, 850 sacks of salt, and Kyong-won city, the amount of trade was limited to 50 head of cattle, 48 cows, 55 pots.[15]

Learning the situation of trade at the border cities between Korea and Manchurian, the Russian wanted to participate in the transactions. Tae Won-Kun's administration enforced a strict law against trade with the Russians, and punished Koreans who violated it. For instance, Kim HongSun and Tsoe Sun-hak who had secret trade with the Russians were prosecuted by the local authority, Yi Yu-wan.[16]

About this time, a large number of Russians arrived at the city of Kyonghing; they claimed that they brought official documents from Russia and demanded trade. The Koreans, however, rejected them. Later seven left with some sort of documents and promised to return within 90 days. This news arrived at Ujongbu or the legislative branch of the Korean government. Korean government sent out a strict order not to associate with the Russians.[17]

The Korean Christians who were aware of the fact that Tae-Won-Kun was worrying over the border trouble with Russia, suggested that he discuss the matter with the French missionaries.[18] Tae Won-kun knew that the Korean government alone would be unable to persuade the Russians to keep out of the Korean territory and offered to the French missionaries the freedom to conduct their missionary work if they would keep out the Russians from Korea. A French Bishop Berneux who represented the missionaries, refused to accept such a bargain. Prior to Tae Won-kun's approach to Berneux, the Catholic missionaries smuggled into the west coast of Hwang-hae province,[19] four additional missionaries; in violation of the public law of Korea.[20] Tae Won-kun knew this fact, yet rather than make an issue of the smugglings, preferred to make their entry legal by having the French missionaries accept his bargain.

From October to November in 1865, about three score of Russians came to North Korea.[21] In January of the next year, a Russian gunboat arrived in the harbor of Wonsan, the eastern harbor in South Hamggong province, and sent a message to the Korean court demanding free trade with Korea. Tae-Won-Kun was now certain of Russian's determination to share in Korea's trade. At this time, the Korean Christians, Hong Pongju and Kim Myonho who represented the Roman Catholic church, went to persuade Tae-Won-Kun to negotiate a treaty with Britain and France instead of with Russia. Further, Hong and Kim assured Tae-Won-Kun that the treaty could be negotiated through the French missionaries in Korea. Both of them were very confident, because they were under the advice of Bishop Berneux, had secret contact with the French consul at Peking. They were trying to prevent Russian activities in Korea with the support of France and Great Britian. Hong, the closest associate of the Bishop, went to Peking in order to guide French missionaries to Korea. At this time, the Roman Catholics made use of the consequent uneasiness at the Korean court to suggest that the only way to thwart Russia was by making an alliance with England and France.[22]

This plan by the Christians was something impossible for Tae Wonkun to carry out for the following reasons: First, Tae Won-kun was not in favor of making any alliances with any foreign countries. He believed that any type of close relationship with a foreign state or states would bring disaster to the nation; therefore, he was opposed to the idea of an alliance as a whole. Secondly, the Dowager Queen Cho, who appointed King Kojong and Tae Won-kun to power, was strongly anti-foreign. Thirdly, the higher officials of the Korean administration, particularly Cho Tu-sun and Kim Pyong-hak were very much anti-Christian and anti-foreign. When under such circumstances Tae Won-kun was being encouraged to negotiate a treaty with England and France, he thought the Christians as the national traitors who were advocating the idea to sell the country down the river. At this time, Tae Won-kun was informed of the Christian persecutions in China. A letter came from the Korean embassy in Peking stating that the Chinese were putting to death all the Christians found in the Chinese empire. It gave the anti-Christian party, now in full power at the court, an incentive to make like proceedings, but Tae Won-kun warned the court that such actions would lead to entanglement with Europe.[23]

The persecutions began in December of 1865, and on February 23rd of the next year, Bishop Berneux was arrested and lodged in prison.[24] When the court brought him up for trial, he said that he had come to save the souls of the Koreans and that he had been in the country for ten years, that he refused to leave the country except by force. Further, at the personal interview with the regent, Tae-Won-kun who had high regard for him, but Berneux failed to address his Highness in the punctilious form of words demanded by court etiquette. It showed Berneux had an obvious superiority complex. [25] It was not the first time that the French national left a poor taste at the Korean court. Other French Catholic missionaries violated Korean laws during the early stages of their mission work, and gave a bad reputation among the Korean officials. Catholic mission works were initiated at the middle of the eighteenth century by the Koreans who returned from Peking. Peter Sung-hun Yi was the first Korean to be baptized by Jesuit missionary grammant in Peking, and returned to Seoul to organize a church. The Korean Catholic church was organized by a group of Koreans with Peter Yi as their leader. The Catholic church suffered very little at it's early stage due to good nature of King Chongjo (1752-1800) in spite of illegal existence of the church.

Receiving the news of the successful organization of the church in Seoul, Pope Pius VI instructed Bishop Alexandre Gouvea in Peking to give aid to the Korean church. Starting with Father Chu Mun-mo, a Chinese, numerous French missionaries secretly arrived in Korea. The result of the mission work was good. By the end of the century, there were about nine thousand Christians including some members of the yangban class.

The first persecution took place immediately after the good natured King and his prime minister Chae Je-Kong, who belonged to the Nam-in or the South-Men faction, in 1800, left the Palace. The second persecution took place in 1839. The bigger persecutions however, were to come, due to the government's fear of alien domination of the country. The situation got worse when the French missionaries refused to obey the law of the land. The first victim was, naturally, Berneux, the uninformed and arrogant leader of the church.

The death warrant of Berneux read as follows: "The accused, who gives his name as Chang, refuses to obey the King; he will not apostatize; he will not give the information required; he refused to return to his own country. Therefore, after the usual punishments, he will be decapitated.[26]

A few days later, Petinicolas, Peouthis, Davelby, Aumeitre, and Huin were put to death along with the thousands of Korean Christians who were also being persecuted.[27] Three French priests, Calais, Faron, and Ridel remained secure in hiding, but the last was chosen to take a message, giving information of these terrible events to the French authorities at Peking. When the French authorities were informed of the persecutions in Korea, they declared:

The government of his Majesty cannot permit so bloody an outrage to be unpunished. The same day on which the King of Corea laid his hands upon my unhappy countryman was the last of his reign; he himself proclaimed its end, which I in truth solemnly declare today. In a few days our military forces are to march to the conquest of Corea, and the Emperor, my august Sovereign, alone has now the right and the power to dispose, according to his good pleasure, of the country and the vacant throne.[28]

This was written to Prince Kung of China by a French deputy minister to China, M. DeBellonet, on July 13,1866. The vigorous language which he used is perhaps the reflection of Louis Napoleon, the commander of the French fleet in Pacific, Admiral Rose, sent three boats to the Korean coast to make a preliminary survey of the situation. DeBellonet and the French authorities sent the forces to Korea without waiting to hear from the government at Paris. DeBellonet dispatched the fleet and made war on his own responsibility.

Simultaneously, the French Counsel immediately requested the Chinese government to take certain actions in regard to the persecution in Korea. The Chinese government, however, declared that Korea was not under the Chinese rule, but that she was an independent state. Therefore, the French authority had to deal with the matter directly with the Korean government. This is significant in the diplomatic relationship between Korea and China. This was the first time that China ever declared officially that Korea was not a dependent of China.

Meantime, the Chinese government, who had refused to take any responsibility for the actions of the Koreans, sent a message to the Korean government   in regard to the French expedition to Korea. In response to the Chinese government, Korea reported to China that the French missionaries were violating the country's law, learning the native language, changing their name and clothes in order to hide their identity, assembling the bad elements of the Korean citizens, and planning the unlawful things. The Christians were traitors to Korea in the eyes of the Korean official who named them traitor Chun, Jang-Un, traitor Tsoi Hyong, traitor Nam Jong-sam, etc.

At the same time, the government of Korea prepared to meet the French expeditionary forces. The remainder of the French missionaries acted as interpreters, and three Korean Christians guided them to the French fleet which was forced to withdraw by Korean attack. Nine months later, the French returned with seven warships to the Han River; anchored, and flew the French flag in front of the Korean capital. Thousands of Koreans came out to see these black warships which to them were a spectacle.[29]

Tae-Won-kun proclaimed a national emergency and fortified the island of Kanghwa which is located in the mouth of the Han River. This island already was supplied with a force of some five thousand men, consisting for the most part, of tiger hunters and other hardy fighters who took their stand in a strongly fortified Buddhist monastery near the south side of the island some twelve miles from where the French were stationed. By this time, the French troops had already won several victories over the Koreans. After the french fleet left from the nearby Capitol, the Korean government was very confused by the situation, General Yi Nam-sik was appointed to take charge of the affairs and Pak Ju-an was appointed to take charge of the mountain castle and to defend the coast line. When a force of 160 French marines were assigned to attack the Koreans at the Buddhist monastery they thought it would be like another picnic day. The French soldiers, with their lunch boxes packed on horses left early in the morning heading for the monastery. At 11:30 they arrived near the fortress, when someone proposed lunch. Others jauntily declared it would be very easy to capture "the pagoda", and then dine in the hall of Buddha; this suggestion, however, couldn't be carried oui for the group met with an unexpected attack and defeat.[30]

Arriving before the walled fortress that was approachable only up a steep hill in the face of a double flanking fire, the French rushed up to attack; but a withering fire of musketry and of rule cannon, made from models taken from the French wreaks, put nearly one half of the small French force instantly hors de combat.

After this miserable defeat, the French admiral, Rose fired on the town of Kanghwa, stole books and silverware, then sailed away to China.[31] Upon his return to China, after the unsuccessful expedition in Korea by Admiral Rose under Bellonet's order he received news of his government's disapproval of Bellonet's ambitious venture. Napoleon III had other pressing need for his military forces in Europe, and had no intention to follow up the Korean incident at that time.[32]

The result of this expedition was most disgraceful to the French prestige as well as to the Europeans in the Far East. It also encouraged the national isolation policy of Korea because Tae Won-kun thought that the Korean force actually defeated the French, which gave over-confidence to the Koreans. Tae Won-kun probably believed that his force could defeat any invading foreign forces.

During the fighting in the capital it was posted on the gateposts of the palace that whoever should propose peace with the French should be treated as a traitor and immediately be executed.[33]   After the French force was withdrawn from Korean waters, the persecution of the Christians continued until about 1870. The Christian persecutions made an ugly page in Korean history and since then Tae Won-kun became known as anti-Christian.[34] Besides the isolation policy of Tae Won-kun, the imperialistic policy of the Napoleonic French government and the missionaries who violated the law of the sovereignty also helped to bring about the persecution of the Christians in Korea.

As a result of this persecution, the Korean progressive movement was also hindered. The progressive Korean scholars who had close association with the Catholic missionaries were engaged in the various scientific studies.

Among scholars, Park Je-hyong of the Kojong period pointed out the inseparable relationship between the scientific studies and the Catholic religion at that time.[35]

Yi Sunghun was even baptized at Peking by a European missionary, and imported many Western scientific books and tools. The famous scholar on science of the day Jung Tsai-san was well-learned in the field of Western science and has written *Chosun Sukyongsa,* one of the oldest authentic works on the Korean geography, which consisted of fifteen volumes. Jung and his two brothers were baptized.

By this persecution of Tae Won-kun, these progressive scientists were attacked by the anti-Western group including Hong Nak-An and his party. The Western scientific books were also burned. Furthermore, laws prevented the importing of any Western books as well as the censoring of the existing ones. Thought control began. This reactionary policy isolated Korea from the world for some time.

Besides the French expedition, there were some other Western powers also interested in opening trade with Korea. On February 15, 1866, E. Oppert, a Prussian merchant, landed at Tasan county, Chung-chung-do on an English ship mastered by captain James Morison. Mr. Oppert sought permission of the local official to present a gift to the King and to make his desire to open trade be known. However, the local official refused to have anything to do with him.[36] Mr. Oppert, however, not discouraged by his first try, returned to Korea with the same English captain, and local official to open trade. The local officials, Kim Ing-Jip again refused him on the basis of the national isolation policy. Oppert insisted that he be permitted to go see the King personally, but he was never granted this permission. The Korean official was afraid that if he allowed one English ship, it would probably be followed by many others later; then there would be bound to be many troubles.

On May 12, 1866, the American schooner, *Surprise* was shipwrecked at Tsulsan, Pyong-an Nam-do, on the west coast of Korea. The *Surprise* was heading for Lieuchu Island from Shantung. The Korean government treated these American sailors well and Yi Yang-Jun, a Korean official, in spite of the isolation policy, lead them to Peking. The following statement gives a clearer picture of the situation:

Captain McCaslin and his men with their Chinese cook, were kindly treated and well-fed, and provided with clothing, medicines, and escorted on horseback to Uju and after being feasted there, were conducted safely to the border gate...[37]

Two months after the *Surprise* incident, the American ship *General Sherman* arrived at the mouth of the Taedong River on Jun 7, 1866. The surprised Korean local officials[38] asked them reasons for their arrival. The answers were that the English, the American, and the Chinese merchants were seeking trade with Korea. They wanted Korean paper, rice, gold, ginseng, and leather in exchange for western clothes and dishes. They claimed to have no desire to harm them and that they would leave Pyong-yang as soon as the trade ended; otherwise, they would go to the capital and make an effort to see the King. Rev. Robert Thomas, an English protestant missionary, aboard ship, understood a little Korean. The Korean officials stated that trade is prohibited by the national law, therefore, they could not move further up the Taedong River nor to Pyongyang. The group of the foreigners did not pay any attention to the warning, and inquired about the treasures and physical situation of the city of Pyongyang. Meantime, the group of foreigners threatened the Koreans by saying that many more ships would come later.[39] Many local Korean residents were fascinated by the big black ship and made friends among them; the Korean officials, however, prohibited any type of intercourse with the foreigners on the *General Sherman,* and declared they would defend the national coast line.[40]

The *General Sherman* arrived at the city of Pyong-yang and spent the night of the 11th of July there. Meantime, the high officials[41] of the city and the prefecture inquired into their arrival. Rev. Thomas and other Chinese (Cho Neung-Pong, Lee Pa-Shiang, and Cho Pan-Ryang) acted as spokesmen since they knew the language better. The foreigners further demanded to know why the Korean killed the sevens foreigners and persecuted the Roman Catholics. In addition they claimed that their religion is the Gospel of Jesus, which is entirely different from the Roman Catholic. Besides these threats they also mentioned that the French fleet was on its way to the capital of Korea. The Korean officials. however, refused to accept either the Gospel of Jesus or the Roman Catholic, and rejected any type of trade which the foreigners proposed.

The *General Sherman* anchored at Taedong River and refused to leave the city. Two Korean officials, Yi Hyun-Ik and Shin Ta-ke went to the ship and explained to them again that the local officials had no right to trade with the foreigners unless the central government of Seoul approved. The Korean government would, the officials said, be willing to give all possible needed assistance to ships in distress. The English missionary Thomas and the Chinese merchant Cho Neung-Pong seemed to understand the difficult position of the local officials, but the owner of the ship (or the Captain) and the businessmen were determined to have trade and didn't pay any attention to the local officials. They simply ignored the local officials' appeal to them, and completely misunderstood the position of the local officials who had no right to negotiate a trade with foreign countries, beside the central government's policy was not to trade with the foreigners at that time. Meantime, the *General*

Sherman was tied up on the Taedong River as result of low tide.[42]

The local government officials, simultaneously, proclaimed that any citizen who associated with foreign ships would receive capital punishment. Rev. Thomas with three other companions landed at Man-Kyong-Dae which is located in the south of the city for observation. The mayor of the city persuaded them to return to the ship.[43] On July 16, 1866, six foreigners from the *General Sherman* rowing close up to the heart of the city, where Yi Ik-Hyun, the local official, chased them with a small boat. They were having a difficult time rowing up the river because of the rough waters.[44] At that time there were many Koreans assembled along the bank, who were calling to the *General Sherman* to return their official, Yi. Simultaneously, the angered Koreans were throwing stones at the ship. The five foreigners in the small boat became frightened and rushed back to the ship. A junior military officer, Pak Tsun-Kwon caught this small boat and rowed to the *General Sherman* with two other junior officials in order to rescue their superior, Yi. They rescued Yi but the two junior officials, were thrown overboard and drowned.[45]

On July 20, the *General Sherman* still remained on the west shore of Yang-gak Island at the river. The head or the governor of Pyong-An prefecture, Mr. Pak Kyu-sun, ordered several high officials including the mayor of the city, to investigate the condition of the *General Sherman*. The report was that the ship had no intentions of leaving the river. On top of that, the ship's crew stole rice and other foods from the local people and threatened them with gun-fire, killing seven and injuring five more Koreans.[46] Mr. Pak, the governor, who was among the mass near the bank and who felt the hopelessness of persuading the foreigners that there would be no hope of opening trade, appointed two officials, Paik Nak-You and Shin Ta-Ke, to direct the fight against the *General Sherman*. The fight continued all day but the *General Sherman* still remained without any sign of departure. After three days of desperate fighting, the *General Sherman* caught fire and all the passengers aboard died.[47]

The governor of Pyong-An prefecture gave special rewards to those officials and soldiers who fought against the *General Sherman*. The *Gerenal Sherman* incident was reported to the Chinese government through Ujongbu or the legislative assembly.[48] At the same time the Korean government declared the strict national isolation policy; prohibited the use of al] foreign books and goods, and proclaimed that anyone who violated this statute would receive capital punishment.[49]

On the other hand, the officials or the citizens who promoted this national policy would receive special rewards. The Korean government established a special naval defense budget of 30 thousand Ryang (Korean money), and distributed it to the local naval bases and many mountain castles were also built along the coast lines.

The disappearance of the *General Sherman* caused a great disturbance to the Westerners in China. The American minister to China immediately inquired of the Chinese authority and requested an investigation of the *General Sherman*. Meantime, the commanding officer of the American Asiatic Fleet, Bell, sent out the *Wachusett* to Korea in order to investigate about the *General Sherman*. Captain Shufeldt of the *Wachusett* contacted the local officers at the west coast and sent out the documents but left without receiving any reply from the Korean government.

The Chinese government received detailed reports from the Korean government, and transferred them immediately to the American authority at Peking, According to the Korean reports, the disaster happened due to the faults of the foreigners themselves. They arrived in Pyong-yang, harmed the Korean citizens, stole food and treasures, distributed alien literature, and disturbed the peace in the country. The Korean government reminded the Peking regime again that they don't intend to open trade with any foreigners and refused to accept any foreigners in the future.

The Korean reports stated further that they did not have trade wi;h the English and the French, but maintained the peace. On the other hand, when the French soldiers came to Kangwha Island, they burned the castle, destroyed the treasures of the country, and stole what was left of the remaining goods. The report further said, "Is that the way foreigners make trade?" and, "Is that the way religion teaches?"[50] If damage has to be paid to the foreigners, it should be arranged accordingly; but on the other hand, how can the Korean government estimate what damage the foreigners have done to the Koreans? These questions were raised among the high officials of the country.[51]

In December, 1866, the Russians also arrived at the city of Kyong-won near the Tuman River, asked again for trade, but the local government officials refused them.[52] In January of the next year, five Russians returned, took Korean animals and disturbed the peace.[53] The biggest disturbance among the many cases was caused by several groups of Russians when they crossed the Korean border and arrived at the cities of Kyong-hing, Insang, Kyong-won, etc. on December 18,1866. The local Korean militia under the leadership of Kim Ya-yon, the governor of Hangyong prefecture, and Jong Ji-won, head of the special military mission to the north, chased the Russians away. The Korean government gave special awards including Insam (or Ginseng) to those injured persons and arranged special plans to prevent future disturbances in the northern border. The Russians, however, constantly crossed the border and in many cases they influenced the Koreans to move out from Korea to

Manchuria and Siberia. Approximately one thousand families ran away from their native land to seek richer lands and a prosperous future. The local inhabitants suffered very much through the double taxation plan and the conscription to the militia in order to defend the northern border. The Korean government tried to enforce the law that anyone who crossed the border would be shot to death.[54] This law did not prevent them from escaping Korea. The Korean settlement in Manchuria and Siberia at the present day began from these adventurous group of the early days. Many of them never crossed the border, but were shot by the Korean border patrolmen on the way. Those who crossed the new land made the best of their lives in their adopted lands, and they began to cultivate the rice farm which was first introduction to those lands by these Koreans.[55]

With all these incidents with the foreign countries, the Korean government under Tae Won-kun was still as stubborn as ever, and did not settle the incident of the *General Sherman*. The American Consul General William S. Seward thought that the case of the *General Sherman* could be utilized in opening trade in Korea. In a report to the State Department of the United States on the case, he proposed[56] first, that the Korean envoy come to Shanghai in order to explain to the Americans the causes of the *General Sherman* incident and to explain to the French why the Roman Catholics had been persecuted in Korea: that the Korean envoy was also considering sending Korean envoys to Europe; secondly, that there were still survivors of the *General Sherman*[57]; thirdly, that the American warship, *Shenandoah* was heading for Korea to investigate further the *General Sherman* case. In spite of this report, the report of the Korean envoy in Shanghai was proved to be untrue. There was no indication of such a move by the Korean government at that time. This rumor was spread by the American adventurer, F.B. Jenkins who was associated with the Prussian merchant Earnst Oppert. Two of them even dug out Korean tombs in search of jewels. It was a Korean custom to bury all the personal jewelry when a person died. The ship *China* arrived at Hanju county in Tsung-tsung prefecture on April 18,1867. Both Oppert and Jenkins, and a French Catholic father, led by the Korean Christians, Tsoi Son-il and others, landed at Kumanpo port. They claimed to be Russian soldiers, and attacked several towns with guns ignoring the protests of the local officials. They arrived at Kadong where they dug up the tomb of Tae Won-kun's father as revenge against Tae Won-kun's isolation policy. That was one of the worse revenge methods they could employed against any Korean at that time. This action did not help the Korean situation. The foreigners and the Korean Christians left Kumanop port after attacking several inhabitants to steal their food. The governor of the prefecture, when informed of this incident, immediately despatched about 100 soldiers after them. This incident caused considerable uneasiness at the capital, Seoul.[58] The Oppert group even went as far as to Yongjong castle and sent a warning to Tae Won-kun that if he won't open trade, his country would meet with a national crisis. In a few months several warships come to attack Korea and she must be engaged in a fight with them. In spite of such warning, Tae Won-kun was not frightened. The Oppert group was forced to leave Korea for Shanghai.

The Secretary of State of the United States answered this report on June 27, 1868 advising first the rescue of those surviving aboard *the General Sherman,* but there was no survived members of the ship; secondly, to find the causes for the violence and to investigate the conditions of the ship; then to sue for damages and get a formal apology; thirdly, to make a treaty to open Korean ports to the United States and other nations and to protect the foreigners's lives and their properties in Korea. At the same time, Seward was appointed to negotiate the matter with the Korean government directly. The State Department gave him directions to make a similar treaty with the Koreans as the American-Japanese treaty. Seward, however, realized that there was no chance to make a treaty with Korea without having the aid of military forces. The United States revoked his suggestion. Seward's idea of opening Korea was delivered by F. F.Low, the American minister to China: Minister Low, with the permission from the State Department at Washington, interviewed the Chinese authority at Peking in regards to trade with Korea; he also sent a note to the Korean government that there were two unfortunate incidents; the *Surprise* and the *Sherman* in Korea. The Korean government treated the first case to the satisfaction of the American government, but the second case was not as satisfactorily dealt with. In fact, the American government was not too sure that the Koreans even recognized the American flag. The second of the note stated that the American government was sending her minister and naval officer with a warship to Korea in order to investigate the situation, and to discuss the matter of future trade and the shipwrecks on the Korean coast. Thirdly, that the American government sought a peaceful settlement, but should the Korean government refuse this offer, Korea would be inviting unfriendliness.

The Chinese government meantime, declared again that the national policy of Korea was her own and that China had no control whatsoever over Korea. This attitude of China was also reported to Korea by Peking government. Minister Low was using Commodore Perry's tactics.[59] The five American warships under the commanding officer John Rogers arrived near Yangjang Island where they anchored on May 30,1871.[60] The American envoy Low immediately contacted the local officials, but had no success. Meantime, the central Korean government sent out a note to the Americans that the Korean government had treated all the Westerners who were ship-wrecked well and giving them the needed help, and were also guiding them to Peking; that in the future too, she would continue the hospitality. The unfortunate incident of the *General Sherman* had been explained several times to various groups and was being repeated again so that the Korean people would not harm any foreigners who did not harm the Koreans, The ship *General Sherman* met her fate at the Taedong River in Pyong-Yang as a consequence of her own action. The Koreans did not initiate the incident as the evidences has proved. "If one wishes to have friendly relationships one should approach with the will of the virtuous, but the foreigners lacked this part. If one opens the commercial trade, it might lead to more troubles."[61]

The Korean government sent out the junior officials to the *Colorado* where Minister Low was staying and delivered the message sent by the Korean legislative assembly. The American did not interview these junior officials because of their low rank, the commanding officer, Rogers, ordered that the *Palso* and the *Monocacy,* with four other small boats, to survey the coast the river. Meantime, the Korean government proclaimed a national emergency and was busy building the forts all along the coast lines. This was for coast defense.

On June I, 1871, the *Palso* and the *Monocacy,* appeared near the capital through the Han River. The Korean forts fired upon the American vessels which returned the fire. The American warships, like *General Sherman,* were violating the national law of Korea when they approached the capital through the Han River which is under the sovereignty of the Kingdom of Korea. The Americans probably did not understand the geographical situation. The Han River was no longer the high seas, and it is quite a long distance from the high seas, to the capital. Minister Low and others perhaps misunderstood the location of Seoul as in the case of Tokyo which is located close to the same seas. The Low group perhaps planned the same tactics as did Commodore Perry in Japan. This, however, could not be applied in the case of Korea, and they were responsible for the violation of the national law of Korea.

The American marines, on June 10, landed under the protection of the United States naval gun fires, and occupied one part of the land. It was another clear indication of American Navy's adventure in the Far East, and Washington government was not willing to support the aggressive naval policy. The Korean government complained that "She (the United States) is talking peace in the mouth, but violates the law of the land, and threatened with armed forces."[62] As far as the Korean government was concerned, the

Westerners, the French, the Russians, the Americans, whom they dealt with violence are all-alike. The Western imperialists lacked respect and common decency, and condemned as people without virtue.

The government informed in detail the Westerner's activities to China, and the Westerners were fully informed of the Korean national policy. The Western imperialists, however, paid no attention to the law of the land which they wanted to trade with.

The failures of the two major expeditions of the French and the Americans to Korea encouraged more of the national isolation policy. Tae-Wonkun actually believed that the Korean defense forces chased the foreigners away from Korea. He had no idea about the strength of the two powers. In June 1869, when the Prussian minister to Japan, Van Brandt, arrived at Pusan on a Prussian merchant ship, with the aid of the Japanese, and asked for trade, the local government officials not only refused to receive the Prussian documents, but at the same time boycotted the Japanese settlement near Pusan as long as the black ship remained at Pusan. Tae-Wonkun had now stronger confidence in his policy, and the isolation policy had to continue with more courage and vigilance. Temporarily Western intervention had ceased, leaving the Hermit nation alone, until her aggressive neighbour, Japan, came with more determination and violence.

Tae Won-kun, meantime, pioneered in developing a conventional type of nationalism which opposed all alien contacts. Later events will indicate the futility of his efforts.

Notes

1. *Chosen-shi,* Book No. 6, Vol. 4, page 430; Choi Hojin, *Kindai Chosen Kezai-shi or An Economic History of Modern Korea, is* an excellent study of this aspect. See chapters nine and ten of above.
2. Wang Myong, O-*Tsol-Nyun-sa or* a *Collection of the Korean historical stories of the past five thousand years, p. 189*
3. Among the elder statesmen, there were Cho Tu-sun, the prime minister, Kim Jwa-Kin the brother of Queen Sunjo, Kim Pyong-Ik, son of the Kim Jwa-Kin, Kim Hing-gin brother of King Tsol-Jong's wife, Kim Pyong-Hak, King Tsol-Jong's brother-in law.
4. King Sun-Jo crowned when he was only 11 years old after his father, King Jong-Jo died. King Sun-Jo's grandmother or the wife of King Yong-Jo was to administer the government for the young king. She invited Kim Jo-sun, a scholar, to advise them. Kim managed to marry off his daughter to the

young king and he became the father-in-law of the king. Following approximately 60 years were governed by the Kim clan.

5. Sands, W. F., *Korea and the Korean Emperor, Century Magazine, p.* 577-584. Mr. Sands was an American counselor for the King.
6. Lowell, Percival. *Choson, The Land of the Morning Calm, a Sketch of Korea,* p. 159
7. Hulbert, H. B., *History of Korea,* 11 p. 204
8. *Ilsongnok,* May 10, 1865; *Chosen-shi VI* Vol. 4, p. 52
9. Oda Shogo and Sugimoto Seikai, *Outline of Korean History,* Recent period, p. 18
10. *Tsol-Jong'Kisa,* vol. 164, April; *Chosen-shi, op. cit. p.* 44
11. Hulbert, H., *The Passing of Korea, p.* 114
12. Bishop, 1., *Korea and Her Neighbours, p.* 38
13. *Ibid, p.* 256
14. Griffls, W. E., *Corea: The Hermit Nation, p.* 375
15. Tsoe Nam-sun, *Kosatong,* (a History), p. 173
16. *Chosen-shi, Revised Diary, p.* 21
17. *Ibid . p.* 61 Quoted from *Tsol Jong Kisa,* Vol. 164, November
18. Yi Ning-hwa, *Korean Christianity and the Diplomatic History,* and Pere Dallet, *Historie de l'Eglise de Korea,* for full story of the activities of Roman Catholicism in Korea.
19. Oda and Sugimoto, *op. cit., p.* 25
20. *Ilsongnok,* Jan. 11, 1866. Not only the missionary Berneux, but any Korean who had associated with him was also arrested. Hong Toma was arrested with Berneux, and Yi Soni was called a criminal because he aided the missionary. See Dallet, *op. cit., pp.* 525-26
21. *Ilsongnok,* Nov. 10, 11, 1865; Kemp, E. G., *The Face of Manchuria, Korean, and Russian Turkestan, p. 91,* Kemp reported that the aggressiveness of the Russians in the north in 1866 goaded the Korean emperor into a fierce determination to exterminate the Christian once and for all.
22. *Singjongwon, op. cit.,* Jan. 20, 1866; *Honcho Kiji, V.* 185, Jan. 20, 1866; Dallet, *op.cit.,* vol. 11 p. 521-25
23. Griffis *op. cit., p.* 374
24. Hulbert, *op.cit., p.* 115; Dallet, *op.cit., vol.* 11, p. 526-29- Berneux, Hong Pongju, Yi Son-l, and others were put on trial while the Catholic books were accumulated and burned. 20th, Yi Son-l was freed, but others were found guilty.
25. Griffis, *op.cit.. p.* 374
26. Hulbert, *op.cit., p.* 116. Berneux stayed and preached at Seoul, Kwagju, Nongin; *Ilsong nok,* Jan. 20, 1866; Dallet, *op.cit., p.* 531

27. *Ilsongnok,* Jan. 24, 1866; *Chosen-shi, op.cit., p.* 68

28. U. S. *Dip. Cor.,* 1866, p. 536, 1867, p. 416, pp. 419-426

29. *Tongmun Hwigo, The Condition of the Foreign Ships; Tongmun Kwanji V.* 11 cont. ed. 1 866

30. Griffis, *op.cit., p.* 384

31. Hayashi, *Chosen Tsushi, p.* 530

32. U. S. *Dip. Cor.,* 1866, p. 536; 1867, p. 416, 419 426

33. The original photostat copy in *Shiguku, Vol.* 11 No. 1

34. For a detailed study of the Christian persecution, see Dr. George Paik, *History of the Korean Protestant Church;* ''Chosen Kiristokyoshi Kenkyo'' in *Seikya Cakusho,* No. 2, 3,4,5.

35. Hong l-Sop, *Chosen Kwahaksa,* or *History of Korean Science, p.* 262

36. *Ilsongnok.* Feb. 18,21,22, 1866; Oppert, A *Forbidden Land: Voyage to the Corea.*

37. Griffis, *op.cit.,* p.391

38. The local officials were Jong Tai-sik, the high officials of the city of Hwangju, his assistance Shin Yong-han, his interpreter was Yi Yong-suk, and military official was Jl-Myong-sin.

39. *Papers Relating to Foreign Relation of the U.S., part 1, 1867, No.1867, No.124, p.426-428*

40. *Singjongwon Revised Diary,* July 10, 1866

41. Pak Kyu-su, the head of the Pyongan prefecture, Yi Hyongsik, the second head of the prefecture, Pang Ik-yang, the military official, Shin Tai-ke, the mayor of the city. The Chinese were Cho Neung-pong, Lee Pa-shiang, and Cho Pan Ryang.

42. When the *General Sherman* reached the bank of Taedong River, near the city of PyongYang, it was high tide, but the foreigners didn't know the tide situation. *Ilsongnok, July 18, 1866*

43. *Pyong-An Pyong-yong Kerok* or *The military record of Pyong-An,* July 15, 1866

44. *Ilsongnok,* July 22, 1866

45. *Ibid,* July 23, 24, 25, 1866; *Chosen-shi op.cit., p. 90*

46. *Singjongwon op.cit.,* July 27, 1866, Paullin, *Diplomatic Negotiation of American Naval officers* 1778-1883, p. 284

47. Rev. Thomas and Cho Neung-pong came out to the deck of the ship and asked to be rescued but the angered Koreans shot and killed them. Rev. Thomas who is now respected by the Korean protestants as a saint, had planned to come to Korea with the French Fleet which was under Rear Admiral Rose but changed to the *General Sherman* because the French Fleet was delayed and the *Sherman* desperately needed a Korean interpreter;

Rev. Thomas learned Korean at Peking. There is St. Thomas Memorial church near the place where he was killed.

48. *Tongmun Hwigo* original edition, "The Condition of the Foreign Ships"; *Tongmun Kwanji,* VII. cont. ed. 1866.

49. *Singjongwon,* July 30, 1866

50. *Chosen-shi, op.cit., p.* 128

51. *Tongmun Kwanji, V.* 11, cont. ed. 1866

52. *Ilsongnok,* Dec. 12, 13, 29, 1866

53. The Russians took away two cows which belonged to Jong J-Ok, returned one and insisted upon a quick reply from the local authority on opening trade, etc. *Ilsongnok, Jan. 2, 1867*

54. *Tongmun Hwigo,* orig. ed. "The border crime"

55. The rice farm was first introduced to the lands by these Koreans.

56. *Foreign Relations of the U. S.,* 1870, no. 281, N9, 282

57. Since there were rumors that some of the crew aboard the *General Sherman* were still alive, the American depute minister Williams, and the British minister, Aloock, inquired to the Chinese authority who in turn inquired the Korean government. *Ilsongnok,* March 18, 1868; *Tongmun Hwigo, op.cit.*

58. *Chosen-shi, op.cit., p.* 234

59. Dennett, *American in Eastern Asia, p.* 453

60. *Papers Relation to the For. Rel. of the U. S.* 1871, p. 115-21

61. *Ilsongnok,* Feb. 21, 1871

62. *Ibid.,* Apr. 28, 1871

2

The Opening of Korea, the Treaty of 1876 with Japan

In turning to the Korean relationship with China and Japan, we find that their relationships were peculiar in nature. Korea paid tribute to China during the long period since the Manchu invasion in order to keep a "friendly" relationship between the two nations; she kept her independence until a new power emerged in the Far East at the end of the 19th century.

Since Hideyoshi's invasion in 1592, the Tokugawa Shogunate had tried the soft pedal policy on Korea and sent a number of envoys on a mission to Korea in order to open trade but without success. For instance, in 1860, the Japanese government sent the news in regard to the Japanese treaties with the Western powers. In 1867, Hirayama of the Tokugawa Shogunate intended to develop a good relationship between the United States and Korea, but Hirayama was not able to go to Korea. According to the original message which Hirayama was to carry, the relationship between Korea and Japan was so good in the past, and there was no reason two nations should not renew it. On top of it, Japan is genuinely concerned over Korea's future due to the foreign threats, especially of the French. [1]

After the fall of the Tokugawa Shogunate, the new government of the Meiji sent an envoy on mission to Korea, but the Korean government did not trust her neighbour's "peaceful" intention in spite of Japanese friendly approach at this time.

In 1866, the first year of the Meiji Restoration, the Japanese government sent a message to the Korean government that, the old policies would change completely and would start with mutual understanding. [2] The Korean government, however, refused to recognize the de facto situation of new Japan.[3] The main reason for the refusal of the message by the Korean government was that the Japanese message used the words "Hwang" meaning "Imperial", and "jwa-kin-hwi-sojang" meaning "the general who served to guard the emperor, and "pyongjo-shi" or a "high official", and other similar words and phrases in the documents. All the terms could only be used in referring to the Chinese emperor who was regarded as the highest ranking among all the rest of the kingdom.

These words used by the Japanese authority were unacceptable by the Korean government. Because such words and phrases like "the imperial envoy" of Japan made Japan seem superior to Korea, they thought.[4] Since these words were used only in reference to the Chinese emperor by the Korean government, they could not accept the documents by the Japanese officials. The Japanese officials in the foreign affairs department, in order to convince the Korean officials, further explained the difference in the old tradition and the new developments in the international situation; particularly the aggressiveness of Czarist Russia.[5] In September, 1870, the Japanese officials of the foreign affairs department, Yoshioka, personally delivered the documents to the local officials in Pusan port, and Yoshioka remained in the city a year and a half without any reply from the Seoul government.[6] In January, 1872, a Japanese in the foreign affairs department carried the documents which were sent by Mune, the lord of Tsushima, to the local official of the cities of Pusan and Tongnae. As it is noticed here, the Korean relations with Japan in the past were carried through the local officials in Pusan and Tongnae but not through the central official in Seoul. The lord of Tsushima was the official Japanese receptionist, since the Meiji restoration, when Japan dissolved the feudal system and established the prefecture, the lord of Tsushima became an important figure in the Japanese foreign office as Kaimu Taisho or the minister of the foreign affairs, since he was the one to deal with Korea, and relation with Korea was an important factor in new government of Japan. These Japanese officials under the leadership of Moriyama asked for a reception, but the Korean local officers again refused to do any official business with them.[7] In August of same year, the high Japanese foreign official Hanabusa arrived in Pusan port with two warships protected under the name of the Japanese residents at Pusan. The Japanese residents near Pusan port had been established since Hideyoshi's invasion, however, only the Tsushima people were permitted to reside in the settlement. Sometimes foreign groups misunderstood this Japanese settlement to be a Japanese colonial possession. R.Alcock, British Consul-general at Yedo, referred to this Japanese settlement of Tso-ryang as a part of "belonging to Tsushima". Alcock was interested this problem because he preferred Pusan port and Tsushima for her strategic importance as a trading port rather than Yedo or Niigada.[8] The Korean official, however, refused the proposed conference by Hanabusa so long as the Japanese official threatened them with warships. Under the circumstance, Hanabusa's mission was also a failure. Tae Won-kun replied to these proposals: "A determination to cease all relations with a renegade from the civilization of the Orient."[9] The insistence of the Japanese government to open trade with Korea was due to the fact that there was a considerable amount of trade already engaged in, in spite of the non-existence of an official treaty between Korea and Japan. Since 1868, the amount of trade reached about 120 thousand yen annually between the Tsushima Island and the local Pusan port.[10] This fact was an indication of the prosperous trade between the two nations. The local Korean officials were little interested in regard to this trade but more concerned over their national isolation policy. Meanwhile, the militarist group of the Japanese government was impatient with the stubborn isolation policy of the Korean government, and advocated "Seikanron" or "theory of conquer Korea". The extreme group which included Saigo, Koto, and Itagaki, all former members of the cabinet, protested the policy of "peace" of the Iwakura, Ito, Okubo group who had an intimate knowledge of the world situation. As a matter of fact, the Iwakura group had just returned from a trip to Europe and advocated the advancement of democratic affairs rather than the conquering of Korea.

The Japanese cabinet was in a critical situation because of the conflicting view on the policy over Korea. The Hanabusa group on a mission to Korea reported formally to the Japanese cabinet on October 14, 1873. On October 23, the Japanese government decided to stop discussing further on the Korean mission. Next day, Saigo, a strong leader of the "war" group, resigned from the cabinet in protest. On the 25th, Itagaki, Fukujima, Koto, and Goto also resigned.[11] The Iwakura's peace party, nevertheless, triumped at that time. But Saigo's war party protested the Japanese government policy of Korea, since they advocated the conquest of Korea instead of the soft pedal peace policy, many war-like groups joined with Saigo's. The famous Satusma rebellion soon followed against the present government of Japan.

Meanwhile, Tae Won-kun's sudden changing of the old traditional system of government surprised the royal and official classes and made many political enemies among these government officials, particularly, when after four years of his administration, Tae Won-kun chose his daughter-in-law from among the common class. Tae Won-kun was consciously thinking of selecting his daughter-in-law, the queen, since the young king was ready to get married according to the tradition of the times. He did not want any strong in-law influence at the palace again as was the case previous to his administration.

He was looking for a potential queen from among the insignificant families.

Min Tsi-rok, Tae Won-kun's brother-in-law, was rather a poor man and had a young daughter. Tae Won-kun one day asked his wife about Min Tsi-rok's young daughter and he was satisfied with his wife's remarks on the future queen, and asked her to invite her over some day. Tae Wonkun said to his wife; " . . . is about fourteen years old; how is her disposition?" The wife replied," she is indeed of an unusual character although she was raised on a farm, she had learned the 'Siao-hsioh' (or Minor studies by Confucius) from her father at the age of six and was well-versed in 'Ssu-shu' (or Four documents by Confucius) at the age of ten. She was now fourteen years old and had finished learning the 'Wuching' (or Five Documents) under the guidance of Sing-ho."[12] That was enough for Tae Won-kun. He made an arrangement immediately, and young king married the young intelligent woman with the sanction of the dowager queen Cho. The marriage was a happy occasion at the palace.

The young king, however, was not too happy about his marriage because he already had a mistress at the palace.[13] The king, in fact, visited his mistress more often than the new bride, the queen Min. As a matter of fact, the young king actually lived with his mistress and she had a child by him. The queen Min who was still young and concentrating more on her reading, suddenly realized the unhappy situation and determined to chase out the king's mistress and the baby. She succeeded in her plan with the aid of her brother Sing-ho. Thus the unpleasant married life of the queen Min ended after five years. The queen then immediately raised some serious problems to the king and asked him to think of the national affairs more seriously and devote his time to the matter. One day, the queen said to the king; "Your excellency, what do you think on the following matter? Since the beginning of the Tae Won-kun administration, the country has been isolated from the great powers. The scholars are complaining because of the closing of the institutes all over the country. Our nation is facing the most critical times since the birth of our state."[14] The queen further emphasized that the king should take at once the administration from his father and concentrate more in the national affairs rather than wasting time with his mistress. The queen also said that if the king did not change his mind immediately, some of the ministers might ask help from the Chinese emperor. Whether the queen's aim was to threaten her husband to leave the mistress or planning already against her father-in-law, Tae Won-kun, or both, there was a definite significant move from her part. The king graciously apologized for his behavior and asked for her aid in carrying out his mission as a king. The King's attitude toward the queen had changed completely since that night although the king had visited his mistress again. The queen's influence gradually increased at the palace and her relatives under the leadership of Min   Sing-ho, the queen's brother, were holding the important high officials in the government.

Jo Song-ha and the other high military officials requested Tae-Wonkun to sell some of the government's reserve gold to meet the critical financial situation and to pay the unpaid salary of the soldiers. Tae-Wonkun consented although he did not favor the plan. The queen felt that the issue was significant enough to insist on punishing Jo Song-ha, a high official of Tae Won kun's administration, who initiated the plan, and opposed the plan vigorously. It was a very obvious political issue in opposition to Tae Won-kun and his group. Min Sing-ho, as leader of the anti-Tae Won-kun faction, conducted successfully against the Tae Wonkun administration. Eventually, the Min family came into power and Tae Won-kun was forced out of the office after ten years of strong and conservative, but revolutionary domestic administration from 1864, to 1874. After his forced retirement, queen Min who had a strong character and great ability, now began a Min-dominated administration during the next twenty-three years, 1874 to 1896; the political struggle between the factions, however, had continued.

In June 1874, when the Japanese official Moriyama arrived at Pusan port again, the official attitude of the Korean government was somewhat changed. In fact, the Korean government officials recognized the Japanese mission and officially received them at Pusan. This was the first time although it was the local officials', the Korean officials recognized the Japanese diplomatic envoys. On January 19, 1875, the Japanese envoy, Moriyama, and others arrived again at Tongnae on a warship with a new communication. The local Korean official this time refused to see the Japanese envoy on the grounds that they came by warship. In the documents, there were still the words such as "Kijo" or the "imperial", "Dai Nippon" or the "Great Japan", although they carefully avoided the words "Tenshi" or "the son of the heaven". The envoy insisted that it was impossible to change the word "imperial" and "great". On February 5th, the head of Tong-nai city, Hwang Jang-yu, received and forwarded the documents of the Japanese foreign minister to the Korean central government and treated the envoy Moriyama and the vice-envoy with a special banquet.[15]

Three months later, the same envoys again came to Tong-nae; this time the envoy wore Western clothes. He also insisted on using the main gate to the city.[16] The Japanese official attitude seemed to have changed in the eyes of the Korean people. At the palace in Seoul, opinion was divided as to whether or not the Japanese envoy should be accepted. Tae Won-kun's influence was still strong although he was retired from the palace. Meanwhile, the Japanese government in Tokyo sent out a message to the Japanese official in Seoul to find out what was going on in Seoul.[17]

In August of 1875, Inouye, captain of the warship Unyo, came to the west coast of Korea and surveyed its coast line without official permission from the Korean government. Captain Inouye tried to reach Yong-Jong castle near Chemulpo by a small boat in order to get some fuel and water at the coastal station, but the Korean marine who was on watch at Jungdai, fired at the Japanese warship because he was afraid of a foreign invasion. As a consequence, the Japanese fired at the Yongjong castle, burned it and returned to Japan. Captain Inouye reported the incident to the Navy department of Japan, and the Japanese government immediately held an emergency cabinet meeting.[18]

In the meantime, Tae Won-kun who was waiting for an opportunity to return to the palace, instigated some of the Confucian scholars, who might had been protected by Tae Won-kun during the period of the close-up-Confucian institutions, in the southern states to favor his opinion that the Min clan had failed the administration and that he should be returned to the palace. The Confucian scholars had been successful and as a result, the public favored Tae Won-kun's return to power. There were several cases where the Confucian scholars were punished by the Min administration because they advocated the resuming of the Tae Wonkun administration. Min's government declared that anyone who advocated Tae Won-kun's return to power would be given severe punishment.[19]

Tae Won-kun took advantage of this opportunity and immediately moved into the palace after three years of retirement. The public expressed it's opinion by the demonstrations. He assembled the ministers and in his address to them he stated that the reason for his return was that he was needed in order to rescue the nation from corrupt politics. He further stated that the ministers should now speak up if they objected to his return or to his policy. The ministers obviously did not wish to commit themselves or get into trouble. Tae Won-kun again came to power although he had to share it with the Min group at this time. As soon as he felt that he was in power again, he immediately released the Confucian scholars, who were arrested by the Min group on grounds that they advocated Tae Won-kun's return.

Meantime, the Japanese came back in December of the same year under the guidance of Lieutenant-General Kuroda Kiyotaka as envoy, and Count Inouye as vice-envoy for the purpose of negotiating a treaty. There were a considerable number of problems before the Japanese cabinet in regard to selecting an envoy to negotiate a treaty with Korea. Conflicts between the warlike party and peace party as well as the political jealousy between the Satsuma clan and the Chosu clan brought many problems in selecting the envoys. At first, Count Kido, who belonged to the peace party, was selected as the envoy, but withdrew from it, because of poor health. Kuroda, who represented the war-like party, was appointed as next choice; and Inouye, a member of the peace party as well as the Chosu clan, was required to represent the peace party; thus the envoys represented both political factions in Japan. General Kuroda with two men of war, three transports and three companies of marines, or about eight hundred men in all, arrived at Pusan and anchored within sight of Seoul as next stop on February 6th.

　　Arrival of the Japanese black ships within sight of Seoul aroused considerable excitement among the high officials of the Korean government. In the Korean government, the high officials had a stormy debate as to whether Korea should negotiate the treaty with Japan or not. Tae Wonkun advocated the usual isolation policy while the Min group advocated the opening of the country. Actually, there was no other course than to negotiate a treaty with Japan because Japan was determined to get through the negotiation even she had to use forces of arms. "The Japanese government must use force in settling the Korean intercourse . . . now," was the declaration of the imperial councilor of Japan after they learned about the Unyo incident in Korean water.[20] In spite of the fact that China knew of Japan's plan in Korea, China was unwilling to help the kingdom of Korea "so long as Japan confined her action to forcing Korea to make a treaty. [21]

　　Meanwhile, the Japanese envoy in Peking, Mori Arinori, was inquiring about the treaty with Korea. The Japanese envoy inquired of the Chinese government whether or not the Chinese government would accept the responsibilities for the Korean government's actions on the Japanese citizens and properties. If the Chinese government refused to recognize them, the Japanese claimed it was only in words that Korea belonged to China. China's stand toward Korea was the same as before in the cases of the French and the Americans. As a matter of fact, Li Hung-chung had already confidentially suggested to the Tsung-li Yamen or the Office of Foreign Affairs that it had advised Korea to receive the Japanese officials.[22]   Li Hung-chung was responsible for the Chinese diplomatic relations with Korea, and was in a position to give advice to the Korean government. It is doubtful that he could have been able to change certain inevitable situations already developing between Korea and Japan. China was unable to stop or prevent the Japanese aggression in Korea and elsewhere in the Far East. The Japanese envoy first arrived at Pusan port where they asked the local officer to inform the Korean government that the Japanese envoys were approaching Kanghwa city in order to make a treaty with Korea. After this warning, they arrived in Kanghwa city; Moriyama and Yasuda went to prepare the hotel for the envoy group which consisted of four hundred persons.[23]

The Korean government in the meantime, sent out Shin hyon as the chief officer of the reception and Yun Jai-sing as a vice-chief. On February 11, 1876, the conference between the Japanese and the Koreans began.[24] The Japanese envoy, Kuroda, said that the purpose of this meeting would be to restore the three hundred year old relationship between the two nations. Further he inquired of Shin Hyon why the Korean government had treated the Japanese envoys as such in the past years and fired at the Unyo ship. The Korean envoy, Shin, replied that the Unyo incident occurred because the Unyo was mistaken for a Western ship since it didn't carry the identification of a Japanese ship. Besides it came directly toward the Korean port which was strictly a restricted area. The Korean envoy further stated that, according to news reports, Japan insulted the kingdom of Korea, in saying that Japan would conquer the Kingdom. The Korean envoy was referring to an article which was written in Shanghai by a Japanese, Yaho Junshuku. The article said that about 80 Japanese ships were ready to invade Korea. The Chinese government took the matter very seriously although it was a baseless rumor. This was one of the reasons that the Korean government refused to accept the Japanese envoys at this time.[25]

The vice-envoy of Japan, Inouye, stated that Japan had sent numerous official documents to the Korean government during the past eight years, but the Korean government never once replied to them. Why had the Korean government taken such an attitude? He further insisted that the Korean envoy should apologize for Korea's misbehavior in the past. The Korean envoy, Shin, however, refused to do that; in fact, he protested to the Japanese that, Korea does not approve of coming by the black ships, and the use of words like "imperial" or "imperial order" in the previous documents. These things, Shin pointed out, made Korea suspect Japanese motives. Thus the first day of the conference ended.[26]

At the second day of the conference the Japanese envoy, general Kuroda, put out the twelve drafted articles which he had brought along with him and asked Shin to look them over. Shin delivered this draft to Seoul since he was not authorized to make any kind of a commitment. Shin promised to reply within ten days. General Kuroda warned him that the Korean government should neither refuse the treaty nor delay in answering within the given period, otherwise some very unfortunate affair might take place. The Japanese draft declared Korea was an independent state and an equal to Japan and other nations. There would also be freedom for the Japanese to survey the Korean coast. provide government protection to the citizens of each country in Japan and Korea, and to negotiate a commercial treaty between the two nations. The

Korean king called his ministers and discussed with them about the proposed treaty. Some of the ministers were in favor of the treaty while others opposed it. After considerable discussion at the palace the Korean envoy came back with several suggestions: first, to use only the name of the country, but not to use the title of the sovereigns such as the emperor or the king. The Koreans thought the rank of emperor to be higher than that of king, and it was not clear to them why the term emperor was used for Japan and king for Korea while they were talking of a treaty based on equality. The second point, the Korean envoy raised, was that the word "great" of "great Japan" should be avoided in the case of "Dai Nippon". However, a compromise was made by using the word "great" in reference to "great Korea"in place of Korea. The third point was that Korea refused to have a resident minister of Japan at Seoul, but proposed an exchange of envoys whenever the necessity arose. This question continued even after the treaty was completed. The fourth point was the prohibition of importing opium into Korea; the fifth point was the prohibition of foreign missionaries; the sixth point was the prohibition of trading privileges at the Korean open ports to foreign traders under Japanese jurisdiction. The last three points were accepted by the Japanese envoy; the first and second points were compromised and the third point was refused.[27] One of the most difficult points of the whole negotiation was that the Korean envoys insisted that the Korean king would not sign any kind of documents since it was not the custom of the country. The Japanese envoys objected, and General Kuroda said, "the King's sanction is the main point of the whole treaty; it is most difficult to make any report to the emperor without the King's sanction. It is regrettable to block the treaty just because of the sanction." The Korean envoy replied. "In our country, there are no occasions for the Korean king to use his honorable name in connection with foreign communications."[28] General Kuroda refused to continue the conference any longer and returned to his black warship. Kuroda's action was a threat to the Korean envoy. Meantime, Count Inouye remained at his hotel secretly to observe the Korean's reaction toward Kuroda's action. General Kuroda's action was not unexpected due to the Japanese determination to use force of arms if it needed. When Count Inouye arrived at Pusan, where he had a difficult time with the local officials, he sent a wire to Tokyo to send two additional companies. Inouye said in the telegram: "Thinking of the future, Korean government has not awakened yet; approaching Kanghwa, there will undoubtedly be gun attack, send two companies of soldiers quickly. . . " This telegram was sent to the Prince Ito. The Tokyo government, however, did not sent any additional soldiers. It would have been too obvious to the world that Japan was more interested in conquering Korea than negotiating a treaty. The negative reply was sent to Count Inouye by Sanjo, and Nomura was sent to make further explanations to him. Meantime, Ito sent an official letter to Count Inouye which said: "Count Kido is getting well . . . in case of unsuccessful treaty at this time, wish to make a trip (to Korea). Future plans should not be made public at this time. Count Sanjo and Count Okubo are discussing the future plans . . . General Yamagada is on the way to Bakan in case of emergency (arising between Korea and Japan.)"[29] Ito's letter gives enough evidence of what the Japanese government was planning in case the conference with Korea should fall. In order words, Japan was ready to use military force if necessary to force a treaty with Korea.

The Korean envoy, Shin, immediately reported the critical situation of the conference to Seoul and the Korean government had no choice but to finish the treaty under the circumstances, Inouye, who sought to complete this treaty form the beginning even if should mean war between two nations remained at Kanghwa city, and later was rejoined by General Kuroda on February 26th when the Korean envoy was ready to resume the conference. On February 27, 1876, Korea signed the first treaty in her history with Japan. The treaty was made up of twelve articles, and the significant part of the treaty was in Article I:

"Chosen (Korea) being an independent state enjoys the same sovereign right as does Japan in order to prove the sincerity of the friendship existing between the two nations, their intercourse shall henceforth be carried on in terms of equality and courtesy, each avoiding the giving of offense by arrogance or manifestations of suspicion..."

Besides the treaty, the Japanese envoy received the sanction of the Korean king, and the Korean legislative assembly delivered a friendly letter to General Kuroda. The King's sanction stated that the Korean envoy, Shin Hyon, and others have a conference with the Japanese envoys at Kanghwa. They made a treaty which the King sanctioned. The treaty was made to gain permanent friendship and the officials were to act on matters according to the articles of the treaty. Thus the spirit of the treaty was to be permanently followed.

The envoys of both countries completed the work; a banquet was provided by the Korean officials. The Japanese envoys left for Japan the next day spending eighteen days at Kanghwa, and made a report to the emperor of Japan on March 15th. The Japanese emperor said to the envoys, "You, Kiyodaka, and Kaoru were sent to Korea with a heavy burden. You completed the mission well. The new treaty was exchanged with the friendly spirit of two nations. I am very glad about it.'' And he gave two thousand yen to General Kuroda and one thousand five hundred yen to Count Inouye for their contribution as envoys.[30]

The Japanese envoys gave some special gifts to the Koreans before they left. Among the gifts, there were various types of guns and ammunition. Two Japanese, Miyamoto and Nomura stayed in Korea in order to complete the unfinished details of the treaty.   Meantime, the Korean government proclaimed that the national emergency was over, and sent out officials to each of the ports to explain the new situation. The legislative assembly explained the nature of the treaty to the governors of the provinces and the commanders of the ports; and especially to the Tongnae official, to recognize the Japanese ships and their national flag when they passed the Korean coast and not to violate the provision of the treaty.

The Korean envoys, Shin and Yun, were called to the King, and Shin explained the international situation saying that the national isolation could no longer be carried out in Korea, that ''Sadae Kyorin'' policy or ''the policy of respecting China and the good neighbor policy to Japan'' should he carried out accordingly and the King agreed with Shin. In spite of this Sadae policy, the Chinese government did not interfere with the negotiation of the treaty. The treaty was significant only because of the recognition of Korea's independence, the change of Korea's status quo to China, but also because it was the beginning of Japan's ambition to expand in Korea. This fact, however, was not realized either by the Korean government or the Western powers at that time. Mr. Rockhill commented on the treaty: ''Marks the beginning of a new era in the history of Korea, its entry into the family of nations.''[31] Korean entry into the family of the nations was not as real as it appeared on the surface; it merely gave an opportunity to Japan in her aggressive policy.

Queen Min's party, the political enemy of Tae Won-kun, meantime advocated the treaty with Japan in order to be opposed to Tae Won-kun's policy, was actually not in favor of the treaty. She was bitterly anti-Japanese and was very much pro-Chinese throughout her administration. Queen Min followed the traditional line of the Sadae policy. Many scholars, however, sometimes mislead her into believing that Queen Min's pro-treaty attitude was a genuine progressive one. Mr. Vinacke said;''The Queen's faction became the party of progress, advocating the opening of the country, and the ascendancy she gained over the King helped to bring about the reversal of the anti-foreign policy of the Regent (Tae Won-kun). The making of the treaty of 1876 with Japan, and establishment of Japanese legation at Seoul''[32] Mr. Dennett, another leading scholar on the Far East, said in his well-known book, *American in Eastern Asia;* ''He (the King) married into the Min family, and thus acquired as Queen a strong-minded, aggressive woman, somewhat disposed toward progress and violently opposed to Tae Won-kun.... The treaty of 1876 had been signed with the approval of China which in the midst of its wavering policy toward Japan, was for a moment, seeking conciliation.[33] "Dr. Nobel said; "The Tae Won-kun went into retirement, although not entirely out of power. The intensity of the ex-regent's hatred for all things foreign gave his powerful enemies a convenient issue for opposition to him, and made possible the treaty with Japan in 1876."[34] In spite of these observations, there was no evidence that Queen Min was more progressive than her father-in-law.

The Korean government sent Kim Ki-su to Japan in order to return the visit by the Japanese envoys to Korea. The Korean envoy arrived at Tokyo where he immediately delivered the message of the Korean foreign office to the Japanese foreign minister. The Korean envoy also called upon the Japanese Emperor. It was very different situation in Tokyo where they welcomed the Korean envoy even to the palace, whereas the Korean government did not even allowed the Japanese envoys to Seoul, not to mention of the Korean palace, and the treaty was signed at Kanghwa city, not in the capital of Korea. After a visit of about three months in Japan, the Korean envoy returned to Pusan where he talked with the Japanese officials there in regard to commercial trade, and the envoy immediately made a report to the Korean King, who was fascinated about the situation in Japan, appointed the high officials for the further conference on the trade, which was a supplement to the treaty of 1876.

In June of 1876, Japanese foreign official, Miyamoto Okadzu, arrived at Tongjin in Kanghwa Bay, where he was welcomed by Yi Son-won and Jo In-hi, the Korean special envoys, in order to consult with the Japanese foreign official. Miyamoto proposed to the Korean special envoy, Jo, that Japan would like to construct a highway through Korea to China and establish adequate supply stations along the highway. Secondly, he proposed the opening of eight major harbors in Korea for the purpose of commercial trade with Japan. The Korean envoy, Jo, explained that the Korean people do not understand what was meant by open port, open highway, and that because of this fact, it might bring about unfortunate incidents, and that the Korean government, therefore, could not accept the Japanese proposal. Thus the discussion continued for sometime, but finally both sides compromised and negotiated a supplementary treaty which formed the eleven articles between Korean and Japan.[35] The Korean government did not allow the use of the highway but promised not to charge tariff, for several years in order to encourage the merchants. The treaty was signed by Jo representing the Korean government, Miyamoto, representing Japan, on August 24, 1876, at Seoul. The changing of the conference sight from Kanghwa to Seoul indicated the changing attitude of the Korean government. As a consequence of this supplementary treaty, the Japanese subjects came to enjoy special privileges in Pusan port as well as within a radius of ten ri (Korean measure) from that port. Since the supplementary treaty, the Japanese merchants flowed into Pusan area where many of them violated the local laws and disturbed the peace. The Korean government, therefore, refused to allow additional Japanese to enter the country.

Prior to this incident, Kim Hongjip, the Korean envoy, went to Tokyo where he was to settle the tariff problem at Pusan. According to the document which the Korean foreign minister sent to Japan, it said, that Pusan port had been free of tariff in the last few years, but that now it was about time to collect tariffs, that the Korean government would proceed after a discussion on the treaty articles with the Japanese government. The Korean envoy drafted the statement on the tariff and initiated the conference with Hanabusa who was appointed by the Japanese government to handle the matter. Kim proposed five percent tariff on the import and the export goods, and prohibited the export or the import of rice. Kim further said that the tariff must be fair and that five percent was the standard all over the country. According to the newspaper, however, the Japanese government had planned to collect ten to thirty percent tariff. If this was true, the Korean government wished to do the same as the Japanese; and that the matter of preventing the export of the Korean rice was a serious one which the Koreans wished the Japanese government to understand even though it was not stated in the treaty.

Hanabusa refused any tariff at this time, but agreed to the prohibition of the export of rice. Kim further insisted upon the recognition of these matters by the foreign minister, and Count Inouye. The latter agreed to the five percent tariff, but stated that the export and the import of rice should also continue since about half of the trade was rice. Kim failed to accomplish any agreement on the matters and he returned to Korea. The envoy brought back a letter of introduction from the foreign office. The letter introduced the United States to the Kingdom and advised her to open treaty with her. Meantime, Inouye also advised Kim that the main problem of the Korean government was to prevent the Russian aggression in the Far East. The letter did not impressed the Korean government at that time. The Korean government, meantime, collected tariff at Pusan after August of 1879. Since then, only the licensed merchants were allowed, thus reducing the Japanese merchant considerably. Since the Pusan port was opened the Koreans brought cotton goods, tin-plate, glass, dyes, tools and machinery, clocks, watches, petroleum, flour, lacquer work, iron, hollow-ware, and foreign knickknacks, On the other hand, the exports consisted of gold dust, silver, ox-hides, and bones, beche-de-mer fish, rice, raw silk, fans, cotton, bamboo, paper, ginseng, furs of many kinds, tobacco, shells for inlay work, dried fish, timber, beans, peas, hemp, jute, various plants yielding paper-stock, peony bark, gall nuts, varnishes and oils, and a variety of other vegetable substances having a universal commercial value.[36] Through opening trade with Japan the Koreans learned a great deal concerning modern trade.

Hanabusa, meantime, came to Seoul in September, 1878 in order to survey the two open ports and to prepare the way for the Japanese minister to Seoul according to the treaty of 1876. He discussed the matter of the establishment of a Japanese embassy in Seoul. The Korean government informed him that the Japanese merchants did not heed the laws of the nation, and violated the local laws constantly. The Korean government would be willing to open additional ports but that it would not be necessary to have the Japanese embassy in Seoul. The Japanese envoy also should use Tong-Jin as the way to the capital. Hanabusa refused these counterproposals, and left Seoul.[37]

Again, there was the problem of the trade so the Japanese government sent a warship, *Amashiro,* under Lieutenant Commander Matsumura Yosutane, to Pusan to survey the southern Korean coast line and to select the proper ports. The commanding officer also brought a note to the Tongnae envoy, Yun Tsi-hwa, from the Japanese foreign minister in regard to the establishment of a Japanese embassy in Seoul.[38] Hanabusa again arrived at Pusan with a warship escort in order to protest the Korean tariff practice in Pusan. Hanabusa asked Yun Tsi-hwa to dismiss the custom duties, but Yun refused this request since he had no authority to do that. Hanabusa, with the cooperation of the commanding officer of the warship, landed with armed forces and the Japanese sailors remained in town.[39]

Under the circumstances, the Korean government was forced to dismiss the custom duties at Pusan. Hanabusa warned the Korean government that he would ask for the damages later. The tariff rate was reasonable and the Korean government had a right to collect it. It was not in violation of the treaty as Hanabusa insisted. In fact, the Japanese envoy violated the spirit of the treaty, and forced Korea in a dictatorship fashion, rather than in the spirit of the terms of the treaty which both had just signed. The Korean residents of Pusan and its neighbourhood were angered by the misbehavior of the Japanese and there were conflicts between them from time to time. For instance, on March 24, 1880, when the Japanese sailors were marching towards Tong-Nae city, the Korean people threw rocks at them. Such action, naturally, brought conflict between two peoples. Hanabusa arrived at Pusan by the Japanese warship, *Takao,* on March 1880.[40] He inquired about the damages which was supposed to have been done by the Korean government at Pusan. He claimed that the Japanese businessmen lost business because of the tariff at Pusan, he wanted the damages to be paid. He also passed through a number of the Korean ports and arrived at Yong-Jong port. Then he entered the capital where he resided at the Tong-su-gwan, which became the temporary legation of Japan in Seoul. The Japanese minister immediately called upon the Korean foreign minister, who appointed Hong U-tsang to discuss the problems which Hanabusa brought over. Hanabusa first suggested the opening of the port of Wonsan. Hong refused the Japanese suggestion on the grounds that there were many kings' tombs around the port; therefore, it was impossible to establish trade at the nearby harbor. The kings' tombs were guarded carefully by the officials according to the old tradition in Korea. The Japanese minister further suggested the opening of Chemulpo (Inchon) in spite of the unsettled problem of Wonsan. Hong rejected Hanabusa's suggestion vigorously and said that it was regrettable to hear such a suggestion, that Chemulpo was out of question since it was too near the capital. The Korean people would have been shocked if the government had allowed the opening of Chemulpo. Also, it would have disturbed the national defense.[41] The Japanese minister talked to the Korean foreign minister, but received the same reply from him.

After long debate at the Korean palace, the Korean government decided upon opening Wonsan port, but refused Chemulpo. This information was given to Hanabusa. After the news of the opening of the Wonsan port, the Korean people of the neighbouring cities, Tokwon, Anpyon, Muntson, protested this action to their government. Meantime, the Korean ministers continued their debate on the problem of Chemulpo. Yi Yu-won, a high official of the Korean government, advocated the opening of that port but his opinion was not accepted in the palace and the opening of Chemulpo was delayed some three years. The opening of Wonsan alone was significant for trade. It is one of the best harbor on the Korean east coast. The Japanese trade at Pusan was mainly in foreign goods which were imported from the Western countries. Since there was no trade between Korean and the Western nations, the Western goods came into Korea through China and Japan. The Japanese government, however, was more interested in introducing the Japan-made goods to Korea than importing the Western goods. For this purpose, Wonsan was the ideal port for it was a new location and distant enough from the already opened port of Pusan. The problem was that the Japanese were not willing to go there and settle down for business as they did in Pusan area; the Japanese government actually brought them by force over to Wonsan, and financed their business.[42]

After the treaty of 1876, one of the major changes in the Korean government was the reformation of the military system. Among the many instructions to Hanabusa by Count Inouye, the foreign minister, there was a statement as follows: ''The sending of rifles to the Korean government by us (Japanese) at this time, is showing precisely that we encourage the reformation of the Korean military system. We will provide the rifles any time if the Korean government wishes to have them.''

Count Inouye, with the approval of the army sent five pieces of each type to the Korean government. The Korean government invited Lieutenant Horimoto, the Japanese military attache to the Japanese legation at Seoul, to be military instructor of the Korean army. Yun Ung-nyol, one of the members of the Korean good-will mission to Japan, visited Lt. Horimoto several times, and asked many questions in regard to the military affairs. Yun himself held a high position in the Korean army, and also was trusted by the King. Yun who was one of the leading men who had initiated the reformation of the old Korean system of drill to the new system which was patterned after the Japanese system, was trying to introduce the Japanese military system as quickly as possible in Korea. Lt. Horimoto immediately began to train eighty selected young men. This was the beginning of the reformation of the Korean military system. There were five branches in the Korean military department; protection, training, prohibition, a palace guard, and general duty. These five branches were abolished and two were established, general military and training department. As soon as this new system was introduced to Korea, many of the old military officials as well as the old-time professional soldiers lost their positions and were waiting for an opportunity for revenge. These discharged soldiers were to have been compensated by certain numbers of sacks of rice by the government. A high officer who was in charge of the military affairs, Min Kun-ho, trying to avoid future trouble had the government pay one month's compensation to these soldiers during the month of June in 1883. Unfortunately some culprit had mixed great quantities of sand in the sacks of rice, and consequently embittered the soldiers to such an extent that some five thousand of them began a fight against the Min dominated government. The government, only able to pay one month's pay out of the thirteen month period, did not satisfy the former soldiers. An officer who was in charge of the warehouse mixed the sand in order to confiscate some of the rice for his personal use. The dishonesty of the government officials included those of all ranks. The soldiers killed Min Kun-ho and, Lt. Horimoto, the Japanese military instructor. The embittered soldiers thought that these two were responsible for this inhuman act. During these turbulent days, Queen Min escaped through disguise to her relatives at Tsungju in South Korea. She disguised herself as a palace girl and fled when the ex-soldiers entered into the palace. The Japanese minister, Hanabusas fled to Chemulpo where he received help from the British and went to Japan on a British survey ship.

Tae Won-kun, who was seeking for an opportunity to gain power at the palace, saw his chance with the critical condition of the Min-dominated administration. Tae Won-kun also had influence over the former soldiers. He secretly instructed Kim Jang-son, and Ryu Tsung-man of the anti-Min faction to camouflage their clothes as ordinary citizens, and lead the former soldiers into the government warehouse to get guns. The ex-soldiers released the former national guards, Kim Tsun-yang, Ryu Pok-man, Jung Ji-gil, and Kang Myongjun, who were imprisoned by the Min faction, from the Seoul prison. The ex-soldiers were divided into three groups: one group was to attack Kim Po-hyon, the governor of Kyong-gi province, and the military warehouse; the second group was to attack Min Tae-ho another of Min's high officials; the third group was to attack the military instructor Lt. Horimoto and the Japanese legation. These attacks followed and simultaneously many high officials including General Yi Kyung-ha, Sim Sun-tak, were dismissed from their post because these high officials were also the targets of the former soldiers. Tae Won-kun appointed Yi Jai-myon, General of the Army, and warned him of the gravity of his responsibility if a such critical situation reoccurred. Tae Won-kun restored the old system and appointed his men to the various posts. Yi Jai-myon became general of the training, Shin Jang-hi became the general of the Palace guard, besides them, Jo I-sun, Im Sangjun, Yi Hojong, Jo Kyong-ho, Shin Ingjo were also assigned various positions in the government.

Meanwhile, Queen Min sent a secret messenger to the King with news of her safety and that she was temporarily staying at her relative's in Tsungju city. The message was brought by Pyon Won-kyu, a government interpreter who was at the city, and no one at the palace was aware of her safety until the message had arrived. The Queen simultaneously sent word to the Korean envoy, Kim Yun-sik, in Tien-tsien stating that the revolt was led by Tae Won-kun in order to further his political ambitions and that the government needed help from China in order to settle the revolt. Kim immediately forwarded the Queen's message to Li Hung-chang. Li, who was watching the Japanese activities in Korea very closely, saw the opportunity had arrived, and sent five thousand soldiers under the leadership of Wu Chang-ching and Ting Wu-chang to Korea as soon as he received Kim's message. The Chinese soldiers arrived in Korea and the revolting group had been suppressed following Tae-Won-kun's arrival to the palace.

Prior to the Chinese arrival, the Korean government also sent a message to the Japanese government. The message read: "This incident was entirely a domestic affair in which many high officials were killed and in which your legation also was involved. The government was unable to control the mob since the soldiers were among them. We are very sorry that we were unable to protect your legation.'' The Japanese government had an emergency cabinet meeting, they decided: first, to send one warship to Wonsan and one to Pusan in order to protect the Japanese citizens; second, to send Consul Kindo of Pusan to Chemulpo in order to investigate the situation; third, to send three hundred soldiers and sailors to Seoul with Hanabusa; fourth, that the minister would settle the matter at Seoul; fifth, that they should avoid war by following a defensive policy, but that if there were no other alternative save war, the minister must report to the government as soon as possible.

Inouye arrived at Shimonoseki where Hanabusa was waiting for instructions on August 7th, after he heard all the detailed reports from Hanabusa, he advised him in addition to follow a peace policy as much as possible. Count Inouye further to]d Hanabusa that in case the Korean government refused the Japanese proposals and was unwilling to cooperate with Hanabusa, the Japanese government was going to ask for either Kumun Island (Hamilton Island) or the Song-do Island, and that the Korean government should dismiss all the pro-revolt group, and punish them. Inouye further stated that in case of an important incident, they would demand heavy damages. By this time, the Korean government had arranged a meeting with the Japanese envoys including Inouye.

As a consequence of the meeting, Korea made another treaty which is known as the Chemulpo Treaty after the name of the city where it was signed. According to the treaty, Korea was to pay an indemnity of five hundred thousand yen on a five year's installment basis; Japan was to keep three hundred Japanese armed soldiers in Seoul; and to send a Korean envoy to Japan for an apology.

Tae Won-kun secretly sent a copy of the Japanese requests to the Chinese officials, Ma, and asked him to be arbitrator for the Koreans and the Japanese. Rather than arbitrating the dispute, the Chinese officials, Ma and Ting called upon Tae Won-kun at his home, and suggested that he see the Chinese emperor in order to apologize for the unfortunate riots.

Commodore Ting arrested Tae Won-kun when he refused to follow Ma's suggestion, and took him to the Chinese warship; later they took him to Tien-tsien. This action of the Chinese officials could hardly be understood since Tae Won-kun was ready to cooperate with China, rather than act against her. No others than the Japanese officials were happy to see Tae Won-kun's disappearance.

The disappearance of Tae Won-kun from the Korean political scene was a great help to the Japanese who were trying to settle the problem of the revolts. On August 28, the Korean government sent message to the Japanese minister saying that they were sending the Korean plenipotentiary, Yi U-won and the vice-envoy Kim Hongjip to meet Hanabusa to negotiate the dispute.

Later, the Korean government sent Kim Hong-Jip again to Tokyo on a good-will mission. Kim was received by the Japanese Emperor and met many outstanding Japanese statemen of the days and was welcomed with a special banquet. He had several conferences with many high ranking officials of the Japanese government in regard to trade between the two nations. Thus Kim tried to pave the road for normal trade relationships between Japan and Korea. Korea now became a member of the trade nations of modern days through Japanese effort, although they were forcefully engaged, nevertheless, she opened her door for first time to the world as a treaty bounded nation. What this means to Korea we will examine in the following chapters.

Notes

1. *Tongmun Hwigo,* "The Condition of The Foreign Ships"
2. *Chosen Kosho Shimatsu,* Vol. 1, 1868
3. *Okuhira, op.cit., p. 33*
4. *Ilsongnok,* April 12, 14, 1875
5. *Chosen Kosho Shimatsu, Vol. 1,* 1868
6. Okuhira, *op.cit., p. 34*
7. *Chosen-shi, op.cit, p. 277*
8. *Public Record Office,* Alcock to Earl Russell, Yedo, March 17, 1862, No. 23. Confidential Foreign Office 46-51.
9. Brinkley, F., *A History of the Japanese People, p. 683*
10. *Chosen Kankei Kosho Hishu,* Dec. 9, 1875
11. *Seigai Inouye Koden, Vol. 11, p.* 598-620, 655-683 *Seikan Jitsuki o or The Real Situation of the Seikan,* (conquering Korea), Chapter on "The 17th Cabinet Meeting of Japan".
12. Wang Myong, *op cit., p. 193*
13. The young king's secret sweetheart was Yi Sang-sung, a palace girl.
14. Wang Myong, *op cit., p. 196, 199*
15. *Ilsongnok, August 9,* 1874; *Singjongwon Revised Diary,* August 9, 1874; *Honcho Kiji,* V. 195, August 10, 1874
16. The main gate of the city was used only by a superior envoy from the central government by one of equivalent rank. The local Korean officers were not willing to treat the Japanese officials on the same levels as their Korean superiors.
17. *Ilsongnok,* May 10, 25, 1875; *Chosen Kosai Shimatsu, Vol.* 3
18. *Seigai Inouye-Ko Den, p. 684*

19. Singjongwon, op.cit., Mar. 2, 6, May, 17, 1875
20. Seigai Inouye-Ko Den, Vol. 11, p. 686-694
21. *Ilsongnok,* August 2, 23, 1875
22. *Okuhira,* op.cit., *p.* 43
23. *Chosen Shi, op.cit. p.* 385, also see, Ariga, N. "Diplomacy" in Alfred Stead (ed) *Japan by the Japanese, p. 176*
24. *Tongmun Hwigo, op. cit..* Wang Yun-sheng, *Liu-shin-nien Lai Chung-kuo Yu Jih-pen,* or *Sixty Years of Relations between China and Japan, Vol. 1, p.* 124
25. *Ilsongnok,* Jan. 5, 1876
26. Ibid., Jan. 15, 1876
27. *Chosen-shi, op. cit., p.* 398
28. *Tongmun Hwigo, op. cit., Chosen-shi, op. cit.,* p. 399
29. *Seigai Inouye-Ko Den. Vol. 11,* p. 700 703, 704
30. Okuhira, *op. cit.,* pp. 50-55, quoted from the *Nishi, Monji* or the *Letters of the Japanese* Mission, Vol. 1
31. Rockhill, W. W., *China's Intercourse with Korea, p.* If; see Sir Harry Parke's report, the British to Japan, to the Earl of Dearby. Yedo, March 27, 1876. Japan no. 1, 1876, p. 17ff
32. Vinacke, H., A *History of the Far East in Modern Times, p.* 131
33. Dennett, T., *American in Eastern Asia, p.* 466
34. Noble. H., *Korea and U.S. Before 1895, Vol. 1, p.* 54. Noble's doctorate thesis.
35. Chung Henry, *Korean Treaties, p.* 209
36. Grifts. *op. cit., p. 4-6*
37. *Ilsongnok,* Nov. 17. 18, 1878
38. *The Diary of the Japanese Mission,* April 15, 17, 18, 1879, quoted in *Chosen-shi, op.cit.,* p. 458
39. *Chosen-shi, op. cit., p.* 479
40. *Ilsongnok,* second March, 4, 5, 1880. According to the Chinese calender there were two months of March is that year.
41. *Chosen-shi, op.cit., p.* 495
42. *Seigai Inouye-Ko Den, Vol.* 111, pp. 436-437

3

Korea Opened to Western Powers, the 1882 Treaty

The Korean national isolation policy continued even after the Treaty of 1876. Many Western powers attempted to open Korea, but all failed. After the expedition to Kanghwa in 1871, the United States, too, called off the Korean problem. In 1878, United States Senator Aaron A. Sargent of California introduced a resolution which requested the President to "appoint a commission to represent this country in an effort to arrange, by peaceful means .... a treaty of peace and commerce between the United States and the Kingdom of Corea." At the same time the Senator justified the action of the Korean government in respect to the *General Sherman,* and condemned the attacks upon the ports by the navy in 1871.[1] There was no formal action taken on the resolution, but the following year, Commodore R.W. Shufeldt was sent to the China Sea with instruction to make, if possible, a treaty with Korea. Commodore Shufeldt visited Pusan in 1880 like many others did in the previous years and experienced the same refusal that other foreign officers had. Commodore Shufeldt stayed at the American legation in Peking until 1882. Prior to Shufeldt's visit, a British vessel was wrecked on the Island of Jeju or Qwelpart in 1878, and the Koreans rescued the crew, salvaged the cargo, provided transportation to Nagasaki, Japan but refused to accept any compensation for their services. The British secretary at the legation in Tokyo tried to use this opportunity to establish a permanent relationship with Korea, but failed. Russian, British, and French vessels touched at different ports, and sought to communicate with the Korean authorities at Seoul but failed including an Italian man-of-war at Wonsan and Pusan.[2]

Li Hung-chang who was alarmed by the treaty of 1876 between

Korea and Japan, which recognized the Korean independence, set promptly to work in checking the Japanese activities in Korea. Li, therefore, encouraged Korea to enter into treaty relations with Western powers and simultaneously urged the Western powers to open trade with Korea.[3] Li writes thus to a high official of the Korean government:

> You may say that the simplest way to avoid trouble would be to shut your self in and be at peace. Alas, as far as the East is concerned, that is not possible. There is no human agency capable of putting a stop to the expansionist movement of Japan, had not your government been compelled to inaugurate the new era by making a treaty of commerce with them? As matters stand, therefore, is not our best course to neutralize one poison by another? You should seize every opportunity to establish treaty relations with Western nations of which you should make use to check Japan.[4]

By this time the Korean government was forced to realize that it was impossible not to make treaties with the Western powers. Commodore Shufeldt learned these facts about the Korean intention and went to Korea accompanied by three Chinese naval vessels. Prior to this adventure, the Secretary of State of the United States, instructed John A. Bingham, the U.S. Minister to Japan, to ask for the aid of Japan to contact the Kingdom of Korea.[5] Commodore Shufeldt received a letter of introduction addressed to the Japanese consul at Pusan from the foreign minister, Inouye. Shufeldt contacted the local officer at Pusan, and the head of Tong-Nae city, through the aid of the Japanese consul. The Korean officials, however, refused to deliver Shufeldt's message to the King because the trade was open only to Japan. After the failure of this attempt, Shufeldt went to Tokyo and the minister Bingham contacted Inouye for help. Inouye sent a message to the Korean foreign minister, Yun Ja-sing, on May 29, 1880. Inouye requested that Yun answer his letter within sixty days. Inouye's message was that the Korean government would no longer be able to continue the isolation policy and that it would be much wiser to open trade with other nations. He also introduced Commodore Shufeldt and explained what had happened at Pusan. He further explained that such incidents like in Pusan might have brought a serious international incident, and isolation policy was impossible due to the changing international situation of the day. Not only had Japan followed this step, but also had China that the United States was respecting this courtesy and that the American envoy was anxious to hear from the Korean government.[6] On August 11, 1881, Kim Hong-Jip arrived at Tokyo and returned the American message which was still sealed and not opened. Evidently, they didn't even read the American message".[7] After returning the American message to the Japanese foreign office explaining that the Korean government had no desire to open trade with the United States or any other foreign country, Kim further explained that improper words were used. The American addressed Korea as "Tae Koyro" or "The Great Korea", and "O-ran" or "Honorable Look". These terms had been used in reference to China and her emperor. Japan had faced the similar problems as we have noticed previously. The Korean government, therefore, did not even wish to open the letter'.[8]

The Japanese foreign minister, on the other hand, encouraged the Korean envoy to open the country and manufacture ammunition to defend the nation, and to select talented young men in the military and the cultural fields in order to train personnel. Kim later followed Inouye's advice. While Kim was staying in Tokyo, the Chinese minister to Japan, Ho I-chang and the councilor, Whang, came to see Kim often. Kim received a letter from them stating that there was no other problem more critical than that of preventing Russian aggression in the Far East. Korea should be friendly to China, negotiate with Japan and make associations with the United States in order to build a strong country. The letter further stated that China would help Korea in case of war with a foreign country, but since Japan was not able to help Korea in any case, it would be to Korea's advantage to maintain a closer relationship with China rather than Japan. The United States was a country of courtesy and did not intend to invade foreign lands or to tell lies to people and interfere with other nation's political affairs. The United States had helped small nations. Since the United States was China's favorite nation, China distinguished the United States from European nations; the Chinese believed that the United States had no other intentions than "to have trade".[9]

The Chinese officials advised Kim Hongjip that the Korean government should treat the American envoy well and seek to make a treaty. Thus both the Chinese and the Japanese governments encouraged the Korean government to make a treaty with the United States. Not only the Chinese government, but also the Japanese government was afraid of the Russian aggressiveness in the Far East. Inouye told Kim Hongjip that the trouble between Russia and China would affect Japan as well as Korea that the desires of the Americans, the British and the French to open trade in Korea were not so much for the trade itself but because they feared Russian domination in Korea.

Meantime, the Korean government sent Yi U-won to Tientsin with selected groups of people who were to be trained in the manufacture of munitions. Yi agreed with Li Hung-chung that the Korean government should ask for advice from the Chinese foreign officers in matters connected with foreign nations in the future. In spite of the 1876 treaty with Japan, the Korean government was still inclined to go along with China in a traditional "big-brother" relationship. Kim Hongjip, meantime, returned to Korea from Japan, and reported to the King personally. The King asked him which way the Russians would enter China in case Russia attacked China. Kim replied that the Chinese minister was worried over the Russian problem and that he was willing to cooperate with the Korean government. He hoped that the Korean government would be prepared to meet the national emergency although China would be willing to help Korea. The only problem being the unsettled condition of the Korean foreign policy. The King, who was personally worried about the international situation was anxious to find out all the details in regard to the situation.

From here on, the King took more active interest on the matter of foreign policy, and began to think seriously of opening Korea to the Western powers. The King appointed Kim Hong-Jip to pursue such a possibility.

Commodore Shufeldt, after receiving a rejection from the Korean government, went to Nagasaki, where he waited to make his next move. The Chinese consul in the city hearing about Shufeldt and his mission, made a report to Li Hung-chang. Li Hung-chang was much surprised at the news of Shufeldt and his mission and invited him to China. Shufeldt accepted Li's invitation and arrived at Tientsin on August 25, 1880. It was an obvious political action of Li who disliked the Japanese recognition of the Korean independence in the 1876 treaty, did not want to see another Korean treaty through the Japanese government. On August 26th Shufeldt had the first conference with Li which lasted for three hours. Commodore Shufeldt reported that at first he asked for help from China in order to succeed in making the treaty between the United States and Korea. Further he pointed out that Korea seemed to be a poor country, therefore, there would not be much trade between the two nations, but her strategic position would help the Americans in case of a shipwreck. Shufeldt also discussed the significant strategic military position of the Korean peninsula in relation to China, Japan, and Russia.

Besides the Korean question, the two men discussed the matter of naval affairs, and the Sino-Russian crisis. Li was concerned over the Russian aggression in Korea and Manchuria, and mentioned the possibility of war between China and Russia. Commodore Shufeldt advised Li that China had no winning chance in case of conflict and that China should follow a peace policy at any cost. Li took his advice and avoided a war.

Commodore Shufeldt left China after a satisfactory conference with Li and arrived at San Francisco on November 8, 1880 and immediately left for Washington, D.C.. Shufeldt made a detailed report to the State and the Navy

Departments on his trip and requested to return to China to finish the treaty between Korea and the United States. The secretaries of the State and Navy granted his request, and Shufeldt went back to China on July 1, of the next year. It is significant to observe here that Commodore Shufeldt was appointed to negotiate one of the most difficult treaties in Far Eastern history in spite of many trained. diplomats in Washington. This fact indicated his talent as a diplomat as well as a naval officer. The Secretary of the State instructed the U.S. minister to China not only to have an immediate interest in regard to the treaty between Korea and the United States, that it was necessary also to have an intimate knowledge of the general political conditions in the East. Therefore, Commodore Shufeldt made reports to the State Department as soon as he received all the available news from Tientsin on the way to Peking. He was to report to the American legation at the same time. If there was any further news, that too was to be reported immediately''.[10]

Meantime, Li Hung-chang contacted the Korean officials who was at Tientsin at that time. The Korean officials, O Yunjung, the head of the machine and the engine construction department, and Yi Jo-yu went to Tientsin in order to inspect the works of the Korean students who were there to study the technical matters.[11] Li suggested that the Korean official should make an inquiry of the Korean government's minister plenipotentiary in regard to a treaty with the United States. Li explained to O Yunjung the importance of the treaty with the United States. The Korean official went back to Seoul where he delivered Li's message. The Korean government, by this time, abandoned it's traditional isolation policy, and looked for the opportunity to make a treaty. The King and the government officials expressed such desires and looked for the proper opportunity since Kim Hongjip's report from Tokyo on the Russian problem.

The Korean government sent her envoy, Kim Yun-sik, and the interpreter, Pyun Won-kyu, to China. The envoy carried a secret letter which was delivered to Li Hung-chang. The secret message from the Korean King stated that the King had heard about the strong and rich United States, who loved peace, and wished to negotiate a treaty with her through the office of Li Hung-chang. The King, however, was fearful of his advisors who still disliked the foreigners. In order to make a successful negotiation, the King believed that the Chinese Emperor should force the high officials of the Korean government to accept the Chinese advice by proclaiming the necessity of such a treaty at this time. The King's message had indicated his inferior position and reduced his dignity as a ruler of the nation in order to gain aid from the Chinese Emperor, but aid was not coming.

Li Hung-chang who was aware of the 1876 treaty between Korea and

Japan, wanted to avoid unnecessary conflict with Japan at this time, and advised the Korean envoy not to follow the King's suggestion. Li suggested a treaty between Korea and the United States, and had sent a letter of recommendation to Seoul to this effect. Among the high officials in Seoul, the strong anti-foreign faction in the cabinet was still resisting such a proposal, and expressed a fear of Russian invasion in the event of the Russo-Chinese War, although the Russo-Chinese treaty was already signed on February 24 at St. Petersburg in order to avoid such conflict. Thus, the debate on the treaty continued in Seoul.

Besides the Korean problem, there was another unfortunate development for Commodore Shufeldt. The foreign diplomats, especially the French minister, did not like the close relationship between Shufeldt and Li Hung chang. Li called off his close friendship with Commodore Shufeldt under the circumstances. The American minister, Angell, and the deputy minister, Holcombe, advised Shufeldt, to leave China since the situation was unfavorable to Shufeldt. Li not only stopped talking about Shufeldt's position as a Chinese naval adviser but even stopped asking him for advise concerning naval matters.[12] Meantime, the American government appointed Shufeldt as the American plenipotentiary to negotiate a treaty with the Kingdom of Korea. The Secretary of State sent a long instructive letter to Shufeldt. The letter said that the American government would feel very dissatisfied if a situation should arise where the Korean should misjudge American freindship to Korea. An attempt for negotiations should not even be started, unless there were assurance for complete success.[13] The Secretary further instructed that the process of the treaty should follow the United States-Japanese treaty of 1857, and that it would be wise to bring out the case of the shipwreck as the first and the main purpose of the treaty. Secretary Blaine, had knowledge of the *General Sherman* incident. He admitted that he was not sure whether the President's personal letter to the Korean King would help the situation or not. He also wasn't sure which port would be the most desirable and the one most likely to be opened. He mentioned the port of Pusan as one possibility. As Blaine stated, the whole problem had to depend on Shufeldt. Commodore Shufeldt, meanwhile, was informed by Li Hung-chang that the Korean envoys, Kim Yun-sik and Yi Tong-in were in the city in order to discuss the treaty.[14] Shufeldt immediately sent news to Washington.

On January 17, 1882, the new Secretary of State, Frelinghuysen, sent the following wire to Shufeldt: "Congratulate Shufeldt on prospect of successful negotiation." The Secretary also sent instructions to Shufeldt that the main purpose of the treaty should be for protection of the American lives in case of a shipwreck on the Korean coast. He also added that it would be well not to try to gain too much at first. The treaty should be simple and on a small scale, as otherwise the treaty might not be made at all. The treaty could be gradually extended as the need arose. In general, his instruction was similar to the previous message from Blaine.[15]

Commodore Shufeldt immediately set to work on the treaty by visiting the deputy American minister, Holcombe, as the latter was to participate in the treaty conference. Holcombe had mastered the Chinese language, and his participation would avoid any personal feeling with Li Hung-chang, since Shufeldt was no longer interested in talking on a personal level as before. Shufeldt checked at the Chinese foreign office to find out if Li was an accredited representative of the Chinese government. He found Li to be the official representative. Li came to Tientsin where Shufeldt was waiting for him.

The first conference on the treaty was held March 25, 1882. Li assured Shufeldt that the Korean king and his ministers were agreed on opening Korea to the foreign countries and that they hoped to discuss treaty plans with the United States. There were, however, the enemies of the King and his ministers, and those opposed to opening the country. Recently, the King sent his envoys to Li and they were to negotiate the treaty under Li's supervision. Li allowed Shufeldt to send this message to Washington, which Shufeldt immediately dispatched. The strange feature of the conference was that there were no Korean envoys present although the treaty was with Korea. The Korean envoy, Kim Yun-sik, secretly informed Li Hungchang that he could represent Korea. Kim was mainly concerned with the opposite group of Koreans at home. Shufeldt might have felt the strange air at the conference. Shufeldt who was to negotiate the treaty according to the international law, had to know a little more concerning the background of what was going on between Li Hung-chang and the Korean envoy.

This strange feature can be explained thus; the drafts of the treaty were presented by Li Hung-chang and Shufeldt at the second conference. The main problem at this conference was the first article of Li's draft, which stated: "Chosen (Korea) being a dependent state of the Chinese Empire.[16] This first phrase of the first article was not included when the Korean envoy, Kim Yun-sik, brought it to Li, but Li, dissatisfied with the Korean draft, added the phrase later".[17] Shufedlt after careful study of Li's draft, objected to the inclusion, "dependent state", and Li refused to continue further discussion if Shufeldt rejected the "dependent state" clause. Li further stated that his government would not send envoys and the warships to Korea with the American envoys. Shufeldt calmly presented the prepared letter to Li, and said that the United States had a right to deal with Korea if she was exercising her own sovereignty in all matters of internal administration and foreign relations.[18] The U.S.

government did not wish to accept any statement which referred to the relationship between China and Korea in the treaty. Li explained that even if they avoided the "dependent state" phrase, the Korean King would add it later. It seemed that Li was speaking for himself, not for the King or the King's envoy when he referred to the King's action or used the phrase "dependent state" in the draft. Li's intention was obvious that he wanted to discredit the 1876 treaty which recognized the independence of Korea from China.

Thus the second conference ended without solving the problem of the "dependent state" phrase.[19]

At the third conference, the "dependent state" phrase was still the main problem. Both Shufeldt and Li Hung-chang did not compromise or give in, but held on their to original positions. Meanwhile, Holcombe went to visit the Chinese foreign office at Peking, and explained the fact that the United States government would not give in to the "dependent state" problem; therefore, in order to make a successful treaty, the Chinese government must compromise in this matter. Holcombe suggested to the foreign officer to advise Li Hung-chang to compromise on the problem of the "dependent state." Holcombe as the interpreter of Shufeldt advised him on many issues. He knew more about Chinese politics than Shufeldt or any American then. After Holcombe found out that the Chinese government would give in on the matter of the "dependent state" after he talked with the Chinese foreign officers privately, Holcombe immediately advised Shufeldt to stubbornly oppose Li's original suggestion; Shufeldt certainly did as he was told by Holcombe. Holcombe's diplomatic talent was a great contribution to the treaty. His knowledge of China was indispensable to make a successful negotiation with China. On April 19, the draft was completed except for the "dependent state" phrase in the first article.[20]

The Korean envoy, Kim Yun-sik, though in Tientsien all during the time of the conferences between Shufeldt and Li Hung-chang never attended the conferences. Li conferred with Kim from time to time whenever necessary. As soon as the draft was completed Shufeldt was ready to leave for Korea in order to complete the treaty. Li Hung-chang sent two Chinese officials in order to prepare to welcome the American envoy.[21] Li also wrote a letter to Hing In-kun, the brother of Tae Won-kun, that Korea should negotiate a treaty with the United States, and gave all the details about the conferences between Shufeldt and himself.

While the conference was proceeding, an unexpected problem arose. Li Hung-chang was informed by his friend in the United States that Shufeldt had written on the China situation and had stated that only power could be appreciated in China. Li instantly suspected Shufeldt's action, and questioned

Shufeldt in regard to the article. Shufeldt's article was originally written to U.S. Senator Sargent of California, from Tientsin on January 1,1882. This letter appeared in the newspapers in San Francisco as an open letter, which was reprinted in the *North China Daily News,* on May 9, 1882. Shufeldt's letter said: "Six months residence in this city (Tientsin), the political center of the Chinese government, and an intimacy rather exceptional with ruling element, has convinced me that deceit and untruthfulness pervade all intercourse with foreigners; that an ineradicable hatred exists, and that any appeal across this barrier, either of sympathy or gratitude, is utterly idle. The only appeal or argument appreciated is that of force."[22] The points Commodore Shufeldt had endeavored to make in this letter were: "that China has no real aggressive military or navel strength; that there is and can be no affinity between the people of the United States and China; that the government of the United States, as the government of Europe, should insist upon its rights in China, concerning no more than is granted and trusting no more it is trusted; that although the two countries are so situated as to invite trade, there never can be any intimate political or commercial relations between them, except upon the basis of such as the United States may demand."[23] The main reason Shufeldt addressed it to Senator Sargent was he remembered that "You were the earnest opponent of unlimited Chinese immigrations into the United States both as Senator and citizen of your state." Thus the letter almost caused the unhappy ending of the treaty. Holcombe, the deputy minister, stated to Frelinghuysen that it was fortunate that the letter was published after Commodore Shufeldt left for Korea for it might have prevented the success of Shufeldt's mission to China if the Chinese government had known of it before hand.[24]

The Korean government appointed Shin Hyon as the chief envoy, Kim Hong-Jip as the vice-envoy and So Sang-u as the secretariat. The U.S. plenipotentiary minister Shufeldt arrived at Chemulpo by the U.S. *Swatara,* with three Chinese warships on May 12, 1882.[25] The Korean envoys, Shin and Kim went to meet Shufeldt and the other Chinese officials. Shufeldt returned to visit the Korean envoys the next day. It was a friendly visit, and the goodwill of the Koreans was expressed by their gifts which included rice, eggs, chickens, pigs and other food stuffs.[26] On the other hand, the American envoy also brought such gifts as tea sets, tobacco, and others to the Koreans. At the Korean banquet, Shufeldt remarked that in speaking of a country, one must know their food because it tells about the land and the customs. Those Korean foods were so tasty and the best he had ever tasted. The friendly visit of the American envoys to the Korean banquet helped in creating the hospitable atmosphere. Shufeldt made a good impression on the Koreans.

On May 17th, two Chinese officials, Ma and Ting, visited Shin and

Kim, and the Korean envoys suggested to the Chinese officials that there should be a statement in regard to the rice export as in the case of the 1876 treaty. The rice export was the main concern of the envoys since it was the topic of the day discussed by the ministers as well as the Korean people. The people were afraid that the export of rice would bring starvation to the nation. On the same afternoon, the Chinese official Ma went to confer with Shufeldt in regard to the rice export. On May 18th and 19th, Ma with five others went to Seoul in order to investigate the market condition. On May 20th, Shufeldt landed at Chemulpo with Captain Cooper of *The Swatara,* and other naval officials to visit Shin and Kim formally. As soon as the ceremony ended, Shufeldt and the Korean envoys inspected each other's certificates. Shufeldt gave the envoy the personal message of the President to the King of Korea. They agreed upon the contents of the treaty, and decided on May 20th for the date of signing. On May 21st, they prepared the documents which included three copies in English and three in Chinese.[27]

On May 22, 1882, nine-thirty in the morning, Shufeldt, with fifteen assistants and twenty sailors landed at Chemulpo where the Korean envoys were waiting for them. After the brief greetings, the Korean plenipotentiary Shin Hyon and the vice-envoy Kim HongJip signed on the six copies of the treaty; after which the American plenipotentiary minister, Robert Shufeldt signed.[28] Both Ma and Ting also arrived, but they did not attend when the actual signatures were exchanged. In fact, they requested to leave the room as a matter of courtesy. Hanabusa, too arrived at Chemulpo. When the American envoy entered Korean waters, Hanabusa paid a visit to Shufeldt, but like the Chinese, did not attend the ceremony.

After the ceremony was over, the American warship fired twenty-one gun salute in respect of the King of Korea; a banquet followed at the Chinese warship which was attended by the Korean and the American dignitaries. Article one of the treaty was significant in the Korean relations with the United States. It read:

> If other powers deal unjustly or oppressively with either govern-
> ment the other will exert their good offices on being informed of the
> case, to bring an amicable arrangement, thus showing their friendly
> feelings.[29]

The two countries were to be opened for residence to the citizens and subjects of each other to pursue their callings and avocations.[30] Another significant point of the treaty was that it acknowledged the independence of Korea as it appeared in the treaty of 1876 with Japan, and the treaty was negotiated as an independent state. This meant a direct loss in China's prestige over Korea.[31]

A new phrase, not in the original draft which was agreed upon between Shufeldt and Li Hung-chang, in article eight of the treaty read: "But it is to be understood that the exportation of rice and bread stuffs of every description is prohibited from the open port of Inchun(Chemulpo)". The phrase was suggested by the Korean who had insisted upon the same thing in the 1876 treaty and accepted by Shufeldt. On May 23, the Chinese officials, Ma and Ting, gave Shufeldt the Korean King's reply to the President of the United States. The letter dated May 21st, or April 5th according to the Chinese calendar read: "Having heard that the administration of your government was just and upright, we have long desired to establish friendly relationships with you, but to our deep regret have had no opportunity to do so . . ." and it continued, "having now received the envoy whom you have sent to us for the purpose of negotiating a treaty, we have appointed Shen of the Board of Foreign Affairs as our minister, and Chin(Kim), also of the Board, as his assistant to discuss the business with him. They will be able to sign the treaty at an early day which can be carried back and presented to you by Commodore Shufeldt. We beg that it be ratified quickly and an envoy sent hither to exchange the ratification in order to enable our two governments and peoples to mutually enjoy the benefits of the cordial friendship which shall flow from it, which is our sincere desire."[32] The King pointed out that the American envoy and the Korean envoy would discuss the business and would be able to sign the treaty at an early date. He further said, "we beg that it be ratified quickly and an envoy sent . . ."

After receiving this letter, Commodore Shufeldt replied that there have been thirty years of trade between the people of the East and the West. The general life of the peoples is the same although they are a different race. He continued that the principle of trade is to contribute to.the intellectual and the cultural development of the people as well as for the nation to gain wealth and strength. Shufeldt indicated that the purpose of his mission was also to strengthen the goodwill relations between the two nations, and he assured that there was no other reason than this peaceful will in his mission.[33]

On May 24, Commodore Shufeldt and his group left Chemulpo for Shanghai. The Koreans were impressed by the Americans and so the Koreans invited them again in 1886. When Shufeldt met Li Hung-chang at Tientsin, Li showed him the letter which was of an entirely different nature than the letter which Shufeldt had already received. This letter, too, was addressed to the President of the United States, but dated May 16th, seven days before the treaty had been signed. The Korean King's letter was delivered to Shufeldt two days after the treaty signature; therefore, it seemed at that time that Li Hung-chang tried to impress upon the United States that Korea is a tributary state to China through the Korean King's personal recognition of the Korean political status quo, since Li was unable to insert "dependant state" in the treaty. Li was aware of the fact that Korea's loyalty to the relationship between Korea and China could no longer be preserved for it involved more than just two nations. Li, therefore, tried to obtain by legal evidence which in the Western eyes, embraces international law, to indicate Korea's subordination to China. Li was familiar with the Japanese-Korean treaty of 1876 and its implication. Commodore Shufeldt, on the other hand, paid little attention to the King's letter for he was mainly concerned with the treaty. Shufeldt, therefore, agreed to accept the King's letter which included the "dependent state" phrase rather than one which the King delivered to Shufeldt two days after the treaty signature. The officially recognized letter said:

> His majesty, the King of Chosen herewith makes a communication. Chosen has been from ancient times a state tributary to China, Yet, hitherto full sovereignty has been exercised by the Kings of Chosen in all matters of internal administration and foreign relations. Chosen and the United States in establishing now by mutual consent a treaty are dealing with each other upon a basis of equality. The King of Chosen distinctly pledges his own sovereign powers for the complete enforcement in good faith of all the stipulations of the treaty in accordance with international law. As regards the various duties which develop upon as a tributary state to China the U.S. has no concern whatever. Having appointed envoys to negotiate a treaty it appears to be my duty, in addition there to, to make this preliminary declaration to the President of the United States, May 15,1882".[34]

Commodore Shufeldt, commenting on the King's letter to the President said that letter concerned the tributary status to China, and was written before the signing of the treaty.[35] Shufeldt further commented that this mistake happened because the fact that they lacked a good interpreter. He said that there was no significant meaning to the whole matter except for the fact that it was breaking of their promise between Shufeldt and Li Hung-chang. Shufeldt, however, knew that some of the misunderstanding in the treaty process was due to the lack of a good interpreter. Professor H.H. Dubs underestimated the language capability of the American envoy Shufeldt and the interpreter, Holcombe. Professor Dubs comments: "Both Shufeldt and Holcombe really paraphrase this letter (King's letter) instead of translating it exactly, thus securing a more readable translation and gives an impression that is misleading. In my translation I have tried to be literal and to give the impression the letter would make upon an educated Corean of that date."[36] Shufeldt and Holcombe, however, did not translate the King's letter, or other documents, word for word; it would be impossible to maintain the original meaning by this method. Two translations of Shufeldt and Holcombe give sufficient idea of the King's letter although they used legal terminology non-existent in the Far Eastern language at that time. Contrary to Professor Dubs's view, careful study reveals that Shufeldt understood the general political situation in China and Korea, and handled the situation very well.

Another conflicting matter after the treaty was that concerning the appointment of a Korean minister to the United States. Li Hung-chang did not wish to see a Korean minister with the same rank as the Chinese in Washington. Li insisted that the Korean minister apply in all important diplomatic matters to the Chinese minister and who would give the final approval. Secretary of the State Bayand who was informed of this matter instructed the American minister in Peking to protest the Chinese action, and gave notice to both governments that "as the United States have no priority with the interrelations of China and Corea, we shall treat both as separate governments customarily represented here by their respective and independent agents."[37] The Korean minister at Washington was later received without Chinese intervention, and there was no further question on the subject although China did interfere with the Korean internal affairs until the Sino-Japanese War. The friendly disposition of the Korean government towards the United States was indicated soon after the treaty in a number of ways. Besides the exchange of diplomatic courtesies; American missionaries were allowed to work in Korea in spite of the fact that the guarantee of the missionary to work was lacking in the treaty of 1882.

The President of the United States appointed Lucius H. Foote as the first American minister to Korea. Minister Foote arrived on February 27, 1883 at Seoul where he exchanged certificates with the Korean minister, Min Yong-mok. By request of the U.S. Senate the Korean government granted the rights of transportation of the American exports and imports in Korean ports. This special right was in addition to a similar one to the American-Japanese treaty and the American-Chinese treaty. One interesting fact in the State Department paper was that Thomas Edison wanted the right to place and operate electric lights and the telephone in Korea. Edison wrote to Foote who reported to the Secretary of the State: "on behalf of Mr. Thomas A. Edison, I sometime since applied for the exclusive right to place and operate electric lights and telephones in Corea; as the result of this, together with the observations made by the Corean envoys while in the U.S. an order has been given to Mr. Edison to place his system of electric lights within the palace grounds and building at Seoul."[38]

As soon as the news of the U.S.-Korea treaty spread among the diplomatic circle in Peking, the Western diplomats were surprised and anxious to follow the pattern of the U.S. Sir Thomas Wade, the British minister to China, contacted London immediately, and visited Li Hung-chang for help in negotiating a treaty with Korea. Li was unable to help Sir Thomas, because of his mother's death. Li, however, instructed Chang Shu-shen that the Chinese government would not help Sir Thomas if the British government wanted the same type of treaty as the U.S.-Korea treaty. Li clearly indicated here his dissatisfaction of the U.S.-Korea treaty. Sir Thomas agreed to Li's suggestion and received a copy of the Chinese text of the U.S.-Korea treaty and also a letter of introduction to Ma Kun-tsung of China, who remained in Seoul after the treaty of 1882.[39] The British plenipotentiary, General George Willes, the commander of the British China fleet, arrived on May 27, 1882 at Chemulpo.

General Willes contacted the Korean officials Shin Hyon and Kim Hong-Jip through the Chinese official, Ma.[40] The main problem in the discussion was again the "dependent state" phrase which Ma insisted upon to General Willes replied that he was not authorized to insert the phrase and that he was on}y to follow the Shufeldt treaty.

On May 30, the Korean plenipotentiary Jo Hyong-ha, the vice-envoy Kim Hongjip with the Chinese official, Ma, went to see the British pleni-potentiary, General Willes, at the *virginia,* the British warship. The British envoy said that the Shufeldt treaty was too general and that he wanted more detail in the treaty. The British envoy was unable to convince either the Chinese or the Korean envoys. The British envoy also suggested the Island of Kumun for their warship's stop-over place but this was rejected by the Koreans.[41] Without any extra gain, the treaty was signed between Korea and Britain four days later. According to the treaty, at first, three Korean ports--Pusan, Wonsan, and Chemulpo were to be opened; second, warships were not to enter any Korean port; third, the British would survey the Korean coast. Simultaneously, the Korean King was to declare Korea a tributary state to China, which would be similar to the contents in the letter to the President of the United States.[42] This treaty, however, was not ratified by the British government. The treaty was not ratified because it seemed that the Korean government asked a high tariff; according to the U.S.-Korea treaty, the tariff rate ran from 10% to 30%. The British-China treaty, however, was as low as 5 % except on tea, silk and opium. The British were not willing to pay a high tariff. Secondly the Korean government refused to import any amount of opium which was one of the main items. It is not too clear that the British had insisted to export opium to Korea or not, but the American minister, Foote, observed the probability of the British plan, since the British was exporting it to China heavily at that time. Thirdly, the nature of the treaty was too liberal compared with the British treaties with China, Japan and others in Asia. It seemed that the British government figured that such treaty between Korea and the British might cause other future treaties to be made along the lines of a similar progressive nature which would be in conflict with the traditional British conservative policy of the day. Thus the liberal and progressive policy of the United States and the conservative policy of the British was in conflict in Korea.[43]

Meantime, on June 5.1882, the French warship also arrived at Chemulpo. The French consul, Dillion, at Tientsien, was the French plenipotentiary. Dillion already began to negotiate a treaty with Korea through the Chinese official, and was as successful as the Americans and the British. As the American deputy-minister, Holcombe, predicted the French were not able to convince either the Korean official or the Chinese since the French did not have much trade in the Far East, but desired to spread the Roman Catholic mission.[44] The French mission failed in Korea, and Dillion returned to Peking where he reported to Boree, the French minister to Peking. One of the main reasons of the failure probably was the existence of the unfriendly relationship between China and France at that time. In spite of China's protest, the French troops remained in Indo-China. This situation did not help to make a treaty with Korea.

On June 20, 1882, the German plenipotentiary minister, M. von Brandt, the German minister to China, arrived at Chemulpo by *the Stosch,* the German warship. Von Brandt had special encouragement from Shufeldt before he left China. He also contacted the officials at the Chinese foreign office. Three days later, the Chinese officials, Ma and Ting, again arrived at Chemulpo. The Korean government appointed Jo Nyong-ha as the chief envoy, and Kim Hongjip as vice-envoy, and two sub-officials.[45] On June 27, the Korean envoys arrived at *The Stosch* where the envoys presented certificates. On June 30, they signed the treaty which was exactly the same as the previous treaties with the U.S. and the British. At the ceremonial banquet which was held on *the Stosch,* the German minister said, ''All the Asiatic countries have had diplomatic relations; now at last Korea joined. More than ten years ago, the French ship entered the Han River where she lost more than half of her soldiers. The British ship arrived at southern Korea and requested Korea to open trade but received no reply. Later American ships came three times in the same attempt but all failed. But now during these few weeks three treaties have been made. All of which could not have been achieved without the help of the Chinese.[46]

After Sir Harry Parkes was transferred to Peking from Tokyo, he arranged with the Chinese government for a treaty with Korea. Sir Harry arrived at Chemulpo on October 26, 1883. At the same time the German plenipotentiary Zappa, the German consul-general at Yokohama, went to Seoul for the same purpose. Both of them succeeding in negotiating new treaties with Korea. At this time, the tariff rate was 5% to 20%. Britain's main export was cotton which had a tariff rate of 7.5 %. Sir Harry Parkes was appointed as the British minister to Seoul later.[47] The new German-Korean treaty was similar to the British-Korean treaty. Following these British and German treaties, other European countries to came to Korea to make treaties. The Korean government negotiated the treaties with Russia on June 25, 1884, with Belgium on June 26, and with Austria-Hungary on June 23, 1892.

Among all the treaties with the Western powers, the 1882 treaty with the United States was most meaningful for the "Hermit Nation". Most of the Americans who dealt with the Korean problem were sympathetic although there were some who were not. A new Minister from the United States to China, John R. Young, who advocated an active American policy in the Far East was such an exception. Mr. Young said," We have little to loose whether Corea becomes a province of China or is annexed to Japan or remains indepen-dent."[48] Young cabled the Department of State asking that a naval vessel be sent to Korean waters.[49]

The *U.S.S. Monocacy,* under Commander Cotton, was promptly placed at the disposal of the American Minister. Young's instruction to Commander Cotton was to offer his friendly good offices for the settlement of the riots while maintaining an attitude of strict neutrality, according to the first clause of the 1882 treaty.[50] The American good offices was to help in settling the dispute in Korea peacefully. Meanwhile, the treaty had received the approval of the American Senate on January 9, 1883. The New American Minister L.H. Foote was sent to Seoul where ratification was exchanged. The Korean King had special interest in the treaty and received the American Minister enthusiastically.[51] Having negotiated treaties with the Western powers, especially with the United States, the King was now eager to learn about the modern things as much as his progressive ministers in the govern-ment.

The King, through the state council, appointed the plenipotentiary minister Min Yong-ik as head of the mission to the United States. Min Yong-ik was the son of the Prime Minister, and Queen Min's nephew. The envoy was instructed to confer with the President of the United States in regard to the matters of the postal services, the public school systems, the custom services, as well as the diplomatic affairs. Thus the Korean diplomatic relations with the United States and other Western powers began with enthusiasm. The ancient "Hermit Nation" opened her door wide with good will and hope.

Notes

1. *Congressional Record,* Pt. III, p. 2324, 2600
2. U. S. *Foreign Relations,* 1879, p. 612; Griffis, *op.cit., p.* 426, 428.; Foster, *op.cit.,p.* 321-22
3. For Li Hung-chang's distrust of the Japanese in Korea and his advice to the Korean high offlcials with regard to the treaty relations with Western powers, see the text of Li's advice to Korean high officials on October 23, 1879, text is in H. F. MacNair's *Modern Chinese History: Selected Reading, p.* 511; also Chosen-shi, *op.cit., p.* 501-504; Bland, Li *Hungchang, p.* 159
4. Bland, Li *Hung-chang, p.* 159
5. Okuhira, *op.cit., p.* 68
6. *Zenrin Shimatsu, vol.* 5; *Tongmun Kwanji, vol.* II, continued edition 1881
7. *Tongmun Kwanji, op.cit.,* "The Foreign Ships"
8. *Chosen-shi, op.cit., p.* 432
9. *Ibid., p.*538
10. *Ibid. op.cit., p.* 75. Quoted from *Ijonghakje-illok* in Dr. Imanishi's home library
11. See James Blaine to James Angell, May 9, 1881, *China Instruction, vol.* 3, no. 94 confidential
12. Paullin, *op.cit., p.* 306-7
13. Blaine to Shufeldt, Wash. *Foreign Relations of the United States,* Nov. 14, 1881, China Instruction, vol. 3
14. *Tongmun Kwanji, vol.* 12
15. See Frelinghuysen to Shufeldt, Wash. *Foreign Relations of the United States.* Jan. 6, 1882, China Instruction, vol. 3
16. Shufeldt to Frelinghuysen, Tien-tsien, Apr. 10, 1882, no. 5 *Foreign Relations of the United States;* Shufeldt sent his own draft and Li's draft to Frelinghuysen. The U.S. draft was compiled with the help of Deputy Minister, Holcombe, at Peking. Li's draft was supposed to be from the government of Korea and modified by Li. According to the first article, it said; "Chosen-being a dependent state of the Chinese empire, has nevertheless hitherto exercised her own sovereignty in all matters of internal administration and foreign relations. After the conclusion of this treaty, the

King of Chosen and the President of the United States shall treat with each other upon terms of perfect equality and the subjects and citizens of the two nations shall maintain perpetual relations of friendship If other powers deal unjustly or oppressively with either government, the other shall render assistance and protection, or shall act as mediator in order to preserve perfect peace.

17. *Ilsongnok.* March 15, 1883; *The Collection of Li Mun-tsung-kang,* vol. 43, "The U.S.Korea treaty."
18. Shufeldt quoted from Li's own draft, article 1.
19. Shufeldt to Frelinghuysen, Tientsien, Apr. 10, 1882, no. 5, *For. Rel. of the U.S.*
20. Li suggested to Shufeldt that if the State Department agreed to restore the phrase it should be included. Li also suggested that the addressing word "Dae Chosen Kunju" or "The royal master of great Korea" should be changed to "Kunju" or "the master of the country." Shufeldt agreed to change it.
21. *Tongmun Kwanji, vol.* 12, *op. cit.,* 1883
22. *North China Daily news,* May 9 1882
23. *Ibid.*
24. Holcombe to Frelinghuysen, Peking, May 22, 1882, no. 103, confidential, *For. Rel. of the U.S.*
25. *Singjongwon Diary,* Mar. 25, 1883
26. Shufeldt to Frelinghuysen, Shanghai, Apr. 28, 1882, no. 7, *For. Rel. of the U.S.*
27. See for the detail story of these affairs *The Real Record of the American Trade,* or *Miguk Tongsanggi.*
28. *Ilsongnok* Apr. 7, 1883
29. Chung, H. *Korea Treaties,* p.4; *Treaties of U.S. p.* 216
30. Commodore Shufeldt's report, May 29, 1882, M.S.S. Dept. of State; President's message vol. 8,111; Curzon, *The Problem of the Far East, p.* 202- Griffis, *op.cit, p.* 325.
31. Bayard to Denby, Feb. 9, 1888, *For Rel of the U.S.,* 1888, vol. I, p. 3255
32. The Korean officer, Yi Ingjun delivered the two letters of the Korean King to Ma and Ting on May 22. One letter used the name of the King which was more personal, the other one used only the name of the country, which merely read "The King of Korea." Ma chose the latter one. Yi who was sent by Shin and Kim of the Korean envoys, asked Ma to deliver the letter to Shufeldt.
33. Shufeldt once said, "the feat of bringing the last of the exclusive countries within the pale of Western civilization" and he accomplished this. see

Appenzeler, H.G., *The Opening of Korea:* Admiral Shufeldt, *Korean Repository, vol. 1, p.* 62, 1892

34. The original copy in Chinese is found in Okuhira, *op.cit.*

35. Shufeldt to Frelinghuysen, U.S. Naval Hospital, Mare Island, California, August 23, 1882, *For. Rel. of the U.S.*

36. Nelson, *Korea and The Old Orders in Eastern Asia, p.* 147

37. After the treaty was made, Shufeldt sent a report to Washington, stayed in Nagasaki for a few weeks while waiting for an appointment which he never received. Returning to the United States on July 29, he stayed in California. The American public and even the Washington officials including President Arthur did not pay much attention to what Commodore Shufeldt achieved. In spite of his successful service, Commodore Shufeldt was practically unknown compared to Commodore Perry.

38. Foote to Frelinghuysen, Sept. 4, 1884, Seoul, *For. ReL of the U.S.*

39. Chester Holcombe to Frelinghuysen, Peking, May 29, 1882, no. 117, confidential, *For. Rel. of* the U.S.

40. *Tongmun Kwanji, op. cit.*

41. Chosen-shi, *op cit, p.* 614

42. *Ilsongnok,* Apr. 22, 1883; *Singjongwon Diary,* Apr. 22, 1883; Honcho Kiji, vol. 2, Apr. 23, 1883; Also see Treaties, Regulations, etc, between Corea and other powers, 18761889; published by order of the Inspector-general of customs, 1891, p. 53f

43. Foote to Frelinghuysen, *For. ReL of* the U.S. confidential, no. 23, 37, Oct. 30, 1883.

44. Holcombe to Frelinghuysen, May 29, 1882, no. 117, *For. Rel. of the U.S.*

45. *Singjongwon Diary,* May 7, 1883; *Ilsongnok,* May 7, 10, 1883

46. M. Von Brabdt, *Drei-und-dreissig Jahre in ost-asien.* Bk. 111, p. 238

47. Parkes, Harrv, *Life of Sir Harry Parkes, Vol.* 11, p. 214

48. U.S. *Foreign Relations,* 1883, p. 172;

49. Pollard, *op.cit., p.* 429

50. *Treaties of U.S., p.* 216; Chung, *Korean Treaties, p.* 4

51. Foote to Frelinghuysen, May 24, 1883, U.S. *Foreign Relations;* Tso Namsun, *To-sa-tong, p.* 213

4

Kim Ok-Kiun's Modernization Movement Failed

In accordance with the treaty of Chemulpo with Japan, the Korean government sent a mission to Japan. The mission consisted of Pak Yong-ho, the chief envoy, Kim Ok-kiun and Kim Man-sik, two vice-envoys. Upon arrival in Japan, the young Korean diplomats were greatly surprised and impressed by the modernization of Japan, They learned soon that Japan had acquired all these modern things from the West. These things which Korea was fighting to avoid—the import of railroads, steam vehicles, warships, etc. The Japanese foreign office in Tokyo entertained, amused, and startled the Korean envoys by showing them their warships, factories, and offices equipped with steam and electricity. As Mr. Griffis put it, "the ripened fruit of the seed planted by Perry in 1854.[1] Then naturally, these Korean envoys felt that Korea had much to learn from Japan immediately and made immediate contact with the higher officers of Japan to take measures in restraining the Chinese intervention of the Korean government and to reform the Korean administrative policy. The young Koreans demanded that China's intervention be abolished in order that Korea might progress and become modern. These youth with aristocratic background were all under the influence of Yu Taijun who was a well-known scholar in Korea. They even dreamt of chasing Russia out of Manchuria (former territory of Koguryo Kingdom of Old Korea), and establishing a new young country.

China, since 1637, for two centuries and a half, tried interfering with Korea until she got into trouble herself with Japan in 1894. In the middle of the 19th century, China suffered through the activities in Manchuria by Britain, France, and Russia; therefore, China repeatedly proclaimed Korea an independe. ᵗ nation. When she saw that Korea was coming into closer bonds with Japan day ·y day, after the treaty of 1876, she was certainly worried about Korea's relationship with Japan. Although China refused to take the responsibility for Korea, she was still anxious to retain Korea as a vassal because of her vital strategic importance and other traditional reasons as well as the economics. On the one hand, Japan wanted to see the complete independence of Korea, not because she desired Korean independence for Korea's sake, but to serve their own purposes. It was therefore, a great opportunity to the Japanese to have these young enthusiastic Korean patriots in planning Japanese future interference in Korea.

China, on the other hand, after the affair of 1882, Yuan Shin-kai, with his two thousand Chinese soldiers continued to supervise the Korean high government officials. Yuan's status as a Chinese resident in Seoul was not clear as he demanded special privileges: for example, the right to attend every one of the King's meetings with foreign diplomats, to be carried in his chair accompanied by his attendant, through the central gate to the palace when he came for an audience with the King; other diplomats were compelled to leave their chair at the gate and walk more than a half mile to the hall of residence. Li Hung-chang also sent P. G. Mollendorf, as advisor to the Korean government.[2] The Chinese government, like the Japanese, had negotiated a treaty with Korea. The Korean envoy, Jo Nyong-ha and Kim Hongjip went to Tientsien where they negotiated a Sino-Korean water-land commercial treaty. The main issue of the treaty was not commercial, but political in nature. In this treaty, China insisted to have a "dependent state" clause, and they agreed. Such a contradiction was the position of the Korean government in their negotiation of the international treaties.

In order to achieve the modernization of Korea, the King sent selected student to both China and Japan. Fourteen students, led by a youth, So Jai-pil (Phillip Jaison) were sent to a military academy in Tokyo. In Tokyo these young students were under the supervision and leadership of Kim Ok-kiun, a great revolutionist of those days among the progressive Koreans, and who had great influence over the young students. Meantime, Pak Yong-ho, who went to Japan as a special envoy, resigned his official position and trained about six hundred soldiers in modern military tactics under his own guidance in order to meet the coming crisis. These progressive youth were secretly preparing to revolt against the conservative Min-dominated government. The leaders of this group were in high governmental positions and were in an excellent position to plan and execute such a plot. Leader Kim Ok-kiun returned with some of the students in 1883 to Korea and organized the progressive group which began to publish a newspaper, *Independence,* supported by Japanese government through the Yokohama Specie Bank.[3] Takezoye, a man well-learned in Chinese classics, was sent to Seoul as a Japanese minister to-aid Kim Ok-kiun. Now the aggressive Hanabusa was replaced by a cultured diplomat.[4] Through *Independence,* the progressive group actively advocated the complete independence of Korea from Chinese interference and urged the importation of the new Western civilization as Japan had done.

The principle leaders of this group were: Kim Ok-kiun (age 34), Hong Yong-sik, son of the conservative leader, Hong Sun-mok, Pak Yong-ho, the former envoy to Japan, So Jai-pil, the youth leader, So Kwang-pum and Yun Kwang-ryol. So Kwang-pum who was sent to America and Europe on a special observation mission by the King, reported emphatically upon his return that Korea must have a constitutional government. While staying in Japan, Kim Ok-kiun from the envoy group of 1877 made close contact with such members of the Japanese high officials, including the former Premiers, Okubo, Inukai, and the leader from the former Samurai group, Toyama, who once called Kim Ok-kiun the Sun Yat-sen of Korea. On his return to Korea, Kim organized a political party called Progressive Party.

The Progressive Party also welcomed the Christian missionary works. They believed that missions were a "civilizing" influence which would impel Korea toward the culture of the Western world, and as a result, toward the culture of the new Japan which was rapidly adopting the Western ways. While Underwood and Heron, the two pioneers of Christian missionaries in Korea, were passing through Japan they had been much impressed by Kim Ok-kiun's partisans. Heron studied Korean language under Pak Yongho; Underwood came to Korea bearing letters of endorsement from the progressive leaders. The Korean King who relied on Kim Ok-kiun and his friends, had promised to help build a Methodist school and hospital in Seoul.[5]

The Progressive Party was a small minority which had won the royal confidence and which the Japanese were willing to finance. The Progressive Party, however, was overshadowed by the conservative forces, anti-foreign, non-progressive as well as anti-Christianity groups. Since Korea had slumbered for many centuries, it was a natural reaction for the conservative group to object to the sudden change, especially since it was sponsored by ambitious, aspiring Japan. Besides the Japanese government's sympathy for the progressive party there was a civilian group which had secret plans to support Kim Ok-kiun and his group. This group was led by Oi Ken-taro, one of the organized leading socialists in early Japan. Oi's plan was to organize a secret group among the Japanese, and to support Kim's group in overthrowing the conservative influence in the Korean government. And simultaneously to take over the Japanese government by revolution.[6] The conservative group, headed by Tae-Won-kun who now returned from China, and the Min family had no definite political platform but were interested only in the welfare of their factions. The conservatives fought each other for their own selfish motives, and were opposed to the progressive group for identical reasons.

The conservative party was still the majority party, and preferred conservative China as a favored nation in 1884 because of the similarity of culture and along friendly relationship. Since the "Sino-Korean water-land trade treaty", the Korean merchants were restricted to Peking, whereas the Chinese merchants were free to visit Seoul. In some cases, the Chinese soldiers misbehaved in Seoul by stealing and destroying Korean properties. The Korean government protested to Commodore Ting and asked him to arrest the soldiers, but the Chinese didn't even reply. Instead, Li Hung-chang requested the Korean government to prevent the publishing of the newspaper which printed news of the Chinese soldiers' misbehavior in Seoul.[7]

In spite of such Chinese misconduct, Queen Min and her group who were wedded to the Chinese-flavored past, dominated the Korean government while Tae-Won-kun remained an isolationist. Certainly there was no trace of progressiveness in either the Queen or her father-in-law.

On his return to Seoul, after a tour of the world, Min Yong-ik cooperated with the conservative group in which he was surrounded by close family ties, but the envoy, So Kwang-pum, had been converted by Western civilization and joined the progressive party. Since the return of these envoys, the Korean relation with the United States became closer, and Ensign George C. Foulk was appointed as U. S. Naval attache at Seoul and exercised a great deal of influence on Korean politics from the time of his arrival in Seoul.[8] It is interesting to note that Min Yonk-ik's statement in spite of such experience and atmosphere of the capital, he said to Mr. Foote, '' I was born in the dark, I went out into the light, and now I have returned into the dark again; I must as yet see my way clearly, but I hope to see on.[9] Min, however, did not see it in time.

In October 1883, the King appealed to the American government to send him an advisor for the Office of Foreign Affairs and also an army instructor. As a matter of fact, Min Yong-ik, while he was in Washington, had approached Admiral Shufeldt to become political adviser, but Shufeldt refused. He refused the invitation on the advice of his friends. Li Hungchang was opposed to Shufeldt's presence in Seoul since Shufeldt consistently advocated Korean independence.[10] The King's plan for progressive reform was to be carried out with the cooperation of the progressive Koreans and with the aid of the American advisors. The former group was willing, but the latter group refused.

The conservative group was ready to change their strategy and also to eliminate the progressive activities in Seoul when they found out that the King openly favored the progressive minority. The King made Kim Okkiun, the chief of the Progressive Party, a baron, the conservative group resented the King's action. This fact made a showdown inevitable, a strength between the progressive and the conservative parties had to be tested openly, and at the same time, between Japan and China. The progressive group under Kim Ok-kiun and the military students under the leadership of So Jai-pil set December 4, 1884 as the date for their attack on the leaders of the conservative group. With the King's cooperation, they reasoned, quick action might bring victory; delay was likely to mean complete elimination from the government. They must strike at once, "for the sake of Korea" one said to Foulk of the United States, "the leading Chinese sympathizers will have to be killed."[11]

This was the day that the new post office building was to be inaugurated and Hong Yong-sik, the postmaster general, and also one of the leaders among the progressive group invited the guests including many high officers, conservative leaders, and foreign representatives for a dinner party. Among the conservative guests were Min Yong-ik, the leader; Mollendorff, a German, Pro-Chinese and anti-Japanese as well as Anti-American; Chinese commissioner Chen Shu Tang. The neutrals were also in attendance: British consul William G. Aston and American minister Foote with his private secretary and interpreter.[12] The progressive's plan, at first, was to report that the palace had been set on fire thereby rousing the reactionary group from their banquet seats, shooting them as they left the party. However, this plan which was to have taken palace at ten o'clock failed in that only Min Yong-ik, conservative leader, was badly wounded, the other conservative did not attend the banquet. Min dragged his bleeding body back indoors and staggered into the arms of Mollendorff muttering, "an assassin has killed me." Mollendorff, Foote, and Aston stayed with Min.[13]

The progressive group seeing this failure in the first step of their revolt against the conservative party, sent a group of young officer cadets to the palace and killed those conservative ministers who had not attended the banquet. These included Min Yong-mok, Min, Min Tai-ho, Jo Nyong-ha (the Queen's cousin). The Japanese soldiers under Captain Murakami, the commander of the Japanese garrison at Seoul, came into the palace in order to help the progressive group.[14] Mollendorff who took charge of affairs in spite of his personal danger, called for chairs to take Min to a safe place, his headquarters. Mollendorff, though anti-missionary himself, called Dr. Allen for help. Dr. Allen, with a guard of fifty Korean soldiers, arrived at Mollendorff's and found

92

his royal patient in very bad shape– ''all blood and gore.'' Dr. Allen saved Min's life through the aid of a physician from the Japanese legation, Min recovered three months later.[15] It made a curious scene: two practitioners of Western medicine saving the life of a major foe of Western institutions, an American missionary doctor working on an anti-Christian politician, a Japanese physician laboring with an anti-Japanese Korean at the center of opposition to both Japan and the United States, Mollendorff's headquarters.

At the palace, the King sent a note to Takezoe, the Japanese minister, stating that the King and his royal family needed protection immediately. Takezoe was ready and eager to do the job if it meant curtailing Chinese influence.

After their altered plans were executed, the progressive group organized the new cabinet by the order of the King and next morning proclaimed the reformation of the administration and the national sovereignty. The new cabinet declared fifteen major policies including: 1. Discard the vague formality of paying tribute to Ching China; 2. Abolish the caste system and legislate, in its place, the equality and rights of the people. Government positions shall be filled with competent persons regardless of social status; 3. Reform land taxation policy in order to prevent irregularities among government officials, eradicate the hardships of the people and increase state revenue; 4. Punish those officials who greatly harm the state; 5. Businesses pertaining to government finances shall be administered by the Ministry of Finance and other existing financial offices shall be abolished; 6. All government offices, other than the six ministries, shall be closed; and 7. The reorganization of the military system. Meantime, the Queen Min already had communicated with Yuan Shin-kai. Yuan of China at first hesitated to offer aid to her for he had instructions to avoid a clash with Japan. China at that time was busy with France, and Viceroy Li Hung-chang knew all too well about his country's fighting forces. It was better to oppose the Japanese as China had done in 1876 and 1882. Yuan, however, could hardly let the Japanese control the King, and Yuan could not accept the measures of the new progressive government which was determined to repudiate Chinese suzerainty, so he brought in his troops to take revenge and to overthrow the progressive government. The Japanese minister, with about one hundred fifty soldiers, fought against about two thousand of Yuan's men. The Japanese, after bitter fighting, decided to retreat. The Japanese, and a handful of progressives then smashed their way through the Chinese forces and arrived at the Japanese legation. Yuan, now had the King and other members of the royal family. He now stopped pursuing the fleeing Japanese soldiers as it would not profit him, and it would mean certain war between China and Japan. The King, under the influence of the Chinese troops appointed a new member of the cabinet including Kim Hongjip, Sim Sun-tak, Kim Yun-sik, and thus the Korean government fell into the hands of the Chinese again through Yuan's maneuvers. The reformist cabinet collapsed and was overthrown after three days because it lacked necessary. preparations and conditions of the time to back up its movement.

The leaders of the progressive group, Kim Ok-kiun, Pak Yong-ho, So Kwang-pum fled to Japan. The pro-Chinese government declared Kim, Pak, So, to be national traitors, and said that they should be punished. Hong Yong-sik, a progressive leader, was killed during the riots.[16]

During the trouble of 1884, a Japanese captain, Isobayashi was killed and several others wounded; the Japanese legation set afire; and the new postoffice building destroyed. While the Japanese were in trouble, the American legation became their place of refuge. Later, at the request of Foote who acted according to the Korean King's request, interviewed the Japanese minister with the German commissioner on December 10, 11. Foote was asked by the King to use his influence in bringing peaceful settlement with Japan. The American with the King's blessing, authorized Ensign Bernadau to join the Chinese and the Korean authorities to escort the Japanese refugees to Chemulpo from the American legation.[17] On the morning of December 9th, Ensign Barnadau was left in command of this mixed escort and they arrived safely in Chemulpo on the next day. With the Japanese minister were the leaders of the riot, Kim Ok-kiun, Pak Yong-ho, So Kwang-pum. They all went to Nagasaki, Japan.

The Japanese minister Takezoye reported to his government immediately about the conditions and the government took immediate action sending Count Inouye as a special envoy with Lt. General Takashtma Heinoseke with two battalions of soldiers, and Rear Admiral Kabayama with seven warships. They left for Chemulpo on December 26, 1884 from Shimonoseki and arrived on the 31st then went to Seoul in spite of the arguments of Mollendorff, who sought to delay them. Count Inouye demanded that Korea apologize and pay an indemnity of 110,000 yen to Japan as well as 20,000 yen for the construction of a new Japanese embassy, and provide barracks for the military guard on the grounds adjacent to the legation. The conference between the Korean envoy, Kim Hongjip, and the Japanese envoy, Inouye, lasted from January 7 to 9, 1885. There wasn't much compromise although much discussion. The Korean government was to accept whatever Inouye proposed. The Chinese officials were trying to interfere with the conference, but the Japanese envoy refused to talk with the Chinese officials, the Japanese envoy stated that he was to follow the agreement in the treaty of 1876 where Korea was recognized as an independent nation. The agreement was reached, and the treaty of Han-sung was born on January 9,1885.[18]

After backing out from the 1884 rebellion, Japan had repeatedly announced complete independence of Korea, but her talk of Korean independence was only superficial. Japan was waiting for a proper time to drive the Chinese out of Korea, and monopolize her influence there. Japan was neither concerned about her treaty commitment nor observing Korean law. For instance, Japanese fishermen had been given certain fishing rights in Korean waters, but they overstepped their rights by becoming officious in the waters around Cheju Island where a curious custom prevails: the Korean women do the fishing and dive into the water almost nude to gather seaweed and shellfish, therefore, all males are prohibited by law from the area. The Japanese fishermen, however, refused to obey the law and insulted the women. The Korean government took the matter before the Japanese government which refused to take any action to ease the friction.

China, at this time was in the midst of the Tong-king trouble with France, and was not in a position to support Yuan's forces against the strong modernized Japanese forces; on the other hand, Japan, too, was not ready for further action because the peace party was still in the ascendancy in Japan. Therefore, neither of them wanted war at this time. Besides, the United States, through the good office of the American minister, John A. Bingham, in Tokyo, contributed in settling the Korean affair peacefully between China and Japan. Bingham talked ith Prince Ito, head of the peace group in Japan, in which he suggested that a war between China and Japan should not be inaugurated, and that the two powers should agree to withdraw their military forces from Korea, and recognize the rightful and exclusive autonomy of the government of Korea within its territorial domain This suggestion brought considerable influence upon the two powers as the later events show, particularly of the Tien-tsien treaty.[19] Meanwhile the original policy of the United States was somewhat changed. Foote who had contributed so much for peace settlement in Korea, was reduced from the rank of minister and received two lesser positions minister-resident and consul-general by the diplomatic and consular act of July 7, 1884.[20] He left Korea in resentment to the change in his diplomatic status; so Lt. Foulk took charge of the American legation for a year and a half. They requested American military advisers in spite of this uncertain policy of the United States in Korea. The Korean King's request was transmitted to Congress by President Arthur on January 30, 1885, and the necessary resolution was introduced in the Senate by Mr. Sewall, the chairman of the committee on military affairs on February 26th. The new president, Cleveland had repeated the recommendation of his predecessor in his first annual message to the new congress in December.[21] Three American instructors arrived in April, 1888, but the long delay in the American action had shaken confidence in the United States. This arrangement was made without passing through the hands of the Chinese.

Meanwhile, the British seized Port Hamilton (Kumun-do) on April 14, 1885 in order to oppose the Russian action in Korea, where she seized Wonsan in 1884, and the British flag was hauled down on Feb. 27, 1887. The Russian arrival in Korea was arranged by Mollendorff without the knowledge of the King. Wonsan bay was leased to Russia as a naval base and Mollendorff was dismissed from his official post, an adviser to the foreign affairs, as a result of his action.[22] After that Russia again began to show her interest in Korea. Under the circumstance, both Li Hung-chang of China and Ito of Japan felt that they should prevent war in Korea between two nations, and stop the Russian aggression in the Far East. Both men worked successfully and negotiated the famous treaty of Tientsin on the 18th of April, 1885. The agreement was in three articles: 1. Each power would withdraw her troops then stationed in Korea, within a period of four months; 2. The prospective powers bound themselves henceforth not to send any of their own officers to Korea as military instructors, but they mutually agreed to invite the King of Korea to instruct and drill a sufficient armed force for public security; 3. In case of any disturbance occurring in Korea which necessitated the respective countries or either of them, to send troops to Korea, they would give prior notice to each other in writing of their intention to do so after the matter had been settled they would withdraw their troops and not station them there.[23]

Both China and Japan withdrew their army from Korea giving her a golden chance to carry on her struggle for complete independence. The Korean King could not trust any foreigners except the Americans who were kindly helping the King personally rather than officially. For instance, Lt. Foulk, while acting as American charge, was willing and anxious to render service in many directions. He also advised the government in the ordering of rifles, munitions, and other supplies for the army. The King, therefore, wanted close relationships with the United States because he felt that the United States had reasons for not wanting to interfere with the Korean independence; not only because of the 1882 treaty, but also because of the distance between Korea and the United States. At least that was the King's attitude at that time.

In the summer of 1886, there was a plot to dispose of the King, now known as pro-American, and deport him, his consort and the crown prince.[24] Tae Won-kun, who had been deported from Korea in 1882, was presumed to have learned respect for China's authority during the three years exile in China, was then to be replaced in power once more as Regent. This plot was encouraged, if not originated, by a Chinese resident Yuan, and Li Hung-chang was fully informed concerning the details of the plot.[25]

This plot, however, was discovered and exposed by the foreign diplomats with the help of Min Yon-ik.[26] This plot of Yuan brought the King closer to the American adviser. Lt. Foulk was relieved, perhaps under the Chinese pressure, and William Parker arrived as the new American minister. Parker proved to be unfit for the position and it was necessary to have Lt. Foulk resume it again. But Lt. Foulk was relieved again because Li Hungchang and Yuan Shin-kai disliked him.[27] Removing Lt. Foulk, who was known as anti-Chinese, from Seoul served to rapidly strengthen the Chinese influence in the Korean government. Yuan condemned the establishment of any new Western institutions such as hospitals, the purchase of steamships and other things, and urged the institution of moral reform based on the Confucian pattern. He promised the King that if the two countries remained on intimate terms as before no foreign nation would be able to interfere and Korea would be safe forever. Neither the King nor the Americans agreed with Yuan. In Washington, Secretary Bayard stated the American position by declaring that "if country (Korea) to the expectation of this government, the progress of Chinese interference at Seoul should result in the destruction of the autonomy of Corea and a sovereign state with which the United States maintains independent treaty relations. . ."[28]

The King, meanwhile, was planning to send the envoys to the United States and Europe. This plan, however, was disturbed by China when the news reached Yuan who immediately communicated with Li Hung-chang. Li complained about the King's plan and an imperial order from Peking reached the Korean King: "She (Korea) has certainly to ask our permission and after getting it, to send them . . .[29] By this time, China again brought out the problem of the dependent state, thus ignoring the Korean treaties of 1876 and 1882. The American minister at Seoul promptly spoke to Yuan and reminded him of the agreement in the treaties, " . . . the high contracting powers may each appoint diplomatic representatives to reside at the court of the other . . ." Yuan, however, insisted upon more recognition of the letter from the King, accompanied by Shufeldt which acknowledged Korea's dependent status rather than the treaty term itself.[30] Secretary Bayard was willing to let the Chinese action ride, but on the other hand, he was unwilling to agree to the Chinese demands.

The weak-minded King finally submitted to the humiliation memoir to the Chinese Emperor and accepted the Chinese demands; and diplomatic representatives were sent to the United States and Europe according to the previous arrangement. The Chinese Emperor agreed to the Korean King's memoir on condition that rank of the Korean envoys be only minister-resident while the Chinese envoys carry the rank of minister plenipotentiary. The King offered a compromise that the first envoy who was already named remain as minister, but he be recalled as soon as he performed his duties, then be replaced by a charge d'affaires. The Korean representative, Pak Jung-yang, and his American assistant, Dr. H. N. Allen, who carried the title of American Secretary left for Washington on November 13, 1887 on the *U.S.S. Ossipes* through Japan. Dr. Allen was the "only available person" a man the King could trust to choose as adviser and to do the real work of a two million dollar loan which was an important program of the King's government. Besides, Dr. Allen wanted to visit his home after long tiring work in a strange land.[31]

Upon the arrival of the Korean minister in Washington, he immediately requested an interview with the Secretary of the State who received him promptly. The Chinese minister who had instructions from Li Hung-chang and was to have introduced the Korean minister to the Secretary of the State missed out, perhaps due to Dr. Allen's intelligent arrangement in Washington. The Korean envoy in Washington was treated as a representative of a sovereign state although the dependent state problem was not clearly understood by the officials in Washington. In fact, Denby said frankly that the existing relationship between China and "her dependent state" will remain unclear in modern international law.[32] However, he accepted the co-equality of Korea with the United States, and he even suggested to Bayard of Korea's possible relations to Japan and Russia, England, and China if complete independence of Korea be assured by the U. S. Denby's suggestions were agreed to by Bayard and he stated further that the United States government was not interested politically, but sought merely the protection of the American citizens and their commerce.[33]

Yuan, meanwhile, was instigating the Korean foreign office to raise the question of the right of residence at Seoul. According to the 1882 treaty, there was no clause including such matters; nevertheless, they understood the spirit of the most favored nation treaty.[34] The King himself favored it and welcomed the American missionary to engage in their work. The Korean foreign office, however, was now influenced by the pro-Chinese faction through Yuan, and these officials opposed the activities of the missionaries particularly of the growing evangelistic work outside the city of Seoul, and the proposal by the newly arrived French missionaries to erect a building on a site immediately overlooking the royal palace. The French Catholic missionaries claimed that the treaty of 1886 between France and Korea guaranteed their religious work in Korea. The clause stated that "Frenchmen resorting to Corea for the purpose of their studying or teaching the written or spoken language, science, laws, or arts, shall in testimony of the sentiment of good friendship which animate (s) the high contracting parties always receive aid and assistance.''[35] The Korean foreign minister, Cho Pyong-ik addressed a letter to the American minister on April 24, 1888 in which he stated that: ''Teaching religion and opening schools of any kind are not authorized by the treaty; therefore, we forbid severely any school whatsoever except it be authorized by our government, and we will not allow religion to be taught to our people.''[36] This declaration was a beginning of the anti-missionary demonstration which was to come in June, 1888 in Seoul.

The last chapter of Kim Ok-kiun was a tragic one. Kim Ok-kiun fled to Japan during the 1884 rebellion and was preparing to go to the United States in 1895. When he was informed about the Tonghak rebellion, he changed his p]an, and went to Shanghai; from there he hoped to sail for Korea. He already had informed the Tonghak group ~discussed in chapter seven) that he was on his way to Korea.

Kim Ok-kiun left Tokyo with Wada, his Japanese servant. They stayed in Osaka under an alias in a small Japanese inn.

Lee Il-sik, Kwon Tong-sun, Kwon Ja-sun, and Hong Jong-u were sent to Japan by the Min group, their orders were to assassinate Kim. They went to see him at his hotel; it was a mystery to Kim how they had been able to find him. Kim knew of their mission but he was not afraid of them.

Kim assured his servant boy, Wada, ''The Kwon brothers, Lee and Hong are here to kill me. . . However, I am not a person who would be killed by those fellows, so don't worry.''

After hearing this, Wada was very much worried about Kim's safety. In a latter account, Wada said, ''Mr. Kim's courage was most surprising. He told me about the assassins, but he was very calm when he was with them.''[37] Wada continued, that one day he had lost track of Kim, and when he found him, Kim was at his second wife's home drinking with Lee Il-sik, one of the assassins. Kim spent about three weeks at Osaka and then on March 25, 1894, sailed to Shanghai from Kobe with Hong Jong-u, another of the assassins, Wu Ch'ing-lcan, an interpreter from the Chinese legation, and Wada. Kim and his company arrived in Shanghai on the twenty-seventh and registered at Hotel Tunghwa. Kim and Wada occupied a single room. The next day, while Wada was out, Kim was reading a book. Hong, who was watching for an opportunity to perform his duty, shot Kim from the hall. Kim died immediately and thus, his revolutionary life ended abruptly.

After the assassination, Hong fled, while the proper disposal of Kim's corpse became a problem. While Wada was discussing the matter with the shipping company authorities and the Japanese consul, Kim's corpse disappeared from the Shanghai pier. Later, it became known that the local Chinese police turned the corpse over to Hong who took it to Korea where the

Mins displayed the corpse in public as a warning to other would be national "traitors".[38]

The story of this political murder of Kim Ok-kiun is very significant for two reasons: First, the Japanese consul refused permission to bring Kim's corpse to Japan. Second, the Chinese police protected Hong, the assassin, and even sent him to Korea with Kim's body. According to these facts, we see two things clearly: First, the Chinese government was definitely in favor of the Min administration and against any type of progressive movement in Korea. Second, Japan was not ready to meet China, and was not ready to have a war; in fact, she was afraid of a crisis. Although the Japanese government had no secret agreement with Kim, Kim had many Japanese friends among the officials and the extreme nationalists. When the news of Kim's death arrived in Japan, his friends were very much angered. Toyama, led his followers in an unsuccessful attempt to pressure Prime Minister Ito into declaring war on China.

It appears that Kim Ok-kiun was the first Korean nationalist in modern sense, but he was born too early as Koreans would say about him.

In spite of the national crisis, the Korean leaders were split in their attitude toward modernization of their country. The progressive minded young leaders welcomed the American missionaries who started to transplant the new civilization. Even the King was much excited over the possibility of the modernization, but the traditional conservative Confucian system was too strong to overcome at this time. The struggle, however, did not end between the conservative group and the progressive group. A group of far-sighted young intellectuals like Kim Ok-kiun, nourished with modern thoughts, determined to develop their feudalistic country into a modern nation. The seeds of modern nationalism had been well planted in the minds of these young leaders. The mass, however, still had to be awakened from their long sleep. The society remained a feudalistic one.

Notes

1. Griffis, op.cit., p. 424
2. *Ilsongnok,* Nov. 5, Dec. 6, 1883
3. Inouye, op.cit., Vol. 111, p. 499
4, Ibid, p. 496
5. Harrington, *God, Mammon and the Japanese, p. 13; Pail, Protestant Mission in Korea, p. 73,* quoting *letters* from Foote to Maclay.
6. Inouye, op.cit., Vol, 111, p, 744

7. Hansung Sunpo, no. 10, 11; *Chosen-shi, op.cit., p.* 711
8. Frelinghllysen to Foulk, Nov. 12, 1883; Dennet, *Political Science Quarterly,* XXXVIII p. 89; Pollar, op.cit., p. 434
9. *U.S. For. Rel. July* 17, 1884, p. 126
10. Pollard, *op.cit., p.* 436
11. Harrington, *op.cit., p.* 21
12. The U.S. recognized Korea as an independent state while England and Germany looked upon her as a tributary state of China, therefore, those later two had consulate service instead of diplomatic.
13. Harrington, *op.cit, p.* 23
14. *Ilsongnok, Oct.* 17, 1885; *Zenrin Shimatsu, op.cit.*
15. Allen, *Things Korean p.* 70, 196
16. Chosen-shi, *op.cit., p.* 740
17. U.S. *For. Rel.* 1885, p. 332
18. *China Customs, op.cit., p.* 317; *Singjongwon, op.cit.,* Nov. 24, 1885
19. Brinkly, *History of the Japanese People,* p. 700
20. Dennft, *Politlcal Science Quarterly,* XXXVIII, p. 93 note
21. *House Exec.* Dec. 163, 48th Congress, 2nd season
22. Morse, *The International Relatlon of the Chinese Empire,* p 572
23. Carnegie Endowment. *Korean Treaties and Agreement, p.* 76
24. Pollard, op.cit., p. 441
25. Congressional Record, XIX- p. 8139; Li Hung-chang told his agent, O. N. Denny, formerly of the American consular service in China.
26. O. N. Denny, H. F. Merril, and the British consul-general were responsible for this exposition, see Pollard, *op.cit., p.* 443
27 Dennet, *op.cit., p.* 99
28. U. S. *For. Rel.* 1888, p. 236
29. *Yuan Shin-kai to Korean Government,* Sept. 4, 1887
30. U. S. *For. Rel.* 1888, p. 435
31. Harrington, *op.cit., p.* 226, from *Allen Manuscript*
32. U. S. *For. Rel.* 1888, p. 236
33. *Ibid,* Dec. 1887 p. 255
34. Hulbert, *History of Korea,* II, p. 245
35. Foster, *American Diplomacy In the Orient, p.* 331
36. U. S. *Foreign Relatlons,* 1888, p. 446
37. Kim Jin Ok, ''The Memoirs of Kim Ok-kiun's Death by Wada Eijiro'' in *Pyolgangon, no.5*
38. *Ibld.*

5

The Tonghak Peasant Rebellion and the Sino-Japanese War : 1886~1894

Among the common people who were governed by the yangban class, there were two sub-classes: the free people, and the slaves. The slaves were considered as the property of the yangban class, and the law allowed slaves to be used in trade and they could be inherited as one's property. The offspring of the slaves were naturally to be slaves. In 1485, there were ninety thousand five hundred eighty-one households which were classified as slaves in the country according to the eminent historian, Tso Nam-Sun. This meant that about half of the population belonged to the slave class. The system was preserved with only minor changes until 1887, when King Ko-jong abolished the system. The feudal system was not profitable when it met the challenge of the capitalistic system. Social change, however, was not easy to come by. The Min clan, which dominated the government of Korea resisted the demands of the social forces, and attempted to be more friendly to the Chinese authorities and concentrated more on a centralized and an absolutist government in order to oppress the people. Therefore, the peasants were looking for a chance to overthrow the Min administration. Yuan Shin-kai, a resident of the Manchu Empire at Seoul and the British authority, which cooperated with the former empire, enforced all the extra-territorial rights and extended their jurisdiction to include Koreans who displeased Yuan. His men even beat up Korean officers. China interfered "with a rod of iron," and the Koreans were forced to "kiss the hand that smites them – even the King."[1] China violated the Treaty of 1876 (Korea and Japan) and that of 1882 (Korea and the United States) and ignored the repeated denouncement of the suzerainty of Li Hung-chang over Korea. Neither France nor Germany saw any reason to give assistance to Korea while England found it convenient to help China. On the other hand, some Russians had the idea of acquiring an ice-free port in Korea. The United States represented by Dr. Allen had no chance to obtain complete independence for Korea, although he fought against unreasonable Chinese interference.

During 1892, there was a severe famine throughout Korea and the peasants were faced with great hardships. During these days, the government did nothing to help the peasants, yet the people were forced to pay heavy taxes to the central government and to the local government. In the southern parts of Korea, the peasants suffered the greatest, there, the local officials were extreme in oppressing the peasants. The Min family which had seized and held practically all of the high governmental positions, as well as all the national wealth, was bitterly hated; the people blamed them rather than China or Japan for their plight. In regards to the Korean situation of those days, Lord Curzon who had traveled throughout the Far East commented in Chapter VI of his well known book, *The Problem of the Far East*:[2]

" If the people, the scenery, the capital, the Court of Korea have each an individuality that distinguishes them from similar phenomena in other countries, there were yet in the Korean polity, viewed as a form of government, before the war inseparably associated with the Asiatic system and recognizable in every unreformed Oriental State from Teheren to Seoul. A royal figurehead enveloped in the mystery of the palace and the harem surrounded by concentric rings of eunuchs, Ministers of State, officials and retainers, and rendered almost intangible by the predominant and office-seekers, who were leeches in the thinnest disguise a feeble and insignificant army, an impecunious exchequer; a debased currency, and an impoverished people...these are the invariable systems of the fast vanishing regime of the older and unredeemed Oriental type. Add to these the first swarming of the flock of foreign practitioners, who scent the enfeebled constitution from afar,and from the four winds of heaven come pressing their pharmacopeia of loans concessions, banks, mints, factories, and all the recognized machinery for filing Western purses at the expense of Eastern pockets, and you have a fair picture of Korea as she stood after ten years of emergence from her long seclusion and enjoyment of the intercourse of the nations. She was going to purchase her own experience, and to learn that, while civilization is a mistress of rare and irresistible attractions, she requires to be paid for in coin of no small denomination."

Thus, Lord Curzon pointed out how the already corrupt politics and economy became more so. The life of the farmer more miserable and he often showed resentment towards the government officials. His resentment was a natural reaction for an oppressed class of people and the continuous civil war was also unavoidable under such conditions.

Because Korea opened her ports to Japan and other countries, the cost of living became higher. This was especially noticed in the price of rice, but the income of the average population did not rise correspondingly. Southern Korea was hit the hardest because the landlords rather than the farmers themselves held most of the land. The opening of the country and the invasion of Japanese capitalism, added momentum to the corruption of the agricultural economy of Korea. The peasants who had to face the contradiction of the feudalistic mode of production came face to face with the significant problems of the new society--the capitalistic society.

Previously, Tso Su-un, the founder of the Tsontokyo, a native politico-religious teaching, began to organize an underground movement among the common people against the Min group. He preached a new doctrine to the people in southern Korea.

On the mankind who exists in the corrupted earth: Where is the plan for the defense of the nation and the security of the citizens people?...This world is not contented by the ethics of Confucious and Mencius and the politics of the Emperors Yao and Shun.[3]

After twenty years of private study, Tso Su-un stated his famous doctrine "Man is God." This has also become the principle doctrine of Tsontokyo or the "Heavenly-way-religion" in Korea today.

The birth of this new religion is interesting in that it appeared as a result of the dissatisfaction of the people of their internal and external affairs. Their internal affairs, especially the Confucian scholars in the Min period during the Yi dynasty, were most corrupt. Professor Hulbert comments ". . . that under the hideously corrupt regime of such men as Min Yongjun, the country had been going from bad to worse until the people found it utterly impossible to endure the oppression any longer."[4] In their external affairs, the constant interference of the Western sea powers, the increasing power of the Western civilization, and the Christian mission through China confused the common people's life. The people were waiting for a new outlook, a new social phenomena which would enlighten their daily life. It was at such a moment that Tso who studied the people and the social conditions declared a new hope for them with his new doctrine. This new religion which in actuality was a secret popular movement was not safe when the government discovered its existence. They punished the founder, Tso Su-un. In spite of this the government was unable to quench the burning spirit of the founder and the movement continued with even greater fervor. In 1891, this underground movement emerged as a politico-religious party known as the Tonghak Tang, or the Eastern Learning Party, which first spread extensively throughout the southern part of Korea, and later to the central area. Its activity was strong and there were frequent clashes between this group and the royal class, yangban, which was protected by the government. The Tonghak movement came about as a reaction against the corrupt government the feudalistic system in Korea. Among the Western scholars, however, the Tonghak movement was misinterpreted as an anti-Christian and pro-Japanese movement. It is true that the Tonghak party was anti-Christian and anti-foreigners; but it is not true that the party was originally affiliated with Japan as was alleged.

This becomes quite evident when one finds that the Japanese government fought against the Tonghak movement. Professor Harrington states that ". . . perhaps Japan went further to create the crisis of 1894. The Tonghak rebellion reached its peak at a time convenient for Nippon, and that was not quite accidental, for the Japanese appear to have poured funds into the movement." He states further that the Tonghak uprising was thus tied up with Tokyo.[5] These statements are groundless. The Korean peasants, particularly in the southern provinces, who suffered severely under the ruthless feudalists, rose against the feudalist class. The peasants needed no advice from the outsiders; they themselves had plenty of experience and there was no alternative but to fight against the feudalists. As in many European countries, it was a typical peasant war which represented class struggle between the peasants and the feudalists. This peasant uprising was not only against the corrupt feudalistic system of the Yi dynasty, but also a fight against the foreign powers.

In April, 1893, some representatives of the Tonghak party went to Seoul and presented their petition to the King, asking for legalization of their party as a religion and reported the local problems which they faced. Unfortunately, their petition was refused. Here, Chun Pongjun had a secret agreement with the Tae-Won-kun to co-operate with the Tonghak troops when they attempted to occupy the capital, neither group carried out its part of the plan.

The Min government finally decided to take a more active step and sent orders to governors Kim Mun-hyun of Cholla and Yi Yong-sik of Kyung-sang, to suppress the Tonghak party. Later, a special envoy, O Yunjung, was sent to the governors on a wartime mission to assist them.

The revolt was brought about by the chief of Ko-pu county in Cholla. when he called upon the local citizens to repair a state-owned canal. The local people labored resentfully in repairing the canal under county control. In ordinary practice, the county official collected a water tax from the peasants and used that fund to provide for the necessary expenses of running the canal. Che Pyung-gap, the new chief of the Ko-pu county, disregarded the old practice and kept the water tax for himself. The local people protested against this selfishness of the county official and petitioned the governor of Cholla province. The governor refused to listen to the peasants' protests and instead, he jailed them. The peasants who heard of this unreasonable action by the governor, immediately revolted against the county and the provincial government. The peasants, who were isolated from each other until this time, began to mobilize as a collective unit, and found their allies in the Tonghak Party.

In March 1894, in Ko-pu county, the peasants led by two outstanding leaders, Chun Pongjun and Kim Kae-nam began the fight against the government force. For their motto, they used the slogan ''Save the people from the corrupted government.'' They proclaimed:

> "we humbly hope that everyone, within one common resolution, will combine their efforts, and will select loyal and patriotic gentry to assist them in carrying out the wish of the country. This is the earnest prayer of millions of people. we shall save the common people from the corrupted government..."[6]

The leadership of the Tonghak movement consisted of the intelligentsia and the upper class group who had been disappointed with the government policy, and had all sorts of complaints against it. The founder of the Tonghak party himself was a scholar. The Ko-pu county peasants gave them an opportunity to act against the government. The Tonghak party recruited more volunteers than they could handle. The volunteers were mobilized throughout the provinces of Cholla and Kyungsang and Tsung-tsung. They were able to keep peace and order in the community with very little force. The members of the Tonghak Party were not allowed to smoke or drink. And they were empowered to punish any member who disturbed the peasants or did damage to the community. They claimed that the party was to reform the corrupted government; to get foreigners out of the country; and to plan for all people's interest and well-being. The volunteers were welcomed wherever they went. The Tonghak Party again proclaimed:

> "The highest thing in our society is the ethics...the government officials do not think of the people's interest; on the contrary, they bribe the ones in high official positions, waste their wisdom, condemn the honest scholars...there is no outstanding talent among the officials,

foreigners crowd into the government circle. The resentment of the people against these things increases everyday...we cannot be patient any longer. We will fight to save the people, and will fight to death....[7]

The main complaints against the government policy were: First, the government should abolish unfair land taxation, and tax the lands of the upper class as well. Second, the government should abolish the unfair and irregular income taxes in the cities and the towns. Third, the government should punish those foreign merchants who were dealing in contraband. Fourth, the government should solve the problem of the salt tax.

At the first mobilization, there were about four thousand peasants, about half of them were armed and one hundred cavalry. From the outset, the disciplined action of the soldiers impressed the people favorably. The peasants asked the central government to solve the above problems but, they met with fighting. The contradictory feature of the situation was that the peasants were asking a favor of their enemy, the government.

As soon as the government was aware of what was happening, eight hundred soldiers were sent under the command of Hong Ke-hun and ordered to resist the Tonghak troops. They failed in their mission and the Tonghak troops occupied Chonju, the local capital of Cholla province. Spurred by this victory, they moved towards Seoul, the national capital. Hong Ke-hun, the commander of the government troops, reported that the situation was very serious and that the government should ask the immediate support of China. The Korean government which was still under the influence of the Min group, had two alternatives. To take advantage of Yuan's advice and get military help from China. Or, to meet the Tonghak Party's demands and compromise with them. The government hesitated to take the second choice because the government was afraid of the Tonghak Party's popularity, and Tae Won-kun's influence which was still strong in Korean politics. The first choice meant the appearance of Chinese troops in Korea which would bring Japanese troops as well. Such a situation would create a national crisis in Korea. In spite of the coming of such a crisis, the government took the first choice.

Min Yongjin reported the serious military situation to Yuan Shin-kai. Yuan visited Min Yongjin, the Prime Minister, on May 26, 1894 and persuaded him that the Korean government force needed help from the Chinese government. Min guaranteed Chinese forces within ten days. The North China fleet had just finished great maneuvers at the Yellow Sea under the observation of the English and other Western powers and Yuan, therefore, knew China would be able to send her troops on short notice.[8] Prime Minister Min asked Yuan for help without first consulting the King; the King dismissed the Prime Minister for his rash action, but that did not help to stop the Chinese troops from coming to Korea. Yuan immediately reported the situation in Korea to Li Hung-chang. Li had to consider several important points before he took any action: first of all, if he acted, he would violate the Tien-tsin Treaty and there would be no opportunity for Japan to send her troops to Korea following the Chinese pattern. Even if Japanese troops appeared in Korea. China would control the situation in Korea. These points were of immediate concern to Li in the consideration of sending troops to Korea. Li delayed sending troops for about a month, but later sent fifteen hundred Chinese soldiers under the leadership of Yeh Sze-Ch'ao and Yeh Sze-chang to Korea in order to help the government forces against the Tonghak rebellion. This was in violation of the Tien-tsin treaty. The Chinese government failed to notify the Japanese until after the Chinese troops were on their way. Li reported the fact to the Japanese government as required by the Tien-tsin treaty on June 7. The Japanese government, however, already was informed by Sugimura, the Japanese deputy minister at Seoul, on June 2.

The Japanese government called an emergency cabinet meeting at the suggestion of the Foreign Minister. The members of the Japanese cabinet unanimously agreed to request that the Japanese chief of staff send troops to Korea. Thus, Prime Minister Ito, and Foreign Minister Mutsu, took the initiative to send troops to Korea.[9] They sent the minister to Korea with four hundred marines.

Japan, like China faced two main problems in Korea: first, to keep foreign influences out of Korean government; second, to keep the Korean market for Japanese economic expansion. By this time, the Japanese leaders recognized the necessity of an intensified armament program for her Empire. Japan was afraid of Russian expansion in the Far East; The Siberian railroad was a direct threat to Japan. There were, however, several reasons for the immediate presence of Japanese troops in Korea: to protect the Japanese residents and their interests in Korea, and to prevent Chinese intervention in the Korean government. Japan also remembered the significant case of Kim Ok-kiun, a popular Korean leader in the Japanese political circle who was murdered by an agent of the Min group. Count Hayashi wrote that it was Yuan Shin-kai who originated the scheme to murder Kim.[10] In any event, Kim was murdered by the reactionary force of the Korean government which was still under the influence of the Chinese government. As a matter of fact, when Kim was assassinated in Shang-hai, the Chinese officers turned Kim's body over to the Min agent instead of Kim's secretary. The Japanese friends of Kim were angry and tried unsuccessfully to send the Japanese troops to Korea for revenge. Thus Kim's murder case played an important role in sending the

Japanese troops to Korea..

The friends of Kim, who failed to get the war with China at the time of Kim's assassination, volunteered to join the Tonghak troops.[11] In Tokyo there was a strong group headed by Toyama who supported the revolutionary volunteers, Among the Japanese volunteers were Suzuki, Yoshikura, Ozaki, Tanaka, Shiroju, Takeda, and Uchihara Ryohei, the leader, who later became head of the Black Dragon society. At first, they went to meet Marshall Chun of the Tonghak troops; he refused their support, because he could not trust them. The Japanese, however, convinced him that they came to revenge their good friend's death. The volunteers joined the Tonghak troops and fought, encouraging Japan to send more troops. Japan had the legal i.e. treaty right to send her troops to Korea according to the treaty of Tien-tsin, and also in accordance with the Japanese-Korean conventions of 1882 and 1885. Japan let this fact be known to China.

Besides the Kim Ok-kiun incident, there was another basic reason for Japan's interference in the Tonghak rebellion. Japan was already engaged in heavy trade with Korea at that time, and Korea had already become an important market for Japan. In Japan, there was no land reform, in spite of their adaptation of the Western capitalistic economic system; as a consequence, reproduction of products was immensely hampered. In order to solve the economic problem and to develop the domestic industry of Japan, the Japanese needed the Korean market.[12] Japanese capitalism which accumulated capital now began investing in Korea. Japan could not afford to overlook the significant development of the Korean internal politics.

Even at this stage, Japan began to dominate Korean trade. Chinese interference of the Korean domestic policy interrupted the Japanese economic interest in Korea. Furthermore, if China alone helped to settle the Tonghak rebellion, the Chinese merchants would have eventually dominated the Korean trade. Japan, therefore, was unwilling to leave the Korean market in the hands of China.[13] Thus, the Japanese government sought to send troops before China did. The Japanese policy in Korea was to give close attention to: 1) the development of the Tonghak movement, 2) the Korean government policy toward this movement, and 3) the political relationship between Korea and China. Meantime, Yuan Shin-kai kept close contact with high officials in the Korean government. China, like Japan, had every intention of dominating the Korean trade as well as to hold the political hegemony in the country. In order to achieve these ends, China wished to settle the Tonghak rebellion in favor of a pro-Chinese Korean government. China was competing with Japan for Korea's market which inevitably brought about the political and military conflict between the two nations.

The significant role of the Chinese economic policy in Korea is generally overlooked. China's claims over Korea as her tributary state was not simply based on the "oriental prestige" of China. The close relationship between China and Korea was a matter of economics as well as of culture.

Yuan Shin-kai, who represented Li Hung-chang in Seoul, was a big landlord himself. Li Hung-chang was one of the richest landlords in China at that time. Li's family owned a huge plot of land around Ahnwei and Honan provinces, and Yuan owned about one-third of Changteh county in Ahnwei province.[14] Both Li and Yuan were planning to invest commercial capital in the Korean market with the assistance of the English industrial capital.[15] From the Chinese point-of-view, her investment in Korea was desirable in order to isolate Korea from the outside world. This, however, proved impossible because of the treaties of 1876 and 1882. It is true that the trade between Korea and the others was limited in the beginning of the treaties, but initial practice changed rapidly; not that the Korean market was open to others. This fact had to be recognized by China, and this was the main concern of Li Hung-chang on Korean problems. Professor Dennet pointed out these facts of the situation:

Li Hung-chang had failed to accomplish his purpose. Indeed in the end, he had been led to approve a convention in which the Chinese claim to suzerainty was specifically ignored. The supplementary letters which he had demanded were worthless. Li had evidently come to the conclusion that Korea could not much longer be kept in seclusion and that regardless of Chinese pretention, it was to the advantage of both Korea and China the first treaty be made with the United States.[16]

It seems very significant that both Korea and China agreed to have the United States be the first Western power with whom a treaty was to be concluded. The reason for their selection of the United States is quite an interesting factor. Professor Dennet comments:

Had the first treaty been with France, there would probably have been a religion toleration clause in it such as had given so much trouble to China; and had the first treaty been with England, it might have been difficult to exclude a provision for the legalization of opium. The treaty would be a model for the others, and the United States was set a liberal standard. But Li Hung-chang came bitterly to regret his mistakes in permitting this Shufeldt treaty".[17]

It seems generally agreed that Li Hung-chang made a great political mistake in his long diplomatic career from his own stand point. As Professor Dennet pointed out, the Shufeldt Treaty was a step toward the dismemberment of the Chinese Empire. It was an unintended blow dealt at the security of the Chinese Empire.[18] This, however, was also an unavoidable situation for China. Regretful of this past mistake, Li Hungchang now wished to recover Chinese influence and did not wish to share with Japan or any other powers in Korea. The Tonghak rebellion brought such an opportunity for Li to try his latest adventure.

The French activities in the south of China occurred simultaneously with the Russian action in the far north. The English expansion program in China added up to a major concern of Japan at the time. The situation was most clearly expressed by the leading Japanese militarist, General Yamagada, head of the Privy Council, in his report to the Japanese Emperor.[19] General Yamagada advocated the armament program for national emergency. The reason for this armament program was, no doubt, to save Korea from China. The Prime Minister, spoke to the Japanese businessmen's group in Osaka in May 1895. He said that the Japanese Empire had a long future and must pay close attention to the progress of the business which was of prime concern for national prestige. The Prime Minister further stated that the Japanese businessmen should concentrate on both Cochow and Hong-chow areas, among the richest fields in China.[20] In other words, in order to establish the Japanese industrial capital, she needed the Korean market immediately, and China later. In order for China or Japan to have permanent domination of the Korean market, it was imperative to wage war between the two powers. Prime Minister Ito and the Foreign Minister Mutsu, representing the peace party of Japan which had been trying to avoid war with China, now came to an agreement with General Yamagada, a leading war advocator of Japan. It and his followers knew that war with China would bring economic chaos to a newly developing cotton industry in Japan. Japan imported about one half of her raw cotton from China[21] and China and Korea were the main markets for her finished products. The fact was that the Japanese cotton industry would not be able to carry on without the Chinese raw materials and its market. Yet the Japanese government was preparing for a war against China. Many Japanese newspapers predicted that a war with China would bring economic depression to the industries and consequently to the nation. They warned the government over and over again to deal with China with great caution.[22]

In case of a war with China, Japan also had to face the problem of iron and steel. China had plenty of iron which interested Japan. The Japanese militarist advocated the expanding of armaments, but there was not a sufficient amount of steel in Japan.[23] The answers to all these contradictions of the

Japanese government policies were that the victory after the war with China would bring four hundred million customers and the most favored nation treaty for Japan. The struggle between the peace party and the war party continued; both parties were trying to save and expand the Japanese imperialism on the continent in their own manner. There were no disagreements on this main principle; the only difference was in the tactics and the strategy. The two parties had not disagreed on sending troops to Korea in order to save her interests. The main concern of the peace party was not to violate the treaties, particularly the Tien-tsin Treaty. The problem of relationships was not so much with China, but with the second and third powers.[24] The war party did not pay much attention to the treaty commitments and both parties refused to recognize Korea as a tributary state to China in spite of the advocacy of Lord Curzon.[25] It was a known fact that a war against China would be opposed by the British government. The Japanese government. however, was ready to send her troops to Korea as soon as the Chinese government sent hers. A group of Japanese militarists under the leadership of General Kawakami had already gone to China through Korea as soon as they heard about the Tonghak rebellion. They did not waste much time in taking aggressive action against China. Even the peace party led by the Prime Minister could not prevent their actions.[26] General Kawakami, a member of the General Staff, opposed the position of General Yamagada who wanted to wait until the Chinese troops arrival in Korea. He advocated that they take the initiative and send the Japanese troops regardless of the Chinese hesitance. Kawakami, who had first hand knowledge of the Chinese troop situation had confidence of victory in a war against China and wanted to initiate the fight. The Japanese fleet left from Yokosuga for Korea on June 5, 1894, just two days before Li Hungchang's note arrived. General Kawakami's "preventive war" theory was carried out, even Mutsu, the Foreign Minister, supported Kawakami.[27]

On June 10, both the Japanese and the Chinese troops landed on Korean soil. The Japanese troops came "to protect" the Japanese legation and the Japanese citizens. The Chinese came at the official invitation of the Korean government.

The Korean government prohibited any troop movement by the Chinese or the Japanese in Korea for the time being because of the fear of impending war. Later, the Japanese and the Chinese troops participated in Korea's civil war. In the meantime, the Korean government sent fifteen hundred soldiers from Seoul and three hundred men from Pyong-yang to the south where they attacked Chonju castle and had regained it. The Tonghak troops marched north and fortified the city of Nonsan, making it their new headquarters. The climax came when the Tonghak troops attacked the city of

Kongju on October 25.

In the fight between the Tonghak and the government troops which had the support of both Chinese and Japanese, the latter was favored to win. Since the Kongju battle, the Tonghak troops began their retreat, and the civil war was over at the end of the year when Marshall Chun Pongjun was captured by the government forces. This civil war lasted exactly one year from January to December. Both the Chinese and Japanese helped the Korean army to defeat the Tonghak forces.

The Tonghak party rose with the popular support from the peasants. The cause of the Tonghak party's revolution cannot be overlooked, because it was a most serious people's movement during the last five hundred years of the Yi Dynasty. It was different from the Revolution of 1884 in that the Progressive Party was against the feudalistic conservative government of the Min's. In other words, it was a social, economic revolution based on a democratic spirit which attempted to revolutionize the Korean government. It is significant to note that if the Tonghak Party had succeeded it would have meant the changing of federal monarchy system of government to the "democratic system," and could have brought about a new civilization with the new era.

The main causes for the failure of the Tonghak revolution were: 1) that the mass was unorganized and 2) that the troops consisted of volunteers who lacked proper military training. Had Marshall Chun strongly fortified the city of Chonju as the main headquarters, and concentrated upon the occupied southwest district instead of on further offensive engagement, the battle might have been prolonged and the national forces brought together. For later, militia groups sympathizing with General Chun sprang up throughout southern Korea.

On the other hand, the opponents of the Tonghak troops, particularly the Japanese, were well-trained, well-equipped professional soldiers. Also, Tae Won-kun organized the pro-Japanese cabinet under the Japanese Minister Otori and asked the Japanese force to suppress the Tonghak revolt in the south.[28] It seems that Tae Won-kun did not care for political competition with the popular revolutionary leader Chun. This brought about a very interesting political picture; the anti-Japanese as well as anti-Chinese, Tae Won-kun, with the help of the Japanese troops and the Chinese troops, had suppressed the Korean people's revolution. On the other hand, the Tonghak troops received much technical and material support from the Japanese volunteers in the native, fascist-minded group.

One of the Japanese volunteers, Tanaka Shiro, went to see Chun who was waiting for prosecution at a Seoul prison and told him that he would arrange for Chun's escape from prison to Japan and prepare to fight again if he so desired, but Chun replied that in the first place, he would be unable to escape because of his wounded leg, and in the second place, he did not trust the Japanese government which crushed his troops. Chun received capital punishment.[29]

Both Chinese and Japanese troops arrived in Seoul after crushing the Tonghak rebellion. During the middle of June, the Japanese forces arrived in Wonsan and Pusan where there were Japanese residents. During this crisis the Korean King and his government had very little influence in stopping the increasing demands of China and Japan and the struggle between China and Japan. The following note by a Korean minister explains well the situation of those days:

During this moment the troops of two nations, namely China and Japan are in occupation of Korean soil. The first by invitation to aid in quelling a rebellion; the other without invitation and against the protest of the Korean government, but as represented to me, on account of solicitude for the safety of her own subjects resident here. The necessity for the presence of both of these has now ceased. The Chinese authorities under these circumstances are now willing to remove their troops from Korean soil, provided Japan will remove hers. But Japan refuses to remove her troops until the Chinese have been removed and neglects to entertain any proposition for the simultaneous removal of both.[30]

The minister saw the danger of the conflict between China and Japan in Korea had to plead to foreign powers to help the Korean government to remove them. Thus, the minister continued:

...I respectfully submit to the foreign representatives and their governments that at a time when Japan and Korea are at peace the presence and holding of Japanese armed troops in Korean territory in extraordinary numbers is not in accordance with the law of nations. I am directed by His Majesty to ask that the foreign representatives, being fully acquainted with the facts of the situation, will use their friendly offices, as proffered by treaty, in effecting an amicable solution of the present situation.''

No one responded to this plea. Because the peasant war was unsuccessful, the foreign powers gained special opportunity to stay in Korea. This situation made a military struggle between China and Japan for the Korean market inevitable. China was more anxious to withdraw troops from Korea than Japan was, because China wished to retain her influence in Korea without war with Japan besides, she already had her influence in the Korean court.

Among the Japanese leaders there were two major differences of opinion in regard to the withdrawing of troops from Korea. The Japanese minister Otori held to the Japanese government's intention of withdrawing of troops with China simultaneously. As a matter of fact, Otori agreed with Yuan that they would recommend to their governments the withdrawal of troops from Korea.[31] Sugimura's group made up of the junior ranking officials in the Japanese legation, however, strongly opposed Otori's policy for a peaceful settlement. They raised the problem of Korea's absolute independence at this time. Sugimura's group represented the extreme military group at home and abroad[32] and took advantage of this opportunity in actually advocating an immediate war against China. The Japanese policy gradually changed to the latter policy[33] and looked for more excuses to retain her troops in Korea rather than to withdraw them.

The Japanese official proposal was to reform the Korean government. Why did the Japanese government suddenly suggest the reformation of the Korean government? Did the Japanese government really mean to reform the corrupted feudalistic set-up of the Korean government or did the Japanese government try to raise a political issue in order to retain her troops in Korea?

The Japanese Foreign Minister Mutsu answered all these questions without hesitation. Mutsu stated that the Japanese public unanimously supported the idea of the reformation of the Korean government as soon as the government declared the policy. Mutsu was successful in the initiation of the new policy. As he pointed out in his memoirs, there were various groups that supported this policy because of various reasons. First, the reformation of Korea was an excuse for the expansion of the Japanese Empire. Second, the completely independent Korea should be a peaceful neighbor to Japan. Third, Korea should be a neutral state in case of war between Japan and China, or Japan and Russia. Fourth, inviting the powers to make Korea a neutrality like Belgium or Switzerland. At any rate, Mutsu thought that they all had one thing in common, that was to help a weak force against a strong one, one of the basic ethical issues which the Japanese government could well have taken advantage of.[34] As far as Mutsu was concerned, however, the issue was a political one and nothing else. He said:

> ...I don't think there is any other meaning besides the political necessity in the case of the reformation of Korea...We should not go

beyond the interest of our country on the problem of the Korean domestic reformation. It is not necessary to sacrifice our interest for the sake of the reformation in Korea...The reformation of the Korean domestic policy is proposed in order to solve the difficult problem between Japan and China.[35]

In other words, Mutsu's proposition was clearly not aimed for the benefit of Korea. Thus, it became clear that the design of the Japanese government was to retain and to add troops in Korea. It is doubtful at this particular time, that Mutsu thought of a war with China, since he mentioned that he did not see the necessity of sacrificing the Japanese interest for the sake of what he considered merely a political issue.

June 14, the Japanese cabinet decided that the reformation of Korean domestic policy be proposed at the initiative of Prime Minister Ito. The carefully studied proposition of the Foreign Minister, Mutsu, that the Japanese cabinet should adopt a policy which was to be enacted in case of failure of cooperation from China. Prime Minister Ito suggested: First, the Korean civil war must be stopped by the collective efforts of the SinoJapanese military. Second, after the settlement of the civil war, in order to reform several domestic policies, both Japan and China should send several members of a standing committee to Korea. Their function would be to investigate the financial situation of the central and the local governments of Korea and to establish a necessary police force to keep peace and order in the country. Third, after adjusting the financial condition, to sell national bonds, for the purposes of national interest. The main points of Mutsu's suggestions were the same as Ito's, but Mutsu made it clear that Japan should seek to cooperate with China and to bring China to an agreement to reform the Korean government. In order to bring China into this political cooperation. Mutsu suggested that Japan should initiate a new conference with China on commerce. Mutsu was willing to try the new suggestion. His personal letter to Count Inouye, the Minister of the Interior, indicates that he was trying to avoid conflict with China or at last to delay it. His intention of a peaceful settlement was expressed and he was successful in being able to keep the situation under control[36] Japan wished to expand her empire and planned to reform the Korean government for her own political reasons. The Ito-Mutsu-Inouye cabinet, however, did not wish to engage in a war with China. It seems that their main interest was to keep a balance of power between the two nations in Korea.[37] In the meantime, Japan also wished to extend her economic influence in Korea as peacefully as possible. Mutsu requested Otori, minister at Seoul, for a Japanese proposition on Korea, even though the Chinese government probably would not agree with it. Mutsu proposed to use this opportunity to ask the Korean government for concession of a telegraph between Pusan and Seoul; and the abolition of a regulation protecting grain. Even though China should not agree to the proposals, the Japanese would establish rule anyway and prepare for the later action.

Li Hung-chang, who had been informed of the Japanese proposal, protested strongly to the Japanese government that he had agreed with Ito in 1885 that as soon as the troops finished the mission, they should be withdrawn. Further, that since the Japanese government recognized the self-government of Korea, she had no right to interfere with the Korean domestic policy.[38] Li suspected a Japanese double policy; the agreement of withdrawing the troops and the proposal of the reformation of the Korean government.[39] Li strongly advised Yuan that he should try his best to prevent the Japanese troops from landing at Chemulpo. About five thousand Japanese soldiers arrived at Chemulpo, about half the size of the Chinese forces. Li also advised the Chinese Minister at Tokyo to discuss the Korean matter and protested the Japanese proposals. Through the Chinese Minister, Wang, the Chinese government made this three point counter-proposal to the Japanese government: First, the Korean civil war has ceased and there was no need of discussion on the suppression of the rebellion by two nations. Second, the problem after this settlement should be handled by Korea herself; China should not interfere with the domestic affairs. Japan also had no right to interfere with the Korean domestic affairs since she recognized Korea's independence. Third, withdrawal of troops after the affair has been decided, there would be no need of further discussion on the matter.[40] This strongly worded message did not mean Li was ready to go to war with Japan. On the contrary, Li was trying to avoid a war through a third power influence if not by China herself.

Within the Chinese government, as in the Japanese, there was a group that advocated an immediate fight against Japan, and opposed Li's diplomacy of a peaceful settlement.[41] The Japanese government replied to the Chinese counter-proposals by saying that China did not agree to the initial Japanese proposal, and that Japan would not withdraw her troops from Korea.[42] The Japanese government held an emergency cabinet meeting in the presence of the Emperor and other leading military personnel on June 22, and the national crisis was mutually understood. On June 23, additional Japanese troops were already on their way to Korea.[43] Even in view of the inevitable war, Mutsu was still concerned with the peaceful settlement. Foreign Minister Mutsu and many leading Japanese newspapers, firmly advocated Korean independence. The advocacy of Korean independence was being used as the basis of unity of the Japanese nation and to save Japanese prestige among the nations.[44] Mutsu made no mistake on what he really meant by Korean independence. He said:

...Our government introduced Korea as an independent state to the world, and proclaimed not to damage her independence by this affair. The European powers are watching carefully the future course of the Japanese policy in Korea. If we make a mistake at this time we will fall into the future of having enemies around us. Therefore, we must consider very carefully when we insist upon the reformation of the Korean government. Korean is the center problem only in name, but the attitude of the third power on every single problem is the real center of the whole affair.[45]

One June 24, the Korean Foreign Minister Cho Pyongjik, officially requested the Western powers to interfere in the critical situation of Korea for the sake of peace in the Far East. The Korean Foreign Minister said in his prepared statement:

The presence of a large army in time of peace, the landing of cavalry and artillery, the placing of batteries, and keeping a guard at strategic points after internal quiet is assured is a dangerous precedent for other nations and a menace to the peace and integrity of His majesty's realm.

This clear and concise official observation, however, was completely ignored by the powers. He was right in stating that peace was in danger; under this situation, Korea lost her prestige as a sovereign state. The Korean official statement had some influence upon the powers, at least, the American, British, French, and Russian representatives in Seoul. The jointly requested peace and that the existence of both the Chinese and the Japanese troops in Korea would seriously endanger the interests of their government. The statement was issued on June 25.[46] On the same day, the Russian minister initiated her complaint to the Japanese Foreign Minister in Tokyo. Minister Otori, meanwhile presented the prepared statement to the Korean King, and offered further consultation with anyone designated by the King. The full statement was a very friendly one and did not mention any specific reformation. There were a number of Korean progressive elements, including Kim Kajin, Yu Kiljun, Cho Ili-yun, and An Sa-su, who were willing to cooperate with the Japanese in order to carry out the reformation program. Their political influence in the court, however, was not strong enough. Otori, failed to receive any cooperation from the Korean government.

Meanwhile, the Chinese Minister to Tokyo, used the words "protected dependency" in a written message to the Japanese Foreign Minister in reference to Korea. The Japanese foreign office protested that "protected dependency" not only violated Korean sovereignty, but that it also raised the serious problem of the Chinese intention in regard to the Chinese troops in Korea. To get a clearer meaning of "protected dependency," Otori demanded an explanation by the Korean government in Seoul. In Tokyo, the foreign office was simultaneously protesting to the Chinese Minister.

The Korean minister of foreign affairs answered on June 30, that the Korean-Japanese Treaty of 1876 recognized the independence of Korea, and guaranteed the equality of the two nations. Since the treaty, the intercourse between the two nations had been equality. The Minister further stated that the Korean affairs were handled by herself and were free from any other powers. China too, realized this fact since the enacting of the treaty. He insisted that the Chinese Minister to Tokyo should not interfere with the relationship between Korea and Japan, and he wanted to deliver this message to the Japanese Foreign Minister.[47] The Korean Foreign Minister's answers did not satisfy the Japanese demands; and Otori protested again to the Korean government. Otori's strong protest to the Korean government of June 30 caused the second Russian protest to the Japanese government. This time, the Russian words were stronger than any previous protest received by the powers. The Russian statement said, "We advise that the Japanese government must take full responsibility if the Japanese government refuses to withdraw the troops simultaneously with the Chinese government."[48]

The Japanese government took this warning very seriously because it implied Russian military interference. What would the Ito-Mutsu cabinet decide on the matter? Mutsu immediately consulted with Ito, and Itois attitude was very clear when he said, "How can we withdraw our troops from Korea at this time on the basis of the advice from Russia?"

Mutsu replied, 'I agree with you. The hardship of the future affairs belongs to both of us; there is no need of future discussion. Mutsu immediately advised and reassured the Japanese Ministers to Russia, England, and China of their strong position.[49]

The Korean government had tried to bring the other powers, particularly the Americans, into the situation without any success. The Korean Minister to Washington presented a telegram from the Korean government to the American official. The telegram stated that the foreign representatives at Seoul had held a conference. The Japanese Minister refused to withdraw their troops and hence, the Korean government asked the President of the United

States to settle the conflict.[50] The Washington officials were reassured by the Japanese Minister that Japan had no intention of invading Korea and would withdraw the troops as soon as the Korean government was ready to protect her own interest. The minister further stated that Japan wanted peace and recognized the independence of Korea. The Washington officials accepted the Japanese intentions as good, and refused to interfere any further in the case of Korea.

While Russia was warning Japan, England also advised China. England disliked the Russian expansion in the Far East, and was willing to prevent the Russian expansion. Japan understood these Anglo-Russian relationships when Ito and Mutsu made up their minds to refuse the Russian "advise." Ito and Mutsu hoped to get sympathy from England against Russia if it was necessary.[51] England's position became unclear when Japan approached England with an anti-Russian policy. Li Hung-chang also criticized England's confused attitude.[52] China now had to stand by herself without expecting the third power that she had previously hoped for. China too, now had to prepare to meet the coming conflict.

On July 3, the Japanese Minister suggested on his own behalf, to the King of Korea that the Korean government should select Korean officials on equal basis; improve the financial situation; justify the court; reform the police; and reform the educational system. The King accepted these suggestions. These significant reforms brought important changes in Korea: the class system of the feudalistic land ownership changed to capitalistic, politically, economically and socially. It was not a change of one form of society to another, but to a progressive change similar to that in Japan. The important point in this transformation was that the changes were brought to Korea, not by the Korean people themselves, but by an outside force, the Japanese capitalists.

Among the Korean officials were the fair-minded Kim Hongjip, the former Korean Minister to Japan, and Kim Sa-tsol, who vigorously opposed the Japanese proposals on grounds that the Korean, government must carry out the reformation through her own initiative, not that of the Japanese or any other power. Kim Sa-tsol reported to the Korean government that Japan would not be able to conquer Korea so long as the Koreans resisted. Kim's estimation of Japan's strength was obviously mistaken as later events have indicated. Even this late moment, Li Hung-chang was holding an optimistic outlook on the whole situation. His optimistic view was primarily based on the latest development between China and Russia.

On July 5, the Russian Minister to Korea, Waber, visited the Chinese foreign office on his way to Seoul; he informed the Chinese government that the main purpose of his going to Korea was to settle the dispute between Japan and Korea. He did not say between China and Japan. The Chinese Foreign Minister asked him to see Yuan at Seoul as soon as he got there. Li actually believed that Russia might lend her troops to Korea in case Japan refused to accept Russia's advise on the matter.[53] Li informed his representative in Seoul of this matter immediately. Russia wanted a part to play in this international affair with China and Japan. England, however, did not wish to have Russia interfere in this dispute. England, therefore, advocated that the dispute should be settled by China and Japan; otherwise, she advocated an all powers interference, including the United States and Germany.

On July 7, Otori sent a second notice to the Korean government and urged them to state their position in regard to the reformation. Under this pressure, the Korean government finally set up an investigating committee for the reformation under the leadership of Shin Jong-hi, the Minister of the Interior, and two assistants, Kim Jong-han and Cho In-sing. On the same day, through the initiative of England, the third powers raised the neutrality problem of Chemulpo. The British Minister to China had an interview with the Chinese Emperor and raised four basic questions for which he asked direct answers: First, does China approve.of the domestic reformation of Korea? Second, would China send a high official to Korea in order to discuss the reformation? Third, would China and Japan jointly protect Korea against any invasion of the Korean territory by a third power? Fourth, would the Chinese government treat the Japanese merchants in Korea the same as the Chinese merchants in Korea? The Chinese Emperor gave vague answers to all those questions, and did not encourage the settlement of the British proposals.[54]

The official attitude of the Chinese government indirectly strengthened the Japanese position. On July, 13, the Russian Minister at Tokyo visited the Japanese foreign office and informed them that the Russian imperial government was satisfied with the Japanese reply of Russia's request of June 30, and wished luck in the settlement of the dispute between China and Japan. On July 2, the Japanese government answered the Russian Minister's request of June 30, that the Japanese government had no ambition for any part of the Korean territory, and that she would withdraw the troops as soon as the civil war ended. The Russian government was satisfied with this reply.

The reason for the changes of the Russian imperial government was that she did not want to fight against Japan with China. Russia did not want to see China become a big power through this war. A strong China would mean a threat to the ambitious Russian empire. The revised Anglo-Japanese treaty on July 14, and Russia's changed attitude prompted Japanese action without further hesitation. After a long conference between Otori and the Korean Committee for the reformation on July 10, the Japanese Misister proposed a detailed plan, divided into three different categories: The first category had to be initiated within ten days; it included such items as building the railroad between Seoul and other main cities, setting up the telegraph line between the main cities, etc.. The second category had to be carried out within six months; those included such matters as setting a regular uniform salary system among the government officials, reforming the currency system. The third category had to be carried out within two years; it included such areas as reforming the military system, establishing of schools and sending selected students abroad for further study.

The Korean officials appreciated the Japanese proposals and promised to carry them out to the best of their ability. On July 15, at the third conference of a joint meeting, Shin Hijong, the chief Korean delegate, presented the official Korean statement that Korea had been neglecting all the reformation all this time although the government had plans in mind for the last ten years. Since the Japanese proposals were all beneficial to the Koreans, they would be glad to carry them out. In fact, the government set up a number of committees to carry out these proposals. Shin stated, however, that his government did not think the Japanese government should press the Korean government for the reformation for it was a violation of the spirit of the 1876 Treaty. Shin feared that the other treaty powers might also make requests of Korea, and bring disaster to the Korean government, should the Japanese proposals be accepted by Korea. He urged the Japanese Minister to withdraw the troops from Korea, and to abolish the set time limit on the proposals. Shin's statement upset Otori's plan and Otori immediately wrote to the Korean government that from now on the Japanese government would not take care of the Korean interests, but would only look after her own interests. His angry words did not influence those stubborn Korean high officials.

The Japanese Minister of the Navy, Saigo, asked Foreign Minister Mutsu, whether it would make any difference in the Japanese strategy if they took the initiative against the Chinese battleships in case the Chinese increased her troops in Korea. Mutsu replied simply that there would be no difference in the diplomatic program. Thus, the Japanese military forces were ready to fight as soon as the war broke. Three main naval strategies were agreed upon with the army forces in Japan. First, in case of a complete victory of the naval affairs, the army should invade Peking. Second, if the Japanese navy should be unable to defeat the Chinese navy, the army should not go beyond Pyongyang in North Korea. Third, in case of a complete failure of the naval battle, the land forces should retreat from Korea and defend the mainland of Japan.[55]

The Japanese Minister demanded that the Korean government should force the Chinese troops to withdraw from Korean soil in three days.

The Korean King had asked the Chinese to leave, but they refused to leave until after the Japanese left.[56] Japan demanded war with China, not only because of her interest in Korea, but also because of her domestic troubles. Professor Dennet writes:

> Japan reached a very ominous crisis in its domestic affairs in which a foreign war would be a very welcome diversion to the repeated interference of the Diet in the affairs of the government. On June 2, 1894, the Diet had been dissolved by the Emperor for the third time since December 25, 1891.[57]

For many years in Japan, there had been a strong movement in the political world which demanded the revision of the Japanese treaties with foreign powers, and the retrocession of the treaty ports. Count Hayashi believed that under the current Japanese circumstances, a large force thrown into Korea would temporarily appease the Japanese populace. In fact, had the withdrawal of the expedition been requested of China or Korea, the situation in Japan would have resolved itself diplomatically into a status quo ante, while politically, it would have meant ruin for Ito and Mutsu. On the other hand, a successful Korean campaign would not only have united all parties in Japan, but would have distracted public attention from the question of the treaty revision.

In China, Chang Pein-lun, later son-in-law of Li Hung-chang, advocated war with Japan believing that Great Britain and the powers would support. China Chang presented his views to the throne hoping for the Chinese government to take action--this message was, in turn, forwarded to Li Hung-chang for his advice. Li, though doubting that the European powers would give them support, replied, "I think that in the event of conflict between China and Japan, the foreign powers would be on her side."[58] According to Count Hayashi, the Japanese foreign office was fully aware of China's intention of finding some excuse to wage a war against Japan. The Japanese government was preparing herself for that day and was determined that she herself would decide the time of the conflict.

How should the war start so Japan could make excuses to the Western powers? It was imperative to have a pro-Japanese Korean group to initiate the coup d'etat at the Korean palace in order to get around the international legality of who would be the logical leader for this movement among the Koreans. He would be Tae Won-kun, the political enemy of the Min group that was still in power at that time. Who could approach Tae Won-kun successfully? There were several Japanese civilians in Seoul who represented the extreme war party of Japan: Okamoto Ruynosuke, Fukumoto Nichinan, Tanaka Kenjo, and others who had been waiting for such an opportunity.[59]

Okamoto was assigned to visit Tae Won-kun and explain the plan in detail. The plan was that on July 23, at three o'clock in the morning, the Japanese soldiers would escort Tae Won-kun to the palace and let him take over the government. At the same time, the government officials would be impressed by the Japanese military strength.[60] The pro-Japanese Korean group was to cooperate with this plan and to support Tae Wonkun's administration. Kim Kajun, Yu Kiljun and An Sa-su agreed on the plan. Meanwhile, Fukumoto and Tanaka went back to Japan in order to recruit their comrades and raise some funds. They met many leaders of the extreme war party and raised thirty thousand yen immediately. Tanaka and Fukumoto also met Pak Yong-ho, a Korean progressive leader who remained in Japan waiting for an opportunity to come back.

On July 23, two o'clock in the morning, the Japanese Minister sent an ultimatum to the Korean government that since the Korean government ignored the Japanese requests that from here on, the Japanese government would follow its own course. Simultaneously, the Japanese soldiers and several civilians under the leadership of Okamoto already arrived at Tae Won-Kun's residence. At this time, Tae Won-kun hesitated to take part in spite of his close Korean associates' advice.[61] Sugimoto, the Japanese secretariat at the Seoul legation, with Otori's approval advised Okamoto that "It is all right to use a little bit of force if it is necessary to bring Tae Won-kun to the palace. The only thing that matters being to achieve the purpose speedily."[62]

Tae Won-kun refused to cooperate with the Japanese on the grounds that they might invade Korea at this time. He wanted certain agreements before taking any collective action. Sugimoto had to sign a statement which promised that Japan had no ambition to invade Korean territory. Tae Won-kun also mentioned that Sugimoto could not go to the palace unless invited by the King. Sugimoto sent a man to arrange for that condition. Tae Won-kun arrived at the palace at about eleven o'clock. Yu Kiljun and An Sa-su arranged for Tae Won-kun's entrance into the palace. As soon as the Japanese soldiers marched into the palace, the Min families and the officials ran away. Tae Won-kun was angry with the King, his own son, saying that the King mislead the nation. Later Tae Won-kun thanked Otori for his assistance on getting him to return to the palace and helping him.

Tae Won-kun now began to reform the country under the close supervision of the Japanese officials. The new cabinet was organized by Tae Won-kun and there were both the conservative and the progressive group represented.[63] The Min group now left the palace and Tae Won-kun again stepped into politics. Japan stood firmly on Korean soil. The third powers were still working for peace, but much of their efforts were wasted. Meanwhile, Yuan Shin-ikai, seeing the changed situation, left Korea and returned to China.

On July 25, the battleships, *Akitsushima, Yonshino,* and *Naniwa,* among the best of the Japanese Navy, were ordered from Sasebo to Asan. Two days later they encountered and disabled the Chinese warships *Tsi-yuen* and *Kwang-ki* in the vicinity of Pung Island of Asan forcing them to withdraw towards Wei-hai-wei. While the Yoshino was pursuing the Tsin-yuen, she encountered the *Tsae-Kiang* and the British steamer, *Know-shing* carrying about fifteen hundred Chinese troops being attacked by *Akitsushima* and Namiwa which resulted with the drowning of more than a thousand Chinese. Thus, the war between China and Japan was legally declared on August 1, 1894.[64]

In the early stage of the war, the Japanese were encouraged because of their early triumphs. The northern section of the Chinese Army landed on Korean soil near the mouth of the Yalu River, and advanced to the city of Pyong-yang which was a main defensive fortification in northern Korea. Pyong-yang was a natural fortification for the Chinese Army, and it would be difficult for the Japanese to break through. On August 16, the formal act of casting off Chinese suzerainty took place. On that day, the Korean government declared all treaties heretofore signed between herself and China would be null and void and that all political connection between the two countries would be severed. On August 19, Lt. General Nodzu arrived from Japan with the reinforcements for which General Oshima had been waiting. Oshima sent a detachment towards Pyong-yang while additional Japanese forces landed in both Chemulpo and Wonsan. After bitter fighting in Pyong-yang, the city was occupied by the Japanese on the fifteenth of September. The land battle of Pyong-yang and the sea battle on the Yellow Sea gave Japan a decisive victory over China in spite of the fact that China had many advantages over Japan: China had several war-vessels that were far superior to anything which Japan possessed; China had unlimited population from which to recruit her land forces; she enjoyed the technical assistance of many foreign military and naval men; and she had the sympathy of Great Britain. The Japanese troops chased the Chinese from Pyong-yang to the Yalu region on the further side and could block the advance, China was unable to conquer the powerful and victory-inspired Japanese troops. Thus, the war was not fought on Korean territory for a period of ten years. This was the last chapter of Chinese imperialism in Korea, and the strengthening of Japanese imperialism.

At the beginning of the war, practically all the leading Japanese newspapers emphasized that the purpose of the war was not a selfish desire of the Japanese empire, but for the purpose of maintaining peace in the Far East, and above all, to defend and preserve the integrity of the Korean independence.[65] These stories, designed to deceive the Japanese people began to crumble when the confession of the real aim of the war was made public in a leading editorial statement.

The real aim of the war was not the upholding the spirit of righteousness or to protect Korean interests, but for the benefit of the Japanese empire and above all, to assure a market for Japanese goods.[66] The war was an imperialistic war; it had to come because of the rising Japanese empire which had to expand or die out. The failing Manchu empire had to face the war, because she could not forfeit Korea and let her market fall into the Japanese hands. This war proved to be the opportunity for Japan's industrial capital to be established, supplemented by extraordinary military preparations, and for landlords to concentrate on agricultural lands. There was also the differentiating of classes in Japan; such conditions invited a distinct lowering of the Japanese workers' living conditions and brought about the exploitations of the colonial people. On the other hand, the Japanese workers gradually realized their role in the Japanese economic life, and thus, the beginning of the modern trade union movement in Japan started. The scholarly study of socialism also started in Japan at this time. The Association for the Formation of Labor Unions was established on July 5, 1897, for the purpose of "realizing harmonious labor-capital relations in the interest of promoting industrial development; fostering an independent spirit among workers." The Union of the Japan Railway Engineers, and the Printers Union also was formed in the following year.

Korea, like Japan, changed slowly towards a semi-feudalistic type of state. The change was necessary since the feudal state could not serve the exploiting power as conveniently as it could otherwise. Korea became a victim of imperialism. Why did Japanese introduce the progressive reform in Korea? The Japanese certainly had no desire to reform the Korean government in order to benefit the Korean people; on the contrary, the Japanese forced the reforms on Korea because they foresaw that the bourgeois type of Korean government could support the development of the Japanese capitalistic enterprises through efficient trade between the two countries. Korea also could supply the raw materials for the Japanese industries. Also, the agricultural products which were exported to Japan within a short time were quickly commercialized and it was impossible to expand commercialization in the feudalistic society. The process of the "colonial system" of the Japanese exploitation in Korea was almost systemized after the Sino-Japanese war. The poverty of the Korean peasants, the class distinction of the agricultural society was created from then on, the feudalistic land ownership continued under a more efficient capitalistic mode of production. James Mill, who had described colonies as ". . . a vast system of outdoor relief for the upper classes," wrote, "The mother country, in compelling the colony to sell goods cheaper to her than she might sell them to other countries, merely imposes upon her a tribute; not direct, indeed, but not the less real because it is disguised."[67]

Not only the matter on the purchasing problem, but also on the matter of selling goods to the colonies, the mother country was able to make the colonies pay more for the goods than they were worth. On the other hand, the Korean people gradually woke up and began to fight for their life and freedom.

Notes

1. Harrington, op cit., p. 243
2. Curzon, Lord, *The Problem of the Far East,* Chapter VI
3. Original words in Korean see *Pyolgangon,* vol. 111, no. 4
4. Hulbert, *History of Korea vol.* 11, p. 265
5. Harrington, op. cit., p. 250
6. Tsa Sang-tsan, "Memory of Tonghak Revolution," in *Pyolgangon,* III, no. 2; Kim Pyong-su, "Tonghak Party and Marshal Yun Pongjun," in *Pyo/gangon,* 111, no. 4; Pak Tal-song, "A Great Man and an Effort," in *Pyolgangon,* vol. V, no. 3
7. *Tokyo Nichi-nichi Shinbun,* May 26, 1894
8. Wang Yun-sheng, *Lin-shin-nien Lai Chung-kuo Yu Tih-pen, or Sixty Years of Relations Between China and Japan, vol.* II, p. 3-10
9. Mastu Munemitsu, *Kenkenroku, p.* 15
10. Hayashi, Count T., *Secret Memoirs of Count Hayashi, p.* 38
11. Kim Pyong-sun, "Tonghak Troops" in *Pyolgangon,* III, no. 4 That these extreme Japanese nationalists volunteered to support the revolutionary forces of the "colony" was an interesting phenomena, the same group also supported the Chinese revolution on the republic side. Dr. Sun Yat-sen was a close friend of Toyama Mitsuru.
12. Nobuo, Kiyosaburo, "Japanese Industrial Development Before Sino-Japanese War," in *Science of History (Rekishi Kagaku),* no. 10, vol. IV
13. *Tokyo Keizai Zasshi* or *The Economic Journal of Tokyo,* June 16, 1894
14. Murakami, Shiriyuki, *Before and After the September* 18, p. 170
15. See Professor Witefogal's statement on China, Chinese Economic and Society, vol. 11, p. 367

16. Dennett, Chapter XXV in *American in Eastern Asia* describes about Li's diplomatic action in regards to Korea.

17. *Ibid*.

18. Later, the Anglo-Korean Treaty gave a decisive blow to the Chinese position in Korea. Article four states: British subjects shall be allowed to go where they please without passports within a distance of one hundred Korean ri from any of the ports and places open to trade, or within such limits as may be agreed upon between the competent authorities of two countries.

19. The detailed report of General Yamagada, see Tokutomi Soho, *Biography of Count Yamagada, vol.* 111, p. 99-104

20. *Kokumm no Tomo* or *Friends of the Nation.* no. 252, June 5,

21. The list of the cotton export to Japan on the year of 1893: from China....5,858,294 (kan), kan is equivalent to 3.75 Kilogrammes from India....4,924,518 (kan), from U.S.A....1,058,074 see, *Jiji Shimpo* (daily) July 27, 1894, Tokyo

22. For detailed editorial, see *Chuagi Commercial Daily News,* Aug. 7, 1894; Jiji *Shimpo,* July 23, 1894

23. The Japanese navy minister, Karayama, said that Japan must not be dependent upon foreign countries for the very bases of a strong military force and the most important weapon, the battleships and the guns. *Dai Nippon Teikoku Cikai-shi, vol. 1, p.* 1491; also see Tokutomi, *op cit, vol.* 11, p. 815.

24. *Tokyo Nichi-Nichi Shimbun,* Apr. 18, 1893.

25. The statement of Lord Curzon in the *Problem of the Far East, p.* 372, 377, 309

26. The details of General Kawakami and his group's trip to China and Korea is available in the following newspapers: *Tokyo Nichi-nichi Shimbun,* Apr. 23, 1893; *Kokumin no Tomo,* vol. 12, no. 189, May 3, 1893

27. Oju Tunichi, *Dai Nippon Kensei-shi* or *A Japanese Constitutional History, vol.* IV, p. 151

28. Kim Pyong-sun, ''Tonghak Kun'' in *Pyolgangon, vol.* III, no. 4

29. *Pyolgangon,* no. 14, p. 20

30. *Foreign Relations of the U.S.,* ''Cho Piang-chik to Still,'' 1894, appdx 1, p. 23f

31. Sugimura, A *Record of Suffering Minds in Korea, p.* 10

32. A certain section of the Japanese businessmen supported the militarists on the grounds that victory from China would permanently bring the Korean market to the Japanese hands. This theory was expressed in *Hochi Shimbun* on numerous occasions; e.g. on June 21, it said ''sending out the troops

(Japanese) at this time should not just protect the Japanese residents here and there'' it further states the raising of the problem of the Korean independence and at the same time Japan should not allow China to interfere with Korean internal affairs. *Tokyo Nichi-Nichi Shimbun* which was more or less the spokesman for the government at that time, did not agree with the above statement and advocated that the purpose of sending troops should be only to protect the Japanese citizens and their property, and "to keep equal power with China."

33. Many serious conflicts between the Department of War and the Department of Foreign Affairs was bitterly expressed by Foreign Minister, Mutsu, in his memoirs-Kenkenroku, p. 33-34.

34. Mutsu, op cit. p. 45

35. *Ibid.*

36. Inouye, *op cit, vol. IV, p.* 385

37. *Tokyo Nichi-Nichi Shimbun.* June 13, 14, 16, 23, 24

38. *Ching, Kuang-hsu Ch'ao Chung-jih Chiao-she Shih, liao, vol.* 13, no. 997

39. Li *Wen-chunk Kung Ch'uan-shu, vol.* 15

40. *The Congressional Record of Japanese Empire, vol.* 11, p. 27

41. Wang Yuan-sheng, op. cit., vol. 11, p. 81

42. *The Congressional Record of the Japanese Empire, vol.* 111, p. 1805

43. The General Staff Office (Japan), *Sino-Japanese War, vol. I, p.* 112

44. *Tokyo Nichi-Nichi Shimbun,* June 22, 1894; *Hochi Shimbun,* June 23, 1894

45. Mutsu, op. cit., p. 60

46. *Foreign Relations of the U.S.,* 1894, appdx 1., p. 23f

47. *Chiao-she Shin-liao, vol.* 13, no. 1063

48. Mutsu, *op cit, p.* 60

49. *Ibid. p.* 61

50. *Foreign Relations of the U.S.* 1894, appdx. vol. p. 30

51. Mutsu, *op cit, p.* 60-61. This idea clearly expressed in the telegram to the Japanese Minister to England, Aoki, by the Foreign Minister, Mutsu, on June 30, 1894.

52. *Chiao-she Shia-liao, vol.* 13, no. 1057

53. *Chiao-she Shih-liao, vol.* 14, no. 1087. Russia was advocating a three nation conference in order to settle the dispute.

54. For the detailed record of the conversation on this subject, see *Chiao-she Shih-llao, vol.* 14, no. 1148, Wang Sheng, *op. cit., vol.* 11, p. 38-41. Through this conversation and the London Times editorial on July 15, 1894, expressed clearly that the main concern of the British government was

Russia's ambition in Korea.
55. The Naval Strategy Department of Japan, *History of Sino-Japanese War, vol. I*
56. *Foreign Relations of the U.S.*, 1894, p. 21
57. Dennett, op. cit., p. 497
58. Hayashi, *op. cit., p.* 43
59. Okamoto, a leading man of Genyosha, a first fascist association of Japan, was sent to Korea by this group, Fukumoto was sent to Korea by Tobo Kyokai or the Eastern Association; Tanaka was sent by Kumamoto Liberal Party. They were sent to investigate the Korean situation. see Nobuo, *op. cit., p. 119*
60. Sambo Honbu, *op cit. vol. 1, p.* 119
61. Tae Won-Kun's secretary Jung said to Okamoto that there is only one person who can persuade Tae Won-Kun to take action, and that person was Jung Un-bong, who was in prison when the Japanese soldiers asked him to go with them, Jung refused to go out with them saying that he could not be released without the King's orders. Jung was moved out by the Japanese ;md brought to Tae Won-kun who refused to take Jung's advice. *Ibid. p.* 50
62. *Ibid. p.* 54
63. Kim Pyong-si, Jung Pomjo, Jo Pyong-se, Kim Hongjip, Shin Jong-hi, Pak Jong-yang were the former cabinet members, and Jo Ui-yong, Kim Kajin, Yu-Kiljun, An Sa-su, Kim Hak-u, Kwon Yongjin were the new members or the cabinet. Sugimura, *op cit, p-* 55
64. Wang, *op cit, vol.* 11, p. 79; Nobuo, *op cit, p. 525;* Vladimer, China-Japan War, app. D.
65. *Tokyo Nichi-Nichi Shinbun, Aug. 5, 1894; Jiji Shimpo,* July *29, 1894;*
66. *Jiji Shimpo,* Mar, *22, 1895*
67. Elements of Political Economy, 3rd ed., p. *213*

6

The Activities of the Independence Association : Japanese Interference 1894~1905

Japan, as a growing capitalist nation, needed the Korean market more than China, but China was unwilling to give Korea up without a fight. Thus the Sino-Japanese War broke out in Korea. While the war between China and Japan was raging, the Japanese Minister, Otori, insisted on negotiating another treaty with Korea. He succeeded in drawing up the treaty on July 25, 1894, known as an Offensive and Defensive Alliance.''[1] In order to practice this treaty, Japan sent several advisors and counsellors to draft many detailed rules and regulations which included such things as regulating the size of sleeves, the color of clothes, and the method of dressing the hair, etc., by which the Koreans, were to conform.

The pro-Chinese Prime Minister, Min Yong-Jun, and his cabinet now forced to resign under the changed circumstance; Min fleeing to the city of Tsun-tson about sixty miles east of Seoul. Meantime, the new leadership of the Korean government combined forces of Tae Won-kun and the liberal group. Tae Won-kun still had considerable influence over Korean politics, and the Japanese wanted to utilize his political influence while it was installing Kim Hongjip, a strong personality and a leader with a high standing in the liberal group as the new Prime Minister. Both Tae Won-kun and the liberal group disliked the Min group, but at the same time, there was not exactly an amicable relationship between the two; as a matter of fact, Tae Won-kun and the liberal group were politically opposed to each other. Thus the situation artificially created political confusion in the palace. Besides Kim, several other leading men with progressive ideas were appointed by the King to take over the administration of the government which now consisted of members of both the

131

progressive and the conservative group.[2]

The absolute monarchy now became constitutional and the Japanese were the makers of the rules. The Japanese, who respect the merit system, gave a rank to all the officers including even the housemaids of the palace, and issued many rules which caused complains by the Koreans. The Japanese, not only made the rules, but closely supervised the government, especially the palace. The Korean government felt that was a disgrace to the King, and made a protest to the Japanese government whereby the Japanese government commanded the Japanese legation to withdraw the Japanese soldiers from the palace. The growing aggressiveness of Japanese activities in the Korean government embittered the Korean people against the Japanese. The Min family which was enjoying many rights over the common people as rulers of the country felt the Japanese pressure even more, but neither they nor the people had the power to do anything about the actual problem. The people, however, protested continuously against the Japanese interference in the palace, as a result, the Japanese Minister, Otori, was recalled to Japan in September 1895, and replaced by Count Inouye. One of the main complaints was that of the Japanese military guard about the palace. As soon as the new minister, Inouye, arrived in Seoul, he proposed "the twenty reformations bill" drawn up by the Japanese, and tried to win over the Korean popularity, but the Korean people throughout the country revolted unsuccessfully in 1895, as a protest to the Japanese interference.

Pak Yong-ho, who was one of the leaders of the coup d'etat of 1884, and also known as "pro-Japanese" at that time returned to Korea from Japan where he spent ten years. Pak had been declared an arch-traitor by the Korean government, his house had been razed to the ground and his family dispersed. After he returned to Korea, he sent a long memorandum to the King, and convinced him that he was always loyal to his Majesty and was willing to serve him again if he should get the opportunity. The King gave him a pardon and Pak resumed his status as a Korean citizen. The pardon of Pak had been the sign for a general amnesty to all those who had forfeited their rights in 1884. Not only Pak Yong-ho, Dr. So Jai-pil (or Philip Jaisohn) who had been in America for many years also returned to Korea and was awaiting an opportunity to make Korea a modern government. So Kwang-bum, another leader of 1884 revolution, also had returned from Japan and the progressive movement was already on its way in the middle of December. The King moved to form a new cabinet composed almost entirely of men who had been foremost in the attempt of 1884: the ministers were Kim Hongjip, Pak Yong-ho, Yu Kiljun, So Kwang-bum, Tso Hu-yon, Sin Ku-son, Om Se-yong, O Yunjung, Kim Yun-sik, Pak Jung-yang, Yi Jaimyun, and Dr. So was employed as adviser to the privy council for a term of ten years. Meanwhile, the war ended, the treaty of Shimonoseki was negotiated between China and Japan in 1895. The treaty of 1895 at Shimonoseki, which provided that "China and Japan recognize definitely the full and complete independence and autonomy, and guarantee the complete neutrality of Korea" gave the Koreans an opportunity to strengthen their government. The Korean government now turned toward the progressive group for its leadership in order to reform the government. Dr. So more than any other individual became active and utilized his official position as an adviser of the privy council, and was anxious to promote reform and education in order to introduce a democratic progressive political system which he learned about while he was in the United States. The progressive group now held the political power, and the King wasn't totally unhappy about it since Pak Yong-ho was a close relative of the King and trusted by him, and it was natural for the King to attached to Pak. Pak too had no reason for desiring a complete change in the status of the ruling house, besides, he was a determined political enemy of Tae Won-kun.

However, the progressive group wanted to reform the administration and make a progressive government, they were not left alone to do what they wished. Japan now could give more attention to Korean politics since the war was over in her favor. Japan didn't intend to forget what she fought for. Pak who was known as "pro-Japanese" was no longer able to stay as Prime Minister because he refused to comply with the suggestions of the Japanese Minister, Count Inouye. Count Inouye drew up several special rights for the Japanese in Korea. Inouye and his staff found that they had misconstrued Prime Minister Pak and his liberal party's views which merely advocated the revolutionary spirit and admired the spirit of the Meiji restoration to mean that they entertained the idea that Korea should be under Japanese protection. Not only the Japanese, but the conservative group under the leadership of Tae Won-kun too had tried to remove Pak and his group from power. Tae Won-kun laid before the King certain grave charges of treason against Pak, which though not believed either by the King or Queen Min, convinced them that it would be impossible to defend him from probable destruction.by his opponents. Tae Won-kun was well aware that the people were still regarding Pak as a "traitor" in spite of the King's blessing. Under these circumstances Pak resigned his position as Prime Minister and escaped again to Japan. This again crippled the progressive movement.

After Pak Yong-ho left the cabinet post, Queen Min, with the support of Russia's forces, re-emerged into the political picture and began to advocate anti-Japanese movements against the close association with Japan which was the progressive group's policy. Japan could not carry out her ambition in Korea so long as the iron-willed Queen was on the throne. The Japanese, therefore, decided to remove the Queen from her position. The Japanese Minister, Count Inouye, tried his utmost to remove the Queen and having failed, felt that there was no alternative but to use a mean method to get rid of her. Inouye was recalled and succeeded by Viscount general Miura, a man of a different stamp: an old soldier, a Buddhist of the Zen school and an extreme ascetic. Miura's responsibility was to remove Queen Min; he came to Seoul with a Japanese Soshil (or professional assassin) to carry out the plans of the Japanese Imperial government. As soon as he arrived in Seoul, he called on Tae Won-kun, the chief political enemy of the Queen, and tried unsuccessfully to get his cooperation.[3] Finally, Miura called his secretary Sugimura, and Okamoto, an adviser to the Korean Army Department, discussed a plan for disposing of the Queen; then called Tae Won-kun again and threatened him to cooperate with their plan.[4] Before Count Inouye's departure to Japan, he assured the King and the Queen of Korea that the Japanese would be willing to protect the Korean Royal house in case of danger. He gave the following report in the Japanese parliament upon his return to Japan: "I explained to the Queen that it was the true and sincere desire of the Emperor and the government of Japan to place the independence of Korea on a firm basis and in the meantime to strengthen the royal house of Korea. In the event of any member of the royal family, or indeed any Korean, attempting treason against the royal house, I have the assurance that the Japanese government would not fail to protect the royal house even by force of arms."[5]

Both the King and the Queen felt confident that the promise from a distinguished Japanese statesman could be relied upon. The words of Count Inouye, however, did not bear truth. Early in the morning, on the 8th of October, 1895, the citizens of Seoul heard unexpected firing at the palace. This was in time of peace. The Kurentai with the Japanese instructor, marched up and down on all sides of the palace during the night, which caused some alarm within the palace. General Dye and Mr. Sabatin[6] saw the Japanese soldiers with fixed bayonets standing there. When those soldiers and the Kurentai broke into the palace, the two foreigners had little to do but watch. The soldiers and the Japanese assaissns swarmed into the palace from all directions, demanding the whereabouts of the Queen, hauling the palace ladies about by the hair to compel them to point out Her Majesty's quarters, rushing in and out of windows and doors, throwing the ladies-in-waiting from the seven feet high veranda into the compound, cutting and kicking them, and brutally murdering; they had thus secured their victim''.[7]

Meantime, Tae Won-kun, in exile from the court, was under Japanese guard, at his country house. Evidently the Japanese didn't trust him. The

King's second son, Prince Oui-wha, begged his mother to escape with him by a little gate which yet remained unguarded by the Japanese, through which they might pass disguised to friends in the city. The dowager Queen, however, was too old and too weak to go along with them, and Queen Min, refused to leave the dowager Queen alone to the terror which the occupation of the palace by foreigners would insure; meantime, trusting the positive assurances of protection that had been made to her through Count Inouye before he left for Japan.[8] The Soshi and officers who wore in Japanese uniform passed through the room where the King stood trying to divert attention from the Queen." One of the Japanese caught him (the King) by the shoulder and pulled him about, and Yi Kiung-chick, the Minister of the Royal household, was killed by the Japanese in his majesty's presence. His royal highness, the crown prince, was seized, his hat torn off and broken and he was pulled about by the hair, the Soshi threatening him with their swords while demanding the where-abouts of the Queen."[9] Mr. Sabatin too, was questioned and threatened with death. "[10] At last they found the Queen and killed her with theirs words. Even though they had killed the Queen, they were not sure of their victim, so they then covered her body, and brought palace women to identify it; one of them suddenly cried out with horror, "the Queen, the Queen" when they took off the cover, They were sure then that they had the right victim.[11] Then they threw a bed wrap around her(probably not yet dead) poured kerosene over her, piled faggots of wood around, and set all on fire.[12] In spite of such inhuman action, some people are trying to justify the incident by saying;". . .that the murder of the Queen, with all its unhappy consequences, although the crime was undoubtly concocted by Min's implacable enemy, Tae Won-kun, the Japanese government never sought to evade the share of responsibility imposed upon it."[13] This evasive statement was no longer held true when the Westerners, especially the American missionaries, knew the facts of the Queen's murder first hand, and a famous American newspaper man, Colonel Cockerill, of the *New York Herald,* came to Seoul and wrote with utmost frankness about what he learned.[14]

The Japanese Minister, Miura, arrived at the palace at daylight with Mr. Sugimura, who had arranged the details of the plot, and a certain Japanese who the King had seen apparently leading the assassins, and actively participating in the bloody work, and had an audience of the King, who was profoundly agitated.[15] At the same time, all the foreign representatives had audience with the King. Contrary to custom, the King grasped the hands of the representatives, and asked them to use their friendly offices to prevent further outrage and violence.

Ten days after the tragedy at the palace, the Japanese government, which was soon proved innocent of any complicity in the affair, recalled and arrested Miura, Sugimoto, and Okamoto, Some months later, they were placed on trial before the Japanese court at Hiroshima along with fortyfive others. At the trial, Miura and others were acquitted on grounds that there was no sufficient evidence to prove that any of the accused actually committed the crime originally meditated by them''. In fact, Miura told the court an entirely distorted story of the actual murder. Miura had his title removed temporarily but it was restored within a short time.[16]

In the meantime, the Korean government composed of the pro-Japanese elements, was holding the King and the Crown Prince as prisoners in the palace. The foreign representatives at Seoul were in sympathy with the King and showed much indignation over the cruel assassination of the Queen. Mr. Waeber, the Russian Minister, and Dr. Allen, Charge d' Affaires of the United States were most trusted by the King. For sometime, they visited the palace everyday; perhaps, they felt obliged to see the King personally in order to know his wishes and policy. On the other hand, they themselves wanted to get more information, and perhaps to keep in check any plans of violence toward the remaining members of the royal family.[17] Nearly a month after the assassination of the Queen the conditions were so bad under the rule of the new cabinet, that an attempt was made by the foreign representatives to terminate it by urging Count Inouye to disarm the Kurentai and to get the Japanese soldiers to occupy until the loyal troops could be drilled, the efficiency on which the King might rely for his personal safety. Count Inouye, who probably felt that step required armed reoccupation of the palace by the Japanese would be liable to bring about a serious misunderstanding, and very grave complication, so the proposal was not accepted then. Meantime, the Russian Minister, Waeber, a man of great ability had close contact with the King, and schemed to move the King and the Prince to the Russian legation. The Russian plans were carried out on February 11th of the following year. The King and his son were courteously received and housed in the best portion of the legation building as one might have expected. It evidently opened the Russian intrigue, and the new cabinet was organized at the legation and Pak Jung-yang became the Prime Minister. It had obviously done more harm to the nation than the frightened King could have imagined at that time.[18]

Meantime, on his return from the United States, Dr. So had organized ''The Independence Association'' which was initiated as a social club of the cabinet members which included Jo Pyung-sik, a pro-Russian leader, and many other political leaders of the day. As soon as the Treaty of Shimonoseki was declared, the members were more enthusiastic about politics than socials at the club. By the majority vote, ''A Social Club'' changed to its name to ''The

Independence Association'' and advocated carrying the Korean independence movement to the common people. The Crown Prince contributed a thousand dollars to the Association for this purpose and the King gave his consent to Dr. So approving of the movement. The aims of this organization were very obvious: to make Korea a strong, free nation able to stand alone before the world powers, and made a progressive democratic government pattern after the government of the United States where Dr. So spent more than ten years learning the principles of the U.S. a strong free nation meant eliminating foreign influences including those of Russia, then Korea's overlord, Japan and China, and against any foreign powers' interference; but to stand by the rights of the people "Korea for the Koreans" was their gospel. It insisted upon a still more liberal government, in the shape of a genuine constitutional monarchy, in which the royal prerogative should be largely curtailed and the element of paternalism eliminated. Dr. So and his associates devoted to reform the entire social system of the country, not just the government. Because of this changed situation, the cabinet members who had been enjoying their socials at the "club" no longer participated in the meetings and the liberal groups now dominated the "Association" completely. The most well-known leaders among them were: Yi Sangjai, Namgung Ok, Yun Chi-ho, besides Dr. So himself. They severely criticized the government's foreign, domestic policies at the public meetings, especially the foreign policy; they were very much anti-Russian as well as anti-Japanese.

The "Association" was very popular with all classes and many of the nobility as well as the commoners were members of the Association. Their followers consisted quite largely of impulsive, eager young men; many of them Christian, many of them students, and probably including the majority of the brilliant, energetic, and sincerely patriotic young men of the country.

Dr. So now resigned the position of adviser to the Foreign Minister of the Korean government, and he and others were trying to reform the government through the popular movement of the Independent Association. The primary basis of his whole reform idea was based upon some of the leading Western political philosophers. Dr. So said; "At first I tried to help the Korean government in the capacity of the Privy Council, as they offered me a five year contract to serve them in this manner. I accepted the offer and gave some advice. For the first month or two some of it was accepted by the Emperor and his cabinet officers, but they soon found that if they carried out this advice, it would interfere with some of their private schemes and privileges. They informed the Emperor that I was not a friend of his but a friend of the Korean people, which at time was considered treason. My influence was decreasing everyday at the court, and my advice was ignored. I gave up the idea of helping the government officially and planned to give my services to the Korean people as a private individual."[19] As a first job, Dr. So published the newspaper *Independence* printed in Korean and English, the first of its kind to be published in Korea, and issued three times a week under the auspices of the Independence Association. The *Independence* advocated the spirit of independence and public opinion backed the newspaper as well as the Association. Dr. So and his associated were especially encouraged by the warm support of unofficial American friends. Two Americans: Dr. Allen, who had natural ability, was proved to be one of the most able diplomats ever to represent the United States at the Seoul court, was highly regarded by the Korean people and the high officials helped Dr.So and his group; and the second person was Dr. Hulbert who was equally trusted by the Korean leaders and was adviser to the Korean government also helped the Independence Association. If the United States had paid a little more attention to the Korean affair and helped them through men like Allen and Hulbert, the history of Korea might have had an entirely different course, and that might even have checked the growing power of Japanese imperialism which became a menace to the security of the United States.

At this time, an important thing took place in Korea, the most valuable mining concession in the district of Unsan in the north was granted to an American syndicate, represented by James R. Morse, a transaction that proved most profitable to the owner the American. This arrangement was made by Dr. Allen, the American Minister. Allen, as already pointed out, had influence among the high officials in Seoul.[20] The Unsan grant covered an area already "honey-combed by native miners." In the winter of 1896, these men were ordered to stop work to make way for a foreign company, and soon they saw the new monopolist taking what the natives regarded as theirs.[21] The Korean natives wrote the following petition to the United States Minister: "We are gold miners (who) have been engaged in opening quartz mines in the Li Tap Mountain . . . but in the seventh moon last year, American miners took away from us by force all the mines without a single payment, under the pretence that they had purchased the same while we were working them. Also. . . big and little fir trees which we planted and cared for several hundred years in the neighborhood of our houses and our fathers graves were cut down leaving only the bare hills, by the American miners without any compensation. . . Is it in accordance with international law that anyone can take away by force the property of another without payment?"[22] This was a serious incident which brought public attention in regard to the foreigners' activities in the country. In same year, July, the concession for building a railway between Seoul and Wiju was given to a French syndicate which had no desire of pushing through to the finish, but merely to pre-occupy the ground and prevent others from getting it.[23]

The summer of 1896 saw great material improvements in Seoul. The work of clearing out and widening the streets was vigorously pursued and although most of the work was done superficially, some permanent improvement was effected. While the progressive movement was speeding ahead the King who was a moderate person never looked upon administrative changes with real favor, which would weaken his hold upon the finances of the country. In regard to serious matters, he was consulted by many of the leading conservative officials, who saw the establishment of liberal institutions as the end of their opportunity for personal power.

For the King and his conservative advisers, the concept of the government by law was entirely alien; their concept was the government by men. The government policy, therefore, had changed strictly based on the interests of the handful people who around the palace. Naturally, the people who followed the conservative government group, too were the type of the people who would do anything which meant pay and promotion. For instance, Hong Jong-u, the assassin of Kim Ok-kiun, who was violently anti-reform was appointed as the chief of police was given an important strategic position to disturb the progressive movement. Another man who had attempted to kill Pak Yong-ho was made Minister of Law, and from all sides were heard contemptuous comments upon the "reform nonsense" of the progressive group.[24]

Besides the government was once again taken over by the conservative group gradually, the King himself held an ambiguous position. Even after his return to the palace after a long residence at the Russian legation, he kept in close touch with the legation, and the Russian officers were put in charge of the palace guard; particularly the army and the treasury were completely in their hands. At this time, February 1898, the Independence Association offered a petition to the King asking for the removal of all Russians from the army and the government offices. The Russian Minister requested the King to state his wish in this matter, and soon after, being informed in the affirmative, the Russians were all withdrawn. Such crusading activities of the Association were not popular either among the Korean conservatives or the imperialistic foreigners whose only desire was to invade the country when time came. The Russian Minister Waebur was so irritated by Dr. So, he even asked the Russian Ambassador in Washington to seek to persuade President Theodore Roosevelt to call Dr. So away to the United States. It wasn't only the Russian Minister, the Japanese Minister Komura said to Dr. So one day; "I fear you are wasting your time. The Koreans are not ready for the American brand of democracy." Komura himself was a Harvard-educated diplomat.[25] Dr. So finally withdrew from his pioneering work in Korea and returned to the United States where he served as a staff physician in the U.S. Army which was engaged in a war against Spain. His withdrawal from Korea was not so much of his personal danger, but those friends who were closely associated with him were constantly threatened. His works had been sabotaged from all sides.[26]

The Independence Association, however, continued its activities under the presidency of Yun Chi-ho. Yun had studied in Japan, the United States, and Europe, and was a member of the Central Advisory Committee of the government and trusted by the King. Now he too had a golden chance to preach the new civilization to the mass people. Yun, like his predecessor Dr. So, frankly criticized the government policies and emphasized strongly, through the newspaper and mass meetings, the necessity of the reformation of the government. It was evident that the government high officers could not ignore Yun because of his high official position as vice-chairman of the Central Advisory Committee. They got rid of Dr. So to America, but Yun was a member of the royal family. Yun not only dealt with the reformation of the domestic policy, but the foreign policy as well. Especially in the month of September 1898, when the American Consul-General, Clarence Greathouse, brought the rascal[27] group of foreigners from Shanghai in order to protect the Korean palace.[28] There were about 200 mixed nationalities including the British, French, Russian, and Austrian who were paid by the Korean government to stay in Seoul.[29] As soon as this group arrived in Seoul, the Independence Association protested to the government; as a consequence, the government had to dismiss this foreign group after ten days in the capital. Another case which gave encouragement to the thousands of members of the Association was that of Russia when she brought a large number of army officers to Korea to drill the Korean troops. The Association objected to their presence and called upon the government to stop this pro-Russian activity with the result the Russian military officers had to be withdrawn from Korea.[30] These successes made them feel justly proud and triumphant. The Association now grew more influential and held more meetings at which many issues of public affairs were discussed with great freedom, the unsubstantial policies of the government were sharply criticized. At one of the meetings, the people asked the government for seven reforms which included abolishing torture and other objectionable customs, and granting more liberties. The Korean government approved of the written request under popular pressure, the King personally approved of the proposals, and simultaneously he added six more new liberal rules for reform.[31]

Yun Chi-ho, the president of the Association, now was appointed as vice-president of the Privy Council. The members of the Association saw their accomplishments and became more self-confident in their movement. They held another meeting at once at which they distributed thousands of copies of the new rules and regulations. Among those which were suggested and consented to that there be established a kind a popular Assembly: a law-making body, with advisory powers composed of one hundred people, fifty of whom were to be elected by the people, and fifty of whom were to be appointed by the King. This was certainly a jolt to the government which realized this as dangerous to their position as an absolute power. The conservative group was not willing to let this liberal movement interfere with their administration and to limit their political power. The conservatives were patiently allowing the liberals to talk, but didn't want to see any action which would curtail their actions in the government. The night before the first election to this proposed Assembly was to have taken place at Independence Hall, seventeen leaders of the Association were arrested by the police. It was the intention of the Minister of Law to sentence them to death, but the people rose en masse; crowded and exciting meetings were held all over the town. Because of this public pressure, the government had to change its decision. The angered people who were neither armed nor had violated any public laws assembled in front of the government building and demanded the release of their leaders whom the police had arrested. After five days of such threatening demonstration, the police released them. It was another victory of the Independents. The King, however, did not carry out his promises of the reformation. There was a big mass meeting which was the sole weapon of the people under the auspices of the Association as usual in the main street of Chong-no in the capital in October 28th 1898, with thousands of people in attendance and over which Yun Chi-ho presided. This meeting was very important since they passed and presented the significant articles to the cabinet for imperial sanction: they were; 1. Neither officials nor people shall depend upon foreign aid, but shall do their best to strengthen and uphold the imperial power; 2. All documents pertaining to foreign loan, the hiring of foreign soldiers, the granting of concession, etc., in fact every document drawn up between the Korean government and a foreign party or firm, shall be signed and sealed by all the ministers of state and the President of the Privy Council; 3. Important offenders shall be punished only after they have been given a public trial and ample opportunity to defend themselves; 4. To his majesty shall belong the power to appoint ministers, but in case a majority of the cabinet disapprove of the Emperor's nominee he shall not be appointed; 5. All sources of revenue and method of raising taxes shall be placed under the control of the Finance Department, no other departments, officer or corporation being allowed to interfere therewith, and the annual estimates and balances shall be made public; 6. The existing laws and regulations shall be enforced without fear or favor.[32] These six articles were passed not only by the people but also by the cabinet members who attended the mass meeting. This was reported to the King by the Prime Minister, Pak Jung-yang, and the King gladly accepted them and added five extra rules to them: 1. The emperor will accept freely the popular opinion of the people; 2. Will grant freedom of speech and assembly; 3. Laws are to be enforced upon local officers; 4. higher officers are to adhere to laws; 5. Public technical schools will be established.[33] This action further encouraged the people and the Association reached the peak of its popularity; on the other hand, the government feared this mass group and laid plans to suppress it. Five days before the Central Advisory Committee meeting, on the night of November 4th, the government again arrested the leaders of the Association including Yi Sangjai, Namgung Ok, Rhee Syngman, and others. Yun Chi-ho fled when he heard the police at his gate. The night before this incident, while Yun was working at the Independence newspaper office, the King summoned him; he went to the palace had a few minutes conversation then left. Later, he discovered that his Majesty had not summoned him at all but that the new Prime Minister, Jo Pyong-sik, who had planned to have him murdered by the gate-keeper as he entered the palace. The Prime Minister did not know that the gate-keeper would not have committed such an act as he had great respect for Yun.[34]

In spite of this oppression, the people under the new leadership of Ko Yong-hwan held mass meetings and attacked the police station where their leaders were held. Finally, the government had to release them again because they feared the strong popular sentiments might bring revolt against the government, but the government secretly prepared a group of people who were brought in from the outside of the capital to fight against the Independents. This group, headed by Hong Jong-u, the chief of police, was comprised of the old time peddlers' guild who were willing to do anything that would mean pay. These peddlers attended the Independents' mass meetings and disturbed their orderly meetings. The situation was so critical that the Independents had to take a serious step to combat them. The Independents organized their own volunteers headed by Yi Sangjai and fought against the government supported peddlers who initiated the troubles. Such violence was no intention of the Independents, but they were strongly convinced of the integrity of their principles and were ready to take any measures to secure its ends.

On November 26th, during these critical times, the King gave audience to a great general assembly outside the great gate of the palace. The Independents were there in force, and foreign representatives and a large number of other foreign residents.[35] Yun Chi-ho was its spokeman. Yun stated very clearly that in the armed attacks of the peddlers upon the people they intended no violence but only desired the fulfillment of the solemnly-made pledges. Yun urged that the legal existence of his organization should again be established by imperial decree, and that the six measures so definitely promised by his Majesty should be carried out. The King promised again to reshape the policy of the government in line with these suggestions, but it must be remembered that the King's intimate minister was anti-reforms and the Independents had popular support, but had no strategic position in the government, and could not exert influence upon the government policy. The people were not properly organized and also there was no strong leader to guide this determined group who wanted to fight against the peddlers or any group which might hinder their progressive movement. After this controversy, the cabinet members were changed again, and Min Yong-hwan became head of the government. Then the King called the government high officials and the leaders of the Independents. Yun Chi-ho, Yi Sangjai, and Ko Yonghwan, Ko Yongjin with about three hundred of their members in order to conciliate the two groups. There were present, not only the Koreans, but the foreign diplomats; the people felt, therefore, that the government would keep their promises this time. The King and the cabinet members promised to protect the Independence Association and punish traitors such as Jo Pyong-sik, a leading pro-Russian, and Hong Jong-u, in front of a mass group of people and foreign diplomats. But again, it was merely a promise made to tide over an actual and present difficulty. The King was surrounded by men inimical to the reform programs. The government had the police and the army in back of them as well as the peddlers. The Independents had nothing but popular sentiment. Yun said; "the popular meetings have gone beyond the control of the Independence Club, and in the face of strong advice to the contrary, they were resumed on the 6th of December, and their language became careless and impudent . . . on the 16th of December the Privy Council recommended the recall of Pak Yong-ho from Japan . . . the more conservative portion of the people revolted against the very mention of the name, Pak."[36] This argument had weakened the Independence group and the conservative group did not hesitate to take advantage of this opportunity. Because of this argument concerning Pak Yong-ho, the Independence Association lost considerable support from the conservative faction of the people. From this point on, the Association was on its way to decline. The government had not kept their public promise and began to arrest the leaders of the Independents again right after the mass meeting where they pledged to protect the Association. Yun Chi-ho was assigned to Hamgyung province as a district superintendent because that was the only possible way to remove him from his powerful influence over the people and vacate his seat as vice-chairman of the Central Advisory Committee in Seoul. Yun was not in a position to refuse the imperial order. As a result of the departure of Yun, the government now could handle the Independents more freely. The government ordered the dissolution of the Independence Association as soon as Yun left the capital. There were two reasons for the easy dissolution of the Association besides Yun's departure: first, the Korean government was backed by the Russian at this time and the Association was strong anti-Russian, and Japan, too, did not want to see the growth of the Korean independence spirit among the Koreans; second, on the other hand, both Russia and Japan were not happy about the American influence among the leaders of the Independents. The Independence Association founded by Dr. So had sown the seed of democratic spirit among the Koreans and later many of those leaders fled to foreign lands and were active in the Korean independence movement after 1905. Rhee Syngman, Ahn Changho, Kim Kiu-sic are probably the most famous ones among them. Professor Hulbert said;'' And thus came to an end a political party whose aims were of the highest character, whose methods were entirely peaceable, but whose principles were so far in advance of the time that from the very first there was no human probability of success.''[37] It seems that Professor Hulbert's close observation was correct, as later evidence indicated, and the people had done their utmost for their security within a limited scope.

Notes

1. See full text in Carnegie Endowment, P. 10 also *The Tragic History of Korea*, appendix.

2. Names of some of the cabinet members: Kim Hongjip, Pak Jung-yang, Kim Yun-sik, Kim Jung-han, Tsu Hu-yun, Yi Yun-yong, Kim Kaijin, Ahn Kyung-su, Jung Kyungwon, Pak Jun-yang, Yi Won-kong, Kim Ha-gu, Kwon Yongjin, Yu Kiljun, Kim Hayong, Yi Yong-ik, So Sangjip.

3. Professor Hulbert and Mrs. Bishop made the following statements respectively and I differ in my opinion with theirs, for comparison the quotations are following ''His (Tae Won-kun) experience of twenty years had convinced him that there was only one way to accomplish the object which the minister had in view and while Viscount Miura naturally shrank from adopting that course it would seem he too was at least convinced that it was the only feasible plan.'' Hulbert, *op. cit., p.* 287; ''When the well-known arrangement between viscount Miura and the Tae Won-kun was ripe for execution, the Japanese Minister directed the commandment of the Japanese battalion quartered in the barracks just outside the palace gate to

facilitate the Tae Won-kun's entry into the palace by arranging the disposition of Kunrentai and by calling out the imperial force to support them.''
Bishop, *op. cit., p.* 270

4. Yi Kwang-su, (ed) "Korean Relation with Japan" in *A Tragic History* of
   Korea, p. 113

5 Bishop, *op. cit., p.* 270

6 General Dye, iate of the U.S. Army was instructor of the old guard in the
   Korean palace; and Mr. Sabatin, a Russian subject, was temporarily
   employed as watchman at the palace.

7. Bishop, *op. cit., p.* 272. Mrs. Bishop gives first hand information.

8. Underwood, *Fifteen Years Among the Top-knots, p.* 148. Mrs. Underwood
   was one of the intimate friends of the Queen and also the medical attendant
   to the Queen.

9. An official report of "Korean Repository" also quoted by Underwood *Ibid*

10. *Ibid*

11. *Ibid.*

12. McKenzie, *Korea Fights for Freedom, p.* 55

13. Ladd, *In Korea with Marquis Ito, p.* 219

14. McKenzie, *op. cit., p.* 57

15. Bishop, *op. cit., p.* 275

16. Chung, *The Case of Korea,* appdx. p. 322

17. Since the King couldn't trust anyone in the palace, he had his food prepared
    outside by the foreigners, Mrs. Underwood said that she cooked and her
    husband, who was acting as an American interpreter for his country's
    Minister, took it to the King. The King opened the food box himself with a
    Yale key. Underwood, *op cit, p.* 154

18. *Ibid, p.* 209

19. McKenzie, *op cit, p.* 67

20. Harrington, *op cit, p.* 160. Allen to Morse, Apr. 15, on or about Dec. 15,
    1896, and Morse to Allen Apr. 15,1904 in the Allen M.S.S.

21. *Ibid, p.* 163

22. *Ibid, pl,* 162. A petition written by 16 citizens of the Unsan district in
    northern Korea, to the Minister of the U.S., May 1897, in the Allen M.S.S.

23. Hulbert, *op cit, p.* 152

24. *Ibid, p.* 154

25. Liem, *America's Finest Gift to Korea, p.* 55

26. *Ibid.*

27. Term rascal used by Yun Chi-ho himself.

28. Mr. Greathouse probably acted on request of the King, but there is no clear
    indication.

146

29. Yun Chi-ho, "Activity of the Independence Club" in *Tong-gwang*, no. 26, p. 36
30. McKenzie, *op cit, p.* 69
31. Underwood, *op cit, p.* 210
32. Tso Nam-sun, *op cit, p.* 121
33. *Ibid.*
34. Kim Yong-hi, *Yun Chi-ho's life, p. 123*
35. Hulbert, *The Passing of Korea, p.* 165
36. *Ibid, p.* 166
37. *Ibid*

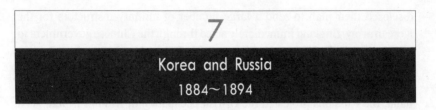

7

Korea and Russia
1884~1894

Russia was not satisfied with Vladivostok which is ice-bound for more than half the year as her outlet in the Pacific. She was seeking a warm port which could serve her the year around and for this reason she was extremely interested in Manchuria and Korea. The Russian Minister, M. Waeber, who was known as one of the most able diplomats in Seoul had secured a secret treaty[1] with the Korean government in 1884 in which Russia was permitted to open a market at Kyung-hing at the border of Korea and Russia[2] and had access to free navigation of the Tuman River which is the frontier of North Korea.

Twelve years later, when the Korean Sovereign stayed at the Russian legation, the Russians concluded another agreement with the Korean government where by the Russians were granted the privileges of mining gold and other minerals for fifteen years, and coal for twenty years, in two districts near Kyung-hing, as well as the right to construct a railway or carriage road from the mines to the shore. In 1884, the Russians seized Port Wonsan (Lazaroff) and on April 14, 1885, the British Commander Hamilton occupied the Island of Kumun in South Korea which he had fortified and established as a signal station, and had started to install a cable to Shanghai.[3] As soon as reports of this affair on the Korean island became known, the Russian Minister Waeber protested to both the Korean government and Li Hung-chang of China through Mullendorf, then adviser of the Korean government. Waeber insisted that if the British were permitted occupation of Kumun Island the Korean government should grant Russia the special privilege of making a highway for commercial purposes from north Korea to Russia. In 1885, the Russians disclosed their plan to send a large number of military instructors for the Korean army. England immediately acted through the Chinese government to interfere with the Korean government. Sir Robert Hart, and other English representatives in Peking promoted this interference.[4] This Chinese interference continued until 1894 when the Sino-Japanese war broke out; on the other hand, the Russians protested the British occupation of Kumun Island. As a result of this protest, the British gave up her ambition in Korea and withdrew her troops from the Island on February 27, 1889.[5] Four years later, Russia secured from the Korean government, an overland telegraph connected between Korea and Siberia.[6]

The new assertion of China claiming to suzerainty over Korea caused alarm to Japan which recognized the Korean sovereignty through the treaty of 1876. The non-compromising attitude of China and the aggressive policy of Japan brought about the Sino-Japanese war. After Japan won the war over China by which a treaty was signed by Ito Hakubun and Li Hungchang at Shimonoseki, both countries recognized the independence of Korea and China was to pay an indemnity of four hundred fifty million yen and give Formosa and the Liaotung peninsula to Japan. The Russian Empire which was watching the action of Japan in the Far East protested to Japan, with the help of Germany and France, that the occupation of the Liaotung peninsula by Japan was a disaster to the peace of the Far East. As a consequence of this three powers intervention, Japan had to return the Liaotung to China and received instead an increased indemnity.[7] The Russian Minister Waeber knew that Japan was weakened by the Sino-Japanese war, and took advantage of her weakness by making close relations with the Korean palace and boasting to Korea of Russia's great, powerful empire. The pro-Russian group became gradually the most powerful element in the Korean government, and the Russian influence grew rapidly while the Japanese influence began to drop. Eventually, the progressive cabinet members were all forced to resign including the Prime Minister Pak Yong-ho who once again fled to Japan. The tragic murder of Queen Min which was schemed and carried out by the Japanese actually benefitted Russia more than any other single action at that time. Waeber looked upon this as a golden opportunity and made plans with members of the pro-Russian group including Yi Pumjin, Ti Hwan-yong, Yi Yunyong, Ahn Ho-suk that the King of Korea should move to the Russian legation for his personal safety from the Japanese. On February 11, 1896, the King and the Prince left the palace and moved to the Russian embassy. From the day the King moved to the Russian embassy, the pro-Russian Korean politicians began gradually to take over the government, and once again the liberal group's dream of reformation was shattered. The King and his ministers carried on their executive until February 11, 1897 from the Russian embassy with the help of the Russians. This gave Russia an opportunity to extend her influence both in Korea and Manchuria. She built the Southern Manchurian Railroad and was preparing a strong fortified naval base in Dairen. Waeber, in inducing closer relationship with the Korean government set about his duty in a very thorough manner. He selected Min Yong-hwan to represent the government and the royalty, and Yun Chiho, leader of the progressive people's movement and now vice-Minister of Education to represent the common people in selecting the Korean representatives to the inauguration of the Russian Emperor, Nicholas II in 1894. The Korean representatives knew that they were merely play things in the hands of the Russian Empire, but there was no escape. It is evident that Waeber choose those two men because he knew that he had to get along with the two groups. The representatives left in March for Shanghai and went to America then to Europe and to Moscow. The Korean group was a bit wary of the warm hospitality given them in Russia. Among the world famous diplomats in Moscow, the Korean group was conscious of the fact that they were treated with special consideration. Russia knew that Korea would be the key to her Far Eastern policy.[8] Nicholas II inherited the job of developing Russia's Asiatic power from his father, Alexander III. He said that he would "follow his father in everything."[9] To achieve this aim, Russia had to meet two powers: Japan and England in the Far East; particularly, in Korea. After Japan showed its power to the world by winning the war, the British Empire, which is isolated in Europe, made treaty with Japan in 1902. Meantime, through the treaty between Japan and Russia, Russia gained influence in Korea. Count Witte said in his memoirs; "this treaty granted us the right to keep military instructors and several hundred of our soldiers in Korea." He continued to say that the agreement;" . . also gave us a preponderating influence upon Korea's state finances. We had the right to appoint the financial counsellor to the Korean emperor, i.e. practically the Korean Minister of Finances."[10] Count Witte refers to the treaty with Japan, but one is unable to find the existence of such a treaty. It was rumored that the Korean representatives at the coronation of the Czar concluded a secret treaty to which the Korean government would undertake to employ Russian military instructors and financial councilors, but that "secret treaty" is yet to be found.

Japan which was closely watching the Russian activities in Korea decided against the favorable opportunity made for the Russian interest in Korea. Therefore, the Japanese representative, Komura, made an agreement with the Russian representative, Waeber on May 14, 1896.

A Russo-Korean Bank was soon organized to transact the financial and economic affairs of Korea, but this failed when a powerful British squadron appeared at Chemulpo. M. Alexieff served as subordinate under Brown; thus, the new Russian Minister, de Speyer lost the prestige which had been so well established by his predecessor, M. Waeber. Meanwhile the anti-Russian sentiment grew so strong that a large number of the Korean intelligentsia joined the Korean Independence Association which has been previously discussed. De Speyer was reported to have written a note to the Korean government on March 7, 1898, asking for a reply within a day to the query of whether or not Korea wanted the services of Russian experts; the Korean government replied in the negative.[11] Three months later, de Speyer was recalled by his St. Petersburg government and the Russo-Korean Bank dissolved. Count Hayashi, the Japanese Minister to St. Petersburg at the time of these disputes, describes in his memoirs his interview with Count Mouravieff, the Minister of Foreign Affairs of the Czar at that time; "At first Count Mouravieff had objected that this happened under his predecessor and that he had nothing to do with it, and finally, after being told that it was a violation of a previous agreement between the two governments, he said: "what I mean is that we have sent these officers to Korea and we cannot recall them immediately. As a matter of fact, we were to have increased their number, but we will not send anymore. We will correct the matter and make amends to you, for it is, as you consider it, a violation of the agreement. But we must have some further time for the matter to be settled in"![12] One cannot imagine that the Foreign Minister of Czarist Russia would make such a statement to the Japanese Minister at that time. Nevertheless there is a record in the latter's secret memoir which is handed down to us today. Meanwhile, the Russian government had leased the Kwantung peninsula, including Port Arthur and Dairen Won from China in March 1898. On the other hand, Russia had negotiated a treaty with Japan on April 25, 1898 in Tokyo. According to this agreement, both Russia and Japan definitely recognized "the sovereignty and entire independence of Korea", and agreed not to interfere in the nation's affairs, nor to take any steps in the nomination of military instructors or financial advisers without having previously arrived at neutral accord on the subject. The Russian Empire was not to interfere with the development of commercial and industrial relations between Japan and Korea.[13]

A former charge at Peking, M. Pavloff, the new Russian Minister to Korea, with the military attache went to Masan in southern Korea in April, 1899, on his way to Russia and met Admiral Makaroff, the famous strategist and the commander of the eastern squadron of the Russian imperial navy, surveyed its port which is thirty miles from Pusan, the finest port in the southern Korea. He made known to the local officials that Russia had intentions of purchasing it as a coaling station. In regard to the acquisition of the Korean port in southern Korea, Count Rosen has to say this; "... perhaps even more so by the proceedings of our naval authorities in connection with the purchase of large plots of ground in places like Fusan(Pusan) and Mozampo (Masan), the erection of hospital buildings, frequent visits to these ports of our Pacific squadron, and similar suggestion of intentions on our part to a possible acquisition of some point in the Korean coast as a naval station. That such intentions were indeed vaguely entertained by our naval authorities, whose favorite dream was the acquisition of Mazampo ... "[14] Baron Rosen was well aware of the aggressive Russian policy in Korea, and had repeatedly warned his government that any such attempt would positively lead to an armed conflict between Russia and Japan. Baron Rosen didn't think the Russian Empire was ready to meet this conflict with Japan and that it would be imperative for Russia to avoid it. Count Mouravieff, however, took the aggressive policy in Korea with the support of the Emperor.[15]

On Pavloff's return from Russia in July, Japan had already purchased the ground which Russia was planning to buy. M. Stein, Russian charge demanded the Korean government to cancel the contract with Japan and sell to Russia, but the Korean government explained that they had no right to interfere with the alienation of private land by its owners within the three miles radius of any treaty port.[16] Russia instead leased the port of Pamguri south of Masan port for the purpose of erecting a hospital, warehouses, and a recreation ground, for the use of the Russian navy. Russia placed her Far Eastern policy under the leadership of M. Kir Alexieff who was then the governor of the Kwangtung peninsula. The reason for Russia's desiring the port in southern Korea was very clear; it would serve them well for a port in the Korean strait is situated between Dairen and Vladivostok and just opposite the Japanese mainlands. In spite of the treaty of 1898 between Russia and Japan, Russia, Count Mouravieff, did not pay much attention to it. On the other hand, there was continuation of the activities of the Russian naval authorities on the coasts of Korea, which was the cause of increasing irritation until the final crisis came. Meantime, the Korean government was suffering sorely between the vigorous demands and the unreasonable protests of the contending powers, while the flexible will of the Korean King, and the discordant and irresponsible Korean ministers, and others were confused with the whole situation . On March 29, 1899, M. Pavloff succeeded in leasing for twelve years, for the use of Count H. Keyserling, a Russian subject, three whaling stations: Ulsan Bay in Kyung-sang province, on the Island of Jing-po in Ham-gyung province, and Jangsing in Kang-won province, in the north-eastern coast of Korea. "[17]

In 1900, the "Boxer Uprising" which broke out in North China, gave the Russians an opportunity to occupy Manchuria. Prior to this, on September

6, 1899, the American Secretary of State, John Hay, declared the famous "open door policy" in China, but the Russian Empire was not ready to accept these principles in Manchuria, and Germany accepted this attitude of the Russian Empire; therefore, Japan was very seriously threatened by the growing Russian influence in the Far East. Eventually, on January 30, 1902, Japan negotiated the treaty of alliance with Great Britain.

In Korea, Yi Yong-ik who saved the Queen's life from the mob in the 1882 rice revolt, became a powerful statesman in his Majesty's government. Yi, a leading pro-Russian, was very unpopular among the people. As a matter of fact, the progressive Independents denounced him as a traitor. However, he was trusted by the King.[18] After all, he saved the Queen's life once. Yi Yong-ik attempted to give the King greater power and to overthrow the progressive movement in the capital. He held complete control over the household treasury while in this position, and even pocketed sums of the government money for his own personal use. When Yi gained complete power in controlling the palace, Russia, too, took many advantages. In 1901, there was an agreement of a five million won loan, which had been signed on April 19, between the Korean government and the French agent of the Yunnam syndicate, M. Cazalis.[19] It nevertheless, was not ratified by the Korean King. If the loan had materialized, a large control over the coinage, mining, and general finance of Korea would have passed into the hands of the French subjects and perhaps also of the Russo-Chinese Bank. The Russo-Chinese Bank in 1902 had offered another loan to the Korean government through its agent at Seoul, Gunzburg and company. The conditions of the loan were that the firm should obtain a permanent monopoly of the famous Korean ginseng, and the right of working certain mines, but it also failed.[20]

In April, 1903, the Russian officials began lumbering in the area above the Yalu River; this was in violation of the secret agreement between the two countries, but Russia insisted upon this region and got it. Professor Vernadski comments on this lumbering matter that the acts were those of an irresponsible group of Russian concessionaires who consisted of a number of doubtful personages who were influential at the imperial court.[21] Nevertheless, they were Russian officials. According to this secret agreement for this concession dated August 28, 1896, when the Korean King was staying at the Russian legation, it had secured for a Russian merchant at Vladivostok the right to organize of Korean lumber company, having a monopoly for twenty-years of the forestry enterprise around the Munsan region, and also on Ullong Island. On Ullong Island, the Japanese already had been cutting for many years, so there wasn't any good timber left when the Russian syndicate took it over. Even the pro-Russian, Yi Yong-ik denied that the lower region was included in the agreement. By this act of Russia, Korea was dispossessed one of its finest sources of wealth and sacrificed future millions for a paltry few thousand won[22] and a promise to pay a share of the profits[23] although no provisions were made for giving the government an opportunity of checking on Russian operations.[24] Thus the failure of the diplomacy in South Korea was successful in North Korea from the Russian point of view. On December 4,1903, the commander of the Russian Far Eastern fleet, came to Chemulpo with its staff and had a conference with the Korean King in Seoul. It was generally believed that Russia requested Korea to lease either Masan or Pusan as a naval base.[25] Meantime, the Russian Minister of the army, General Kuropatkin, one of the aggressive leaders of Russia, who was on an official observation trip to the Far East in the spring of 1903, had passed through Vladivostok and Tokyo and arrived in Port Arthur on June 30. He called a conference on July sixth at the Governor-General's of important Russian officials to formulate Russia's Far Eastern policy. General Kuropatkin on his return to St. Petersburg, submitted a report to the Russian Emperor. Speaking about the Russian activities in Korea, the General said; "... that our enterprise in the Yalu region has become known to the whole world and that the high interest of the autocrat of Russia in the undertaking has also become a matter of common knowledge, both at home and abroad, it is no longer possible to present this enterprise as a purely commercial venture, and in the future it will inevitable preserve a great and alarming political importance . . ." General Kuropatkin made a correct observation on the matter, and he continued; ". . . therefore, however, great the commercial advantages of the enterprise may be, it appears advisable for us to sell it to foreigners if we do not wish to maintain a constant source of danger of a break with Japan." He even suggested the necessary measure to insure good relations with Japan.[26] Count Witte stated in his memo's that the entire cabinet members were unanimous in their negative attitude toward-an aggressive policy in Korea. The Bezobrazov coterie remained powerless in spite of its influence upon the Emperor. However, this situation changed radically when the Minister of Interior Plehve openly joined Bezobrazov. The Emperor now followed the advice of Bezobrazov and his group who advocated the annexation of Korea from the early days won the confidence of the Emperor, persuaded the aggressive policy in Korea with the cooperation of Admiral Alexeyev who became the governor of the Kwangtung peninsula, and the viceroy of the Far East and became the Commander-in-Chief of the fighting forces.[27] Count Witte commented on Alexeyev's appointment saying that the appointment was the height of absurdity for Alexeyev was not an army man, and could not even aide on horseback; nor did he in any way distinguish himself in the naval service.[28] The diplomatic and the economic disputes now came down to military significance; namely, the Yongampo incident which was the climax of the whole relationship between Korea and Russia, and the immediate cause for the Russo-Japanese war which followed.

In May, 1903, forty-seven Russian soldiers in civilian clothes presently increased to sixty, besides a large number of Chinese and Korean under Russian employ arrived at Yongampo[29] located near the mouth of the Yalu River. The Russian aggressive policy in Korea became obvious, and at the same time, the diplomat's influence in the Russian government was diminishing. Count Witte wrote to the Foreign Minister in regards to the Korean problem which was one of the storm centers of Russian Far Eastern policy according to Count Witte's own language he said; "An armed clash with Japan in the near future would be a great disaster for us." then he continues; "furthermore, and that is most important, in the eyes of the Russian people a war with Japan for the possession of distant Korea will not be Justified, and the latent dissatisfaction may render more acute the alarming phenomena of our domestic life, which makes themselves felt even in peace time . . . I consider it my duty to say that, according to my opinion, when the worst comes to worst, it may be advisable to give up Korea altogether . . . between the two evils, an armed conflict with Japan and the complete cession of Korea, I would unhesitatingly choose the second."[30] This letter dated November 28, 1901, represented the typical expression of the peaceful types of the Russian leaders at that time. Because of this belief, Count Witte was dismissed from his ministry, Minister of Finance, in August 1903. Pares on Witte's dismissal states that it was largely because of his dissent from the Emperor's Far Eastern policy.[31]

The Russian soldiers at Yongampo increased from one hundred to two hundred who purchased from the Koreans, under the names of the Korean citizens, some fifteen houses and some twelve acres of land.[32] Meantime, inside the Korean government, there was a difference of opinion concerning the Russian policy at Yongampo and its vicinity. On June 11th, the council of State passed a resolution that the Russian behavior at the frontier did not conform to the treaty between the countries. The foreign office on the 14th, protested the Russian acts in the respective areas.[33] At the same time, the Japanese Minister insisted to the Korean government that Russia should remove the telegraph lines, that she had. Again in July, the Korean Commissioner of Forestry and Baron Guzburg, an agent of the Russo-Chinese Bank at Seoul, visited Yongampo, and drafted an agreement leasing the port to the timber company, represented by Gunzburg himself. The company also granted, in the Korean text, judiciary rights over the residents within the leased area.[34] The occupation of Yongampo and the suspension of the evacuation of the troops from Manchuria, and the active military connection between its army centers and the Korean frontier gave an exceedingly ominous appearance.

The Korean government under the pro-Russian influence, could not strongly resist the Russian activities even if they wanted, simultaneously, she had no desire of help from neither Japan nor any other power, because the government leaders believed that no power would help Korea for benefit of the Koreans. The British, American, and Japanese representatives pressed the Korean government to open Wiju and Yongampo to foreign trade in order to prevent Russian monopoly. The Russian Minister, M. Pavloff, was opposed to the opening of these two ports to other than Russia; because the influence of the Russian diplomats dominated in the Korean government, the Russians had their wishes in Korea. Both Yi Yong-ik and Yi Kwon-taik, two pro-Russian leaders, who had been convinced by the Russians that the great Czarist Empire of Russia would be more dependable than the Island Empire of Japan in case of hostilities between the two powers, they were firm in the belief that Korea would be much better off if Korea relied upon Russia rather than upon Japan.

Japanese diplomacy made much effort to come to a peaceful agreement, and this was only possible if Russia would either evacuate her troops from Manchuria or leave Japan a similar free hand in Korea.[35] But Russia was neither willing to withdraw from Manchuria nor give a free hand to Japan in Korea. It perhaps would avoid the political crisis between Japan and Russia, if Russia accepted Japan's offer, but it would be a temporary settlement if they did because they had similar ambitions in the Far East by their imperialistic nature, In any event, Korea would not had received any benefit from either of the imperialistic powers. Japan, who was rather upset about the whole Korean situation, held a special cabinet meeting (Gozen Kaigi)[36] in the presence of the Emperor on June 26th. A series of propositions were decided upon and presented to the Russian government through the Japanese Minister Kurino, on June 27th. They included: a mutual agreement to respect the independence and territorial integrity of the Chinese and Korean empires, and to maintain equal opportunities in these countries; a mutual recognition of Japan's special interests in Korea and of Russia's special interests in Manchuria; and a pledge to respect the open door policy and the territorial integrity of the countries in question and others.[37]

Russia's reply to Japan's proposal arrived October 3rd through the Russian Minister Baron Rosen in Tokyo. It provided: 1. a mutual engagement to respect the independence and territorial integrity of Korea; 2. the recognition by Russia of Japan's preponderating interests in Korea; 3. a Russian pledge not to interfere with economic undertakings of Japan in Korea, nor to oppose any measures taken for the purpose of protecting such an undertaking; 4. the recognition of Japan's right to send troops to Korea with the knowledge of Russia for the purpose of protecting her interests; 5. a mutual engagement not to use any part of the Korean territory for strategical purposes nor to undertake on the Korean coast any military works capable of menacing the freedom of navigation in the straits of Korea; 6. a mutual engagement to establish a neutral zone on the Korean territory lying to the north of the 39th parallel; 7. the recognition by Japan of Manchuria and its littoral as being in all respects outside her sphere of interest.[38] This reply did not give Japan any satisfaction, but added to her embarrassment with such phrases as "the recognition of Manchuria and its littoral as being in all respects outside her sphere of interest," besides, this point, Russia imposed upon Japan the following new conditions regarding Korea: not to use any part of the territory for strategic purposes; not to fortify the southern coast; and to consider the territory north of the 39th parallel as neutral between the two powers.[39] On top of these unagreeable points, the reply delayed just about three months. The Russians, perhaps, didn't think three months delaying in such an important diplomatic letter was significant, but the Japanese felt that was an act of discourteousness. Japan replied on October 30th with several important concessions. The first important point was the freedom of navigation in the Korean straits (article 5), second, a neutral zone on the Korean-Manchurian frontier extending fifty kilometres on each side, (article 6), third, recognition by Japan that Manchuria is outside her sphere of special interest, and recognition by Russia that Korea is outside her sphere of special interest.[40] On December 11, Russia's rejection arrived. At this time, Russia was silent on the subject of Manchuria, and repeated the same propositions as in October in regard to Korea. Japan, through Baron Komura, proposed to Russia again on the 21st of the same month the entire suppression of the neutral zone in case Russia should be unwilling to admit to one in Manchuria and to admit a mutual engagement not to undertake any military work capable of menacing the freedom of navigation of the straits of Korea on the Korea coast. When Russia's reply was received in Tokyo on January 6, 1904, Russia declared that Japan should recognize Russia's rights in Manchuria and proposed that northern Korea be designated as a neutral zone. Japan requested Count Lamsdoff on January 13th to reconsider their reply, but he gave the same points as the on the previous replies on February 7th. The diplomatic relations between the two countries were severed. On February 9th, there was already the Japanese force, a battalion which arrived in Seoul under Major Hiraoka Hachiro. At the same time, German and French forces were arriving in Seoul; the American and the British forces had been there since January. On the Japanese side, she could put 150,000 men in line at once, because both army and navy had been kept in the closest contact with the progress of the diplomatic debate. The Russians, on the other hand, had in all, only 80,000 field troops with 23,000 garrison and 30,000 railway frontier guards.[41] When the Japanese forces arrived in Chemulpo on February 8th, a war between Russia and Japan was already in progress in the port. The Russian ships *Variak* and *Koryets* were attacked by the Japanese in a port declared neutral by Korea on January 25.[42] Did Japan ignore this neutral port or didn't she care? By doing this Japan secured a free hand for the Japanese troop movement in Korea, and it was at the outset decided in favor of the Japanese. Japanese troops moved speedily to the northern frontier of Korea. Japan thus occupied Korea.

On February 9th, Russia declared war on Japan; Japan declared war on Russia on the following day.[43] Russia lost the war to Japan and the treaty of Portsmouth was concluded. The Russian government was persuaded to listen to a suggestion of peace by President Roosevelt; Count Witte conducted the negotiations with many successes. On the Japanese side, she had come near the end of her reserves in both men and money, and so she had to find a way to compromise although she won the war. According to the treaty, Korea was to be within Japan's sphere of influence; Russia was to leave South Manchuria, including Liaotung peninsula, and to surrender half the Island of Sakhalin. Thus the official relationship ended between Korea and Russia, and Korea then was firmly under the Japanese influence for sometime to come.

Notes

1. *Tokushu Jyoyaku, p.* 731-732

2. *Ibid. p.* 772-775, April 22, 1896

3. In 1721, two Russian officers, Izmailov, Lange, attempted to enter Korea, but were stopped by the Chinese. See Vernadsky, *Political and Diplomatic History of Russia, p.* 240

4. Dennet, *"Early Policy in Korea" in Political Science Quarterly,* vol.XXXVIII, March 1923

5. Nishida, S., *The International Position of Japan as a Great Power p.* 186

6. Curzon, G., *Problem of the Far East, p.* 212

7. Russia was in a favorable position, because the existence of the Franco-Russian entente (Jan. 4, 1894), and the Russo-German Commercial treaty (April 1, 1894). While France herself was interested in both Indo-China and south China, the French backed Russian economic expansion in Manchuria and Korea. Germany too did not want the Russian competition in

158

Europe and Africa. So it was their strategy to support Russia in the Far East in order to their own interests. After the intervention, a Russo-Chinese treaty of friendship, 1896, was declared. China agreed that Russia might construct a railroad line across North Manchuria in order to save mileage on the Trans-Siberian. One can imagine how Japan felt toward the Russian expansion. Japanese militarists advocated successfully to the people that she must prepare to meet the enemy, Russia. It was a good chance to gain the domestic political power for the militarist as they have done in the past.

8. Kim Yong-hi, *Life of Yun Chi-ho, p.* 100

9. Pares, Sir Bernard, A *History of Russia, p.* 404

10. Witte, *The Memoirs of Count Witte, p.* 97-98

11. The Korean Independence Association was not only anti-Russian, but also anti-foreign powers which interfered with the Korean independence.

12. Asakawa, K., *The Russo-Japanese Conflict, Its causes and Issues, p.* 270

13. Rockhill, *op Cit, p.* 433

14. Rosen, *Forty Years of Diplomacy, vol. 1., p.* 155

15. *Ibid, p.* 156

16. Asakawa, *op cit., p.* 275

17. The full text of this contract is available in the U.S. 56th Congress, 1st session, House Documents, vol. 1., pp. 484-488

18. Hulbert, *The Passing of Korea, p.* 179

19. The *Kokumin,* April 23, 24, May 3, June 9, 1901; also Asakawa, *op cit., p.* 279

20. *Ibid,*. October 22, November 17, 1902; also Asakawa, *Ibid, p.* 279

21. Vernadski, G., A *History of Russia, p.* 175

22. The traffic annually aggregated the sum of one and a half million tales; see The *Kokumin,* July 27, 1903

23. The Korean King was to receive one fourth of the profits.

24. Hulbert, *History of Korea,* 11. p. 347

25. Kim Yong-hi, *op cit.,* 162

26. Witte, *op cit., p.* 121

26. *Ibid, p.* 124

28. *Ibid, p.* 127

29. *The Kokumin,* telegram, May 8, 9,1903

30. Witte, *op cit., p.* 117

31. Pares, *op cit., p.* 117

32. *The Kokumin,* telegram, May 22, 25, 1903

33. *The Kokumin,* correspondence, June 19, 1903

34. The contract bore neither a definite period of time for the lease nor fixed the area of the leased territory in the Korean text of the agreement, but

according to the Russian document, the lease is said to have extended over 20 years and covered a space equivalent to 204 acres. see *The Kokumin,* Seoul telegrams, July 6,10,17, 23, 27, August 2, 8,18,1903; also Asakawa, *op cit., p.* 319

35. Pares, *op cit., p.* 422

36. The personnel of the Japanese cabinet in the meeting included Viscount Katsura as the Prime Minister, Foreign Minister Baron Komura, General Temuchi as the Minister of the Army, and the Minister of the Navy was Admiral Yamamoto; and the Privy Councilors were Marquises Ito and Yamagada, Counts Matsukata, Inouye, and Ogawa.

37. Baron Komura's speech before the Japanese Diet on March 25, 1904, see Nishida, *op* cit., p. 233

38. *Diplomatic Correspondence Between Japan and Russia,* no. 17

39. The Russian government explained later, on January 6, 1904, that the creation of a neutral zone was "for the very purpose which the Imperial Japanese government had likewise in view, namely, to eliminate everything that might lead to misunderstandings in the future; a similar zone, for example, existed between the Russian and British possessions in Central Asia." Nichi-Rosen Memorandum, no. 38

40. Nichi-Rosen Memorandum, no. 22

41. Pares, *op cit., p.* 423

42. *New York Herald,* Jan. 25, 1904

43. *London Times,* Feb. 11,12, 1904

8

Korea Under Japan's Domination

Japan annexed Korea in 1910 after two major wars: one against China, 1894-95; the other against Russia, 1904-05. Japan's domination of Korea ended when she surrendered to the. Allied powers in September, 1945. The Korean people experienced much agony and suffering during those thirty-six years under Japanese imperialism.

There are about 50 million people who inhabit an area of 220,845 square kilometers, comparable to the size of South Carolina and Georgia combined. Korea is one of those rare countries that may be called homogenous in the sense that it possesses a common language and a cultural background which dates back to 2000 B.C. The language, a branch of the Ural-altaic family, is one of the most systematic and scientific phonetic languages in the world today. To be sure, however, it is as different from Chinese and Japanese as English is from German or French. The Koreans are from Mongoloid stock; many of them are tall and robust and have a lighter and fairer complexion and more regular features than other members of the Mongol family.

The mountainous peninsula of Korea juts out like the handle of a pot from the. Asian continent and lies in the straits between Japan and China. To the north on the mainland it is separated from Manchuria by the Yalu River and the White Head Mountain, and a small northeastern tip of the border lies adjacent to the Maritime Province of the Soviet Union. The Yalu River is economically important as a source of hydroelectric power. It was in the Manchurian hills across from this river that Kim Il-sung, at the age of nineteen in 1931, started a "Korean Patriots' Band" with eighty men and eventually organized the "Autonomous Korean government" of five counties. There are still more than a million Koreans living in the Manchurian area of new China. Geographically, Korea is in about the same latitude as South Carolina and Georgia, and has a humid subtropical climate. It has a temperature range of 12 degrees below zero to 32 degrees above zero centigrade.

During the Japanese occupation, Korea was predominantly a land of farmers. Agriculture comprised slightly less than half of the total value of production while forestry, fishing, mining, and industry made up the remainder. The farm lands were concentrated in the south while industries were in the north, close to the natural resources of coal and iron ore and other rich mineral deposits.

Relatively little was known of this tiny country, once called the "Hermit Kingdom of the Far East," until the latter part of the past century. Its natural resources and strategic position as springboard to the continent were to provide keen interest to the imperialist Czarist Russia, Japan, China, and Western powers. Korea became a primary factor in the Sino-Japanese War of 1894 and the Russo-Japanese War of 1904. From the very first conflict, Korea was catapulted into the arena of intra-imperialist intrigues and struggles, and fell a victim to imperialism's inevitable and insatiable drive for markets and cheap resources. The Russo-Japanese War definitely established Japan as the sole power in the Far East and, flush with victory, she then proceeded without moral qualms to annex Korea formally as a colony. All these imperialistic activities of Japan were fully supported by the United States through the Taft-Katsura Agreement.

In 1945, after thirty-six years of Japanese rule—rule not altogether without sporadic uprisings and harassments, especially on the border regions--Korea w as liberated by the entrance of the Soviet Army from the north and American troops from the south. The days of slave servitude to Japanese imperialism had ended.

Japanese imperialism began in Korea with the treaty of 1876, the first which Korea ever negotiated with a modern power. According to this treaty, Korea was recognized as an independent and sovereign state, and Japan received the right of extra-territoriality which in turn gave her the first impetus for territorial ambitions on the Asian continent. In 1894-95 the Sino-Japanese War was fought in which Japan defeated China and simultaneously exerted increasing influence in Korea.

The year after this war, Japan found another rival force interested in Korea, namely, Czarist Russia. The Japanese government suggested that Russia should have special interests in Manchuria and she in Korea; however, Czarist Russia refused to accept these propositions, insisting that she should enjoy privileges in Manchuria and Japan in South Korea with North Korea as a neutral zone. No agreement was reached and war finally broke out in 1904 between the two nations.

Japan fought the war with British and American backing while Russia had French backing. President Theodore Roosevelt cooperated as much as possible in forcing Russia out of Manchuria where American financiers had some commercial interests.

Meanwhile, the British government revived the Anglo-Japanese Alliance in which she recognized Japan's "paramount political, military and economic interests in Korea" and further, granted "the right of Japan as she may deem proper and necessary to safeguard and advance those interests always." The United States was the unsigned partner to this revised treaty when President Theodore Roosevelt sent his secretary of war, William Howard Taft, to Tokyo to negotiate a secret agreement with Japan. The result was that the United States approved of Japan's "suzerainty over Korea," while Japan promised not to take any aggressive action against the Philippines. It became quite obvious that both Great Britain and the United States betrayed Korea and violated the Anglo-Korean and the American-Korean treaties.

As a result of her defeat, Russia was forced to recognize Japan's sphere of influence in Korea through the Portsmouth Treaty which stated "The Imperial Russian Government... engages neither to obstruct nor interfere with the measures of guidance, protection and control which the imperial government of Japan may find necessary to take in Korea."

Therefore, the road to Korea was thrown open to Japan, abetted by the major world powers. At that time the Korean government was not aware of the situation nor of the threat of domination by Japan. In March, 1904, Marquis Ito, chairman of the Japanese privy council, arrived in Korea to hold a conference with the emperor. Marquis Ito emphasized to higher officers of the government that the Koreans must learn from the Japanese, the pioneer of the new civilization in the Far East, and advocated the promotion of cooperation between the two nations. After Ito returned, the emperor of Korea dispatched a special envoy, Yi-Siyong, to Japan on behalf of good relations. However, the Japanese had a different plan for Korea.

A few months later, in the agreements of July and August, 1904, the Korean government was forced "to accept a Japanese financial adviser and to consult the Japanese government on all matters affecting foreign affairs." Japanese advisers on police, judicial and military matters followed shortly. In April, 1905, the Korean postal, telegraph and telephone services were taken over by Japan.

The conclusion of the Portsmouth Treaty further enhanced Japan's position in Korea. In November, 1905, Marquis Ito arrived at the Korean capital to present new demands which amounted to the virtual establishment of a Japanese protectorate over Korea. I he Korean emperor and ministers refused to sign the new treaty at first, but when Japanese soldiers were placed around the palace with machine guns and the Korean Prime Minister was dragged out of the conference hall by Japanese officers, the government was forced to accept the terms. I he protectorate w as established and Marquis Ito assumed the post of Resident-General of Korea in February 1906.

The Korean emperor sent a secret mission to the President of the United States, requesting aid on the basis of the American-Korean Treaty. The result was a foregone conclusion: President Theodore Roosevelt ignored the appeal and tacitly approved of Japan's actions.[1]

Japan's imperialist designs on Korea culminated in 1910 when she annexed Korea as a territory of the Japanese Empire. The pretext was the assassination of Prince Ito (promoted from Marquis) in 1909. According to the Japanese, ungrateful Koreans killed Ito in Harbin (Manchuria) and Japan did not really desire annexation but was forced to take this measure because of Korean opposition to the reforms instituted by Japan.

Prior to Japanese annexation in 1910, Korean society was based on an "Asiatic" mode of production in the agricultural slavery system. There were no such groups as the European medieval handicraftsmen in Korea, and the isolated families and tribes-people still had remnants of the feudal domestic handicraft which provided them the necessary and semiprimitive articles. Consequently, there was no real source for the accumulation of capital. The transformation from feudalism into capitalism accelerated when the Japanese capitalists invaded Korea.

Japanese capitalism emerged at the end of the Tokugawa period as the "Meiji Restoration" which was characterized, in contrast to the development in Europe, by a compromise of feudal elements with the rising mercantile class. Industries underwent rapid development, while agriculture remained basically semi-feudal. Characteristic of Japanese capitalism was the strong influence of militarism, which was necessitated by Japan's late entrance into the field of world competition when the other major powers were already entrenched in their colonies and markets.

Korea, one of the backward nations in Asia at that time, was an object of envious interest to Japanese capitalists, but the matter was not so simple because of the close relationship between Korea and China; moreover, other nations had set their eyes on Korea. Consequently, Japan followed the technique of the Western powers in insisting upon opening trade in Korea.

In January, 1874, the militaristic Meiji government had commissioned Count Okubo to investigate the "Korean problem" and secretly planned to pursue a policy of eventually conquering Korea. The treaty of 1876 was the opening wedge for the penetration of Japanese capital into Korea. The Japanese "colonial system" in Korea provided good profits in rice, soy beans and agricultural grains, so much so that capital investments in Korea were given priority because of the decided advantage in exploiting colonial people.

The economy of Korea, as of China and most of the other countries of Asia, is founded on land and agriculture; for this reason, Japan's control over Korean land, especially farm land, meant control over Korea's economic livelihood. Likewise, it also meant economic chaos for the Korean peasants who comprised nearly 85 to 90 percent of the population in 1910.

Because of this fact, the Japanese tried to control the cultivated land through the government, semi-governmental organizations and through individuals. In 1942, of the 4,600,000 jungbo (one jungbo equals 2.45 acres) of cultivated Korean farming land, about 424,000 jungbo were owned by Japanese, excluding the big companies. In addition, about 80 percent of the cultivated land was owned through semi-governmental agencies, especially by the Water Utilization Association, the Village Monetary Association, the oriental Development Company and the Bank of Korean Colonization.

Under Japanese administration, Korean farmers were forced to submit to the demands of Japanese imperialism without the benefit of any aid or protection from the Japanese government. Korean landlords, on the other hand, received encouragement and support, and they became the co-workers and appeasers of Japanese aggression in Korea. Thus, Korea's rural economy was placed wholly at the disposal of the Japanese, leaving the farmers in a tragic economic condition. In fact, since the Japanese annexation of Korea, the agrarian economy was in such a chaotic state that about 10,000 middle-class Korean farmers were forced into bankruptcy, while tenant farming increased by 15,000 families a year.

In 1945, at the time of the Allied occupation in Korea, the class composition of the rural population was as follows:[2] More than two and a half million (2,572,229) or 60 percent of the total cultivated acreage of the 4,475,326 acres was tenant land, and the remaining 40 percent was self-farmed.

Japanese landlords concentrated more in the southern part of Korea than the northern area since there were more rice fields in the south. For instance, by 1931, Japanese landlords held about 90 percent of rice fields in north Jolla Province, while they held about 70 percent of the same in South Jolla.

The following table gives a bird's eye view of Japanese concentration on land purchasing at different parts of Korea during the ten-year period from

1922 to 1931.[3]

Starting with fifty landlords in 1910, the number increased to about 7,000 in 1915, bringing the average acres down to about thirty jungbo. The majority of them were medium-sized farmers. The big landlords, having more than one thousand jungbo, numbered thirty-seven,[4] outnumbering the number of big landlords in Japan proper. There were only twenty-two big landlords in Japan who had more than one thousand jungbo. As a whole, Japanese landlords held about 80 percent of the cultivated land in Korea, and about 70 percent of them were in fertile rice fields.

How did the Japanese manage to own so much in such a short time? There have been no disputes among scholars as far as the number of Japanese holding Korean land. All these statistics were published by the Japanese government. There have been disputes, however, among the scholars on the method used by the Japanese for acquiring land.

The apologists of Japanese imperialism explained that Korea had been waiting for the "enlightened" policy of Japanese imperialism. Sending Japanese citizens to Korea, therefore, was supposed to be good for the Korean as well as for the Japanese.

A leading Japanese economist, Fukuda Tokujo, wrote a series in the Japanese periodical *Naikai Roncho* for three consecutive months beginning in November, 1904, after his brief visit to Korea in 1902. In his articles, Professor Fukuda observed that Korea was about a thousand years behind Japan. He compared the 19th century Korea with the Fujiwara Era (the 8th century to 11th century) in Japan. As a learned scholar, he should have known that the characteristics of the Fujiwara Era were not present in Korea. Korea was a feudalistic society, unlike the Fujiwara Era which was ruled by one family. There were intrigues and conflicts for leadership of the family, but the Fujiwara never needed a united front with another family to rule Japan.

Another characteristic of Japan society under the Fujiwara was the rise of feudalism with its *shoen* system. Privately owned lands which were not subjected to periodical redistribution constituted *shoen*. These were similar to the manors of European feudalism. Small farmers in the country did not receive proper protection from the imperial government as the central government was weak. They saw little advantage in paying taxes to a government which could not protect them. The large tax-exempt estates held by powerful nobles or warrior chiefs provided the answer to their problem; a small farmer could put his land under the warrior chief's estate and escape the payment of heavy taxes. The farmer, of course, worked the land as before, paying a fee which was less than the tax for this privilege. As a result, the farmer gained a powerful protector, and the warrior chiefs expanded their powers in their regions. The practice required   military power and from it came the development of a military class. All this happened before Kamakura Bakufu. None of these features existed in 19th century Korea.

Professor Fukuda claimed that in Korea there was no sense of land ownership by the people. In fact, there were no owners of land. The only landowners were the royal family. The people merely entertained a vague sense of common ownership of land.

Although the majority of the people did not own land, it did not mean they had no sense of ownership. Nor were the landowners necessarily of the royal family; many were feudalistic landlords. Professor Fukuda misunderstood the Korean system. His theme was that Korea, being a prefeudalistic society, was incapable of developing by itself and Japan, therefore, should develop Korea for her.

Professor Fukuda and his successors were more than willing to cooperate with the Japanese government to promote the chauvinistic interpretation of history in order to support Japanese imperialism. His theory was supported by many Japanese scholars, including Yokada Hiroshi, Sujuki Takeo, Moritani Katsume and others.[5]

A recent study reveals that there were several basic methods of acquiring land that Japanese landlords employed in Korea. Asada, in his *Japanese Imperialism and Old Colonial Landlord System,* listed four methods: 1. Japanese used Korean names or bribed Korean officials who made it possible to register land in their names; 2. lending base as a semi-permanent lease type; 3. making official contact without having the buyer's name appear in the contracting papers; 4. double entry of selling papers and mortgage papers, and many similar underhanded schemes.[6]

Evidently the Japanese had no difficulty in buying Korean farmlands even before Japan annexed Korea, in spite of the law prohibiting such action. The purpose of buying Korean farmland was not all for the farming. Many Japanese landlords rarely operated the farms directly. They leased the farmlands to Korean tenants, usually to those Koreans who helped them to buy the land.

As soon as Japan annexed Korea, tricks and bribery were no longer needed. Now the Japanese government-general openly promoted Japanese acquisition of Korean land. Although the attractions were there, most Japanese farmers were not about to leave their homes to go to a strange land to start a new life.

Two groups of people were most attracted: the big landlords and the merchants. The low price of Korean farmland attracted big Japanese landlords while the opportunity to earn high profits in a short time attracted merchant groups.

The choice land near the Kunsan area cost no more than fifteen to twenty yen per jungbo, the second choice between ten to fifteen yen, third choice was ten yen or less. Of course, dry fields were much cheaper. These prices as compared to the Japanese rice lands were less than one-tenth to one-thirteenth.[7] It became evident to the big Japanese landlords that acquiring Korean farmland made good business sense to them; besides, all their investments were well protected by the Japanese government .

Three private groups, a well-known Mitsibishi Zaibatsu, Okura, and Shibuzawa, were active participants in purchasing Korean farmland. Mitsubishi's Higashiyama farm and Shibuzawa's Chosen Kogyo Company were outstanding examples. Shibuzawa, for example, held 16,000 jungbo in 1936, employing 20,000 tenants. As far as the Japanese government was concerned, Japanese immigration to Korea was too slow in spite of all the activities of the big landlords.

The majority of Japanese immigrant farmers owned less than ten jungbo, and their investments were a little over one thousand yen just prior to the annexation in 1910. The following table indicates the situation in Korea at that time.[8]

In order to speed up mass immigration to Korea from Japan, the government-general needed further attractions for Japanese immigrants. The government-general undertook the most infamous land-grabbing project ever witnessed in any colonial policy in history.

During Terauchi and Hasegawa's administration from 1910 to 1919, the government-general of Korea set up the notorious "Bureau of Temporary Land Investigation" which surveyed all the lands and made a definite land demarcation in Korea. The government spent a large sum for the project. The survey classified land into either state-owned or private-owned, the state-owned land being public land, uncultivated fields or private land for which no claim was established at the time of land registration. Through this project the government became the biggest landlord.[9] This act proved unreasonable because a large majority of the farmers who did not understand the Japanese language failed to register their land and land which was not registered in a given period could not be claimed by them. In this way, many farmers lost much of their land.

In addition to this survey, the establishment of the Oriental Development Company brought another tragedy to Korean farmers. T his semi-official company became the second largest landlord next to the government. With the government's support, the company successfully confiscated in 1926 the richest land in Korea, amounting to more than ninety thousand jungbo.

Most of the land was used to support Japanese immigrants in Korea. In other words, the government financed the company to acquire the land from Koreans so it could turn it over to Japanese immigrants. This basic policy, using Korea as the rice bowl of Japan, was essential to Japanese imperialism.[10]

Thus, the Oriental Development Company played an important role in Japanese Colonial Policy in Korea.

Korean farmers were attacked on two sides. On one side was the colonial policy, such as the land survey and the Oriental Development Company; the other attack   came from Japanese merchants. They were ordinary merchants. They were out to snatch Korean purses as quickly as possible. The most effective way to achieve this goal was to engage in the pawnshop business. Through the pawnshops, much of the land was stolen indirectly as compared with the direct methods described above.

The usual interest rate was between 6 to 10 percent per month, and most of the borrowers used the money for emergencies, such as arranging parents' funerals or children's weddings. There was no way they could return the borrowed funds on time. In some cases, when the borrowers returned the principal, the lender made excuses to refuse it.[11] Although land was cheap as discussed earlier, Japanese lenders knew that they could grab it at one-third the normal price if they used pawnshops, and they did.

Most farmers needed cash to buy grains to sustain themselves between May and September. While working their farms, they could not sell their labor for extra cash. Especially when the farmers needed to buy tools and fertilizers, there was no way they could get money, except at pawnshops. They mortgaged their farmland and borrowed cash to buy necessities to maintain their farming. Among borrowers, 80 to 90 percent were never able to return their borrowed money. Thus, they lost their farm land.[12]

It was no wonder then that there were so many Japanese pawnshops in Korea. In 1905, fifty-nine out of seventy-four Japanese residents in Kaesong City engaged in the pawnshop business, while there were forty three in Seoul and twelve in Intsun.

Thus, the Japanese used many tricks to acquire land from Korean farmers, and the exploitation intensified with time.

It was never the intention of the imperialists to improve the lot of the natives. Their job was to exploit the people. Many students of Korean history attempt to bring to the fore the improvements Japan made in Korea. They claim that the infamous land survey was to distinguish the private and public properties. It is true that the private property system of modern capitalism was introduced through the land survey. They claim that farmland has been improved, irrigation systems have been initiated, cultivated land acreage has increased, domestic cattle encouraged, and the silkworm industry promoted, etc.

What they don't tell us, however, is that the Japanese imperialists destroyed the existing irrigation system and set up a new system for big landlords. There were 3,735 lakes and 9,386 ponds throughout the country before the irrigation system was introduced in 1917. As soon as the irrigation system was introduced by the government, farmers suffered directly and indirectly.[13] The production of rice increased, but Koreans consumed less rice than before because of the official price controls. Rice was needed in Japan. Ever since the famous rice riot in Japan in 1919, the Japanese government has had to import about five million bushels of rice a year. The Japanese population, increasing by nearly a million, did not help the situation. As rice production increased, the Korean consumption decreased since rice was being exported to Japan.[14]

Increasing rice production was not meant to improve the economic situation of the Korean farmer, but rather to supply Japan. Korean farmers who submitted to the policy of the Japanese and changed the dry fields to paddy fields were put to great expense and labor; furthermore they were not protected by the government.

As soon as Governor-General Saito took office in 1919, he announced great plans and hopes for increasing rice production in Korea for Japan. His "enlightened policy" is the story behind this rice production. His plan was to improve existing rice fields, to change dry fields to rice fields, and to cultivate more new lands, amounting to 800,000 jungbo in thirty years. Thus, he established a new "land improvement section" in the Bureau of Colonization under his direction to carry out his policy.

The policy was destined to fail because it hurt the people. When Japan increased its own rice production, as in the period 1930-1931 Korean farmers had good crops also and the price declined automatically. Korean farmers were in no position to pay land taxes, irrigation fees, and many other obligations even when they sold their entire crops. When the government-general faced the reality of this price crisis, he simply dissolved the newly created "Land Improvement Section." It had been simply a symbolic means to answer the crisis and not a plan to rescue the farmers. What was the result?

In 1931, there were 1,393,424 households classified as tenants which increased to 1,546,500 such households in 1932. Tenant households increased more than 140,000, and tenants represented then 53.8 percent of the farm population against 48.4 percent in 1931, due to the government-general's deliberate rice policy which worked against the interests of small farmers. Incidentally, there was no status change among the large landlords; they remained about 3.6 percent. The government then advised farmers to convert their rice fields back to dry fields. Again, when Japan needed more rice, as during the Sino-Japanese war in 1937, the produce-more-rice policy was readopted.

Meanwhile, the farmers' livelihood went from bad to worse. Japanese official reports stated that there were 1,147,094 households at starvation levels and 5,439,446 starving persons--27 percent of the total population. This situation was much improved after good crops during 1930-31. The situation in the spring and summer of 1930, however, had been a more normal one as the Japanese official had reported. The following table tells that story. Nearly half of the Korean people were starving during the spring and summer seasons in 1930.[15]

We are compelled to note that more Japanese landlords penetrated the area and more Koreans confronted starvation. For instance, as previously pointed out, the Japanese arrived first in South Korea in Jolla and Tsungtsong provinces and expanded their penetration there. As a result, these areas created more starving peasants even though these areas have the richest rice fields in the country. It was not the shortage of rice that created starvation among the peasants for the rice which the peasants produced was placed in government storehouses. When fewer Japanese landlords penetrated the area, there were fewer starving people. Hamgyung province had only 20.5 percent of the population starving, because there were only twenty Japanese landlords who owned no more than thirty jungbo, and none of them was considered a big landlord.

What the government wanted was to create as many landless farmers as possible in Korea. They were successful in doing that. Close to 1,551,000 families were leaving Korea each year for Manchuria, seeking a livelihood and thus making room for Japanese poor people to move into Korea.

To make this policy more systematic, the government established a company to exclusively handle affairs with the Oriental Development Company. The sole purpose of the Korean-Manchurian Development Company was to handle the Korean immigrants who settled in Manchuria. The Japanese government had more than one reason to have Koreans migrate to Manchuria. First of all, by moving Koreans out of Korea, they made room for the Japanese immigrants to settle at desirable locations. There was another significant political reason behind the movement. The Japanese government wanted to build an anti-partisan movement in Manchuria.

It became evident to the Japanese government that to thwart Kim Il-sung and other Korean partisan movements in Manchuria, it was necessary to cultivate the area where the partisans were active and confront the Korean revolutionary groups with well-indoctrinated pro- Japanese immigrants. At the same time, by providing favorable farming conditions, they thought they could prevent the *Hwajonmin*[16] activities in the border area. The government was trying to save the timberlands which the Hwajonmin were supposed to have ruined. What the government was most concerned about were their political activities as allies of partisan groups.

Thus, the Korean-Manchurian Development Company was established and supported by the government-general with an initial capital of twenty million yen in 1936.

The initial investment was divided among the major companies that had prime interests in Korea and Manchuria. The Southern Manchurian Railway company took 100,000 shares. The Oriental Development Company took 99,900; the Bank of Korean Colonization took 60,000; the Bank of Korea, 40,000; Mitsui Busan, 25,000; the Mitsibishi Company, 25,000; and the Sumitomo Company, 16,000. In other words, the Korean-Manchurian Development Company was financed by semigovernmental companies and the major Japanese Zaibatsu groups. Where the profits involved Zaibatsu groups, they worked closely with the government. their responsibilities in exploiting the people were no less than those of the government officials. Thus the Korean farmers were exploited by the Japanese from the beginning of their arrival until their departure.

As Japanese landlords advanced and occupied major roles as dominating powers on farms, the nature of Korean farm population changed. The surviving Korean landlords were more closely associated with the Japanese, and the alienation between Korean landlords and Korean tenants was similar to that of the Japanese landlords and the Korean tenants.

Through the commercialization of agricultural products by these big landlords, the system depended on the capitalistic mode of production rather than the feudalistic one. This changing system created tensions between landlords and peasants which they had never experienced before. During the time of the feudalistic system, where feudal lords and farmers were the two major classes, their normal relationships were more cordial. Such a simple social relationship, however, disappeared when the new class, the capitalistic landlords, began to emerge as the ruling power.

Japanese agricultural policy changed constantly according to the needs of the empire rather than the needs of the Korean inhabitants. When Japan needed extra rice to supply Japan proper, the government was forced to increase production in Korea. In order to increase the production of rice in Korea, the government had to change dry fields into paddy fields, and establish water utilization systems. This meant that the farmers had to pay heavy water taxes, and gradually turn over their land to the Water Utilization Association for accumulated unpaid debts. In 1929, the association controlled 50 percent of the rice fields in Korea.

The Japanese government's policy regarding rice affected not only the Korean farmer but also the Japanese farmer, because when rice was exported to Japan it affected the production of rice in Japan. Thus, the government had to solve two problems: first, the over-production of rice, and second, the competition between the Japanese rice and that of her colonies. A serious question was raised as to how the Korean government could dispose of the six to eight million bushels of rice formerly used by Japan and now unwanted by them. At this time, the price of rice was higher than that of millet, thus, the Korean peasant could not afford to use his rice instead of millet. A further difficulty was that the rice policy was not constant but changed according to the situation in Japan – if the supply was sufficient in Japan, no imports were needed; if, however, there was famine in Japan, Korea was immediately called upon for rice imports.

For this reason, the Korean government-general changed its policy and advocated a greater consumption of rice at home to dispose of the accumulated rice. But this policy only led to a further dilemma: first, the Manchurian government protested that the million and a half bushels of millet formerly exported to Korea could not be used elsewhere; and second, rice had to be stored in anticipation of famine in Japan. Therefore, while the Japanese stored rice in Korean warehouses for their own consumption, the Korean people, on the point of starvation, were forced to seek roots and grass in the hills to sustain themselves.

In 1933, the Korean government-general under General Ugaki was obliged to change its agricultural policy altogether. General Ugaki advanced his famous slogan: "Cotton in the South, sheep in the north." Could General Ugaki get cotton plants from the paddy fields? It was obviously ridiculous, but General Ugaki insisted that growing rice be replaced by cotton.

There were two reasons for the cotton-sheep policy: first, home industries in Japan needed raw materials; second, Korean cotton and wool did not provide competition with Japan. General Ugaki's cotton-sheep policy had to change again when Japan engaged in war with China, causing a greater demand for rice in Japan. General Minami, who succeeded General Ugaki, decided to increase the production of rice in Korea, and advocated "not to eat rice" instead of Ugaki's "eat more rice."

Imperial Japanese policy regarding the industrial development of Korea likewise showed the classical pattern of imperialist exploitation. Prior to 1920, "the corporation law" made it impossible for a Korean to engage in

174

any industrial enterprise. And even after its repeal, the Japanese government encouraged only those "desirable" small-scale industries using local raw materials, such as mats, lacquers, straw ware, etc., to be produced. A decisive change in policy took place only after Japan had invaded Manchuria. By that time Japanese militarism had already laid plans for future campaigns in Asia, and Korea was to play a strategic role.

However, the so-called "rapid development of Korean industries after 1931" was a relative issue. The subscribed capital in Korea was only 4.4 percent of production in Japan, and of this percentage, "household" industries accounted for a quarter of the output. (A "household" industry is an enterprise conducted at the home of the entrepreneur, by members of his family, usually during their spare time.) This latter figure revealed the undeveloped state of factory industries. Japanese controlled 72 percent of industrial production, while Koreans controlled only 26.5 percent, of which "household" industries were responsible for one-half of the production, indicating the decisive domination by Japan in Korean economy at that time.

The living conditions of the Korean workers were in a pitiful state and were continually aggravated by two factors: first, the Japanese were given preferential treatment and received twice the normal wage given to Koreans; and second, the poverty of the countryside was driving people into the cities, thus adding to the ever-increasing pool of surplus labor.

In conclusion, it is obvious that Japanese imperial policy in Korea brought not one iota of benefit to the Korean people. Rather they were exploited and impoverished. Whatever measures were taken to develop the resources or to increase the production were done only on the basis, and only to the extent, that they aided Japanese imperialism.

Notes

1. For details, see Tyler Dennett, *Americans in Eastern Asia* (New York: Barnes & Noble, 1941), ch. 15 and 16, and by the same author, *Roosevelt and the Russo-Japanese War* (2nd ed.) (New York: Doubleday, 1925).
2. For details, see Harold Hakwon Sunoo, *Korea: A Political History in Modern Times* (Seoul: Kunkuk University Press, 1970).
3. Compiled from the Government-General of Korea's *Chosen-no Nogyo (Agriculture of Korea)*, Seoul, 1924, 1932 editions. In Chong-sik, *Chosen-no Nogyo Kiko (The Agricultural Structure of Korea)* (Tokyo: Hakuyosa Co., 1940).
4. There were ten Korean landlords who had more than one thousand jungho

in all of Korea .

5. Ki-jun Cho, " Transformation and Problems in the Study of Korean Social Science," *Korea Journal,* Seoul, June, 1971, p. 5.

6. Kyoji Asada, *Nihon Teikoku-shugito Kyushokuminchi Jinushi Sei (Japanese Imperialism and Old Colonial Landlord System),* (Tokyo: ochano mizyu shoten, 1968), p. 69.

7. Matsuro Kato, *Kankoku Nogyo-ron (A Study of Korean Agriculture)* (Tokyo: Shyokato Co., 1904), p. 258.

8. *Chosen Shakai Keijaishi Kenkyu (A Study of Korean Social Economic History)* (Seoul: Imperial University Press, 1933), p. 43.

9. Sunoo, op. cit., p. 256.

10. *Chosen Keijai-no Kenkyu, (A Study of Korean Economy)* (Seoul: Imperial University Press, 1929), p. 159.

11. Tokuichi Fujihara *The Old Tales of Japanese in Korea* (Tokyo: Shokato, 1930), p. 190.

12. Yong-hyop Yi, *Hankuk Kuntae Toji Chedosa Yonku (A Study of Korean Land System in Modern Times)* (Seoul: Pomunkak, 1968).

13. See detailed story in Sunoo, op. cit., ch. 13.

14. The Government-General of Korea (Bureau Of Agriculture and Forestry), *Chosen-ni okeru Gosalruni kansuru Sanko jilro Tekiyo (References on the Farm Tenants in Korea)* (Seoul: Bureau of Agriculture and Forestry, 1932), p. 24.

15. Shigeru Kobayashi, *Kinsei Noson Keizai-no Kenkyu (A Study of Modern Agricultural Economy)* (Tokyo: Miraisha, 1968), p. 98.

16. *Hwajunmin* means the people living in the fire-field. The landless peasants cultivate land in the hillside or mountain side by burning the trees down. It was, of course, an illegal *action. Hwajunmin* numbered about 340,000 households and more than 12 million people on about 400,000 jungbo in Korea in 1930.

9

From the very first day of the Japanese imperialist venture into Korea, the Koreans have shown an undeviating will in their struggle to oust the invaders and regain independence.

The sporadic patriotic movement spread at home and abroad. The major military action against Japan was led by Lee Suk-chun and Hong Pum-do in different areas along the northeast border between Korea and Manchuria, and Lee Tong-hwi in Siberia.

The first famous fighting against Japanese forces occurred in May, 1906 in south Tsungtsong Province where more than two hundred of the "Ewi-pyong" or "Righteous Army" declared their campaign to emancipate their countrymen from Japanese domination. From July, 1907 to the end of 1908, 14,566 Korean rebels were killed and 8,728 captured by the Japanese army. After the annexation in 1910, outbreaks continued consistently, but it was a war of medieval weapons against the modern, mechanized Japanese military forces and gendarmerie. Many Koreans were forced to flee to Manchuria and China and, from points along the northern border, they conducted forays into the frontier districts.

The military actions were not the only means employed to protest Japanese aggression. There were several political-diplomatic movements by Korean patriots abroad: the New Korean Youth Party (Shinhan Tsungnyun-tang) in Shanghai led by Dr. Kimm Kieu-sik and Kim Chul; Young Korea Academy (Hungsadan) in Los Angeles led by Ahn Changho; Comrade Society (Dongji-hoe) in Honolulu led by Dr. Syngman Rhee.

The outstanding event in Korea's resistance struggle was the March

First Independence Movement of 1919. on that day, a "Proclamation of Korean Independence" signed by thirty-three representatives was read and half a million Koreans throughout the country held demonstrations. From March first to the end of May, twenty-one cities and two people's militia participated in 1,542 mass meetings.

It was a completely peaceful movement. People ran out into the streets waving the Korean flag and shouting "Mansei" or "Long live Korea." So well organized were the demonstrations and so loyal were the people to their national cause, that the Japanese, despite having a most highly efficient spy system, were completely ignorant of the impending storm until the day it happened. This infuriated the Japanese government, and within two months it ruthlessly suppressed the movement. Seven thousand Koreans were killed, 40,000 wounded, and 50,000 arrested, while hundreds of churches, schools and homes were destroyed.

The national independence movement was started and directed by the leaders of civic and religious organizations and members of the intelligentsia. Ministers of the Presbyterian and Methodist churches were just as active as the Buddhist priests and the leaders of the Tsondokyo, or the Heavenly Way Teachings, an indigenous religion. The bourgeoisie in Korea was greatly influenced by the revolutions in China and Russia and the winning of independence by many small European nations, such as Poland, Finland, and Czechoslovakia. The declarations of independence by small nations and their recognition by world public opinion stimulated the Korean national revolution.

Among Korean leaders responsible for the organizational process were Son Pyonghi of Tsondokyo, Lee Sung-hun of the Christian church, and Han Nyong-un of the Buddhist church. The initial idea of a nationwide nationalistic movement among the Koreans overseas was conceived in Shanghai by the New Korea Youth Party at its regular monthly meeting on February 1, 1919. The group decided to send a Korean delegation to the world peace conference in Versailles to demand independence. To strengthen the delegation's position at the conference, the group planned nationwide anti-Japanese demonstrations to express the displeasure against Japanese occupation of Korea. The group dispatched delegates to key places: Kim Tsol to Seoul, Lyu Woon-hyung to Siberia, Chang Duk-Su to Tokyo, and Dr. Kimm Kieusik to Paris.

The news which Chang Duk-Su brought to Korean students in Tokyo stirred the Young Patriots, and the student associations drafted a Korean "Declaration of Independence," which Choi Pal-yong, Lee Kwang-su and eight others signed.

While they were preparing the nationwide movement, the former King Kwang-mu of Korea was murdered on January 22, 1919, by the Japanese. The news of the king's death shocked the Korean people. The leaders of the nationalist movement decided that the anniversary of King Kwang-mu's funeral would be the date for the mass demonstration.

The 1919 independence movement's demonstrations took place on March first and continued for several months in Korea. Two hundred eleven cities and about two million people, about 20 percent of the national population, participated in the demonstrations. More than fifteen hundred meetings were held between March first and the end of May. Seven thousand five hundred Koreans were killed, nearly sixteen thousand were wounded, and about forty-seven thousand were imprisoned. Besides these casualties, forty-nine churches and mission schools were burned to the ground and more than seven hundred private dwellings w ere demolished.

There was such diversity in the leaders' individual backgrounds that some internecine violence was highly possible. Some of the groups approximated what Professor Karl W. Deutsch has called "pluralistic security communities," since they preserved interunit harmony in the absence of political amalgamation.

In spite of the failure of its immediate goal – national independence from Japan--the nationalist movement attracted worldwide attention and laid the spiritual groundwork for the future nationalist movement in Korea.

What were the significant features of the 1919 patriotic movement? First, the movement was led by religious leaders who advocated nonviolence. No one was to harm the Japanese or Japanese property. The movement's intention was to convince Japanese leaders on the basis of the spirit of justice and goodwill. Their beliefs and behaviors were in the spirit of martyrs. They believed that their physical pains and hardships were necessary parts of the process of the spiritual freedom they sought.

For instance, on the night before the demonstration, twenty-nine of the thirty-three signators of the Declaration of Independence gathered in Myongwol-gwan, a Korean restaurant in Seoul, for a final meeting before the big event. Being fully aware of Japanese militaristic harshness, all of them expected capital punishment, but upon concluding their meeting, they officially informed the Japanese police of their plan for the next day. One of the signators, having arrived too late to participate in the ritual meeting, went to the police station and voluntarily surrendered to the Japanese police. Their spirit is expressed in the following statement:

Our part is to influence the Japanese government, dominated as it is by the old idea of brute force which is opposed to reason and universal law, so that it will change and act honestly and in accord with the principles of right and truth.[1]

The statement is quoted from the *Declaration of Independence*. It indicated the non-violent character of the movement.

Second, the nature of the movement was inevitably a humanistic one. The Declaration did not state any hatred of the Japanese, but rather, a desire to live peacefully as a neighbor nation. It said:

...we tell it to the world in witness of the equality of all nations and we pass it on to our posterity as their inherent right . . if the defects of the past are to he rectified, if the wrongs of the present are to be righted, if future oppression is to be avoided, if thought is to be set free, if right of action is to be given a place, if we are to deliver our children from the painful heritage of shame, if we are to leave blessing and happiness intact for those who succeed us, the first of all necessary things is the complete independence of our people.[2]

The document explains the conditions and the reasons of subjugated people's motives for self-determination. The thirty-three signators pledged and advised the people to follow three terms of agreement:

This work of ours is in behalf of truth, justice, and life, undertaken at the request of our people, in order to make known their desire for liberty . . [Then, it concluded] . . . 1. Let no violence be done to anyone; 2. Let those who follow us show every hour with gladness the same spirit; 3 . Let all things be done with singleness of purpose, so that our behavior to the very end may bc honorable and upright.[3]

Third, the movement had democratic ideals. Korean guerrilla movements continued along the border in the north while various patriotic movements continued abroad. The two major revolutions in Russia and China had stimulated these patriotic movements. It was, however, none other than the Wilsonian idealism expressed in his Fourteen Points that excited the Korean leaders. Wilson announced his policy in a speech to the Senate in 1917. He declared:

...henceforth, inviolable security of life, of worship, and of industrial and social development should be guaranteed to all peoples

who have lived hitherto under the power of governments devoted to a
faith and purpose hostile to their own....[4]

President Wilson thus became the champion of "self-determination." "Every territorial settlement must be made in the interest and for the
benefit of the populations concerned," said President Wilson. This message
found lodging in the mind of every subjugated man; it became the basic thought
and desire for millions of Korean people who did not know that they were words
in a vacuum.

Japanese police and gendarmes used their weapons indiscriminately
against the peaceful demonstrators besides arresting the Koreans. Soon the
jails were filled to overflowing; the Japanese set up temporary jails, but their
efforts to stop the demonstrations were futile. The demonstrators probably
believed that the Korean government in exile would soon return and establish
a republican regime. By now, nearly 200 American missionaries had gained
the confidence of Koreans who regarded them as reliable and friendly,
although some of the missionaries were openly sympathetic to the Japanese
government.[5] The Korean people had no reason to distrust Wilson's "self-
determination" concept. Here is a clear case of a false political promise that
brought premature chaos and tragedy, as the world witnessed more recently in
Hungary in 1956.

It is interesting to note here that none of the national leaders
advocated a revival of the monarchical system in Korea. The democratic
republican form of government was their unanimous choice. An editorial
entitled "The Dignity of Life" appeared in the *Los Angeles Times* concerning
the Korean Declaration of Independence. "In our opinion this proclamation
will stand on a plane of exaltation with our own Declaration of Independence."[6]

So far, we have mentioned three characteristics of the early Korean
nationalism of 1919. Now we should add two elements which do not appear
in the Declaration of Independence.

What the signers did not stress in the Declaration is as important as
those points which they did. The Declaration did not stress such important
conditions of self-determination as the homogeneity of the Korean language
and the economic exploitation of the nation by the Japanese.

First of all, the Japanese had already invaded the Korean market and
dominated Korea's natural resources. The newly organized Oriental development Company took control of the land and the water systems. In other
words, economic exploitation had been initiated, although it was still in its
infant stage. Korean national leaders, however, did not stress the economic

issue as a major factor of their movement.

Early German nationalists like Johann Gottlieb Fichte and Ernest Moritz Arndt stressed the superiority of the German language over the French, Italian, Spanish, English and Slavic languages as a major factor making the German nation superior. Fichte insisted that among the Europeans, the Germans alone spoke an original, not derived, language. Therefore, the Germans alone were destined to provide world leadership. The Korean language is one of the most advanced among modern languages, but Korean national leaders did not even mention the language as a condition of independence. We do find German nationalism as expressed by Fichte or Arndt in Korean nationalists' writings,[7] but there is no hatred of the Japanese as Arndt advocated hatred of the French.

One American reporter, Professor Nathaniel Peiffer of Columbia University, said of the demonstrations of 1919:

> The first line was cut down and ridden down by mounted men, the second came on shouting, "Mansei," or "long live Korea." Every man and woman in the line knew what was before him, every man and woman had seen the penalty paid; it meant brutal beatings, arrests, torture and even death. They did not quiver. When one procession was broken up, another formed and marched straight at the waiting troops, only cheering, waving their flags and cheering.[8]

The eyewitness here reveals the physical pain the people endured and the brutality to which they were subjected. Many American missionaries reported similar stories to the mission boards of the Methodist and Presbyterian churches in the United States. The importance of the national movement, in spite of these most brutal and painful physical phenomena, was in its spiritual aspect.

The leaders of the movement mixed political self-determination with religious concepts. In the Declaration of Independence and subsequent mass demonstrations throughout the country, the entire movement reveals a politico-religious tendency, not only because the leaders of three religious groups led the movement, but because of the context in which the people endured the mass physical suffering and left an immortal spirit of pride and honor to the Korean people. They were more inclined to be free spiritually and have inner liberty than political liberty. "We wish to inspire the government of Japan," was their declaration. The essential nature of their whole action was primarily dominated by spiritual motivation. From the standpoint of political liberation, it was a failure and negative, but from the standpoint of a spiritual movement, it w as a success and positive.

It was successful because of what the leaders felt in their hearts: the existence of liberty and morality preserved by the people. The document expressively accepts the morality, which is not a product of human knowledge, but is the outcome of obedience to a universal law. It states that "... it will change and act honestly and in accordance with the principles of right and truth." Here we detect that the leaders of the movement refer to "transcendental sense" of Kantian freedom, of which they had little or no knowledge.

Morality, they believed, was independent from consequences, and impermeable to rewards. They volunteered to be imprisoned and expected worse, but they believed themselves to be free if their will was free; and their will was free when their actions were in accordance with their inner-directiveness.

Their ethico-religious teachings and attitudes expressed and propagated among the people a new attitude to political questions. They made a new political temper popular among the young intelligentsia. Moral vigor became the hallmark of virtue; political action could not be good unless it was the outcome of deep moral conviction. The Korean nationalists asserted themselves against a world which paid no attention to them, but they had no choice, they felt, their conviction could move mountains and their heads were bloody but unbowed.

The spirit of the March First Movement is now one of the dominating traditions of Korean national culture. The spiritual and inner movement has continued, even though the physical part of the movement ceased under severe pressures by the Japanese. It may sound strange, but the Korean Communist Party was dissolved and the members were forced to join the Japanese Communist Party, at one time under the direction of the Comintern. Such paradoxical actions of the international communist movement have been revealed more than once in the history of Korean nationalism.

After experiencing the complete failure of the 1919 nationalist movement, leaders and youths alike began to reorganize their respective groups to pursue the patriotic movement. Since the youth, especially college students, had taken the leading roles in the demonstrations, they were more disappointed than the older generation with the outcome of the movement. The young generation understood now that future movements must not rely upon support from the West, for it had failed them. The intention of the older generation was, as it is expressed in the Declaration, to let the world know of the desire of the Korean people and expose Japanese imperialistic rule, rather than to achieve immediate independence. They knew that non-violent protest would not bring about national independence, but that only world opinion and approval would help the Korean cause. The pressure of world opinion, especially from the United States, changed the Japanese policy in Korea from military rule to cultural rule, although the latter policy did more damage to the national conscience in the long run. The Korean people did gain some freedom in the area of publication.

The older generation was satisfied, at least temporarily, with the change of atmosphere and the new regime's political leniency. Among the older generation there were two distinct groups. One was known as "Young Korea Academy" or "hungsadan," under the leadership of Ahn Chang-ho, and the other was "Comrade Society" or "Dongji-hoe," under the leadership of Syngman Rhee. The two groups emerged at about the same time and though rooted in the United States, nevertheless they had considerable influence in Korea proper. Ahn's group advocated national independence through strengthening individuals and becoming an organized group. Thus, his group emphasized self-discipline and education. Mr. Ahn knew the shortcomings of the nation, and he wanted very much to teach the group to prepare to be future citizens of an independent Korea. Therefore he and his followers disapproved of the immediate action that General Lee Tong-hwi's military took in Manchuria against Japan. He was afraid that terroristic and military actions would bring about harsh policies against Koreans within Korea, and would jeopardize the educational programs and the cultural activities which had been gained after the March First Movement.

Rhee's group went one step further, by submitting Korea as a possible mandate of the League of Nations. The implication was clear that Korea was not ready for independence in the view of Dr. Rhee. Eventually, this advocacy caused the Korean provisional government in Shanghai to dismiss Dr. Rhee as president of the government in exile.

The failure of this bourgeois revolution immediately raised the problem of the future leadership of the independence movement. The people recognized that the civic and religious leaders were no longer capable of giving adequate guidance to the independence movement. The people waited for a vanguard force which could pursue a consistent revolutionary line and overthrow Japanese imperialism. The young generation lost its confidence in the leadership of the older groups. They were impatient with both Ahn and Rhee. Their groups lacked the action and the dynamic movement which youth found in communism.

The communist movement gradually developed and took over the revolutionary leadership although the party was still young and small in numbers. The failure of the 1919 revolution and subsequent events led to two significant results: first, the bourgeois nationalists as a group began to collaborate with the Japanese – even such outstanding leaders as Ts'oe Rin, Ts'oe Nam-sun, Yi Kwang-su and many others; second, the Communist Party, following a policy of no compromise with the Japanese and consequently suffering the most, was able to demonstrate its sincerity and organizational ability to the people.

There is no doubt that the economic policy of the Japanese was a major factor in the transfer of political hegemony from the nationalists to the communists, for the latter were able to explain the economic issues and economic foundations of Japanese imperialism to the people, whereas the nationalists, basing their fight against Japan on self-interest and emotion, were unable to do so.

The communist movement in Korea came about as a result of several factors: first, the most significant was the economic exploitation by Japanese colonial policy; second, the colonial people's movement throughout the world contributed to the cause of the national liberation movement; third, the numerous proletariat movements in Japan encouraged the Korean labor movement; fourth, the split in the schools of thought within the nationalist groups, especially in the Tsondokyo which had provided such great national leadership and influence. One of the Tsondokyo groups held to an opportunistic tendency in the political movement and leaned towards a compromise with the Japanese administration, which caused the group to lose popular support.

The beginning of the Korean communist movement can be traced back as far as 1918. General Lee Tong-hwi organized that Korean Socialist Party at Khabarovsk in June 1918. This was the first communist group organized in the Far East, antedating even the Comintern. General Lee was a recognized leader through his military activities against the Japanese in Manchuria and was highly respected among his compatriots. When the Bolsheviks engaged the White Russians militarily and the Japanese intervened in Siberia, the Koreans became their natural ally in the struggle, although for different reasons. Disappointed Koreans living in Manchuria and China were glad to join the Bolshevik force, and fought against the Japanese. General Lee Tong-hwi proceeded to Shanghai from Siberia and joined the Korean provisional government in September, 1919 and became premier within a short time. Meanwhile Lee, utilizing his prestige as premier, began to recruit his Korean compatriots for the purpose of organizing the Koryo Communist Party in January 1920. The Korean Socialist Party at Khabarovsk now had virtually moved to Shanghai with him, and recruited such important nationalists as Kim Rip, Lyu Woonhyung, Ahn Pyung-tsan.

While Lee Tong-hwi was organizing the Koryo Communist Party in Shanghai, another Korean Communist Party had been organized in Irkutsk under the guidance of Boris Shumiatsky who was the head of the Far Eastern Secretariat of the Comintern and served as commander of the Fifth Army of the Russian Revolutionary Forces in Siberia. To strengthen the Bolshevik military forces in the Far East, Shumiatsky contacted the nationalist leaders of the Congress of Korean People and organized "The Korean Communist Party in Russia" on September, 1919. Ahn Pyungtsan, who attended the conference, returned to Shanghai, named the Koryo Communist Party as the Shanghai branch of the Korean Communist Party and was assigned to establish a branch in Korea. The committee which was assigned for this task included Lyu Woon-hyung, Kim Man-gyom, Cho Tong-u, and Park Heun-Young was appointed functionary of the Communist Youth Group.

Thus, the Irkutsk group, under the domination of the Soviet agent, challenged the nationalistically oriented Lee Tong-hwi's Shanghai group. Meanwhile, Lee sent Park Chin-sun, his private envoy, to Lenin in Moscow and convinced Lenin that he should support Lee's group; he received one million rubles of the promised two million rubles as aid to the Korean communist movement. Lee's group was; thus, well financed while the Irkutsk group was suffering financially. Lenin either neglected to check with his agent, Boris Shumiatsky, or was anxious to add General Lee to his camp, probably for military purposes. It appears that the latter group, however, had increased its membership to one thousand in the area of the Maritime Province by 1922. Learning of this situation, Lenin dismissed both the Irkutsk and the Shanghai groups by December, 1922, and organized the Korean Bureau in the Comintern to control the Korean communist movement.

In February, 1923, the Korean Bureau was transferred to Vladivostok with Vishinsky as its chief, and Katayama Sen, Han Myung-sun of the Irkutsk group, General Lee of Shanghai group as the members of the Bureau, and Chung Chai-dal was sent to Korea as a secret agent. Thus, the Korean communist movement, once organized by nationalists and communists alike, was short lived, and officially became an integrated part of the international communist movement.

The radical elements of the nationalist group and the communists realized that the working class had to be mobilized and organized. Several organizations emerged. Among the more outstanding groups were the worth Wind Association, the Seoul Youth Association, and the Tuesday Club. The North Wind Association was formulated in 1922 by a group of progressive Korean intellectuals headed by Kim Yak-su. Probably the most active group in the radical movement was originally known as the North Star Association, most of whose members were educated in Tokyo. The second organization, Seoul Youth Association, was formed in 1922 under the leadership of Kim Sakuk and Lee Yong and consisted of four hundred different organizations and represented approximately fifty thousand members. The third group was the Tuesday Club. It was composed of 500 organizations and represented 60,000 members. The Tuesday Club was under the leadership of Park Heun-Young, Kim Tantsi. Of the three groups, the North Wind Association was the strongest and exercised the most influence in the labor movement.

In 1924, the League of the Korean Labor and Farmers was organized with some 180 organizations; and the League of Korean Youth was established with some 220 youth organizations, and so the labor and the farmer movements became unified under radical elements. It was the first successful nationwide unified effort since the 1919 movement and also the first time radical elements were able to get together.

With such a prelude, the Korean Communist Party was officially organized on April 17, 1925, in Seoul. Fourteen leaders of the radical movements assembled at a restaurant at one in the afternoon and discussed organizing the Korean Communist Party and officially announced the purposes of the party. Their goals were: first, Korean independence, and second, abolition of the private property system. Eight of the organizers were selected to form the Central Executive Committee and three were selected for the inspection committee. The Central Executive Committee was to draft the party constitution and also to complete the organization. After several meetings, the committee set up a secretariat, departments of organization, and propaganda. As soon as the Central Committee drew up a party constitution, the group immediately applied for affiliation with the Comintern. The committee members then spread throughout the country to recruit members. They had enrolled fifty-three new members mostly from among the intelligentsia within a year. From then on the party's influence spread throughout the country, focusing especially in the cities.

In May, 1926, the Korean Communist Party sent a group of agitators to Manchuria under the leadership of Cho Bong-am. The group organized the Manchurian branch of the Korean Communist Party in Ningkota. one of their tasks was to aid the families of the professional revolutionaries. Thus the activities of the Korean communists in Manchuria were renewed. The communist activities, however, were soon spotted and about thirty communists were arrested by Japanese police with the cooperation of the Chinese police in December, 1927. These communists were sent to Seoul and imprisoned.

In September, 1928, Kim Tsol-san and forty other communists who had not yet been arrested were also sought out and imprisoned by the Japanese and Chinese police. These two large-scale arrests seriously handicapped the infant communist movement in Manchuria and the result was a complete

188

reorganization of the communist party in Manchuria. The party went underground and organized several front groups, including farmers, students, and
intellectuals, along the more popular issues rather than along outright
revolutionary lines. The old radical names were abandoned and substituted
with League of the Youth of Manchuria, League of East Manchuria Labor, and
others. These popular organizations, however, were supervised by special
communist representatives from Northern Manchuria and also from Irkutsk,
where the Korean communists were still active; these supervisors had close
connections with the Korean communist movement under the direction of the
Comintern.

The League of East Manchuria Youth included forty-eight organizations with a membership of 100,000. The League of East Manchuria Labor
included forty-eight organizations with 2,500 members. Four executive
members of the Koryo Youth Association, one of the forty-eight groups in the
youth organization, were arrested in Changchun and sent to Sinueju, Korea.
The discovery of communist propaganda sheets sent to Korea from Manchuria
aroused police suspicions and resulted in the arrests. Later in 1930, police who
were assigned to the Japanese consulate-general arrested Kang Sok-jun and
122 others associated with the youth group and sent them to Seoul. Following
this incident, the Japanese police dissolved the Korean communist organizations located in Manchuria and prohibited all public meetings there.

Soba, head of the Japanese police of the consulate-general, stated,
"We have sent to Seoul eighty persons who were thoroughly investigated, and
who proved to be real communists. I was surprised by their courage."[9] Thus
the communist movement ceased to exist temporarily in Manchuria, and the
focus of the movement was in Shanghai. On March 26, 1926, Korean residents
in Shanghai organized the Korean Youth Association under the leadership of
Chu Yo-sup. The aims of this organization were: first, Korean independence;
second, to weld the organizations into a united front; third, to make an effort
to establish, as soon as possible, one national movement party; fourth, to
cooperate with the people's liberation groups of the neighboring countries;
fifth, to study the practical policies and ideals of the national movement.

It was a time of compromise between nationalists and communists,
and a time for formulation of the united front movement, and the youth
organization became a front group for the Comintern. The organization
immediately branched out to ten cities in China and received support from the
Comintern for the purpose of unifying nationalists and communists. The
Comintern advocated that Korean communists join the nationalist groups and
work with them for common causes, rather than try to compete with each other.
It was almost imperative for communists to cooperate with nationalists since

they had lost most of their leaders, and besides, the Comintern Far Eastern policy at this time had already been geared toward a united front.

To promote revolutionary activities, the Youth Association organized the Central military committee with the cooperation of all the Korean organizations which surfaced again in Manchuria. The first step in this undertaking was to call an official meeting at Tai-sai-chan of all representatives, and twenty-seven revolutionary leaders, who represented various revolutionary armies in Manchuria. The group elected Kim Cha-jin, chairman of the military committee, as he already had been recognized as the leader in military affairs. Kim's military action against the Japanese disturbed the government's policy more than any others at that time. The group also began the publication of the official magazine *Oltsi* in Korean. *Oltsi* and other propaganda materials were smuggled constantly into Korea.

The Comintern followed the united front policy in China, and ordered Korean communists to cooperate with the nationalists as was the case in China, resulting in the organization of Sin-kan-hoe on February 15, 1927. Since both communists and nationalists were not able to carry out an anti-Japanese movement alone, they welcomed the opportunity to organize the united front. Communists were planning to apply a dual policy–Sin-kan-hoe as a front organization while maintaining the communist movement in the underground. This policy was in accord with the Marxian concept of historical materialism. Korea was not ready for a proletarian revolution and a bourgeois revolution had to take place first. It was the time when the Comintern insisted on Chinese communists joining the Kuomintang (Nationalists) Party, and establishing a united front, rather than fighting against the Nationalists. The major enemy of Korea was not the Korean bourgeoisie, but the foreign exploiter-- Japanese imperialists. Therefore, the logic was clear to communists in Korea, and they followed the order from Moscow.

The principles of Sin-kan-hoe were: first, promotion of the political, economic, and social awakening of the people; second, promotion of national unity; third, absolute refusal to recognize opportunistic (or pro-Japanese) groups. Thus, Sin-kan-hoe was the first united political organization to exist in Korea. The organization was composed of some one hundred and forty various branches in all parts of Korea with fifty thousand members, including most of the intelligentsia, nationalists, and communists.

The organization was revolutionary in name only and failed to carry out many activities because of close surveillance of the strict Japanese colonial policy which had become even more restrictive.

The majority of the leaders of Sin-kan-hoe were well-known nationalists since many of the communists had been arrested, especially during the

190

third communist roundup in 1926. Nationalist leaders of Sin-kan-hoe included Lee Sang-jae, a well-known patriot, first chairman; Kwon Tong-jin, a leader of the Tsondokyo, second chairman; Ho Hyun, a renowned lawyer, third chairman. It was under the leadership of Ho Hyun that the organization attempted a mass demonstration for the first time. It failed as the police arrested the leaders before the plan for the demonstration materialized. The plan was connected with the 1929 student movement.

Sin-kan-hoe was soon dissolved by Japanese police. Communists actively carried out strikes in factories and sabotaged farms. They organized the "Association of the Reconstruction of the Korean Communist Party," and the "League of Young Communists." on the other hand, the nationalists organized "The League of Christianity and Tsondokyo." Thus each group established its own league and undertook activities separately. The communist group led strikes which extended nationwide, involving approximately 250,000 people in the movement. In 1931, Yong-hing Farmer's Union with a total membership of 18,000 sponsored a big demonstration, and approximately 150 farmers were arrested by police in connection with the strikes in the Hong-won area alone.

Nong-tson Tenant Union with a membership of about two thousand six hundred led a starvation sit-down strike, and Jong-pyong Farmers Union conducted a strike which ended with two hundred members being arrested in Yong-hing county during october, 1931. The modern peasant movement began in Yong-hing county. The peasants became the major force, not the intellectuals and certainly not the middle class, in the struggle against Japanese imperialism in Korea from then on. Why this change in leadership in Korea at this particular time?

The peasant class, the landless group but the real producers, was confronted with one major aim as the new stage developed. Subsistence was the chief concern of the peasant. The goal of the peasant class was, thus, simple and direct, while their target, capitalistic landlords, characteristically was more complicated. The dominating landlord elements were not only capitalistic and profit motivated, but also harsh and severe. They had been the biggest landlords in Japan before they came to Korea and they were experienced in dealing with tenants. Their lands were their capital, and they established severe rules and regulations to control their Korean tenants. Japanese landlords were violent, merciless, and not given to humanistic handling of Korean tenants.

To illustrate the treatment of Korean tenants, we cite the case of the Higashiyama Farm which belonged to Mitsubishi Zaibatsu. The following conditions appeared in a Higashiyama tenant contract. First of all, the landlord reserved the right to demand that farmland be returned whenever he so desired; second, the contract could be revised according to the desires of the landlord; third, all damages and expenses were to be paid by the tenants. Under such conditions, the landlord was able to evict any tenant who was not in the landowner's favor.

Conditions which could result in the tenant's dismissal from his land included: delay of the payment of rent; damaged land regardless of whose fault it might have been; changing the farming system, etc. Under these conditions, the landlord could, with validity, boast that he was able to get his land back any time he desired. He merely revoked the tenant's rights and confiscated the land.

In order to keep up his tenancy, the tenant had to spend a great amount of his income for repairs and improvements which only profited the landlord. The Shimadani Farm, another big Japanese farm, had an even more unscrupulous contract. The reasons for dismissal of tenants were: first, damage to the landlord's prestige; second, complaints about the rental situation. In other words, tenants were not allowed to talk about their present contract or about the landlords. Freedom of speech had been prohibited by the contract.

In the contract of the oriental Development Company, when a tenant violated a good custom, the standard of a good custom being set by the landlord, he could be dismissed. These clauses could obviously be interpreted by the landlord in any way he pleased, and the unfairness of the contract was clear.

Other peculiar clauses appeared in the Kumamoto, Nakashira, Ishikawa Farms' contract: first, tenants had to post signs on the premises designating the owner and the amount of land for which the tenant was responsible; tenants had to deliver the entire crop to the place designated by the landlords; the landlords would subtract from the total crop the amount coming to them for rent, interest, dues, etc., and the remainder to be hauled back by the tenant to his home. In most cases, the vast majority of the crop went to the landlord, leaving only a minute part of the harvest to the tenant.

Since landlords held the power of dismissing tenants at any complaint, intimidated tenants registered few or no complaints against their landlords. These conditions existed for these tenants who had written contracts, but the majority of tenant contracts were oral ones. In 1930, 73 percent of all tenant contracts were oral agreements. In Kyonggi Province, 89 percent of the contracts were oral while in North Hamgyung Province 99 percent were oral.[10] The risks tenants took with oral agreements were very obvious. The Japanese official report listed twenty-eight reasons which landlords could use against their tenants. For instance, the landlord could dismiss the tenant when he felt that the tenant was not working hard to raise additional crops; dismissal could result when the landlord thought that the tenant's behavior was undesirable, such as joining an undesirable association; landlords could dismiss tenants who instigated other tenants and disturbed their work. Under such conditions, the dismissals of tenants were frequent occurrences, and it was the landlords' main weapon in intimidating the peasants. In Kyonggi Province, 27 percent of the entire cultivated land's tenantship changed hands in 1930. Similar situations existed in other parts of the country: 25 percent in North Jolla, 20 percent in South Jolla, 35 percent in North Kyongsang, 10 percent in South Kyongsang, 30 percent in North Tsungtsong, 20 percent in South Tsungtsong, etc.[11]

Those who lost their tenancies either left for Manchuria or became Hwajonmin (illegal farmers of the "firefield"). The landless tenants accepted the situation as a natural occurrence of human life. They complained but did not organize themselves to protect their natural right--the right to live. They were not conscious of their personal rights. This situation was not to continue long.

Korean farmers were divided in two classes: one group, although small in number, stayed with the Japanese landlords, while the vast majority became poor tenants. In other words, the capitalistic land system coupled with primitive agriculture methods created these two extreme classes. As the landlords expanded their possessions more and the numbers of the tenants increased, the competition of getting land tenancy became acute. Meanwhile, the landlords made their rules and regulations even more crude. As the landlords' exploitations increased, the peasant resistance increased. This was an inevitable result. The peasants had nothing to lose. They lost their lands, and now their livelihood had been threatened. Even from a pure economic sense, there were enough reasons to anticipate the class struggle between the two extreme classes.

The political and national conditions of the time were cause enough for rebellion. However, as exploited as they were, the peasants were unable to resist the landlords until they were organized by progressive students returning from Japan. These college students had been impressed by the October Revolution and witnessed the peasant movement in Japan. They returned to Korea to organize the tenants. The Tenants' Association and the League of Peasants became the pioneering organizations against the landlord class. As early as 1920, there were fifteen tenant strikes against landlords with 4,000 tenants participating. These were new experiences for them and they created a new situation in Korea. The government-general dissolved these peasant organizations immediately to protect the landlords, but the peasant strikes increased in spite of the suppression.

Following is a table that shows the number of peasant strikes during the years from 1920 to 1932 in Korea.

Not all the tenants' strikes were violent in nature. Some of them were rather moderate and the tenants hoped to settle the matter peacefully. The tenants' prime concern was economic. In 1931, when strikes numbered 667 with more than 10,000 tenants participating, 42 percent of the causes of the strikes were classified as dismissal or increase of tenant fees by landlords. The other reasons for strikes were also closely related with the fees, rent payments, etc. According to official Japanese reports, there was no mention of political and national feeling among the rank and file members of the tenant group. Yet, the Japanese government arrested and imprisoned leaders of the peasant movement saying they were "undesirable elements." This rigid control increased when Japanese militarism expanded to China in 1931.

A similar situation existed in Japan. As the military adventure in China expanded, monopoly capitalism in Japan collaborated with the military adventurists. Landlords had government support to enforce their semi-feudalistic methods on tenants. This system did not help to increase agricultural products. Furthermore, the low-price system of agricultural products was maintained while an inflationary economy continued in the country. The gap between the prices of agriculture products and industrial products was so great that farmers suffered unbearably. The fertilizer price contracted by the monopoly trust forced farmers to borrow cash to pay for the fertilizer, which had been inflated, thus the farmers' debt increased. All these conditions occurred on Japanese farms, as the tenants' struggle against landlords intensified during the '30s.

The main causes of the tenants' struggle were the tenant rent, improving tenant conditions, etc. They were purely economic factors. Lowering the rent, the price of fertilizer, and loan interest rates were economic issues. In 1934, there were 5,828 strikes with more than 100,000 participating in them, but the major grievance remained economics. The nature of the tenant strikes in Tsungtsong and Jolla Provinces were very similar to the tenant strikes in Japan during the '30s. One characteristic of Korean tenant strikes was that the vast majority occurred in the South; including South Tsungtsong, North and South Jolla, and North and South Kyongsang, Kyong, and Kyonggi Provinces.[12] It is clear that those places where the most Japanese landlords penetrated, the most strikes occurred, and the main cause of the strikes was economic, in spite of the biracial situation which existed. The tension between Japanese landlords and Korean tenants was caused by immediate problems rather than long-term political reasons. The peasant movement was, therefore, based on the struggle between capitalist landlords and poor farmers, leaving out the middle-class farmers. It was a revisionistic type of economic struggle.

Due to the nature of the movement, the peasant effort in the south at this time was regional rather than national in scope. This situation reveals a significant factor in the Korean peasant movement. In spite of wide-spread tenant strikes year after year from 1920 to 1932 in South Tsungtsong and the North and South Jolla areas, there were no major political movements among the peasants. In comparing these areas with North and South Hamgyung Provinces. we find some of the major political movements among the peasants, although there were not as many strikes during the same period.

The strike in Yonghing in 1931 is an example. The Yonghing Farmers' Union with a membership of eighteen thousand staged a big demonstration which resulted in the arrest of 150 strikers. After this initiation, the Nong-tson Tenant Union with a membership of two thousand six hundred conducted a starvation-sit-down strike. The Jonpyong Farmers Union joined the strike. As a result, about two hundred members were arrested by police during the month of October in Yonghing County alone. The strike had nothing to do with tenant fees or rents or any economic issue. The cause of the strike was the refusal by police to permit the opening of the village night school.

on the night of October 21, 1931, eight union members organized four separate groups which attacked the county office, police station, railroad station, and homes of landlords where the rioters destroyed official documents and other important papers. They beat up the head of the county and the landlords. Police headquarters of South Hamgyung Province received the news with surprise and sent out armed police forces to Yonghing County. The fight between armed police and farmers continued with heavy casualties and ended with five hundred union members being arrested. This was one of the significant peasant movement events in Korean history.

Why was it that a political movement initiated by peasants occurred at Hamgyung Province, where fewer exploitations had taken place by Japanese landlords, and why did it not happen at Tsungtsong Province or even in Jolla where more severe exploitations took place? Was this simple accident? We can speculate that such a significant movement came about in the north, rather than in the south, because of the degree of exploitation. When tenants were exploited with such extreme harshness as we have witnessed in the south, they were physically exhausted and too busy with eking out their livelihoods to think beyond their immediate needs. While the farmers in the north still remained small self-tamers, the majority of them at least had some leisure time to think and organize themselves to enhance their livelihood as a group. organizing a village night school was such an example.

Another reason was an external one. Being closely connected geo-graphically with Manchuria and Siberia where the Korean revolutionary movement was active, the people of the north were constantly reminded of the anti-Japanese movement as a necessary ingredient of their total struggle for decent living. In other words, the peasants in the north did not separate the economic issue and the political issue while their brothers in the south did.

Japanese imperialist policy in Korea exploited not only the Korean farmers but also produced problems for the Japanese farmers. Japanese landlords were not kind to their people when it became a matter of profits. They had no humanitarian concern over either Koreans or Japanese.

Japanese capitalism destroyed not only the agricultural economy but also small-scale handicraft industries in Korea as well and thereby destroyed the self-sufficient basis of Korean economic independence. By monopoly control of all machinery, tools, fertilizer, and other supplies, two changes were immediately brought about. First, daily living expenses rose and debts were incurred to meet the immediate economic crisis. Secondly, the home industries, which usually kept the peasant employed during slack seasons, were abolished under Japanese control. Thus, with higher farm rent, water taxes, debt interest, and farm supply costs, the peasant did not earn enough for his livelihood after his debts were paid, unless he borrowed more money—only to become more immersed in debts, which, as they gradually accumulated, led inevitably to bankruptcy.

In conclusion, we are able to make the following observation about Japanese imperialism in Korea. First of all, the greater penetration of Japanese imperialism, particularly by landlords in early occupation days, the greater the number of tenant protests occurred, primarily for economic reasons. The political protests, on the other hand, came from the less penetrated areas. Secondly, the number of starving people were in direct proportion to the exploitation of Japanese imperialism and penetration of Japanese landlords into the region. Thirdly, the more the peasant increased his production and produced more rice, the less he became worthy and the less rice was available to him. He actually became devaluated as a commodity, which brought him misery. As a matter of fact he was alienated from his own creation. He was not only totally dehumanized but eventually left his land and his home, looking for a new place and a new hope to live.

Notes

1. Carton Waldo Kendall, *The Truth about Korea* (San Francisco: The Korean National Association, 1919), p. 49.
2. Ibid.

3. Ibid.

4. Ibid.

5. International Review of Mission, Vol. 11, New York, p. 343.

6. *Los Angeles Times,* April 6, 1919.

7. The poem, ''The German Fatherland,'' contains a strong Germanic feeling.

8. Kendall, op. cit.

9 *Tong-A Ilbo or Tong-A Daily News,* Seoul, oct. 28, 1928.

10. The Government-General of Korea, *General Reference on the Farm-tenant in Korea* (Seoul), p. 74

11. Ibid., p. 105.

12. The Government-General of Korea, *Chosun-e Sojak Kwansup (The Tenancy Custom in Korea)* (Seoul, 1933), p. 58.

13. Hoon-ku Lee, *Chosun Nongupron (A Discourse on Korean Agriculture)* (Seoul: Ulgusa Co., 1935), p. 326.

10

Liberation and After

Independence for Korea was decided upon at the Cairo conference of October, 1943, by the leaders of the allied powers prosecuting the war against Japan, President Franklin D. Roosevelt, Prime Minister Winston Churchill, Generalissimo Chiang Kai-shek. Here they declared "in due course Korea shall become free and independent." The words "in due course" were the brake that provided the dilemma. Many leading patriots abroad worked hard to convince the allied leaders that the Korean people were qualified to govern themselves.

President Harry S. Truman, Britain's Winston Churchill, and the Soviet Union's Joseph Stalin reaffirmed Korean independence in the Potsdam Declaration of July 26, 1945, with China later agreeing to it. On August 8, 1945, one week before the termination of hostilities, Soviet armed forces marched into North Korea. On September 2, after the Japanese surrender, the Supreme Commander of the Allied Forces announced that the U. S. and the Soviet armed forces would share in the occupation of Korea. The Soviets were already in their northern zone of occupation; the Americans landed on September 8, and took over the area south of the 38th parallel. This convenient arrangement was for the sake of the military occupation of enemy-held territory. No one, however, foresaw that such a temporary division of the land would bring tragedy to the nation later.

Korea was, like any other enemy-held territory, subjected to government by the Allied forces, and the problem of governing a country like Korea was no simple matter.

World War II produced about the same problems for non-self-governing peoples as did World War 1. Colonial problems have been some of the prolonged causes of international conflicts and wars. The big powers had already mentioned their trusteeship problems at the Dumbarton Oaks Conference. However, the subject was not resolved and this matter was carried over to the Crimean Conference where President Roosevelt and Prime Minister Churchill discussed a possible addition to the Dumbarton Oaks proposals. A final decision on territorial trusteeships again was deferred.

The matter of trusteeships was raised at the United Nations Organization conference in San Francisco. At this conference the task of drafting a plan for a new trusteeship system was turned over to Committee Four of the General Assembly. Three main conceptions of the trusteeship plan were represented at the conference. The American principles concerning dependent territories had already been submitted by Secretary of State Cordell Hull to President Roosevelt, who endorsed them in March of 1943. These principles set forth that all people who aspire to independence should get the cooperation of the United Nations. Specifically, the trustees section of the U.N. was to help the people of such territories unify in preparation for independent national status. The proposal was approved by President Roosevelt two days before his death.[1]

The basic aims of the international trusteeship system, according to the charter of the U.N., are international peace and security and to promote the political, economic, social and educational advancement of the inhabitants of the trust territories and their progressive development towards self-government or independence, depending on the particular circumstances of each territory and its people and their freely expressed wishes. Special circumstances were to be stated by the terms of each trusteeship agreement. These common principles finally were agreed upon and the plan was accepted by fifty-one nations.

The case of Korea came under Article 77, which stated that territories may be detached from enemy states as a result of the Second World War, and a five-year trusteeship system was announced in Moscow by the foreign ministers of the United States, Great Britain and the Soviet Union in December, 1945.

Prior to the Japanese surrender, the Korean underground movement had established the Korean People's Republic under the chairmanship of Lyu Woon-hyung, an old patriot and hero. Immediately after this, and shortly before the arrival of Allied troops, General Abe, then governor-general of Korea, asked Lyu Woon-hyung to protect Japanese citizens and insure peace and order. Lyu accepted the proposals with certain reservations. It is curious to note that General Abe, representative of the Imperial Japanese Government, should approach the recently formed de facto government of his subjects with such supplication. One can only surmise that the People's Government had the unanimous support of the population and consequently had the only authority that might restrain the wrath and anger of the Korean people toward the Japanese in their midst.

Soviet military forces arriving in North Korea immediately recognized the People's Government and cooperated with it in establishing the North Korea People's Interim Committee on a much wider political and social basis than the initial body. Moreover, the Russians gave wholehearted support to the Koreans' initiative in removing Japanese-appointed puppets, dividing the large estates and nationalizing former Japanese industries as the property of the Korean people. With Soviet encouragement, farmers' unions, labor unions, women's associations, and unions of youth began to appear quickly and to participate in the national life of the country.

To the south of the 38th parallel, Lt. Gen. John R. Hodge, commander of the American forces, maintained the People's Republic to be illegal and retained the hated Japanese in administrative capacities. Korean delegates waiting to greet American troops at the port of Inchon were fired upon--by the Japanese. A protest to the American Military Government (AMG) was ignored with the claim that these Japanese soldiers "had the legal right" to maintain law and order! General Hodge then proceeded to create the Korean Advisory Council, consisting of eleven members, to aid the AMG. The chairman of this body was Kim Seung-soo, one of the biggest landlords in South Korea. During the war he had been an active member of the central council of the Japanese government. He was also chairman of the Korean Democratic Party, an organization of landowners and big business men. It was from this party that the members of the American Advisory Council were chosen, although there were numerous more representative political and social groups which were more than willing to help the AMG. An amazing and rapid metamorphosis took place: The pro-Japanese became pro-American.

Within six months the Korean people, who once welcomed the American liberators, were demanding to know how soon they would leave Korea. An editorial in *Chosun Ilbo,* a conservative Korean daily in Seoul, characterized the American occupation "as worse than under the Japanese."

In spite of the Cairo Declaration of December 1, 1943 promising Korea independence, there was no precise formulation of a plan to govern Korea until December, 1945 when representatives of the Soviet Union, the United States and Great Britain met in Moscow. It was agreed there that Korea was to endure military occupation for one year, followed by five years of civilian trusteeship. To assist in the formation of a provisional government, the

Soviet and American military commands in Korea were instructed to establish a joint commission which, in consultation with democratic Korean organizations, was to make recommendations to the Four Powers. The joint commission, in cooperation with a proposed provisional government, was to promote the economic and social progress of the Korean people in developing democratic self-government.

The conservatives, Kim Koo, Syngman Rhee and Kim Seung-soo, violently opposed the decision. Rhee and Kim Koo were in exile for the greater part of their lives and, returning home, they sought to capitalize on the anticipated unfavorable mass reaction to the proposed trusteeship of Korea. Kim Koo started his "fight to death campaigns," calling for national strikes and demonstrations. The supporters of Kim Koo launched a wave of terrorism and intimidation: offices of newspapers supporting the decision were stoned and vandalized; members of democratic organizations were kidnapped and beaten, and oftentimes murdered. These terrorists openly declared they intended to kill Park Heun-Young, secretary of the Communist Party in the South, and Lyuh Woon-heung, a leader of the People's Republic. The handful of conservatives who were anti-Soviet became now also anti-American and anti-United Nations; however, the American Military Government continued to tolerate their activities and recognized them as representatives of the Korean people.

On the other hand, democratic organizations and the vast majority of the population accepted the decision on trusteeship. They thought that Korea, emerging as a weak and relatively backward nation, would again be easy prey for imperialism. They felt that the only way to insure her future independence was to have collective action of the major powers in helping Korea to her feet. In its message of January 2, 1946, to the major powers, the Central Committee of the People's Republic declared that the three ministers' conference was a progressive one and their decision would result in a democratic Korea. They said the gradual fulfillment of Korean independence had been advanced and they pledged to support this progressive agreement.

On January 3, 1946, more than two hundred thousand people gathered in Seoul to "support the Moscow Agreement," while in Pyongyang, one hundred thousand participated in a similar meeting. During this period demonstrations were held throughout the south and north. Among the organizations involved were the Korean Federation of Trade Unions with a membership of three million, and the Youth and Women's Federations, each representing one million members. These massive demonstrations indicated decisively the overwhelming sentiments of the Korean people who were not to be mistaken for political opportunists.

In the midst of this enthusiastic atmosphere, the American-Soviet Joint Commission met for the first time on January 5, 1946. This conference dealt only with the most urgent problems regarding interzonal mail service, allocation of radio frequencies and movement of persons and goods from one zone to the other. The sessions on major questions of policy took place on March 20 between the two military commandants. On the crucial issue of the formation of the provisional government, the growing rift in the overall Soviet-American relations became evident–the cold war freeze was taking hold.

In these discussions, Soviet authorities maintained that consultation on the provisional government should be only with genuinely democratic Korean organizations and not with national traitors and collaborators who aided Japanese militarists during the Japanese occupation. The Soviet position was a reiteration of the Moscow Agreement.

But American authorities held that "all groups should be entitled to state their views," and that the Soviet viewpoint was a violation of freedom of speech and of the Moscow Agreement as it wished to restrict the participation of the Korean people. By this time American authorities sought to justify their already adopted policy of supporting the groups of collaborators and conservatives who would be certain to protect the gradual penetration of American economic and political interests in South Korea. As the Soviet's Molotov showed a year later in a memorandum to the American Secretary of State George Marshall, of the organizations recommended by the American Military Government for consultation, seventeen were opposed to the Moscow decision and a token three supported it. Stated in another way, the American position in the Joint Commission was tantamount to saying that General Tojo should be consulted in the creation of a democratic Japan. The conference reached no satisfactory solution.

In April, 1947 Foreign Minister Molotov submitted a three-point proposal to the U.S. Department of State as a basis for resuming Joint Commission discussions.[2] The Joint Commission reconvened in May only to adjourn once again without any agreement. The point of departure was still the major question regarding the kinds of organizations to be consulted in the formulation of a Korean provisional government.

From these two conferences it became clear to the Korean people that their independence was still in the distant future. The Koreans were forced to conclude that the United States was in principle fundamentally opposed to the international agreement and was using and aiding the conservatives. It seemed to be the American intention to have this articulate group create the impression that the anti-Moscow decision was the true and popular wish of Korea. The United States hoped that the situation would provide the moral justification to

202

abandon in toto the international agreement, making it possible to push through her own economic and political interests in South Korea, as happened in later days. Although the American Military Government in the beginning attempted to maneuver within the framework of the Moscow decision, it soon dropped all pretensions and facades and openly followed its unilateral policy in South Korea.

Failure of American Military Government Policy

The postwar situation in Korea offered ample opportunity for the United States to demonstrate goodwill and friendship by tangibly aiding Koreans in recovering from the oppressive Japanese rule. When American troops landed in South Korea, they were joyously welcomed by the Korean people as liberators. Despite this advantage, the American Military Government from the very outset taxed to the extreme any feeling of friendship the Koreans had for the American occupation troops.

During the first few days after liberation the American Military Government declared a policy of "non-fraternization," forbidding American soldiers to acquaint themselves with the Korean people. It could hardly be argued that health consideration was the sole reason for the measure. And still less could it be thought that Korea was an occupied enemy state where a non-fraternization policy would be appropriate. Soon, American soldiers were engaged in "gook" hunting. "Gook" is an American derogatory term referring to Koreans. It originally came from the word "mi-gook," or "America," which the Americans interpreted as "megook" or "I am a gook" when Koreans welcomed the Americans. The episode was an unfortunate affair which American authorities condoned at the time.

Immediately after the end of the war, Dr. Syngman Rhee, aged conservative political leader who spent thirty-three years of exile in the United States, was flown to Korea under State Department instruction. He had at one time participated in the anti-Japanese struggle and was president of the Korean provisional government in exile. Consequently, the American Military Government sought to use him as "the Korean leader." He was, to be sure, thoroughly oriented towards American interests. As a matter of fact, prior to his departure, Dr. Rhee had committed himself to secret transactions with financiers concerning Korean mining industries worth two million dollars. Thus, the man who was destined to play an important role in Korean politics already had tied himself to the American business world before he got to Korea.

In regard to probably the most crucial economic question in the South, the AMG confiscated 353,000 jungbo of Japanese owned land, which accounted for 83 percent of the total cultivated land. It declared these lands for sale, a maximum of ten jungbo to a person, thus putting the buyer in the landlord category. According to this plan, there would have been created 35,000 more small holders. In practice, however, this theoretical figure was considerably reduced and the position of the large landlords was enhanced. Consider who had money to purchase the properties:

1. Present landlords and big business interests who bought directly and also through black market deals, providing the money and acquiring land under other names;

2. Those able to borrow money from landlords and wealthy people, generally through blood relationships and marriages.

This reconcentration of farm lands had its subsequent effect on the rice policy in the early part of 1946. Despite an extremely good rice harvest the previous year in the South, a 60 percent increase, and the fact that compulsory export of rice to Japan had stopped, the American Military Government's "principle of free enterprise in matters of trade and commerce" virtually choked off the supply of rice to the population. Landlords and merchants hoarded the harvest in warehouses and attempted to raise the price of rice through this artificial scarcity. Consequently, while during the war the people were able to obtain 2.3 "hops" of rice per person a day from the Japanese, in 1946 there was barely one "hop" available. In the midst of plenty, starvation was still rampant.

Similar disastrous practices guided disposition of Japanese industrial enterprises. The American Military Government took over all these establishments and created the "New Korea Company." Shares and interests were sold to individuals and corporations, purportedly to encourage the development of native economic resources and capital. However, this plan was rendered meaningless by the pouring in of war surplus goods which were rusting in the South Pacific, and finished commodities which were either of no practical value or stifled native industries. To illustrate this point, let us take the dispute which arose in May, 1948. Hydroelectric plants in North Korea had been supplying power to the whole of the South, and in payment, which was already two years in arrears, the North Korean government asked the AMG for electrical equipment. There were shortages of such equipment to meet the urgent demands created by the developing economy. The American authority refused and, instead, offered "nylon stockings, tobacco, and Hollywood films." The North simply shut off the electricity and waited.

This American policy of dumping ravaged the economy in the South. Figures for 1948 show the textile industry, largest in that part of the country, declined by 67 percent compared to the previous year; heavy industry and farm machinery suffered losses of 50 percent. Moreover, the AMG, shortly after arrival, completely dismantled six large factories of key importance, either burying the equipment or throwing it into the sea.

In 1948, there were more than 1 million unemployed out of a rough total of 16 million people. Due to inflationary prices, real wages of workers were about one-fifth of that before liberation. The lives of farm-tenants were no better. The attempts of the workers to solve these pressing economic problems were met with rebuff by the American authority. The American Military Government stressed that there would be no jobs if there were no business; therefore, business must be protected first. With the "business first" concept, any agitation from workers was not tolerated. Leaders of the Korean Federation of Trade Union were imprisoned, and members intimidated by mass arrests. Finally, the workers' committees, which were formed in factories after the liberation, were dissolved and replaced by collaborators. Not only the workers but the whole population were angered.

The American Military Government was quick to sense the seriousness of the situation and forthwith promulgated Ordinance 55 regulating the activities of political organizations. Under its dictum, any group of three or more persons constituted an organization and, to conduct any form of political activity, had to be registered as a political party. Furthermore, it required that complete membership lists and addresses, plus financial records be submitted to the American authority. Persons not members of the organization were forbidden to make financial contributions. Violators of this regulation were to be subject to civil or criminal prosecution. The measure was clearly aimed at the resistance of democratic forces in South Korea. The trade union groups denounced this repressive act and described it as "more vicious and severe than the peace preservation law of the Japanese."

The path of political suppression centered first in eliminating the communists. Accordingly, on May 18, 1946, the American authority indefinitely suspended publication of *Haibang Ilbo or The Emancipation Daily*, organ of the Workers' (communist) Party of South Korea. The official pretext was that the building in which the newspaper was located, formerly Japanese property, was under the control of the American Military Government. All former Japanese properties were under the control of the American authority at that time. Besides, the American authority claimed that it found that the Chikasawa Printing Shop which was also located in the same building had printed fraudulent currency.

The Korean Democratic National Front, a broad coalition which developed from the People's Republic, made a statement which denounced as irrelevant the accusation of the currency fraud incident and defended the

Workers' Party and its organ, *Haibang Ilbo*.[3]

The AMG was unable to offer the least evidence to substantiate its charges against the communists but, nonetheless, continued the persecution, eventually driving the organization underground and declaring a reward for the apprehension of its general secretary, Park Heun-Young. Three more newspapers were soon closed up: *Inminbo or People's News, Hyundai Ilbo or Modern Daily News,* and *Chungang Ilbo, or Central Daily News.* Editors critical of the American Military Government were imprisoned. The Americans were now outdoing their Japanese predecessors in filling the prisons with Korean patriots. In American-occupied South Korea, the number of those jailed was twice the number during the Japanese regime for both North and South Korea.

The disastrous chain of events in postwar Korea pivoted around three conservative political figures: Syngman Rhee, Kim Koo, and Kim Seung-soo. Consequently, some have regarded the failure of American policy in South Korea as a simple unfortunate mistake on the part of the AMG in having relied on the advice of these three leaders. The claim has been advanced that the United States was not well acquainted with Korean affairs and badly prepared to undertake the occupation of that country, and therefore, the mistakes were inevitable but not deliberate. There has been a consistency and cohesiveness to American policy in South Korea which raises very serious doubt whether the American authority had any real intention of building a democratic Korea.

In one year after liberation, the Korean people had suffered enough, had experienced bitter disillusionment enough, that outbreaks occurred throughout South Korea in the proportions of a mass, popular revolt. It started in September, 1946 when the Railway Worker's Union submitted a list of grievances to be negotiated with the AMG. The following is a part of the strike diary issued by the Korean Federation of Trade Unions.

On September 15, 1946, the South Korean Railway Workers' Union, a member of the KFTU, submitted its demands to the Transportation and Railway Bureau of the American Military Government and requested an answer within a week. The demands were: (1) Four "hops" of rice per worker per day, three "hops" per day for each dependent; (2) Increase of living cost differential to 2,000 won (Korean currency) and 600 won for family allowance; (3) Abolition of the daily pay system; (4) Withdrawal of the planned cut in the number of employees; (5) Continuation of lunch service; (6) Institution of democratic labor laws, freedom of press, speech and assembly, the right to organize, bargain collectively and right of labor to strike.[4]

On September 21, 1946, the American Military Government ignored the union's demands. Having received no reply within seven days, the union requested KFTU to intercede in its behalf. Two delegates from KFTU called on General Hodge, the American commanding office in Seoul, and requested his mediation. The general denied the request.

On September 23, 1946, 7,000 railway workers in Pusan, largest port in South Korea, went out on strike, followed by the entire membership of eighteen locals of the Railway Workers' Union. There were about 36,000 workers on strike.

On September 24, General Learch, American Military Governor, made a special radio broadcast in which he declared the strike illegal and said all strikers were liable to arrest. He explained that since the AMG was the legal owner of the railway, all railroad workers were government employees and that it was illegal for them to strike against the government.

This summary declaration by General Learch was reinforced by General Hodge who, discarding all pretenses, urged the Korean people "to exterminate the elements who organize strikes and provoke discontent. "

Sensing the threat to the entire Korean labor movement, workers in all major industries joined the strike which quickly developed into a general strike, involving about 330,000 workers in communications, electrical, metal, chemical, printing, transportation, food, textile, and shipping trades. The strike demands of all unions were essentially the same as those of the railway workers unions. All unions demanded an adequate rice ration and all unions stressed their demand for democratic labor laws. The only variations in demands pertained to local situations where the release of arrested leaders and strikers was sought.

Thus, for the first time in Korean history, a general strike affected all areas throughout South Korea, completely tying up transportation and communication and shutting down all plants and factories. In Pusan, seventy armed policemen, seven detectives and three American MPs attacked the strikers in attempts to arrest the union leaders.

On September 26, in Seoul, police launched a systematic attack on all local strike headquarters, arresting union leaders and strikers. The next day, police intensified attacks on workers in all provinces of South Korea and mass arrests took place in all towns and districts. On September 28, armed police surrounded and attacked the workers' dormitories in Taigu City, slaying several workers.

On September 30, more than two thousand armed policemen and American MPs in Seoul attacked the strikers, injuring about forty of them, killing one, and arresting seventeen hundred strikers.

The violence used against the workers only strengthened their determination and solidarity and raised the wrath of the entire population to white heat. By the first part of October, workers, peasants and students of the eight provinces of South Korea were clashing with the Korean constabulary and American troops which were sent under a declaration of martial law to quell the uprisings. An estimated 100,000 students of universities and high schools participated in sympathy strikes.

The case of the students in the city of Taigu will provide an insight into the nature of this movement. On October 2, 1946, the students of the Taigu Medical School, the Teacher's College, and Agricultural College, as well as those from high and middle schools, were having an orderly demonstration through the city, carrying the bodies of several slain workers. The procession was halted in front of the police station where two machine guns were installed and more than a hundred policemen waited, ready to fire a deadly volley into the crowd. The chief of police ordered the demonstrators to disperse. Three more truckloads of police arrived at the scene. The nervous excitement heightened, but the students maintained their ranks solidly and demanded the police force he withdrawn. The police disregarded the appeal, whereupon the students rushed into the police station in waves and occupied it before anyone was injured. They were successful, for the police were uneasy and reluctant to shoot, facing thousands of courageous young people. In fact, many of the policemen threw away their weapons and joined the students. The students quickly made full use of this opportune situation by forcing police to concede to three points: (1) Release of all democrats from jail; (2) No retaliatory action by the police; (3) Police duties to be performed without arms.[5]

Meanwhile, American tanks and motorized units were mobilized in the city and attacked the demonstrators in the afternoon, leaving a wake of mutilated and murdered youths. This was on October second. An International News Service report of october 4 stated twenty-four hours of bloody rioting occurred with thirty-eight police officers and an undetermined number of civilians killed; the city looked like a veritable battlefield.[6] Radio Moscow reported severe fighting even up to October 20.

In the port city of Inchon the workers "arrested" local officials and took over municipal buildings. In Kyonggi Province 10,000 people participated in a virtual armed insurrection. So tremendous was this upheaval in South Korea that in one instance on October 14 the AMG found it necessary to send the Sixth Infantry Division in full battle order to Kyongsang Province, where some 36,000 railway workers were putting the local police to route. The National Chief of Police described the situation as "worse than the 1919 anti-Japanese revolution."

The spontaneous uprising, despite its vigor and popular support, was still a disorganized expression of anger and dissatisfaction. The democratic

208

forces, despite their potential, were not yet congealed into a solid fighting front. Moreover, effective leadership and guidance of the movement were quickly lost through brutal suppression waged by the AMG. For example, by the end of october, the last person in the central leadership of the KFTU was arrested. Within two months from the beginning of the general strike, the uprising, for the most part, was crushed.

Contrary to what General Hodge alluded to be the precipitating factors, "elements who . . . provoke discontentment," the summary by the Korean Democratic National Front laid the full responsibility on the American Military Government.

Why the revolts? There are a few suggestions which could be considered as indirect causes of the revolts. First of all, owing to the scarcity of food, the people were in a state of starvation. Notwithstanding this, the foodstuffs collected to date had not as yet been distributed to the people. Second, without any definite policy to promote the welfare of the people, the American Military Government had employed after liberation the same vicious officials of the Japanese regime. As a result, oppression of the people by these militarists and national traitors was intensified. Third, American Military Government ordinances changed so rapidly, and corrupt officials violated the laws so frequently, that the people simply had no faith in the American Military authority. Fourth, the American Military Government policy in denying fundamental liberties was considered by many worse than that of former Japanese masters.

Against this background, there were two important immediate reasons which caused the revolts. First, despite the reasonableness of the demands of strikers, who reflected the desires of all working people, strikers were illegally shot to death on numerous occasions by police forces. Second, in the summer grain collection, the American Military Government disregarded entirely the welfare of the peasants and, in addition, used unfair and illegal methods in extorting the grain.

Notes

1. U.S. Department of State, *Bulletin,* Washington, D.C., 1945, p. 1004.
2. Molotov's three points were: (1.) The establishment of a provisional Korean democratic government with broad participation of Korean democratic parties and social organizations; restoration of Korea as a democratic and independent state; and development of its national economy and culture. (2.) The establishment of democratic bodies of power throughout Korea by

free elections on the basis of general and equal suffrage. (3.) Aid to Korea to expedite political and economic unity as a self-governed state independent of foreign interference, which fact would eliminate the division of the country into two zones.

3. The statement said: "From political common sense there is no reason for the Worker's Party and its leaders to have been involved in such a brazen act as the currency fraud. The Worker's Party most bravely fought against Japanese imperialism for Korea's liberation and is now faithfully fighting for the establishment of Korean self-government and democracy. All its leaders have sacrificed and given their lives for the Korean people."

4. Statements are based on information sheets distributed by the union during the disturbances.

5. Based on an interview of a former medical student in Taigu city during the author's visit in the summer of 1961.

6 *Internahonal News Service,* Washington, D.C., Oct. 4, 1946.

11

The Cold War Begins in Korea

The American-Soviet Joint Commission held its forty-second meeting on July 14, 1947 in Seoul. This session, as was also true with the previous ones, was concerned with seeking agreement on the list of Korean organizations to be consulted preliminary to the formation of a central provisional government.

The American authorities insisted "all groups" be eligible for consultation, especially those opposed to the Moscow Decision, namely, Syngman Rhee and Kim Koo. Although the American authority insisted "all groups" be available for consultation, Americans significantly excluded the bulk of the democratic organizations, including the Korean Federation of Trade Unions, the Korean Women's Association, the Korean Youth Alliance and the Korean Peasants' Union, which alone had a membership of three million.

The Soviet delegation, on the other hand, insisted on including these organizations. The disagreement was a serious one. It was not purely coincidence that anti-trusteeship elements were also the landlords, big businessmen, and the collaborators who had associated with Japanese interests in the past and were so unprincipled as not to hesitate one minute in doing so again. It would have been very difficult to expect any of these elements to fulfill the wishes, the overwhelmingly popular wishes of the Korean people for a free and independent Korea.

The American Military Government remained adamant, and thus an apparent "impasse" was created. Then, on September 17, 1947, General George Marshall presented a prepared address in the U.N., calling upon the

General Assembly to deliberate on the Korean question. This was an unilateral action entirely unjustified. First, it was outside the jurisdiction of the United Nations organization, and secondly, the problem was far from being as incapable of solution or deadlocked as the United States insisted. Possibilities for a successful outcome of negotiations had not been exhausted. The reason for the maneuver was that in the U.N. the United States could wield its influence effectively over a large number of members of the world body. In short, the United States hoped to achieve in the U.N. what it could not achieve in direct discussion with the U.S.S.R.

The U.N. General Assembly voted to place the Korean question on the agenda and referred it to the First Committee for initial discussion and report.

A few days later in Seoul, the Soviet delegate on the U.S. and Soviet Joint Commission proposed both American and Soviet occupation troops withdraw simultaneously from Korea at the beginning of 1948 and allow the Korean people to organize their own government without outside interference. This suggestion was also submitted to Secretary of State Marshall in October.

The U.S. proposed to the U.N. General Assembly that elections be held in the Soviet and American zones before March 31, 1948, and these elections be under U.N. supervision as a first step toward establishment of a national government. To supervise the elections and to help in the subsequent steps of establishing security forces and organizing a government, the United States proposed establishment of a U.N. Temporary Commission on Korea. The General Assembly approved the American resolution on November 13, 1947.[1]

Andrei Gromyko, debating the resolution before the General Assembly, characterized the American plan as "putting everything upside down." He insisted that the evacuation of foreign troops must precede the election of representative organs and the establishment of a democratic government in Korea, but the evacuation would be considered as the concluding measure in the chain of events proposed in the U.S. plan. He complained that the U.S. proposal contained a formula which did not obligate anybody to do anything. He stated that the elections had to take place while foreign troops were still present in Korea under the United States plan. Naturally the foreign troops would interfere in the elections, he said.

Already enough Korean patriots were imprisoned and enough democratic organizations persecuted, made illegal and driven underground to render meaningless any election as projected by the United States. It was akin to gagging a man and then telling him he had all the freedom of speech he wanted. Also, the experiences of various U.N. commissions, specifically the

Balkan Commission, had provided ample evidence to judge the action of this new body a foregone conclusion.

The Soviet Union boycotted further proceedings of the Temporary Commission on Korea which, the U.S.S.R. delegation contended, was set up without the participation of the Korean people. Earlier the Soviet Union had submitted a draft resolution to invite elected representatives from both North and South Korea to take part in the discussion of the question. The Americans disagreed, insisting that the elective character of these representatives be first assured through a United Nations-sponsored election. In other words, the U.N. should decide the fate of fifty million Korean people and then ask them what they thought of it. The logic of this plan was "to put everything upside down." Consequently, with the Soviet Union boycott in effect, any U.N. election had to be confined to the South, and the resulting government would be a separatist regime, not a national one. That was not the end Korean people wished for, but they were not allowed to express their desires.

The Korean people reacted quickly and indignantly to this new American proposal. All shades of political opinion were united in opposition and refused cooperation with the U.N. Commission. Even before the American proposals were formally acted upon by the General Assembly, twelve major political parties in South Korea assembled to form a Joint Committee based on (1) a demand for immediate recall of occupation troops and (2) calling of a national election for the formation of a united central government. The committee also proposed a meeting to be convened in the near future of representatives from both sections of the country – a significant step to national unity.

The Korean Public Opinion Institute in Seoul showed 71 percent of the people in the South definitely against the U.N. election and only 11 percent supporting it. Press dispatches in February of the following year reported widespread sabotage of rail traffic and telegraph communication lines in protest to the election. AMG authorities announced the death of eighteen civilians and four policemen and the arrest of one hundred fifty in violent demonstrations.

After conducting an initial investigation, Krisna P. S. Menon of India, chairman of the U.N. Commission on Korea, and Victor Hoo, secretary, flew back to Lake Success from Seoul to report to the Little Assembly. They stated the commission was "all but unanimous" in thinking a separate government elected and set up in the American zone cannot be a national government." Whereupon Dr. Phillip Jessup, American delegate, served notice the United States would press for the establishment of a government in the South which would be recognized as a representative national body.

On February 26, 1948, the Little Assembly by a vote of 31 to 8 instructed the Commission on Korea to proceed with preparations for a separate election in South Korea, which was to be conducted not later than May 10 of that year.

During the debate in the Little Assembly, Ralph Harry of Australia, a member nation of the commission, expressed skepticism as to the advisability of the proposed action. He was fearful of the danger in creating "rival authorities in North and South Korea." Lester Pearson, Canadian Under-Secretary of External Affairs, warned the Little Assembly his government might consider withdrawing from the commission should it follow a course which he considered "unconstitutional and incorrect."

Meanwhile, important developments were taking place in Korea. During February the Central People's Council, which as the result of the November, 1946 elections in North Korea assumed the functions of the previous Interim Committee, drafted a constitution to be distributed through both zones of Korea and discussed by the people. The charter called for a popularly elected assembly which would choose a fifteen member presidium as the central administrative organ, provided for government ownership of all mines, forests, utilities and major industries, and abolished absentee landlordism. It was adopted on May 1, 1948, by the Central Council and approved by the Korean Unity Conference.

A few days before, on April 22, 545 delegates from fifty-six political and social organizations of both zones, with a combined representation of ten million Koreans, met in Pyongyang to hold the Korean Unity Conference. This event occurred in the midst of preparations for a separate election in the South and was a tremendous blow to the AMG machinations. Among the many representatives from South Korea, there were none other than Kim Koo, regarded as the second most powerful rightist leader, and Dr. Kimm Kieu-sik, hand-picked president of the AMG Interim Legislative Assembly. The AMG, by way of rather blunt reasoning, branded the Unity Conference as a "strictly communist run and dominated affair" since the meeting was held in Pyongyang. The presence of Kim Koo and Kimm Kieu-sik, two avowed anti-communists, however, contradicted the claims of American authorities.

The Unity Conference denounced the coming election in the South, and advocated national unity, a common appeal strong enough to overcome certain of the existing political differences. The resolution adopted by the conference castigated the U. S. for refusing to accept the proposal of simultaneous withdrawal of troops from Korea and demanded the unlawful, coercive and unreasonable election in South Korea be stopped and that the U.N. commission leave immediately.

After three weeks of full discussion, the Unity Conference proposed: establishment of a unified government for all Korea through a general election in both parts of the country, establishment of a democratic government by rejecting any form of dictatorship, recognition of private property rights and rejection of monopoly capitalism, rejection of military bases for any foreign nation in Korea, and other matters of national concern. The conference was, indeed, an important step toward national unification.

Politics with Terror

On March 1, 1948, Lt. General John R. Hodge, American commander in South Korea, issued a proclamation in which he announced May 9, subsequently postponed a day, as the date of national elections in South Korea. Twelve days later in Seoul preparations for the event began. Cho Byong-ok, chief of the national police, called the heads of the district police forces to brief them on instructions which explicitly stated that the police were to deal severely with anyone opposing the election and support in every way those individuals and organizations which supported it. To implement this policy, the chief established ''Police Election Committees'' consisting of the local chief of police, the local chief investigator, and the local chief of public safety on all district levels.

The constabulary w as mobilized and equipped with the latest American weapons. In April, Major General William F. Dean ordered the formation of ''Hyangbo-dan'' or community protective corps, which were to function as auxiliary agencies to the local police force during the election. On the 30th of April, Cho Byong-ok circulated instructions to all police stations to shoot down anyone obstructing the election. The following day, the AMG issued Order 21 totally prohibiting any assemblage and demonstrations until after the election.

Korean right wing terrorists now went to work. Their special task w as to call on every house and see to it that people were registered to vote and that they cast their ballots on election day. These hoodlums, carrying clubs and baseball bats, played havoc - sadistically beating innocent people and threatening them with imprisonment unless they voted. American troops also cooperated in this campaign by carrying the unconscious victims in their jeeps and trucks to the election booths.

These, then, were the elaborate preparations to insure ''a free and fair election,'' to insure an ''atmosphere conducive to a proper and unhampered expression of the people's desires.''

On May 10, election day, American warships - employed in a similar manner as in the Greek plebiscite–ominously cruised up and down the southern coastline. American fighter planes roared endlessly overhead. In the city streets, heavily armed MPs drove about in their jeeps.

In Seoul, for example, the newspaper *Jayu Shinmoon* or *Free Press* reported "several thousands of police and specially hired civilians in cooperation with the United States occupation forces erected barricades on main roads and intersections of the city, and at every entrance to a back alley of the city were stationed armed police."[2]

At every booth in the city were placed twenty policemen and two detectives, and also the Election Committees were there to supervise the voters. Members of the Hyangbo-dan were seen everywhere, herding the more reluctant citizens to the polls with their menacing clubs.

Despite all the precautions taken by the AMG and the reactionaries, the people resisted. Cho Byung-ok later reported that between February 7 and May 25 more than eight thousand instances of resistance took place, including 44 strikes and 244 demonstrations. Students were particularly active in this movement. The Korean Federation of Trade Unions called two general work stoppages: one in February on the arrival of the U.N. Commission, and the other on May 8, two days before the election.

The most outstanding incident during this period was the outbreak on the island of Cheju, off the southern tip of the mainland. Koreans call it the "Paradise of the South Sea" since there are no beggars, no thieves, no disorders which might disrupt the peaceful life of the island. The inhabitants were hard working and not quickly prone to take to violence. But on April 3, the series of outrages committed by the corrupt officials and gangs of terrorists followed by the announcement of the separate election culminated in an armed uprising by the people. On that day alone, police stations at thirteen points on the island were attacked. Although the AMG hastily dispatched the constabulary, the fighters effectively continued the struggle for months after, until the establishment of a People's Committee in full control of the island.

In all, nearly five hundred people were murdered in South Korea and scores upon scores were beaten and imprisoned.

The newspaper *Jayu Shinmoon* commented: "Although the election day was a holiday, the city was surrounded by an atmosphere of being under martial law. Korean w omen used to put on yellow- or green-colored smart dresses on Sundays and holidays, but on this particular day they put on yellow-whitish dull dresses or slacks. They were seen looking around them as they cautiously went to the election booths.... Throughout the city of Seoul none but children laughed."[3] The conservative Catholic newspaper, *Kyung-hyang Shinmun,* also made a similar statement.[4]

By whatever criterion of democratic procedure, the South Korean election was a far cry from any semblance of a free election. The election regulations were drawn up in such a way as to guarantee the results in favor of the rightist candidates. The Department of State declared that the election received public approval and enthusiasm. If there were any "enthusiasm and public approval," it was the perverted enthusiasm of the Hyangbo-dan and the police; it was the approval of the handful of reactionary politicians.[5]

On June 25, the U.N. Temporary Commission on Korea reported to the General Assembly that a reasonable degree of free atmosphere characterized the election. Despite the dominant and decisive voice of the American government, the unconcealed violations of basic civil rights could not be ignored, and three member nations of the U.N. Commission dissented, refusing to give their full endorsement to this mockery of democracy. James Roper, United Press correspondent, described how in one instance he witnessed members of a U.N. observers team reprimand inspectors at three election booths for illegally searching voters within the designated area of the polls. As an illustration of the mockery of fairness, anyone running unopposed in a particular election district was automatically assured office even if all the votes were cast against him. Consequently Syngman Rhee was elected even before the ballots were counted since his terrorist supporters succeeded in persuading his opponent to withdraw.

The rightists won the election of those elected representatives who formed the National Assembly, forty-eight were landlords and thirty-two were capitalists; not a single worker or peasant was elected. At its first session, the assembly chose Syngman Rhee president of this newly created regime, and he then proceeded to select his cabinet or State Council from the ranks of his faithful followers.

The Americans called them "men of experience in government and politics."

However, in five months a split occurred between these worthy gentlemen of the Assembly and Rhee. The forty-eighth meeting of the assembly charged him with including collaborators in his cabinet, specifically:

Lim Moon Wha, assistant in the Ministry of Commerce and Industry, who had served the Japanese as head of a county and was a high official in the Department of Mining and Industry;

Yoo Jin Oh, assistant in the Ministry of Law, who had participated in the Japanese-sponsored Great Asia Cultural Conference; and

Min Heu-sik, Minister of Communication, who held a high position in a Japanese public high school.

As soon as Rhee took office, as election rewards he began to appoint incompetent individuals to lucrative government positions, especially in the diplomatic service, which was absorbing a great part of the budget. The charges against these three individuals are undoubtedly true, but for that matter all the leaders of the government were implicated in one way or another with the Japanese, or were presently supporting collaborators.

The complete inability of the administration to meet the real and immediate needs of the people began to wear thin the cloak of legality so precariously acquired through the U. N. election. Living conditions had not improved, political suppression had gone unabated, rampant corruption of government officials was tolerated – how could it be reasonably argued that this government represented the Korean people?

On October 20, 1948, members of the 14th Regiment of the National Army of South Korea stationed in Yosu mutinied. The previous day this particular unit received orders to proceed to the island of Cheju, about 170 kilometers off the coast, in a punitive expedition against the population, which was continuing its armed resistance started in the spring in connection with the election.

The soldiers and officers rallied together the people of Yosu and captured all strategic points and buildings. A mass meeting was called. The entire population of Yosu, more than forty thousand people, responded enthusiastically and declared their loyalty to the Korean Democratic People's Republic, which was formed two months before and had its provisional capital in Pyongyang. From October 20 to 26 the elected People's Committee administered and defended the city against the troops,[6]

The strategy of the mutiny was not to hold Yosu but to go to the nearby Chiri Mountains and surrounding districts and establish bases for extended guerrilla warfare. The insurgents left the city as quickly as possible and joined forces with others who had gone ahead and captured Sunchon, a neighboring town, and had enlisted more volunteers. Together – now numbering more than four thousand – they succeeded in arriving safely at their destinations and laid the basis for the national liberation movement which then covered more than half of South Korea.[7]

The people of Sunchon and Yosu, for the most part youths armed with old Japanese rifles, were to hold the towns as long as possible to cover the retreat of the partisans.[8]

Realizing fully that this event might very well kindle the whole South in open rebellion, the government launched a desperate attack to crush the uprising. No longer could Syngman Rhee indulge in wishful thinking that it was merely a sporadic and isolated outbreak. The existence of the People's Republic in the North made a powerful rallying point for the people.

Government troops, equipped with modern American weapons, tanks, armored cars and ten times stronger numerically, attacked Yosu on October 24. They were supported by shell fire from American warships lying off shore. Despite this military superiority, it took the 3rd, 5th, 12th, and reformed 14th Regiments two days of fierce fighting to overcome the rebellious forces of Yosu. The defenders fought to the last man. Not one surrendered.[9]

The retaliation that followed was an orgy of cruel and inhuman massacre. The *Noryukja* or Toiler, an underground newspaper in Seoul, wrote, "Many tens of thousands of innocent people were arrested and stripped naked on the playgrounds of the schools, and then, the enemy took out before the firing squad any person he pleased. Thus, many thousands of innocent people were executed...."[10]

North Korea

On August 25, 1948, elections called by the People's Council in Pyongyang were held in both zones of Korea. In the North, according to Pyongyang, 99 percent of eligible voters cast their ballots, while in the South, 77 percent of the people defied violent opposition to vote through underground election committees.[11]

The Supreme People's Assembly of the gathered representatives was to be the highest body of the republic, and Pyongyang, the provisional capital city. The constitution, drafted in February of the same year and tentatively adopted by the People's Council of the North, was discussed and ratified by the assembly as the basic charter of the state.

In compliance with the request of the new government, the Soviet Union began to withdraw her troops amidst tumultuous manifestations of friendship and gratitude by the Korean people. Evacuation was completed before the December 31 deadline. The same note requesting troop renewal submitted to the United States was ignored on grounds the southern regime asked for prolongation of occupation.

At the second plenary session of the People's Assembly on January 28, 1949, Premier Kim Il-sung stated: "The democratic foundation of the Korean People's Democratic Republic has been firmly consolidated; the most important economic basis for the development of our state laid; the standard of the people's material and cultural life elevated day by day; and the conditions created in which many daily necessaries of the people can be manufactured."[12]

The task now was to defend and strengthen the republic and carry out the unification of the divided nation, he believed. Kim Il-sung further stated: "The Two Year Plan will raise the living standard of the people by strengthening all the more firmly the economic foundation for the northern half of the Korean People's Democratic Republic. Not only that. When our fatherland is unified, this Plan will create basic conditions for a rapid restoration of those factories and places of enterprise as well as the railway transportation services in the southern half of the Republic which have been destroyed. And also it will create conditions in which the living standard of our compatriots in the South, who are groaning under the suppression and terrorism and who are suffering from starvation, can he rapidly elevated."[13]

The plan, for example, envisaged an increase by 143.2 percent in 1949 in industrial production as compared to 1948 and projected another 194.1 percent increase in 1950. In this connection, it should be borne in mind that the mountainous regions of the North afford little opportunity to raise production by the extension of lands under cultivation. Consequently, the problem would have to be solved in the main by improved scientific methods of agriculture and rational utilization of the soil. In education, the plan called for an overall expansion of facilities in 1949 to provide for compulsory education to go into effect in 1950 for the first time in the history of Korea. Also, a goal of 77,700 additional staff members and technicians was set for the end of the plan. This is merely a glimpse into the ambitious program the Korean people set for themselves, imbued now with greater zeal to build a strong and prosperous homeland.

Another historic step forward during this period was the Korea Soviet Agreement for Economic and Cultural Assistance signed on March 17, 1949, in Moscow. The Korean delegation, headed by Premier Kim ll-sung and Park Heun-Young, Vice-Premier and Foreign Minister, met with Premier Stalin and Vice-Premier Molotov during the first week of March.

"In an atmosphere of friendship, with a spirit of understanding and aid, and on an equal footing," Kim said later in his report, "we carried on our discussion with the Soviet delegation."

The result was a treaty valid for ten years, whereby the two contracting countries, on the basis of assistance, equality and mutual interests, vowed to leave no stone unturned in strengthening and developing their commercial relations as well as relations in the fields of culture, science and the arts. A satisfactory arrangement on the list of commodities and raw materials to be exchanged was promised. Because Korean imports from the Soviet Union would exceed her exports, the Soviet government established a credit of 212 million rubles for Korea, starting from July 1949 and extending until July 1952 . The Soviet Union also agreed to lend technical assistance in the reconstruction of Korea, and moreover, to train Korean students in various sciences. A provision was made for common exchanges of experiences in agriculture, industry and culture. The agreement w ás equitable and no party derived any special advantage from it to the detriment of the other. This was an extension of the basic Soviet policy that "The dependent countries should be enabled as soon as possible to take the path of independence."

Compare this treaty with that concluded by the southern regime with the United States in the fall of 1948. As it was, even prior to the agreement, the Americans had gradually crippled the South Korean economy by predatory policies. In the agreement, Americans gained an unchallenged monopoly, for example, over the mining, fuel and transportation industries. Among the strands of the tight network of American interests, the Standard and Texas Oil Companies controlled jointly the entire liquid fuel industry through their Daihan (Korean) Petroleum Company. Further, the United States insured its position by stipulating that private investment by foreigners in Korea as well as entry of private traders of all countries be facilitated. This was simply one of the many clauses making South Korea subject to foreign control again.

The events of the past were not without meaning to the people of Korea. Especially in the South, bitter lessons of experience were deeply ingrained. The artificial division of the country – the very condition which kept Syngman Rhee's dictatorship in power – had to go. Toward this end, the Democratic Front for the Unification of the Fatherland was created in Pyongyang on June 25, 1949, by delegates of nineteen organizations from the North and forty-nine from the South. This body was a loose coalition centered on the premise that for any further progress toward independence, Korea first had to be unified. The main points agreed upon were:

1. Immediate withdrawal of American troops from the South, which is the basis of the puppet regime, the force that maintains it.

2. Recognition of and support to the People's Democratic Republic of Korea as the legally and democratically instituted government.

3. Mobilization of the people in a struggle against traitors who are hindering unification.

4. Struggle to carry out in the South land reform, nationalization of basic industries and the guarantee of the elementary rights of a citizen in a democratic state.

The Democratic Front called for a peaceful unification. It realized fully the entire population was in complete accord with the demand of unification. Indeed, the points raised by the Democratic Front were the crystallized expressions of the masses. Consequently, unification was not a conspiracy that had to be imposed by force.

In its efforts to arrive at a solution, the Democratic Front was even willing to concede its recognition of the People's Republic as the legitimate government. Instead, it proposed an immediate general election in both parts of Korea to decide the issue in a democratic manner. Rhee declined the offer. He was quite aware of his precarious position.

The whole South Korean regime was beginning to shake to its very foundations. The despotism that it was creating by violent force would have to generate its motion of existence. Up to July 1949, 93,000 Koreans were massacred, and 154,000 imprisoned in South Korea. The worst incident occurred on Cheju Island where 30,000 people were slaughtered in one month in the spring of 1948. Demagogic appeals to "patriotism," and "a fight to death against Communism," were used to whip up and bolster the morale of the South Korean troops. The officers were boasting everywhere that they were ready to invade the North at the moment President Syngman Rhee gave the order.

The only "invasions" to the North were sporadic forays into the border regions. They were not military expeditions but simply attempts to harass and spread terror among farmers in small villages. The Democratic Front, investigating the series of border incidents, reported some 432 armed attacks were made by the South Korean Army in 1949. The most shameful atrocities were committed by these brigands; no one was spared in the debauchery. Special service squads trained by the Americans were sent to the North to carry out specific assignments of assassinations of leading figures, to destroy railways and factories, to poison drinking water.[14]

While the South Korean army seemed to be effective in its own back yard, the whole front had flared up in rebellion. The partisan movement which started on the mainland with four thousand men after the Yosu uprising in October 1948 had gained strength. News dispatches in the fall of 1949 reported the number of guerrillas had increased by twenty-five thousand. The total figure, however, is unknown.

The fighters were now militarily and politically well trained, moving in solid groups under a unified command. Even Shin Sung Mo, Minister of Internal Affairs in the South, admitted, "Six hundred of them could withstand six thousand experienced regular troops." Most important, they had the support of the people, without which no guerrilla movement can exist. When the units attacked a car or train, they never touched the innocent passengers and their belongings. When they came down to a village from their mountain hideouts, they helped the farmers in tilling or harvesting. And at places where the guerrillas were established, land reform was immediately instituted together with all the democratic reforms so eagerly awaited for by the people.

Thus, the partisans of South Korea in the fall of 1949 were working in an area of 81 counties, including three cities, out of the total of 130 counties or– more than two-thirds of the South. Their bases controlled the spine of mountains, going from the eastern tip of the 38th parallel–the division between the North and South–running diagonally across to the south-western tip of the mainland. Consequently, this north-east and south-west diagonal completely sliced South Korea into two. People's Committees were established at three points in the Chiri Mountain area– the southern part of the diagonal- -and in the Halla Mountain on Cheju Island off the southern coast. The forces of resistance were spreading quickly throughout South Korea.[15] It required a quick decision for the Seoul regime to defend its life. A war between North and South was inevitable under such conditions.

Notes

1. Harry S. Truman, *Years of Trial and Hope* (Garden City, N.Y.: Doubleday, 1956), p 326.
2. *Jayu Shinmoon,* Seoul, May 11, 1948.
3. Ibid.
4. Kyunghyang Shinmoon, Seoul, May 11, 1948.
5. Ibid.
6. *Noryokja,* Seoul. Jan. 1, *1949.*
7. *Minju Ilbo,* Seoul, Nov. 21, *1948.*
8. President Park Chung Hee of South Korea was a commanding officer of the company which led the rebellious forces at Sunchun on Oct. 20, *1948.* He was sentenced to death but later pardoned. His life was spared in return for a list of names of the leaders. For details, see *Kyunghyang Shinmoon,* Feb. 17, *1949;Seoul Shinmoon,* Feb. 18, *1949;see also Dong-A Ilbo,* Oct. 14, 1963, and *Kyunghyang Shinmoon,* Oct. 8, 1963.
9. *Tass, Nov.* 6, 1948.
10. Noryokja, Jan. 1, 1949.
11. Ibid.
12. *Minju Chosun,* Seoul, Feb. 3, 1949.
13. Ibid.
14. Based on interviews by the author of several army officers who had *participated* in such *activities.* These officers *are* still holding *important* positions in the ROK *army.*
15 *Minju Chosun, op.* cit.

The Korean War : An Interpretation

Korea had been divided by occupation zones, and no one expected the transition from such zones to a joint American-Soviet administration and eventual independence to be quick or easy. The United States and the Soviet Union had made much effort to secure some sort of cooperation in the establishment of a unified Korea, but the two powers were not able to achieve the promises of the Moscow decision of 1945.

In his address to the Overseas Press Club on March 1, 1946, Secretary of State James F. Byrnes declared that the United States intended to prevent aggression, by force if necessary. He tempered his remarks with the assertion that he was "convinced that there is no reason for war between any of the great powers," and added that only an "inexcusable tragedy of errors could cause serious conflict between this country and Russia."

Byrnes suggested a list of "must nots" for the world's nations. As his first point, he said: "We will not, and we cannot, stand aloof if force or the threat of force is used contrary to the purpose of the United Nations Charter."[1] Regarding America's role, Secretary Byrnes declared: "The Charter forbids and we cannot allow aggression to be accomplished by coercion or pressure or by subterfuges such as political infiltration." Then, the American Secretary of State continued, "We must make it clear in advance that we do intend to act to prevent aggression, making it clear at the same time that we will not use force for any other purpose."

Four years later, the American government's attitude in the Far East, particularly with regard to Korea, changed somewhat without any clear indication of a major policy shift. Secretary of State Dean Acheson in addressing the National Press Club on January 12, 1950, on Far Eastern Policy said, "In Korea, we have taken great steps which have ended our military occupation and in cooperation with the United Nations have established an independent and sovereign country recognized by nearly all the rest of the world. We have given that nation great help in getting itself established. We are asking the Congress to continue that help until it is firmly established." Following this sympathetic introduction, Acheson drew a U. S. defense perimeter running from the Aleutians to Japan, to the Ryukyu Islands and then to the Philippines. This put Korea on the outside of the American defense orbit. But Acheson said: "We have a direct responsibility in Japan and we have a direct opportunity to act." As some authorities pointed out,[2] Acheson's statement reflected the views of the Joint Chiefs of Staff, w ho evidently felt that in case of a global war in the Far East, Korea would not be a main theatre of operations and was therefore of little strategic importance. It can be stated that, without political ideological considerations, modern war strategy cannot be understood. Purely military strategic concepts do not explain it.

President Truman asked Congress for a grant of as much as $150 million for economic assistance to South Korea while endorsing fully Acheson's now famous view of the Far East Defense Line. Acheson wrote a letter to the President on January 20, 1950, saying: "The Republic of Korea owes its existence in large measure to the United States, which freed the country from Japanese control. The peoples of the Republic of Korea, the other peoples of Asia, and the members of the United Nations under whose observation a government of the Republic of Korea was freely elected, alike look to our conduct in Korea as a measure of the seriousness of our concern, with the freedom and welfare of peoples maintaining their independence in the face of great obstacles." He added, "It is our considered judgment that if our limited assistance is continued, the Republic will have a good chance of survival as a free nation. Should such further aid be denied, that chance may well be lost and all our previous efforts perhaps prove to have been in vain." Of this letter, President Truman said: "I entirely concur in the Secretary's views as to the seriousness of this action and the necessity for its speedy rectification. I shall take up this matter with congressional leaders and urge upon them the need for immediate action, in order that important foreign policy interests of this country may be properly safeguarded."[3]

Congress reluctantly approved $60 million in aid for South Korea up to June 30, 1950. It previously authorized the same amount for an earlier period. The grant represented a reduction of $30 million from the sum originally requested by the State Department. It is interesting to note a statement in the Korean Aid Bill, "Not withstanding the provisions of any other law, the administrator shall immediately terminate aid under this section in the event of the formation in the Republic of Korea of a coalition government which includes one or more members of the Communist Party or of the party now in control of the government of northern Korea.[4]

Evidently, this clause shares no common ground with other U.S. treaties such as the United States-Australia-China and the United States-Australia-China -Philippines draft resolutions which were approved by the U.N. General Assembly on Dec. 12, 1948, and Oct. 21, 1949, respectively. These seek ''to bring about the unification of Korea,'' and call upon ''member states to refrain from any acts derogatory to the results achieved and to be achieved by the United Nations in bringing about the complete independence and the unity of Korea.'' Thus, we notice two major contradictions in the U.S. policy toward Korea: the first, the Acheson view, and second, the provision of the Korean Aid Bill, which tended to harden the division of Korea against the spirit of the U.N. resolution.

Secretary Acheson defended his position regarding aid to Korea when the Korean War began, saying, ''The defeat of the Korean Aid bill would 'bulk large' as one of the factors that encouraged the Communist attack upon the Republic of Korea.''[5]

Regardless of the hidden desire of Secretary Acheson to support the Republic of Korea, the majority of governments throughout the world were led to believe that the United States was really committed very deeply to saving the Republic of Korea.

The idea that the U. S. was not strongly committed to the survival of South Korea was strengthened when Senator Tom Connally, Chairman of the Senate Foreign Relations Committee, stated in an interview that since Korea was divided by the 38th Parallel with communists in control of the North and since the Soviet Union was close at hand, the North could easily overrun South Korea whenever it wanted to do so. He hinted that the U. S. would probably have to abandon South Korea, and if there were a large-scale military conflict, it was probable that the United States would not intervene.

on the other hand, there were among responsible decision-makers those w ho advocated war. For instance, Secretary of the Navy Francis Matthews advocated ''instituting a war to compel cooperation for peace . . . we would welcome the just aggressions for peace.'' More than any single man, General Douglas MacArthur had influenced America toward a war atmosphere. He spoke of Taiwan as a part of an island defense chain from which the United States could dominate by air power every Asian port from Vladivostok to Singapore, and Major General Orvil Anderson, Commander of the Air War College, said bluntly: ''We are at war.... Give me the order to do it and I can break up Russia's fine A-bomb nests in a week."[6]

General MacArthur's changed Japanese policy created more war tension than any single action by others. He had moved in overseeing Japan's occupation from the original goals of democratization, disarmament, and decentralization of occupied Japan toward a return of the old ruling groups of pre-war Japan in 1948. Japanese militarism was ready to come back under MacArthur's protection.

General MacArthur believed, as he advocated consistently during the Pacific War, that the fate of man's civilization would be decided in Asia, not in Europe, and he saw himself as the man who would dictate such destiny by destroying the newly-born Communist China. MacArthur declared that:

> 1000 American bombers and large quantities of surplus U.S military equipment, if utilized efficiently, could destroy the basic military strength of the Chinese Communists.[7]

Such public statements and a changing policy in Japan to rearm posed a serious threat to the People's Republic of China. It wasn't only MacArthur who followed a hard line, but Secretary of War Henry Stimson also looked forward in 1945 to the creation of a friendly Japan as America displaced the defeated enemy in Japan and Korea.[8]

The hard-line military advocates led by General MacArthur deliberately created the crisis in the Far East, and Korea was to become the battleground of another international war, much like the first Sino-Japanese war of 1894-1895, and the Russo-Japanese War of 1904-1905.

In this tense atmosphere, none other than John Foster Dulles arrived at Seoul, South Korea in June 1950 to give a moral boost to President Syngman Rhee and his government. He gave belated support to Korea in a speech:

> The American people give you their support, both moral and material, consistent with your own self-respect and your primary dependence on your own efforts. We look on you as, spiritually, a part of the United Nations which has acted with near unanimity to advance your political freedom, which seeks your unity with the North and which, even though you are technically deprived of formal membership, nevertheless requires all nations to refrain from any treat or use of force against your territorial integrity or political independence. . .
>
> The free world has no written charter, but it is no less real for that. Membership depends on the conduct of a nation itself; there is no veto. Its compulsion to common actions are powerful, because they flow from a profound sense of common destiny.

>   You are not alone. You will never be alone so long as you continue
> to play worthily your part in the great design of human freedom.[9]

Dulles' speech, however, really gave no definite support to the Koreans. He said nothing about American intervention in the case of an attack from the North, nor did Dulles speak of "more active economic and military aid." Dr. Rhee, however, took Dulles' speech as active support of the Republic of Korea in the event of a military conflict. Dulles' appearance in Korea, although his speech was ambiguous, encouraged Dr. Rhee to fulfill his lifetime ambition for the unification of Korea.

North Korea interpreted Dulles' remarks as an American intervention in South Korea in the Greek style. The Chinese certainly saw America applying the Greek solution to Asia. That's what America had tried with Chiang Kai-shek in China. It failed in China, but the hard liners blamed the Truman-Acheson-Marshall soft policy. Senator William Knowland of California favored sending American troops to fight in Asia.

Thus, the contributions toward war in Korea cannot be blamed on any single person. Rather, many individuals were involved. The establishment of a republic in the South seemed to be motivated by a desire in the United States to have a buffer zone against communism, but the U. S. government policy was indecisive, ambiguous and irresponsible to its commitment to bringing about a democratic government in Korea.

The Korean War was far more tragic than any war between two unrelated sections because it was fought by two politically split camps of one and the same people. A tragic war broke out at the 38th Parallel in the early hours of Sunday, June 25, 1950. When Northern and Southern Korean forces met, it became evident within a short time that the forces of North Korea were far superior to those of the South. Even though the South Korean army was only slightly smaller than the North Korean army, the fighting capacities of the two forces were not evenly matched. The South Koreans lacked tanks, medium-range artillery, heavy mortars, recoilless rifles, and fighter planes. The American support of ROK forces later revealed itself in the inability of South Korean forces to defend themselves against the North Korean army.

The information of the military clash was immediately reported to the United States and the United Nations by the South Korean government. A special meeting of the U.N. Security Council was called and it quickly approved by a vote of 9 to 0 a resolution that North Koreans had committed a breach of the peace, and ordered them to withdraw from South Korea and to cease military actions. President Truman then issued three orders. He directed General Douglas MacArthur to evacuate Americans from Korea, to repel attacks on airports, but to remain south of 38th parallel. General MacArthur also was ordered to get supplies and ammunition to the South Koreans and the Seventh Fleet was to be moved into a position to protect Formosa from attack.[10] Mr. Truman, hastily, without consulting other U.N. members, ordered the preparation of American troops for use if the U.N. should call for action against North Korea.

It was quickly evident that the South Koreans could not cope with the North Koreans. The capital city of Seoul fell on June 28, and the northern forces marched swiftly to occupy most of the area south of the 38th Parallel line. President Syngman Rhee's government was forced to flee Seoul and moved to Taigu, about 150 miles to the south. President Truman feared that a victory in Korea by the communists would put their planes very close to Japan, Taiwan and Okinawa. General MacArthur was directed to aid South Korea with air and naval support south of the 38th Parallel. This support was to come from elements already in his command.

The U.S. 24th Infantry Division was sent to Korea. According to American intelligence, there were about 10,000 U.S. troops and about 25,000 South Korean soldiers holding off about 90,000 North Koreans.

On July 7, the Security Council voted that U.N. forces be united under one command and requested the President of the United States to appoint the U.N. commander. President Truman named General MacArthur to this position on July 8.

This decisive year in the U.N. had started with a proposal to remove the Nationalist Chinese representative from his position in the Security Council. The Soviet Union contended that the communists, not the Nationalist government of Chiang Kai-shek, represented the people of China. When this proposal was defeated, the Soviet Union boycotted functions of the United Nations including meetings of the Security Council. Had the Soviet delegate been present to cast the U.S.S.R. veto, the U.N. would have been powerless to act in Korea. The Soviet delegate returned to assume the powers available to him in August.

On July 31, the U.S. Department of State received a report from MacArthur that North Koreans had no chance of victory. New forces arrived from the United States, the United Kingdom, Australia, New Zealand, Canada, France, the Netherlands, and Turkey, with the U.S., of course, providing the largest number.

Nearly two-thirds of the U.N. members contributed aid of some type, from medical aid and foodstuffs to actual troop commitments. Although the help furnished by the United Nations was considerable, the military action was carried on primarily by the United States. Under the command of General Douglas MacArthur the South Korean Army was regrouped and strengthened and outfitted once more for the field.

Participating U.N. members in the Korean war (or "police action") felt that Northern Korean forces were challenging the charter of the United Nations. They further believed that it was Stalin's strategy to test the willingness of non-communist nations to defend Korea.

President Truman said: "The attack upon Korea makes it plain beyond all doubt that Communism has passed beyond the use of subversion to conquer independent nations and will now use armed invasion and war. It has defied the orders of the Security Council of the United Nations issued to preserve international peace and security." The President concluded, "I know that all members of the United Nations will consider carefully the consequences of this latest aggression in Korea in defiance of the Charter of the United Nations. A return to the rule of force in international affairs would have far-reaching effects. The United States will continue to uphold the rule of law." [11]

The resources which the President had at his disposal at the outbreak of hostilities were not impressive. After World War II the United States and the other non-communist nations had demobilized rapidly, and the United States with the atomic bomb was thinking in terms of fighting a global war. In such a war, it was believed, the bomb and the ability to drop it anywhere in the world were more important than ground troops. In addition, the United States had not included Korea in its defense line against communism. Commenting on the condition of the United States armed forces, President Truman says in his *Memoirs* that the armed forces had been drastically reduced from their wartime peaks, and there was strong congressional pressure to reduce military spending even further. American commitments were many, but the forces were limited. The United States had some occupational troops in Japan, and the only other immediate military resources were air and naval forces. The South Korean Army was armed only for defense, not to fight tanks and heavy artillery.

Considering the reduced state of military forces at hand and the possibility that the United Nations might not support active military aid for South Korea, it would seem that President Truman did make an adventurous decision. In addition, when considering the possibility that United States action might bring the Soviets into the war and precipitate World War III, the Truman decision seems even more dangerous. The United States "frankly did not know" if Russia would become involved, but Truman sent word to Stalin through channels that the United States would keep the peace in Korea even if it meant fighting Russia to do so. [12]

Another limit on President Truman's ability to make decisions was lack of information. At first, it was almost impossible to get any verifiable information, and there did not seem to be any existing plans to respond to an invasion by North Korea. Apparently the possibility of such an act had not occurred to anyone.

The Security Council had already condemned North Korea as an aggressor, and after all the talk of the previous five years about collective security, neither the United States nor the United Nations was willing to settle the situation peacefully, only to meet force with force. The doctrine of containment was a reality. The United States following its doctrine of containment was duty-bound to step into the action in Korea, and the United Nations with its concept of collective security was obliged to participate under American pressure at the Security Council.

"The decision of the free nations to withstand aggression in Korea, is of course, the first and essential step toward the fixing of a firm line containing Communist expansion. Notice has been served on the Russians . . . that any attempt to cross the present frontiers of the non-Communist world by force will be resisted, and will, if pressed home, lead to a general war." [13] This was a typical European reaction to the firm steps taken by President Truman and the Security Council. In light of previous commitments to the United Nations, the philosophy of collective security, the policy of containment, the decisions at Teheran and Yalta proposing an independent Korea, it seemed that President Truman had acted in a consistent manner. He acted, however, on an ideological basis--certainly not on the basis of military necessity.

In addition to the limitations we have been discussing, there were also certain influences which affected the decisions the President made during these first few days of the Korean conflict. It was quite clear that President Truman was going to get the backing of the Security Council, for it had already branded North Korea as the aggressor. He also received almost unanimous support from Congress, and he must have anticipated this before he made public his decisions.

One of the major influences on the President would have been the role played by his advisors. It is clear, for example, that Dean Acheson had great influence on Mr. Truman. Acheson, when he first called the President about the "invasion," suggested a Security Council meeting and Mr. Truman agreed. The following day, Acheson spoke to the President again and made it clear that although the Security Council would probably call for a cease fire, the United States should expect that order to be ignored by the communists. He said that some decision had to be made at once as to the degree of aid or encouragement which the United States government would be willing to extend to the Republic of South Korea. Over and over in his *Memoirs,* Truman indicates how much Dean Acheson had to do in influencing his thinking by his suggestions and command of the situation.

At the first meeting with his advisors, Truman recalls, " The complete, almost unspoken acceptance on the part of everyone that whatever had to be done to meet this aggression had to be done. There was no suggestion from anyone that either the United Nations or the United States could back away from it." He continued, "General Bradley said we would have to draw the line somewhere. Russia, he thought, was not yet ready for war, but in Korea they were obviously testing US, and the line ought to be drawn now. I said that most emphatically I thought the line would have to be drawn."[14] With the views of his advisors, the President took the actions which followed.

The final factor in influencing the President's decision is simply his own perspective. He is alone; he is unique, and only he can really know what goes on in his mind. Truman told of his thoughts in the presidential airplane as he returned from Independence to Washington before he met with his advisors:

> I had time to think aboard the plane. In my generation, this was not the first occasion when the strong had attacked the weak I recalled some earlier instances: Manchuria, Ethiopia, Austria. I remembered how each time that the democracies failed to act it had encouraged the aggressors to keep going ahead. Communism was acting in Korea just as Hitler, Mussolini, and the Japanese had acted, ten, fifteen, and twenty years earlier. I felt certain that if South Korea was allowed to fall Communist leaders would he emboldened to override nations closer to our own shores. If the Communists were permitted to force their way into the Republic of Korea without opposition from the free world, no small nation would have the courage to resist threats and aggression by stronger Communist neighbors If this was allowed to go unchallenged it would mean a third world war, just as similar incidents had brought on the second World War. It was also clear to me that the foundations and the principles of the United Nations were at stake unless this unprovoked attack on Korea could he stopped.[15]

As much as Mr. Truman was willing to support the Republic of Korea, he did not mean to send American troops to defend her. He probably trusted that the Republic of Korea could defend itself with American material aid. After all, the Seoul Defense Minister, Shin Sung Mo, said publicly that ROK troops could defeat the communists within a few days.

The event which involved American troops in the conflict came about through the military and political manipulations of General MacArthur. The opportunity to confront the communists in Asia had arrived, and MacArthur was trying to make the most of it.

In the United States, it was not only President Truman, but conservative policy makers in the Congress, too, who were not thinking in terms of sending American troops to Asia. Senator Robert A. Taft, leader of the Republican party, made clear that American troops should not get involved in an Asian war by saying that the United States was not prepared to use its troops to aid Chiang Kai-shek's nationalist government against communists in China, and he did not agree to using American troops in the Korea War.[16]

Even after clear signs of the Southern Korean armies' defeat, the American government hesitated to commit American troops in Korea. Secretary of Defense Louis A. Johnson made clear that he did not wish to see ground troops sent to Korea.[17] Air power was to be used, although limited to south of the 38th parallel.

As much as the Truman administration was trying to control the Korean situation by not involving American ground troops, President Truman was unable to control the events which followed, and General MacArthur, not President Truman, made major decisions on them. For instance, MacArthur made up his mind to bomb North Korea without Washington's approval.

MacArthur emerged from his private cabin and remarked almost casually: 'I've decided to bomb north of the 38th parallel The B-29's will be out tomorrow. The order has gone to Okinawa.[18]

A similar historical event can be recalled. The Kwangtung Army attacked Chinese forces in Mukden in September, 1931, initiated the "Manchurian Incident" without the Tokyo government's knowledge. The Tokyo government had to accept the Japanese military action and this gradually led to the Sino-Japanese War. Truman and Acheson accepted what MacArthur had committed. General MacArthur intended to escalate the Korean war to an Asian war. He had committed American ground troops to a combat front against the will of the Joint Chiefs of Staff in Washington. The primary reason for sending American troops to Korea by the Joint Chiefs of Staff was to protect the evacuation of American citizens.[19] MacArthur, however, had a different idea. He even made a trip to Taiwan to discuss with Chiang Kai-shek the military problems in Asia without the approval of the White House. Even Winston Churchill was opposed to MacArthur's adventurism in Asia, stating that he would have stopped at the neck of the peninsula north of Pyongyang, keeping clear of the sensitive Yalu River region.[20]   MacArthur wasn't interested in peace either in Korea or with China at this point. Just as he decided to bomb North Korea and decided to commit American troops at the combat front, he decided to escalate war in Korea, in spite of serious opposition in Washington. Later MacArthur became so great an embarrassment that he was relieved of duty by President Truman.

In a military sense, it seems clear that Korea was not vital to United States security, but considering the ideological Cold War which President Truman initiated himself, he now became the prisoner of his own concept. President Truman had to practice what he had been preaching. He wasn't able to see, as President John F. Kennedy saw later during the Cuban crisis, reasonable alternative policies. One of the most important decisions since World War II was Harry S. Truman's decision to take military action against North Korea and this created the most tragic situation in the history of Korea. For whom was the war fought? For the benefits of the Korean people or for the defense of the Truman doctrine?

The war in Korea began with a retreat for United Nations forces. The first United Nations offensive started on September 15 when United Nations forces were coordinated with an amphibious landing at Inchon under the personal leadership of General MacArthur. The landing to cut North Korean communications was a great success and led to the eventual retreat of North Korean forces to the north. It turned the tide in favor of the United Nations forces, which recaptured Seoul on September 28. United Nations forces cleared South Korea and pushed to the 38th Parallel. The government of South Korea returned to Seoul on September 29.

With its forces in the process of securing the 38th Parallel and all territory south of it, the U.N. General Assembly was faced with the question of whether or not to cross the parallel into North Korea.

On September 30, 1950, in a resolution, the General Assembly reaffirmed the U.N. objective of unifying Korea and of holding elections for the establishment of a "unified, independent, and democratic government" for the whole of Korea.

In a meeting at Tokyo with Averell Harriman, MacArthur made known his views on the war. He thought that the North Koreans should be completely defeated as soon as possible, before they could be strengthened by the Chinese or the Soviet Communists. He did not, however, believe that the Chinese or the Soviet Communists had any intention of entering the war directly.[21]

The Truman administration thought it safe to take action in Korea despite threatened interference by Communist China. It was considered that the conflict between the Soviets and China would keep Communist China busy. Secretary Acheson had said, "Now I give the people in Peiping credit for being intelligent enough to see what is happening to them. Why should they want to further their own dismemberment and destruction by getting at cross purposes with all the free nations of the world who are inherently their friends and have always been friends of the Chinese against this imperialism coming down from the Soviet Union I cannot see."[22] There was nothing to fear.

On october 2, MacArthur announced that Republic of Korea troops were operating north of the 38th parallel, and that resistance was light. Thus, his action became official knowledge.

Meantime, Premier Chou En-lai was trying to tell Washington that China wished to avoid war with America, but would not be intimidated by MacArthur's aggression. Premier Chou had informed Indian Ambassador Kimi Panikkar at Peking to convey a message to Washington on China's position:

No country's need for peace was greater than that of China, but there were times when peace could only be defended by determination to resist aggression. If the Americans crossed the 38th Parallel China would be forced to intervene. Otherwise he was most anxious for a peaceful settlement. . .

Ambassador Panikkar then asked the premier, "Whether China intended to intervene if only the South Koreans crossed the parallel." Premier Chou " . . . was most emphatic: The South Koreans did not matter but American intrusion into North Korea would encounter Chinese resistance."'[23]

India's warning of China's intentions drew little reaction. These warnings were credible since the content and channels gave them validity and the means of carrying out the intervention threats were obviously available. Intelligence had reported troops massing in Manchuria for months, and finally, the advantages of intervening outweighed the disadvantages.[24]

On October 3, word was received in Washington that the Chinese would intervene if U.N. troops crossed the 38th parallel.

On October 7, 1950, the U.N. General Assembly passed a resolution by a vote of 47-5 calling for a peaceful settlement of the Korean dispute. MacArthur was given the word and once more a cease-fire proposal was offered to North Korean forces. No reply was received and U.N. forces crossed the parallel. With South Korean forces driving up the east coast, the X Corps set out for another amphibious landing. The United States I Corps moving along the west coast took the city of Pyongyang on October 19. The operation was complete when United States airborne elements were dropped just north of the North Korean capital to cut off a possible retreat. The forces continued northward on all fronts toward Manchuria. By the end of October, 135,000 North Koreans had surrendered and U. N. forces were approaching the Yalu River. In support of these forces were armed contingents from Britain, Thailand and South Africa. The conditions seemed perfect for a final push and victory. But victory was not coming to the U.N. forces.

On October 14, "volunteer" units of the Chinese Peoples' Liberation Fourth Field Army began secret movements into Korea. The final compromise proposal by the Russian delegation to the U.N. had been defeated as U.N. troops had marched into North Korea. The U.N. ignored Peking's warning and accepted its challenge. Great Britain and France, contributing to the U.N. offensive, grew wary of the total disregard of China's warnings. Both, of course, had their own interests to protect: Britain feared encroachment knowing the vulnerability of Hong Kong; France feared a cutback in her rearmament program, and both urged halting the advance at Pyongyang and creating a "buffer zone." To create a "buffer zone" in Korea was not going to solve the central fact of the international status of China at this stage.

Many American militarists and politicians still believed that China would not commit large forces to battle in Korea.[25] Even General MacArthur did not believe in the possibility of Chinese intervention. The general said: "Had they interfered in the first or second month it would have been decisive. We are no longer fearful of their intervention."[26] General MacArthur was basing his judgment on erroneous information. The General's chief intelligence aide, Colonel Willoughby, was fooled by the Chinese Communist usage of the words "unit" and "battalion" to disguise full armies and divisions. Also the general's aerial reconnaissance failed to locate Chinese armies in the daytime because they moved by night and cleverly camouflaged themselves by day.[27]

On the eve of the great Chinese offensive American policy makers were faced with several disillusioning facts. First, China was apparently less the "agrarian reformer" and capable of competing militarily against major forces. In addition, the Chinese, rather than explaining their as-yet-unclear position on Korea, constantly and vehemently branded the United States as aggressor in Formosa. Equally unsettling was that the British and French were completely abandoning the U.S. offensive policy in North Korea.

At this point, there were policy-making disputes between President Truman and General MacArthur, especially in regard to the bombing of Chinese soil. Over the weekend of october 13-17, the President conferred with General MacArthur at Wake Island. When Truman returned, his public statements declared that he had complete confidence in MacArthur and his ability to handle the situation.

In their northward advance, U.N. troops met with increasing numbers of Chinese forces. On November 7, MacArthur reported to the Security Council that U.N. forces had engaged in hostile action with "Chinese Communist military units. " With this development, U.N. members sought to reduce the scope of the war effort. Six members of the Security Council sponsored a resolution suggesting that all nations refrain from supporting North Korean forces. It was emphasized in this proposal also that the U.N. forces would respect Chinese boundaries.

On November 24, General MacArthur issued a statement that the war might well be near its end, that his army had started on a major attack to "end the war," and he promised the troops would be home by Christmas. The general should have known that it was an over-optimistic promise. The next day, Chinese forces engaged several U.N. units in action. Surprised, the U.N. forces withdrew southward. On November 28, President Truman blamed the Soviets for the original attack by the North Koreans, and asserted that the Chinese, who were traditionally friendly toward the United States, were being forced to fight U.N. troops. As later events indicate, Chinese Communists were no more friendly than Soviet Communists. Just as the interpretation of the Chinese Communists as agrarian reformers had been erroneous, classifying Chinese Communists as "friendly" toward the U.S. but forced by the Soviets to fight against U.N. forces, was also false. The Chinese acted very much independently.

General MacArthur wanted authorization to stop "the invaders" in Manchuria, their origin, but it was feared that this might start World War III. Truman, weary of MacArthur's policy statements, ordered all government agencies that " . . . no speech, press release, or other public statement concerning foreign policy should be released until it has received clearance from the Department of State." "And also that "everything relating to military policy must first receive clearance from the Department of Defense." MacArthur's violation of this directive was the basis for one of President Truman's most debated actions.

The U.N. now faced a ticklish situation. The U.N. had passed a resolution labeling the Communist Chinese as aggressors, yet what could it do? The Communist Chinese had their bases in Manchuria, and if the U.N. forces attacked their bases in Manchuria, this would be construed as an act of aggression, and would probably plunge the world into World War III, with the U.S. and others pitted against China, and possibly the Soviet Union. At least, this was the main concern of the Truman administration at this time. On the other hand, the Soviet Union probably enjoyed the situation where she could keep a neutral position while the United States and Communist China engaged in "undeclared war." It had to be an "undeclared war" since there was a military alliance between China and the Soviet Union. The more involved the United States was in the Far East, the less the U.S. could do in the rebuilding of Europe. Korea was not the only place in which communists were active. Communist forces had moved against Tibet, and communist forces were also making themselves felt in Indo-China.

Confronting the Chinese forces placed General MacArthur in a dilemma. He was not allowed to expand the war to Chinese territory and he was not used to fighting "limited war," nor was he in a mood to compromise with opposition. He made it plain that no blame for the defeat should be placed on him or his staff, but should be placed on those politicians who limited the war. He did not believe in "limited wars," and wanted to attack the Chinese full-scale.

MacArthur wanted to use the Korean war to make an Asian war. He proposed that the U.N. continue fighting to unify Korea and change the strategic picture in the Far East by crippling and neutralizing China. MacArthur proposed accomplishing this by a naval blockade of China, aerial bombardment of Chinese airfields in Manchuria and the coastal cities of China and by leading a counter-invasion of Mainland China by Chiang Kai-shek forces from Formosa. MacArthur was advocating a total war against China, not just defending South Korea. MacArthur's concept of the unification of Korea coincided with the destruction of Chinese power. He promised President Rhee, his loyal admirer, as early as 1948 to help the unification and now time had arrived for the unification of Korea. President Rhee said: "When General MacArthur was here on September 29th and had a talk with the president [Rhee] in regard to the 38th parallel, the general wanted to wait two to three weeks and get all the supplies ready and march on. It was the directive from the higher-up not to cross the parallel but to wait for the U.N. decision and act accordingly. The president [Rhee] told him that . . . the Koreans will move on and nobody can stop them.... MacArthur finally agreed..."[28]

President Truman was unwilling to back MacArthur, as were the Joint Chiefs of Staff. General Omar Bradley gave strong support to President Truman's position. Even if President Truman had decided to support MacArthur's position, the United States would have had to go it alone. This was not an acceptable position because it would probably have destroyed the unity of the North Atlantic Treaty Organization.

The rejection of MacArthur's proposal was a rejection of the October 7 decision to achieve a military unification of Korea and affirmation of the original objective of the war, the restoration of the status quo before the war.

When United States forces acted in Korea, the administration wanted to move under the aegis of the U.N. There were two reasons for this. First, by virtue of the "free election" it had sponsored in South Korea, the U.N. had been intimately concerned with the birth of the young state. Secondly, one of the aims of American foreign policy was to associate its cold-war policies with the symbolic, humanitarian values of the United Nations.[29] The United States had to maintain its public image of altruism and acting on moral principles. It had to maintain the image of acting for the public welfare and for the advancement of peace, not for political power and national interests.

On the other hand, United States policy in the United Nations was to get the U.N. to play "follow the leader." On June 25, 1950, the U.S. representative to the U.N. Warren Austin, gave the first statement on the actions of North Korea. The protest by Austin reviewed the efforts of the U.N. to provide ways and means of granting the Korean people the independence which it was agreed was their right.

Strangely enough, many American militarists and politicians believed that China would not commit large forces to battle in Korea. Mirroring the American public's concept of the war's progress was *the Life* magazine article of October 30, 1950, entitled "Hard Hitting U.N. Forces Wind Up War." It said:

> The next day General MacArthur dropped 4,100 paratroops north of Pyongyang to trap what was left of Kim's army–some 27,000 men. Now MacArthur could say confidently, "The war definitely is coming to an end shortly."

On December 16, President Truman issued a Declaration of National Emergency, the idea being to step up production so as to produce by 1952 what had been planned to be produced by 1954. On December 29, MacArthur announced that he felt if he were not going to expand the battle, then America's only recourse was to gradually back off to the Pusan beachhead and then quietly leave, though realizing that this move would leave a most unfavorable impression for Asians in general. He felt that the U.S. could in no way provoke China more, but agreed that it was difficult to tell what the Russians might do if U.N. forces attacked the Manchurian bases. He was frustrated. In March, 1951, however, the Chinese had been pushed back, roughly past the 38th Parallel.

But erroneous estimates by American military leaders of Chinese Army numbers, morale, and capabilities were the critical components of the disaster that befell the U.N. army in the winter of 1950-1951. For example, here was the assessment by an air force general.

It is difficult to believe that the Chinese will commit their forces in major strength unless guaranteed at least the support of the Soviet Russian air Force. And if it is true that Soviet Russia does not want to enter the conflict at this time, the Korean War should be liquidated within a few months.[30]

It was not thought that China would employ all 500,000 troops known to be in Manchuria because the munitions necessary to support a Western-style war were beyond Chinese industrial capability and, the Korean "waistline" could be defended by ten U.N. divisions, against which the Chinese masses would be ineffective, even with supply lines intact. General MacArthur became the target for opposition in the U.N. It was MacArthur's interpreters who failed to understand the Chinese prisoners' demoralization and unwillingness to fight U.N. troops. It was also misunderstanding by MacArthur's intelligence aide, Colonel Willoughby, upon which the general based his judgments during the months of October and November, 1950. General MacArthur commented on possible Chinese intervention:

Very little. Had they interfered in the first or second month it would have been decisive. We are no longer fearful of their intervention. We no longer stand hat in hand. The Chinese have 300,000 men in Manchuria. Of these probably not more than 100-125,000 are distributed along the Yalu. They have no Air Force. If the Chinese tried to get down to Pyongyang there would be the greatest slaughter.[31]

After an initial token attack on November 2, China pulled back to Manchuria. U.N. forces numbering 180,000 troops began their "end-the-war" offensive on November 24 and on November 26 were smashed by a counterattacking Chinese Army of 200,000 who split the U.N. forces into east and west fragments and ended hopes, for the foreseeable future, of either the unification of Korea or MacArthur's dream to destroy communism in Asia.

In the light of the new situation, cease-fire talks renewed. On March 24, MacArthur released a statement on the war. This was directly in violation of the decree by President Truman and the U.S. Joint Chiefs of Staff. MacArthur's statement was contrary to views in a statement prepared by President Truman, his staff, and the heads of several other governments, which had not been released yet.[32]

General MacArthur was replaced by General Matthew Ridgeway as Supreme Commander of Allied Powers and as Commander-in-Chief of the U.N. Command on April 10, 1951. President Truman regarded the recall of General MacArthur as necessary to maintain civilian authority over the military, which is required by the American Constitution. On the other hand, many Americans opposed Truman's action. "The nation and the entire world were shocked by the precipitate action. The free world was stunned," commented one source. It further stated: "The Communist dictators in Russia and China were exultant. The one strong man that they feared, the world's greatest enemy of Communism, had been eliminated from the world combat. It was to them the greatest decisive battle they had ever won."[33] On the eve of this history-making decision, President Truman spoke on a national radio broadcast to restate the government's policy to the people. The President said: "The free nations have united their strength in an effort to prevent a third world war. That war can come if the Communist leaders want it to come. But this nation and its allies will not be responsible for its coming."[34]

With General MacArthur's return to the United States, congressional hearings were held during the months of May and June. Meanwhile, in Korea, U.N. forces moved beyond the 38th parallel, and captured the capital city, Pyongyang, of North Korea. On June 1, the Secretary-General of the U. N., Trygve Lie, suggested a cease-fire approximately along the 38th Parallel. On June 7, Secretary of State Dean Acheson made a similar proposal. On June 23, Jacob Malik, Soviet representative to the U. N . Security Council, suggested that the time was right for discussions to begin between the belligerent.

At the end of a United Nations radio address in New York City Malik said: "The Soviet people believe that as a first step, discussion should be started between belligerent for a cease-fire and an armistice providing for the mutual withdrawal of forces from the 38th Parallel."[35] Obviously China's reaction was important and it reacted favorably but with an exception. The Peking government approved the cease-fire proposal a few days later but said it had not given up hope of pressing its own terms. At first it wasn't known if the statement was to be taken seriously, for many tentative statements of similar nature had been discredited before. But the position was reaffirmed by Admiral Alan G. Kirk, United States Ambassador to the U. S. S. R., after a conference with Soviet deputy foreign minister, Andrei Gromyko, in Moscow on the 27th of June. He had informed Kirk that the negotiations should be by the field commanders and strictly concern military matters, leaving to others political or territorial matters.

The fact that the cease-fire proposal was delivered by the Soviet Union is extremely important. This meant that neither Washington nor Moscow, the two super powers of the world, wanted this engagement fought to a conclusion. Russia, although somewhat materially committed to the Chinese, had no intention of involving its own troops in the war. The U.N. (mainly the United States) had no desire or inclination to extend its losses by advancing past the 38th Parallel in the interest of Korean unity. Western powers were beginning to feel the strain of trying to support a conventional force against the military resources of China and the U.S.S.R. The West welcomed the Soviet proposal.

Secretary of State Acheson now saw it clear to use the reported statements of China as a chance to restate the United States position. While he was appearing before the House Foreign Affairs Committee, Acheson dropped the line that the United States military aims would be satisfied if the communist forces withdrew behind the 38th Parallel and if these forces gave assurances of no further attacks. The United States was then given clear sailing in the negotiations with the communists. This was done when Abraham Feller, the United Nations legal adviser, informed Secretary General Lie that the United States had the right to arrange an armistice or a cease-fire so long as terms of the agreement dealt only with military matters and the results were reported to the Security Council. As a result, General Ridgeway, the Commander-in-Chief of the United Nations Forces in Korea, replied to the Chinese statement on June 29. He said, "I have been instructed to communicate the following: I am informed that you may wish a meeting to discuss an armistice providing for the cessation of hostilities and all acts of armed force in Korea, with adequate guarantee for the maintenance of such an armistice."[36] On this same day Ridgeway was told the principle military interests and the specific details that the United States wanted established in the negotiations. The principle military interests were the stopping of hostilities, an assurance that fighting would not start again and the protection of the United Nations forces. Also sought was a military agreement that would be acceptable over a long period of time. Ridgeway was instructed not to speak on any political questions. Specifically, United States policy-makers wanted a commission to insure the terms of the armistice were met, a twenty-mile demilitarized zone established between the lines at the date of the armistice, no troop buildup except on a one-for-one basis and the quick exchange of prisoners. After receiving this information, Ridgeway appointed his delegation. Admiral C. T. Joy, Commander Naval Forces Far East, headed the delegation. The Communist delegation was headed by General Nam-Il.

On July 10, the first meeting of the delegations began. The meeting place changed from Kaesong to Panmunjom. On July 22, the Chinese halted the talks, demanding that "all foreign troops must be withdrawn from Korea." Unable to achieve the withdrawal of all U.N. troops, the Communists resumed negotiations on August 11. The fighting continued while the talks were going on. On November 27, a cease-fire line was agreed upon.

By the end of 1951 the agenda was complete and the first matter – the adoption of the agenda – concluded. Item 2 fixed a demilitarized zone between the two lines so as to provide a basis for the ceasing of hostilities. Item 3 provided concrete arrangements for the realization of a cease-fire and armistice in Korea, including the composition, authority and functions of a supervising organization for carrying out the terms of a cease-fire and armistice. Item 4 concerned arrangements relating to prisoners of war. Item 5 provided for the withdrawal of troops by stages after a military agreement.[37] As soon as the agenda was agreed to, General Nam proposed that the 38th Parallel be used as the dividing line since it had been so before the war. But Admiral Joy wanted a truce line established by the actual battle lines, not on an imaginary geographic line or on political objectives. The Communists eventually gave way on this point.

There were still four problems to be resolved before an armistice could be signed: the rehabilitation of certain North Korean airfields; control of airfields in North Korea; the exchange of prisoners on a one-for-one basis, and the right of individual choice in repatriation; and exchange on an all-for-all basis.

Before negotiations were suspended in 1952, on the insistence of the United States, the delegations had reached an understanding on three of the four main aspects of the proposed armistice. First, the military line of demarcation was to be established along the line of contact and each opposing force was supposed to withdraw two kilometers from the demarcation line to form a four-kilometer wide demilitarized zone. Supervision of the armistice was to be by a commission made up of officers from the Communist forces and the United Nations forces plus a commission made up of four officers from neutral countries. The United Nations chose Sweden and Switzerland, with the Communists choosing Czechoslovakia and Poland for the neutral commission. The commissions were the Military Armistice Commission and the Neutral Nations Supervisory Commission. The two sides agreed also to recommend a political conference to be held after three months to settle unresolved questions. The fourth point that remained unsettled concerned exchange of prisoners of war.

At this point it is important to point out that the United Nations delegation were all United States officers. Therefore, the decisions they made reflected the wishes of the United States government.

Even though it had been arranged that a prisoner exchange would take place two months after the armistice, it was discovered by the United Nations that 72 percent of the Chinese Communist prisoners captured by the U.N. did not want to be repatriated or exchanged. This was a real blow to the

Communists and they demanded repatriation without exception. The United Nations command, backed strongly by Washington, refused to force anyone to be exchanged. From December 14, 1952, until March 30, 1953, when Premier Chou En-lai broke the ice, the truce talks were at a standstill. Chou En-lai proposed that prisoners who were afraid to return home should be handed over to a neutral state.[38] The proposal did not mean that China or North Korea were bending to the United Nations. Behind Chou's proposal was the Communists' acceptance of a proposal that had been suggested in 1951 for the exchange of sick and wounded prisoners. It had little bearing on the issue of the exchange of healthy prisoners after the armistice but it could be used to gauge the Communists' intentions. This exchange was called "Little Switch" to distinguish it from the general prisoner exchange called "Big Switch."

In 1953 there was a new commander, General Mark W. Clark, a hard-line advocate, and a new party in power in the United States, the Republican party. When the issue of repatriation was taken up again at Panmunjom on April 26, the Communists wanted a chance to question prisoners and hear explanations by them as to why they did not return. The extent of the free hand given to the Communists, which was approved in Washington, prompted the field commander to say, "The Republicans were ready to go further than the Democrats to achieve a truce. " But the Communists seemed less willing, for their first proposal on prisoners was totally unacceptable. The one presented on May 7, however, provided the basis of the armistice agreement. They wanted a commission made up of five neutral nations to hold and take charge of prisoners during a four-month "explanation" period. After studying the proposal, the United Nations suggested a number of amendments. At this General Nam exploded and abandoned negotiations.

General Clark then suggested to Washington that the time had come for action. In reply he was instructed to give way on the matter of the Koreans and other points but to stand firm on the policy of no forced repatriation. He was also authorized to carry the war in Korea on in new ways if the final offer was rejected. The final offer was put forward by the United Nations and accepted by the Communists. This led to the signature of agreed "Terms of Reference" for the Neutral Nations Repatriation Commission established 60 days after the armistice became effective. The terms provided for the five-nation neutral commission headed by India and 90 days were allowed for groups to persuade prisoners to come home. Any prisoner who did not exercise his right of repatriation became part of the post-armistice political conference which was to have 30 days to decide the issues. If there was no decision within these 180 days, the prisoners would have civilian status and their freedom. The neutral commission would dissolve in one month.

President Rhee of South Korea was totally unsatisfied with the truce negotiations, and threatened to release anti-communist prisoners in camps in South Korea as a protest against a "compromise truce." Feeling that he had been "double-crossed," Dr. Rhee released 25,000 prisoners of war. This action greatly embarrassed the United Nations, for the U.N. had promised that these prisoners would be brought before the repatriation committee.

General Clark had earlier favored Rhee's plan and now recommended it to Washington. The United States government rejected the proposal for it did not want to upset the negotiations. The United States government went to great lengths trying to please Rhee but to no avail. Seeing that the delegations at Panmunjom had almost completed their task Rhee released the prisoners. At this crucial moment, the Communists posed some questions: "Is the U.N.C. able to control the South Korean government and army? If not, does the armistice in Korea include Syngman Rhee's clique? And if it is not included, what assurance is there for the implementation of the armistice agreement on the part of South Korea?" Then the Communists recessed the Punmunjom negotiations. Rhee had succeeded in upsetting the apple cart.

The American government induced Dr. Rhee to calm down and cooperate with the U.N. truce team. The inducements were a mutual security pact, military and economic aid and a concession dealing with the political conference to be held three months after the armistice. It was agreed that if nothing was accomplished at the conference table within ninety days, both the United States and ROK governments would withdraw, calling it a hostile trick and a sham. While this was going on, the fighting front was being made ready to be turned over to ROK forces if Rhee decided to fight on alone. The negotiations were resumed in the second week of July. The signing took place on July 27 at three separate sites .

Thus ended, after three years and thirty-two days of fighting and more than two years of negotiations, the military phase of a conflict whose impact on modern civilization had been too strong and too varied to be adequately assessed by any contemporary. Some of the direct costs of the war could be approximated, among them the 300,000 South Korean and 155,000' United Nations casualties, one and one-half to two million Communist casualties, perhaps a million other lives lost in South Korea and three million in North Korea. Under the armistice agreement, the Korean Republic would gain some 1,500 square miles of territory, five million of the destitute, 600,000 destroyed houses, and devastation estimated at anywhere from one to four billion dollars. The monetary cost of the war to the United States was later estimated at $18 billion, exclusive of servicemen's pay.

The armistice had four main provisions. A military demarcation line and a demilitarized zone were established roughly following the line of battle at the conclusion of the hostilities, and lying mainly just to the north of the 38th parallel. The agreement stabilized the military strength of both sides with guarantees and supervision to prevent new forces being added. Repatriation of prisoners of war on the basis of the free choice of the prisoners had been accomplished and there was a call for a "political conference of a higher level" to settle "through negotiation the question of the withdrawal of all foreign forces from Korea." The armistice agreement merely brought to an end the fighting; it did not solve the basic issues involved in the unification of the country. To supervise the truce, a commission composed of representatives of the neutral nations of Sweden, Switzerland, Poland and Czechoslovakia was appointed. Further negotiations planned by the neutral commission failed to materialize as North Koreans insisted on complete United Nations withdrawal and refused to allow U.N.-supervised elections to be held in the north. With a military as well as political stalemate in evidence, the U.N. set up a commission to represent it in Korean affairs. The U.N. Commission for the Unification and Rehabilitation of Korea (UNCURK) was established to carry out the goals and interests of the United Nations in unifying Korea.

Why did Peking choose to intervene in Korea? What were the motivations behind the decision to send "volunteers" to Korea? Was this token payment for their "Korean comrades" who had helped the Chinese revolution during the Chinese civil war? There was no immediate threat to their territories . The threat of a U.N. attack on the mainland would have become more acute with actual engagement, but there was no clear and present danger, at least, in the minds of decision-makers in Washington. The Chinese, however, had a different impression. They felt threatened by MacArthur's manipulations.

Mao Tse-Tung told the West that China was obliged to intervene because first of all, the United States was bent on world domination, as evidenced by the invasion of Korea and Formosa, and the bombing of Chinese towns indicated that China was the next American target. He also charged that "American employment of Japanese troops" in Korea made intervention imperative, in accordance with the Sino-Soviet Mutual Assistance Treaty, and finally, China could not stand by while North Korea was wiped out.[39]

There might be other explanations why China entered the Korean War. For instance, Dr. Hu Shih, a well-known author and a former Nationalist Chinese ambassador to Washington, said: "Months ago I predicted that the Communists would come into the war ... for two main reasons. In the first place the Korean Communists and Chinese Communists, the Korean Red Army and the Red Chinese Army are more than blood relations. They have for years

248

fought together as brothers in distress.'' Many hundreds of Koreans fought alongside Red Chinese forces and some of them held important positions. For instance, Mu Chung, a Korean, was in charge of the Artillery forces of the Red Chinese Army ever since the days of the Long March, and joined the North Korean Army in 1945. The Russian-trained North Korean Army helped China conquer Manchuria. The situation now being reversed, the North Koreans needed help from the Chinese.

According to Dr. Hu Shih, there was a second and more important reason for Red Chinese forces to intervene in Korea. He said: "If the Communist State in North Korea should be permitted to be conquered by the U.N. army, while Soviet Russia on the northeastern border stands by without helping, and the Chinese Communists on the northwestern border stand by without helping, if that were to happen, the prestige of world Communism would fall to pieces. Soviet Russia cannot permit it. Hence Communist China must come in."[40] Dr. Hu Shih's analysis of ideological aspects of intention was reasonably accurate observation. But if it were for purely ideological reasons, why didn't Soviet forces intervene with the Chinese? The Soviets certainly would have been concerned as much as the Chinese, if not more. Who was to play a big brother's role in saving North Korea? Was Soviet policy the determining factor in Chinese Communist participation in the war? Did China, on the other hand, fear aggression in Korea by the Soviet Union and a continuous dominating influence there? It seems that there had been jealousy and uneasiness between the Soviets and the Chinese as to the war in Korea. Since the North Korean forces were not able to defend themselves with the military aid from the Soviets alone, it was inevitable that help was needed from the Chinese "volunteers." This help saved the communist state, and avoided the danger of a major war in the Far East.

It seems that Chinese authorities were undecided whether to believe U.N. officials, who repeatedly emphasized their desire to recognize Chinese territorial integrity, or to believe the "MacArthur-Chiang clique," who were outspokenly desirous of extending the war into China proper. Chairman Mao believed that Manchuria was the teeth and Korea the lips—if the lips were lost, the teeth became cold.[41] It was also entirely possible that Mao was displaying "a screen of foreign intervention and foreign adventure for internal troubles,"[42] hoping to divert neutralists' eyes from China's domestic problems to a front of military might.

Another possible factor in China's decision to enter against the U.N. forces probably was America's reluctance to employ nuclear weapons in the Korean War. Assured by the British diplomatic defectors, Guy Burgess and Donal Maclean, of American intention of respecting China's "privileged sanctuary'' of Manchuria, China was relieved of a primary obstacle to a successful intervention.[43] China could employ her fluid offense against the stabilizing defense of U.N. troops, confident of unharassed supplies and reserves. In any event, Chairman Mao knew the moral criticism that the United States would be forced to bear should she attack with A-bombs, and Mao also was informed that the United States was incapable of effectively delivering its small stockpile and he probably assumed that the Soviets would retaliate in event of a nuclear attack. China's massive population and vast land mass and scattered industry could swallow dozens of nuclear weapons without being decisively affected. Therefore, we can conclude that the final decision to fight against the U.N. forces appears to have been basically a Chinese one.

China did have more than casual interest in North Korea's success. . communist victory would severely damage the American image in Asia. In view of the rapid rebuilding of Japan under the American influence, to destroy the American image was an important political factor. There is no evidence that China participated in planning the war. China observed patiently the development of the war, although her Fourth Field Army was ready to cross the Yalu River at a moment's notice.

Chinese war preparation, originally for the Taiwan invasion, had slowed with the Russian negotiation proposal, but it again became apparent with the U.N.'s crossing of the 38th Parallel. This time Chinese forces were destined for a different location and aimed at a different enemy. When high American officials, particularly MacArthur, began advocating more aggressive action in the Far East, when U.N. aircraft allegedly attacked Chinese territory, and when U.S. President Truman and Representative to the United Nations Austin publicly warned Peking to stay out, China retaliated with bitter diplomatic protests and vicious Hate-America propaganda attacks, exemplified by:

> This mad dog (the U.S.) seizes Formosa between its hind legs while with its teeth it violently bites the Korean people. Now one of its forelegs has been poked into our Northeast front. Its blood-swollen eyes cast around for something further to attack. All the world is under its threat. The American imperialist mad dog is half beaten up. Before it dies, it will go on biting and tearing.[44]

China, sponsored by Russia in the U.N., also protested against American air attacks on Chinese civilians in Manchuria and the American ''invasion'' of Formosa.

The war ravaged most of Korea and a great task of rehabilitation lay ahead for the United Nations Command. It was evident that the same type of united effort that was put together by the member nations during the war was needed desperately for rehabilitation. The war had spread destruction throughout the peninsula. Korean citizens were killed, captured or forced to fight in their own forces. The people were tired and distressed and in need of economic help. The forces which strove to restore peace and order now turned their attention to bringing back this proud people to its rightful state.

During the early stages of the conflict, U.N. aid and service were seen in such organizations as KMAG and the Civilian Relief in Korea program, which financed the bulk of the assistance program. The post-war need for financial aid outside of these American programs came without request for the most part and without delay. By June, 1953, the civilian relief investment and economic aid contributed totaled almost $750 million. The United States bore the major burden of military responsibility in the war, and of this total, it contributed $650 million. The United Nations Korean Reconstruction Agency (UNKRA) added $64 million and other U.N donations added to the total pledged.

The war had intensified health threats which already were serious in some parts of South Korea before the war. Overcrowding, filth and conditions conducive to the spread of disease were the result of destruction and decay. The first step taken by the United Nations Command (UNC) was to innoculate and vaccinate as many as possible. Those who were sick or injured were given primary emergency care and then treated at temporary hospital locations. As a result of these efforts the effects of plague and disease were kept low.

Established sanitation systems had been wiped out for the most part and new ones had to be designed and built. Dusting, construction of wells, and purification of water supplies were only a few of the jobs which had to be undertaken. Medical and sanitation supplies contributed by the U.S. alone by June, 1953, totaled $8.6 million. United Nations agencies and voluntary contributions added up to $1.3 million worth of medical and health supplies.

The Korean War was an unfortunate war, begun as a result of a dividing line intended to facilitate return of Japanese prisoners-of-war in 1945. Why, then, was it not avoided?

Inadequate communications, or the failure to convey accurately to an opponent one's intention and one's probable responses, played a pivotal role between August and October of 1950 in precipitating war between the Chinese People's Volunteers and the United Nations forces.[45]

Was it true that Peking listened to Tokyo and MacArthur too much, to Washington and Truman not enough? Did Chinese appraisals, dependent upon Russian interpretations, exaggerate the threat posed by American policy? America, listening through Indian channels and convinced that China was only trying to increase neutralist pressure on the U.S. through India, diminished the seriousness of the Chinese concern.

In the conduct of military operations (as in any aspect of human behavior), great illusions are born out of a poverty of information coupled with a wealth of confidence that the enemy in any case is unequal to the task of promoting a decisive change in events. This illusion (concerning China's intervention) was nearly complete.[46]

Even had China been assured that her territory would not he physically attacked, she would probably have intervened in Korea at the time she did. There was very little possibility of compromise between Peking and Washington. To China, the ever-increasing aggressive actions of Washington in Asia were signs of troubles. Time had come for Peking to demonstrate to the world that she would not be intimidated by the arrogance of American power.

Mao was dedicated to halting American imperialism in Asia and the time had come. It was Mao's strategy to force the American force to withdraw from North Korea in defense of Chinese sovereignty and her prestige as well as for the interest of Korea's territorial integrity. Ideologically, confronting the super American power in Korea was a significant movement in the development of Maoism. As it expanded later, the Maoistic strategy of world revolution was to increase national liberation wars all over the world wherever American imperialism was involved. To attack the American world position from all directions became an important key in the Maoistic world strategy. Peking was looking for a breakthrough. The concept of driving out American imperialism from Asia, Africa, and Latin America motivated China to intervene in Korea.

As we indicated earlier, the main reason for the United States to intervene in Korea was to contain Chinese communism, or if possible, to destroy it while it was still in its infancy. Saving the Republic of Korea from North Korean domination was an after-thought. Examination of Acheson's public statements which were endorsed by President Truman, probing attitudes among American law-makers, and above all, "the MacArthur school" reveals more than enough to convince us of the U.S. intention in Korea. Consequently, the prime motivation of both China and America in the Korea War was to protect their own national interests. The Korean War was a political war of two big powers, China and America, rather than one based on morals. A Korean proverb says: "A shrimp becomes victimized when two whales fight." The wound of the war has not healed between the two Koreas yet. Two powers should perhaps contribute toward the unification of the two Koreas as a token of friendship.

Notes

1. Associated Press, March 1, 1946.
2. Franz Michael and George Taylor, *The Far East in the Modern World* (New York: Holt, Rinehart and Winston, 1964), p. 770.
3. *The Voice of Korea,* Jan. 27, 1950, Vol. 7, No. 143, Washington, D.C.
4. Clause (b) of Section 3, Korea Aid Bill, quoted in *The Voice of Korea,* March 1, 1950, Vol. 7, No. 144.
5. Glenn D. Paige, *The Korea Decision* (New York: Macmillan, 1968), p. 35.
6. Robert Leckie, *The Wars of America, vol.* 2 (New York: Harper Row, 1968), p. 360.
7. *China Digest,* Hong Kong, April 20, 1948, p. 6.
8. Louis J. Halle, *Civilization and Foreign Policy,* (New York: Greenwood, 1955), p. 243.
9. Soon Sung Cho, *Korea in World Politics: 1945-1950* (Berkeley: University of California Press, 1970), p. 263.
10. Harry S. Truman, *Years of Trial and Hope* (Nev York: Doubleday, 1955), p. 334.
11. Military Situation in the Far East: Hearings before the Senate Armed Services and Foreign Relations Committee, 82nd Congress, 1st session, Washington, 1951, part 5, p. 3369.
12. *Time,* July 3. 1950, P. 7
13. "War and Peace in the Far East," in the *New York Times,* July 16, 1950.
14. Truman, *Years of Trial and Hope, pp.* 334-35.
15. Ibid., p. 332-33.
16. Congressional Record, vol. 96, part 7, June 28, 1950, pp. 9319-9327. See also Paige, *The Korea Decision, p.* 217.
17. Paige, *The Korea Decision, p.* 165.
18. Roy Macartney, "How War Came to Korea," in Norman Bartlet, *With the Australians in Korea* (Canberra: Australian War Memorial, 1954), p. 171.
19. Paige, *The Korean Decision, p.* 246.
20. McGeorge Bundy, *The Pattern of Responsibility* (Boston: Harvard University Press, 1952), p. 266.

21. Truman, *Years of Trial and Hope, p.* 352.
22. John W. Spanier, *American Foreign Policy since World War II* (New York: Praeger, 1973), p. 87.
23. K. M. Panikkar, *In Two Chinas* (London: Free Press, 1955), p. 110. Also see Edward Friedman's "Problems in Dealing with an Irrational Power: America Declares War on China," in *America's Asia,* edited by Edward Friedman and Mark Selden (New York: Random House, 1971), p. 231.
24. Allen S. Whiting, *China Crosses the Yalu* (Stanford: Stanford University Press, 1960), p. 109.
25. Carl K. Spaatz, General, USAF, retired, was quoted as saying he believed that the Chinese would not commit their forces in major strength in a Korean war. *Newsweek, Nov.* 13, 1950, p. 35.
26. Robert Leckie, *Conflict: History of Korean War* (New York: Random House, 1962), p. 165
27. Ibid., p. 159.
28. Robert T. Oliver, *Syngman Rhee: The Man Behind the Myth* (New York: Dodd Mead, 1954), p. 307.
29. Spanier, *American Foreign Policy, p.* 85.
30. Carl K. Spaau, General, "Enter the Chinese Communists," in *Newsweek, Nov.* 13, 1950, p. 35.
31. Leckie, *Conflict, p.* 165.
32. Francis T. Miller, *War in Korea and the History of World War II,* (Philadelphia: Arms Service Memorial, 1955), p. 20.
33. Ibid., p. 33.
34. Truman, *Years of Trial and Hope, p.* 450.
35. Miller, *War in Korea, p.* k-33.
36. Ibid., p. k-39.
37. Walter G. Hermes, *Truce Tent and Fighting Front* (Office of the Chief of Military History, U.S. Army, 1966), p. 31.
38. Richard P. Stebbins, *The United States in World Affairs* (New York: S. and S. Co., 1968), p. 219.
39. "Key to Conflict," *Newsweek, Nov.* 13, 1950, p. 36.
40. "Why the Main War Will Be Fought in Asia--Not Europe," U.S. *News and World Report,* Jan. 19, 1951, p. 34.
41. Dean Rusk, "Security Problems: Far East Area," U.S. Department of *State Bulletin.* Dec. 4, 1950, p. 892.
42. Ibid.
43. Trumbull Higgins, *Korea and the Fall of MacArthur* (New York: Oxford University Press, 1960), p. 77.
44. Leckie, *Conflict, p.* 158.

254

45. Whiting, *China Crosses the Yalu*, p. 169.
46. S. L. A. Marshall, *The River and the Gauntlet* (New York: Greenwood, 1953), p. 14.

13

Syngman Rhee

Winston Churchill, the wartime Prime Minister of England, interestingly described Dr. Rhee as "a self-constituted dictator." Yet, the United Nations, led by the United States, fought a war in Korea to keep Dr. Rhee in power. Why did the United States deliberately ignore the fact that Dr. Rhee was a dictator, and pretend to preserve a non-existent democracy in Korea? Did Dr. Rhee set a trap for America to commit it to a war in Asia? Why did America conveniently overlook Rhee's regime advocating unification by force? Professor Robert T. Oliver, a long-time friend and advisor to President Syngman Rhee, wrote to Dr. Rhee on October 10, 1949 that: "We who are here [Washington] can and will try, of course, to change the opinion that the Republic [of Korea] must not attack the north, but until and unless that opinion does change, . . . either to attack or to indicate that you may plan to do so, would be to take a great risk of losing all support by either the U.S. or the U.N. Meanwhile, if we do lose the `cold war,' that would only result in its becoming `hot' . . . and that may well be the only way in which the issues finally can be settled."[1]

This letter clearly indicates that Dr. Rhee and his American advisor had had serious discussions about the possibility of a "hot" war which could be initiated by South Korea, which would get the United States involved in it. It was a common understanding among Koreans in the South that Dr. Rhee wanted to achieve the unification of Korea in his lifetime. Understanding this, many of his close associates, including Minister of National Defense Shin Sung Mo, openly advocated the unification of Korea by force. Many young Korean army officers believed that the time for the use of force was getting near.

Professor G. Henderson, an American embassy staff member at that time, recorded an interesting conversation with a group of young Korean officers who shared this belief:

> Col. Kim (Paek-Il) laid some emphasis on the great sentiment existing in the army (ROK) for invasion of the north. Col. Kim stated that he felt that the troops needed about six months more training before being really prepared. The implication of what they would be prepared for seemed understood by everyone.[2]

Col. Kim, commandant of the School of Arms, and several other high ranking young officers were interviewed by Dr. Henderson. All of them agreed with Col. Kim's view on preparing for the invasion of the north. Another officer, Col. Kin, was a bright, aggressive young man, according to Dr. Henderson, and stated confidently, "One usually hears the army [ROK] never attacks North Korea and is always getting attacked. That is not true. Mostly our army is doing the attacking first and we attack harder. Our troops feel stronger." The conversation took place in Seoul on August 26, 1949, nine months before the war.

Tragically, Dr. Rhee was as convinced as these young officers and Minister Shin that they could win the war. On November I, 1949, Minister Shin said at a press interview, "We are strong enough to march up and take Pyongyang within a few days."[3] The minister complained about the delay of the invasion saying: "If we had our way we would, I'm sure, have started up already." On March 2, 1950, President Rhee told the Korean people that despite advice given by "friends from across the seas" not to attack the "foreign puppets" in North Korea, the cries of "our brothers in distress" in the North could not be ignored. "To this call we shall respond,"[4] he said. The sentiment of this Korean independence speech w as clearly to unify the country by force if necessary. To create a national emergency, President Rhee employed the unification theme as a patriotic movement. The national emergency was to keep him in power indefinitely .

Wasn't this speech a broad enough hint for American authorities to guard against the possibility of invasion if the Americans wanted peace in Korea?

The problem was that there were conflicting views among American leaders, as we discussed earlier. According to Kim Youngjung, "By violating the constitution, terrorizing the National Assembly and imprisoning its members to retain his position, South Korean President Syngman Rhee is strengthening Communist prestige in the eyes of the democratic people of the world faster than the Commun sts could hope to do themselves. By making a mockery of democracy, he is u idermining the foundation of his country and the American position in all Asia."[5]

A year after the cease-fire between United Nations Forces and the Communists, Dr. Rhee was still trying to maintain his power against the will of Korea and also the very principles of democracy and freedom for which the United Nations Forces had supposedly participated in the war. When Dr. Rhee lacked spontaneous support, he resorted to force. Mounting tension between Dr. Rhee and the assembly finally exploded on May 24, 1952, when Rhee declared martial law "to maintain peace and order." On May 28, the National Assembly voted unanimously not to adjourn until government officials explained the imprisonment of assemblymen,[6] and rescinded the martial law edict. Dr. Rhee ignored the resolution. Vice-President Kim Seung-soo tendered his resignation on May 29 in protest against President Rhee's "assault on the constitution," but it too was ignored by Dr. Rhee.[7] Dr. Rhee said he imposed martial law because of an "international plot" against his government, saying the communists were smuggling money into South Korea. Eight of the arrested assemblymen were accused of being involved. One United Nations source called this charge "eyewash" and said, "The chances are perhaps one in 10,000 that any of these assemblymen are getting paid by the communists."[8]

If Dr. Rhee's accusation of an "international plot" were true, such developments could have well threatened the security of the Korean government and of the entire United Nations effort in Korea, yet Dr. Rhee never informed United Nations military authorities, who would have been vitally concerned. Dr. Rhee's Home Minister Lee Bum-suk founder of the Nazi-type youth movement in South Korea, charged that the communists were plotting to elect Dr. John Myun Chang, former ambassador to Washington and premier of Rhee's government, who would collaborate with the North Korean regime.[9] Rhee's real reason for declaring martial law and cracking down on opposition members of the National Assembly was to maintain his absolute power. President Rhee was elected by the assembly for a four-year term which should have expired in July. The seventy-seven-year-old president was opposed by a majority of the assembly then, and there was no chance for him to be re-elected by the assembly. Thus, Dr. Rhee proposed to change the constitution so the president would be elected by the people instead of the assembly.

On the surface, Dr. Rhee appeared to be a champion of the people. He said that he defended the "will of the people" against the legislators who were "selfish minorities." Some Americans defended Dr. Rhee by saying that United Nations efforts in South Korea would have collapsed without Dr. Rhee as the head of the government. Dr. Rhee's advisor, Dr. Paul F. Douglas, former president of American University in Washington, D.C., said that the United Nations could not afford to intervene because Dr. Rhee had the support of his people. Dr. Douglas added in a newspaper interview on July 14, 1952, that: "Dr. Rhee is staging a one-man revolution' and is determined to change the constitution, illegally if necessary."[10] Dr. Douglas had reason to fear intervention by the United Nations in the Korean internal dispute as it could have caused open warfare behind the lines and collapsed the war against communism. In those extraordinary circumstances, an American editorial commented: "It may be that the sounder–yes, the more democratic cause–is to stand clear and let Rhee, with his solid backing by the people and the Army, revise the constitution in his own way, even though his means appear to outsiders the very antithesis of the democratic process." The editorial continued: "Rhee is not wholly without legal sanction for his program, the constitution providing that: The sovereignty of the Korean Republic shall reside in the people."[11] No one was so naive as to believe in South Korea that Dr. Rhee was the indispensable national leader. On May 29, an American correspondent reported from Pusan: " There are growing signs that Rhee stands almost alone within his government except for the support of Home Minister Lee Bum-suk."[12]

In a parliamentary government system, if the legislators do not represent the people, where do we find the will of the people? Dr. Rhee contended that the time had come for action and he had advocated the revision of the constitution to retain power. He said, "The real struggle for power is between the entire nation and a group of Assemblymen. There is no one more anxious than I am to see this country firmly established as a truly independent and democratic state. This has been the sole objective of my life-long struggle." He might have been sincere, as he had expressed such sentiments, but the words were meaningless when he acted contrary to them.

After he proposed popular election of the president and a two-chamber legislative body proposition was defeated, Dr. Rhee and his supporters went to work in a different manner. Posters appeared in Pusan, wartime capital, and elsewhere demanding the recall of the assembly and holding of new elections. Dr. Rhee said the assembly's action showed it no longer reflected the "will of the people." The constitution made no provision for the recall of assemblymen. Thus Dr. Rhee now had cast aside the Korean constitution. Whether motivated by desires for personal power or not, he had by-passed the law and set himself up as the sole interpreter of what was best for Korea. It should, however, be noted that the constitution itself was only four years old, and was drafted on a somewhat experimental basis. The document was not flaw less, and there was room for improvement. At any rate, this was hardly a time for Dr. Rhee to rip apart the document on the basis of personal gains, in the midst of struggle against "communist aggression."

In Washington, Presidential News Secretary Joseph Short said that President Truman "discussed fully with Ambassador Muccio his concern over the domestic situation in the Republic of Korea." At the same time, Secretary of State Dean Acheson sent Ambassador Muccio back to Seoul because he regarded the situation as "pressing and serious."[13] Meantime, President Truman had sent a strong personal note to President Rhee on June 3, and Prime Minister Churchill also communicated his concern to Dr. Rhee and made clear that British troops were "fighting in South Korea to protect that country from aggression and not to secure the establishment of a self-constituted dictatorship."[14]

In view of the serious political situation, Churchill sent his ministers to Korea to check the condition. The foreign office spokesman announced that Selwyn Lloyd, Minister of State for Foreign Affairs, and R. H. Scott, Assistant Foreign Undersecretary in charge of Far Eastern Affairs, would go to Korea with Lord Alexander, Minister of Defense. They left London on June 6.

Following the lead of London, other United Nations members also protested. A Netherlands foreign office spokesman said in the Hague that the United Nations Commission for the Unification and Rehabilitation of Korea sent a protest to President Rhee, and Richard G. Casey, Minister of External Affairs, said in Canberra that Australia had expressed concern in a note to Dr. Rhee. The French charge d'affaires in Pusan also delivered an official protest note to Dr. Rhee.[15]

U.N. Secretary-General Trygve Lie disclosed on June 6 that he had asked UNCURK (United Nations Commission for the Unification and Rehabilitation of Korea) to express to Dr. Rhee his "deep anxiety" over Dr. Rhee's "arbitrary" acts. Lie stated, "Strict adherence to constitutional and democratic processes are all the more necessary in a country which must nurse and develop all of its resources to join members of the U. N. in repelling aggression and in prompting economic recovery." The United Nations, he said, "and especially those members providing assistance in Korea, cannot remain unconcerned when arbitrary methods are used which threaten to destroy the roots of democratic government." Dr. Rhee responded by countercharging that the protests were made "on the basis of second-hand reports and premature conclusions."[16]

In response to the U.N. Secretary-General's message, Dr. Rhee's spokesman said: " Trygve Lie apparently has leaped to see the conclusion that the Korean government is using arbitrary methods.' It is very regrettable that

Mr. Lie has chosen to arbitrarily evaluate local conditions on the basis of second-hand reports and premature conclusions."[17]

From this point on Dr. Rhee enforced strict censorship, instead of rectifying his authoritarian policy. He banned the June 9 issue of *Newsweek* which carried an article critical of Dr. Rhee's method of running Korea. The *Newsweek* article said: "President Rhee's autocratic action, in the frank opinion of United States and U.N. officials, appeared to threaten the Republic's democratic form of government." It was only the beginning. Even the "Voice of America," an American official broadcast, which had been the official news medium, was suspended as of June 12 because it had been broadcasting American public reaction and editorial comments on current issues in South Korea. "The Voice of America has been broadcasting adverse and distorted news about the feud," the Rhee government spokesman complained, adding the government could not permit its own monopoly radio to "rebuke the government." The ban continued for sixteen days.

Dr. Rhee, facing almost certain defeat for re-election to the presidency by the National Assembly, insisted that the Korean people be allowed to pick the president directly. A constitutional amendment to that effect was defeated by the assembly in April, 1952, 143 to 19. Dr. Rhee charged that the legislature's action violated the "will of the people." Imposing martial law and imprisoning the opposition members of the assembly did not solve the situation. Pressure from members of the United Nations did not allow him any freedom of action.

Dr. Rhee now mobilized the "representatives" of town and city councils and provincial assemblies. Supposedly they represented the "will of the people." There were six hundred of them, and more than eighty assembly members were imprisoned in the hall of the national assembly building by these "representatives." One member of the National Assemby, Pak Sung-ha, was seized and beaten by the mob, and others were pushed, slapped, and forced to return to the assembly hall after some tried to leave. Police stood by and watched the blockade of the assembly without intervening until the Home Minister Lee Bum-suk took charge personally. While this was going on, Dr. Rhee was away on a fishing trip with American Ambassador Muccio. The amicable relationship between President Rhee and Ambassador Muccio left a strong impression on Koreans that the United States government approved Rhee's authoritarian policy, although President Truman registered his complaint openly. The dual policies in regard to the Rhee regime encouraged the dictator to pursue his authoritarian style with enthusiasm.

On June 30, Dr. Rhee issued an ultimatum to the National Assembly to transfer the power of presidential election to the people or face dissolution.

In his message to the assembly, Dr. Rhee said that he could not wait any longer for the Assembly to pass the constitutional amendment bill. He could not wait any longer for the Assembly to take action. He was studying the ways and means of dissolving the National Assembly. He claimed that he must follow the will of the people.

Faced with their own discharge, the assemblymen re-elected Rhee. The *New York Herald Tribune* reported on June 24 that Dr. Rhee would never relinquish his office until he died of old age or an assassin's bullet.

In November, 1954, Dr. Rhee again forced the National Assembly to amend the constitution, enabling him to be president for life, while all successors were to be limited to two four-year terms. He was re-elected with a one-vote margin. In the third presidential election, held on May 15, 1956, Dr. Rhee became the presidential candidate of the Liberal party. A third term was prohibited by the constitution, but Dr. Rhee changed its contents once more to suit himself. The restriction on the number of terms was not to apply to the first president--Syngman Rhee. He was not to be restrained by the national law of which he was the chief administrator.

One of the most significant results of the 1956 election was not the re-election of Dr. Rhee, but the surprising election of Dr. John M. Chang as vice-president. Dr. Chang was   one of several vice-presidential candidates, including Lee Ki-poong, Dr. Rhee's running mate. The number of votes Dr. Rhee received indicated that he might have lost had not his opponent, Shin Ikhi, been dead. A democratic candidate, Shin Ikhi died ten days before the election. He received almost two million votes, and the third candidate, Cho Bong-am of the Progressive party, polled more than two million votes, while Dr. Rhee received a little more than five million votes. Moreover, most of the Liberal party votes came from rural areas which were under absolute police control. The people had been warned not to vote for a dead man and they knew their ballots would be thrown out if they did. The vote for the dead man was a protest against the Rhee government, and it was made under an atmosphere of fear.

Democratic candidate Shin Ikhi charged "only a few hours before leaving for Iri (where he died) that national police were trying to intimidate voters into casting their ballots for Mr. Rhee."[18] On May 15, according to a United Press report, Progressive candidate Cho Bong-am was "in hiding, fearful of his life" for over a week before the election. Cho also charged that his supporters "were subjected to terrorism, their houses were destroyed and property robbed and they were placed virtually outside the realm of protection by the laws," according to a report on May 17 by the Associated Press.

The situation became worse. On December 24, 1958, opposition legislators were locked out of the National Assembly Hall and twenty-two hills were "passed" in their absence. Four months later the opposition Catholic daily newspaper, *Kyung-hyang Shinmun,* was closed down for carrying editorials and news stories of a "false nature."

At the end of his third term, Dr. Rhee decided to run for a fourth term. He needed a new political strategy to fool the people once again.

On February 3, 1960, Dr. Rhee moved up the 1960 presidential election date to March 15 instead of the usual May date, claiming it would be a convenience to farmers. The election date announcement came soon after the chief opposition candidate, Dr. Chough Byong-ok, entered Walter Reed Hospital in Washington for a major operation. Dr. Chough died in the hospital on February 15. Since the constitution provided, in Article 56, that the election should be held "at the latest" thirty days before the outgoing president's term expired, and Dr. Rhee's third term was to end August 15, there was no reason for haste, except to take advantage of his opponent's illness. Dr. Rhee forced through his fourth term on March 15, 1960, which brought an end to the people's patience.

The revolution took place. More than 100,000 students participated in bloody riots all over South Korea against Dr. Rhee's regime. The student revolution was a spontaneous movement without political party involvement. On April 27, student demonstrations were renewed, and threatened the presidential mansion and other government office buildings in Seoul. The situation was uncontrollable. Seeing that Rhee's days were over, Rhee's running mate Lee Ki-poong and his family committed suicide and Dr. Rhee reluctantly resigned his presidency. He was eighty-five years old when he left Korea for exile in Honolulu where he remained for the rest of his life. He wanted so much to be known as the "George Washington" of Korea, but he abused his country's infant democracy more than he could have imagined in his aged years.

The presidency of the Republic of Korea is a constitutional organ heading the executive branch, and as such represents the republic in relations with foreign nations. The governmental organization law, promulgated on July 17, 1948, as the first law of the republic, provided that "the president, as the head of the executive branch, in accordance with laws and regulations, may suspend or repeal administrative orders or dispositions of the cabinet ministers in case such orders or dispositions are deemed improper or illegal." The constitution of the Republic of Korea adopted a presidential system patterned after that of the United States, with some features of the British parliamentary cabinet system added to it. The latter was more characteristic when the Democratic party controlled the government after the April Student Revolution. The Inspection Committee and the Civil Service Committee were established as independent government agencies directly responsible to the president.

A Western-patterned parliamentary system was instituted in South Korea following the first election in Korea in May 1948, and remained through three elections until the military coup on May 16, 1961. Dr. Rhee was elected as first chairman of the National Assembly by an overwhelming majority, then lost his influence steadily as time passed, finally to be overthrown by the spontaneous popular movement.

Dr. Rhee's Liberal party introduced and passed by force a constitutional amendment enabling the first president to run for more than two terms, despite constitutional restrictions, and this act disillusioned the people of Korea who lost faith in the government.

Dr. Rhee was probably the most fanatic foreign supporter of the American struggle against communism. He had received an American education, holding a master's degree from Havard and a Ph.D. from Princeton, majoring in political science. On the other hand, he was also a revolutionary preaching liberty and democracy. The last Korean Royal House sent him to prison for his anti-government activities. He suffered in jail from both the Royal Koreans and the Japanese militarists. They gave him the "water torture"–drops of water at measured intervals dripped on the victim until he was driven to frenzy and madness. The jailers put his fingers between steel rollers and smashed them. He was released from prison in a general amnesty in 1904 as the Russo-Japanese war was beginning–the main issue of which was the domination of Korea. Dr. Rhee fled to the United States where he spent his long exile until 1945 when a United States Army plane brought him to Seoul in mid-October.

Dr. Rhee had been unveiled before the Korean people by Lieutenant General John R. Hodge, then the commander of the United States 8th Army which occupied Korea. Dr. Rhee was merely one of several Korean politicians being tested hopefully by American policy-makers. Dr. Rhee's public statements sounded like Fourth of July oratory. His 1948 presidential inaugural speech was packed with fine Jeffersonian phrases. His American friends were pleased. His actions, however, proved an embarrassment to democratic people. Dr. Rhee adopted a pattern of government that had been consistently dictatorial. Few men in Korea have ever been safe from the coercion of Rhee's large police force. Two of Dr. Rhee's major political rivals were mysteriously assassinated. A third, the American State Department's main choice for the presidency of Korea, fled to the security of a United States Army hospital in fear of his life, and eventually moved to North Korea. Dr. Rhee alone survived.

Men who had been mentioned as opposition leaders usually found one of the following courses advisable: first, prompt disavowal of their supporters; second, a hasty trip to United States territories; third, convenient illness demanding care in a safe hospital. Dr. Rhee believed that he alone could bring the "will of the people" to fruition, since in his opinion other Korean leaders were hopelessly incompetent for the job. Some Americans, particularly generals, including General Douglas MacArthur, liked him and respected his leadership abilities. He was intransigent and intractable. From the outset, he had set himself up on a narrow but very solid platform. He was against the political monstrosity which split his country along the 38th Parallel; he was against communism; and he was for the revival of one Korea. He wanted both American and Russian troops removed from Korea and the nation united, by force and violence if necessary. In commenting on a truce at the end of the Korean War, Dr. Rhee said: "My country today, like Great Britain in 1940, believes that rather than accept a truce of appeasement- the kind of truce we truly believe to be suicidal- it is best to fight on. The alternative is that this monster [Red China], by feeding on its new conquests, will develop power and appetite for all Asia."[19]

Rhee's Korea suffered from economic instability. A characteristic of Rhee's regime was a monopoly control of the economic lite of the newborn nation.

In 1941, 94 percent of southern Korea's capital investment was in the hands of Japanese monopolists. When the American Military Government confiscated enemy properties and redistributed them to Koreans, the redistribution method favored the "haves" rather than the "have-nots." This policy escalated when Dr. Rhee was elected as president of the republic. In other words, Rhee's regime enhanced the position of the monopolists, beginning the Korean monopoly system. As a result, small business enterprises did not grow and the gap between the rich and the poor increased. With the increase of monopoly, free competition was eliminated, and prices were dictated by suppliers rather than regulated by the law of supply and demand, and the nation was confronted with uncontrolled inflation. on top of that, the price of manufactured goods in the city markets went sky high, but the price of farm products went down. During the last days of Dr. Rhee, during 1950s-1960s, the price of fertilizer had gone up 500 percent in five years while farm products went up only 20 percent in the same period. When I visited farmers in the Taejon area in the spring of 1961, a year after the April Student Revolution, farmers were searching for grass roots to substitute for more substantial food in their diets. The starving farmers were ready to revolt against the Rhee regime, and they were more than happy to participate in the April Student

Revolution. The students, of course, were well aware of conditions in the country-side. There were, however, no rewards for the farmers after the revolution.

Failure to deal with social problems was the third characteristic of the Rhee regime. Not able to support themselves on farms, tens of thousands migrated to the cities looking for jobs. There were no jobs for them. As a result, millions of unemployed gathered in the metropolis. Dr. Rhee's government had no policy to cope with this serious national problem. If there was a government policy, it was to ignore the starving and jobless population. The apathetic policy increased tensions between newly created entrepreneurs and the newly created unemployed class. The jobless saw the Rhee regime as the protector of the rich.

Paradoxically enough, these unbalanced conditions simultaneously produced both modern air-conditioned skyscrapers and slums in the capital of Seoul and other major cities. Seoul, for instance, has had everything a modern city should have as the capital of a newly emerging nation: many tall modern buildings, well-trained bureaucrats, disciplined police forces, paved boulevards, a booming tourist business, a center of modern cultural activities, and, of course, many green golf courses in neighboring areas. No foreigner would ever suspect that there could be a revolution in such a prosperous city. Nevertheless, it happened. It happened, because of the more than one hundred thousand jobless men and women from the country-side, added to the tens of thousands of war orphans and widows living in urban slums, and the estimated several million beggars. The Rhee government did not keep statistics on these unfortunates. With high unemployment, war orphans, beggars, and resulting high crime rates, one could not walk safely in the streets of Seoul after dark.

The Korean War, of course, had worsened the situation, but Dr. Rhee's government didn't understand the seriousness of the problem. More and more people were alienated from their government, and the government became more regulative and authoritative, and evolved into a totalitarian regime. Dr. Rhee became a dictator when he declared martial law in the war-time capital of Pusan in July, 1952. The possibility of autonomy for political sections diminished, and the entire governmental system was controlled absolutely by one man. The end of the dictator's regime was inevitable.

The fourth characteristic of the Rhee regime was the style of bureaucratic politics. In spite of laws prohibiting political participation by bureaucrats, the civil servants openly took active roles in politics. They overwhelmingly supported the government they worked for rather than maintaining neutral positions as the law required. As a result, Korean civil servants became inheritors of the traditionally notorious bureaucrat systems of the past—the days of the Japanese occupation, and the later days of the Yi Dynasty.

Under Rhee public administration was primarily a police function, and more and more it was concentrated in the central government. Therefore, public servants' careers depended on the success or failure of governmental control over the public. To preserve their position in the public office, they had to exercise influence over citizens. The situation created an inevitable result. Public servants became the servants of the political party in spite of legal strictures against the practice.

The Korean people had experienced how government operated during the days of the Japanese occupation and the Yi Dynasty, but the public was not experienced in dealing with a democratic system of public administration. When Korea adopted a democratic system, the public was not ready to appreciate the change. Lack of democratic experience by the people made it possible for bureaucrats to follow the autocratic and political traditions of the past rather than to identify with democratic concepts. Consequently, bureaucrats maintained strategic political positions during the Rhee regime and set a pattern for the new system following the old line.

Complaints, mostly unheard by the government, were caused by increasing economic and social problems among the people, especially, intellectuals who had been alienated from the government. The Rhee regime paid little or no attention to the complaints and suppressed them.

The public servants who were nourished by taxpayers worked for Rhee's ruling political party, the Liberal party. An outstanding example is the case of Choi In-ku, the Minister of Interior during the presidential election in 1960. Choi ordered his subordinates, including the national police force, to campaign to re-elect Dr. Rhee. Instead of a fair and just election, the man who was charged legally with enforcing election law actively campaigned in favor of the current president and against his opponents. As a matter of fact, bureaucrats were instructed to ignore violations of election laws, and they justified their illegal actions as it served the incumbent. It was a characteristic exhibition of government by force rather than by law.

Korea's problem, now, was not of communism, as Dr. Rhee frequently claimed, but the treatment accorded the citizens of his republic. He exercised more and more dictatorial power, and became an absolute power with a 50,000-member police force to back him up. Dr. Rhee's regime became a police state. With or without his knowledge, his subordinates became little dictators in their own territories. The nation was ruled by fear and terror. The result of such government is inevitably corruption. Entire government machineries were under the influence of bribery and corruption. The government lost its dignity, influence and ability to function. Since it did not fulfill its duty as a government, it produced anarchy.

Under the Rhee regime, a potential modern and liberal democracy was hopelessly suppressed under the pretense that internal stability and unity of the nation required such suppression. Finally, the government was unable to maintain itself. Remaining were the same autocratic rule, the same corruption, the same indifference to misery and the same misuse of the American aid, which characterized China in the last year of the Kuomintang rule. Dr. Rhee trusted no one, and no business was too petty to escape his attention. For instance, the Korean treasury was under orders to make no foreign exchange allocations in excess of $500 without Dr. Rhee's personal approval. He also had no friends.

Dr. Rhee's speeches were packed with Jeffersonian phrases and his American associates were pleased. His actions, however, betrayed his people too many times. The regime could not free itself from the common practices of graft and bribery. No one expected miracles. No one even anticipated the government would be completely free over night from the age-old practices of graft and bribery. But the people did expect there would be sufficient control so that the nation could survive. Dr. Rhee, like King George III who refused to believe the reports from Boston, had not believed the news of the student revolution. It was, however, too late to take the necessary action when he finally realized that the student revolution was real and discontented citizens were at his doorstep. He was no longer able to control the situation and his political adventure ended.

Notes

1. The Voices of the People, a monthly publication by Channing Liem, New Paltz, N.Y., vol. 4, no. 7, July, 1975.
2. Ibid.
3. *New York Herald Tribune, Nov. 1,* 1949.
4. *New York Times,* Mar. 2, 1950.
5. *The Voice of Korea,* Washington, D.C., vol 9, no. 172, June 20, 1952.
6. Four national assemblymen were arrested on May 26, 1952. Others escaped the crackdown. A government spokesman declared on May 27 that communists were sending secret funds across the border into South Korea to create disorder.
7. Dr. Rhee not only ignored the assembly's protests against martial law, but personally directed the Korean military police to arrest nine opposition

members of the National Assembly. In addition, five assemblymen were sought and a dozen more were afraid to come out of hiding to attend assembly sessions for fear they would be arrested. Dr. Rhee declared: "I am sure there v. ill be more arrests." Report of Keyes Beech in *San Francisco Chronicle,* May 29, 1952.

8. *Associated Press* dispatch from Pusan, Korea, May 29, 1952.

9. Dr. Chang, who resigned on grounds of ill health on April 21, was in the U. S. Army hospital, and his close associate, Chong-won Sunoo, was arrested on the charge of engaging in a "communist conspiracy."

10. Contrary to his strong dictatorial attitude toward his own people, Dr. Rhee was totally dependent on American friends for his survival. He was more than willing to give up his presidential power as the commanding chief of military forces to General Douglas MacArthur. On July 15, 1950, President Rhee wrote a letter to General MacArthur: "I am happy to assign to you command authority over all land, sea, and air forces of the Republic of Korea during the period of the continuation of the present state of hostilities; such command to be exercised either by you personally or by such military commander or commanders to whom you may delegate the exercise of this authority within Korea or in adjacent seas." The letter clearly indicated how much President Rhee was willing to accept the leadership of a foreign general to govern his nation. See *MacArthur: His Rendezvous with History* by Courtney Whitney (New York: Knopf, 1965), p. 338.

11. *San Francisco Chronicle,* June 18, 1952.

12. *Chicago Daily News,* May 29, 1952.

13. *Associated Press,* June 4, 1952.

14. Ibid., June 5, 1952.

15. *United Press. June* 5, 1952.

16. *Associated Press,* June 7, 1952.

17. Ibid.

18. *New York Herald Tribune, May 6, 1956.*

19. Syngman Rhee, "Why I Stood Alone," *This Week Magazine,* August 16, 1953.

14

Park Chung Hee and the Export-Led Development Economy

South Korea, like other former colonial countries, was a backward agricultural, poverty-stricken poor nation. Her developing industries would collapse immediately upon withdrawal of foreign capital, technological skills, and management. Her industries could not survive without the protective barriers which block foreign competition as well as control imports conserving foreign exchange. Such protective barrier policies continued until the commercial normalization treaty with Japan in 1965.

Economic policy of South Korea under President Park Chung Hee's rule (1961-1979) changed drastically in favor of the "open door policy" by inviting direct foreign investments, particularly Japanese capital after the 1965 treaty. The economic policy was initiated, however, not by President Park or any other Korean leaders, but outsiders—American policy-makers with an understanding with the Japanese policy-makers.[1]

Why has economic policy in South Korea changed? The growth of the Korean economy was very slow under American aid to South Korea. The highest growth, 8.7 percent, was experienced in 1957, but declined to 7 percent in 1958, 5.2 percent in 1959, and 2.1 percent in 1960. The U.S. policy was to exploit Korea as her market by selling surplus agricultural products and other commodities. No attention was given to developing basic industries in the country.

When Japan became a major economic power, although she still remains as a junior partner of the U.S., the U.S. decided to share her market with Japan. With this understanding, the U.S. has encouraged Japan to move more aggressively into South Korea and other Southeast Asian countries. The

U.S. high officials laid down the ground work for the normalization of the Japan-South Korea treaty in 1965. Even with such encouragement from the U.S., Japan moved, at least for the first couple of years, back to South Korea very cautiously.

The U.S. shared her Korean market with Japan not simply to help to solve such Japanese domestic economic problems as foreign investment of her enormous surplus capital which she accumulated during the Korean War, but also because of the economic difficulties resulting from American military involvement in Vietnam. The U.S. began to cut her economic aid to South Korea, and wanted Japan to take over some of the responsibilities.

From the South Korean point of view, she needed continuous U.S. economic aid, but instead, the aid had been cut. The Korean "economic miracle" began, therefore, after the 1965 treaty between Japan and South Korea. Under the Japanese aid program to South Korea, which actually began about 1967, the growth of the Korean economy was: 8.9 percent in 1967, 13.3 percent in 1968, 15.9 per cent in 1969, 8.9 percent in 1970, and 16.9 percent, the highest, in 1973,[2] the year after President Park declared his absolute rule which is known as the "Yushin System."

There are three basic characteristics of the South Korean economy. First of all, South Korean economy is an export-oriented economy. Secondly, it is a foreign-capital dominated economy. Thirdly, it is an industrial-oriented economy against the agricultural development.

Export-oriented Economic Policy

The Economic Planning Board of South Korea stated that the annual average increase of Korean exports had been 40 percent from 1961 to 1977. In 1961, Korean exports amounted to $42.9 million but in 1977, they reached $10,007 million. The 1977 exports were 233% of 1961 exports. Korean exports were so successful that she ranked to 17th among the exporting nations within 15 years following independence, and expected to rank within the ten leading nations during the 1980s.

Average yearly growth of exports during the Third 5-year Plan, which ended in 1976, was 45.5%.[3] This had slowed to 39.2% following three years, 20% in the Fourth 5-year Plan Period which ended in 1981. At the end of the Fourth Economic Plan, total merchandise exports amounted to $20.6 billion, 94% of which were manufactured goods.[4]

Not only the increased amounts, but the nature of export goods has also changed. The major exports of the seventies were mostly clothing, textiles, plywood, toys, transistors, and fresh fish, but the nature of export goods in the early eighties were more diversified. The trend towards diversification began to export T.V. radio, and automobiles. In other words, the pattern of export goods changed from labor-concentrated manufactured goods to high technological and capital-concentrated manufactured goods. In its efforts to expand the exports of diversified commodities such as steel, chemicals, transport equipment, machinery, and electronics, Korean businessmen have been aided by a number of factors. First of all, government support, which included subsidized credit, reduction of risks in production, and control of the wages.

Anticipating such changes and the need for popular cooperation to achieve export goals, the Korean government has promoted hard work, savings, and patience. A President Park's political councilor said "We can join the rank of the industrialized nations in the 1980s if we can adjust our international economic competition and win in the export race and technical development.. Let us put all our efforts, courage, creativeness and desires, and let us win in the economic race. Let us continue our attitude of diligence and savings.. everyone will be rewarded when we achieve a high level of the economic development."[5]

What's the purpose of such growth of industry? For the purpose of exports, of course. 1977 exports had increased 23 percent compared with the previous year, and went over $10 billion.[6] How much, then, did the national treasury gain from this remarkable achievement? Not only did Korea not make money, but she lost money by trade.

Korea had import raw materials in order to produce exporting goods. Each year, Korea imported more and more materials, oil, and capital goods in order to accommodate the export program. Consequently, there was a trade deficit. The deficit was $55 million in 1962, $582 million in 1971, $2 billion in 1974, $2.2 billion in 1978, and $3 billion in 1979.[7]

In order to achieve a $10 billion target for exports in 1975, the government granted all sorts of benefits to the industrialists besides allowing lower rates for water, power, and gas supplies. One of the important favors was giving them loans with low interest rates at the government-owned-and-operated banks as well as at the private banks whose license depended on the government. One source indicates that the government subsidized about one-fifth of each dollar's worth or $2 billion. In 1977, the government subsidy for exports went up to 68.2 percent of the entire tax revenue.[8]

During the same year, 1977, twenty leading Korean corporations including Hyundai, Daewoo, Samsung, etc., exported goods amounting to about $4,192,700 million, and one fifth of that amount was government subsidy. For instance, these corporations borrowed huge amounts from the banks at a special rate of interest, 8 percent, while the normal rate was twice that. It is important to point out that the subsidies these 20 corporations received came from the tax revenues the government collected from the common citizens. As the export increased, the government subsidy also increased, and simultaneously, the tax also has increased to subsidize them. In 1971 the tax rate was 15 percent and increased to 20 percent in 1980.

Another important element concerned with the export-import business in South Korea is the overwhelming domination of the Japanese companies there. Two leading Japanese zaibatsu groupsMitsui andMitsubishi, control about three-quarters of Japanese trading business in South Korea. Considering that about 40 percent or more of total Korean trade is with Japan, it is indeed a staggering situation.[9]

In 1977, 81 percent of non-government Korean imported goods were handled by Japanese firms in Seoul. Five leading Japanese firms, Mitsui, Mitsubishi, Sumitomo, Ito, and Marubeni, out of 22 firms, handled 63 percent, or almost $2 billion, of the entire non-government Korean import which 67 foreign firms handled in Seoul. Foreign firms handled about 11.5 percent of the entire importing business including the government's. *The Chosun Daily News,* March 10, 1978, reported that Marubeni Co. alone imported to Korea about $340 million worth of goods during the year 1977. In other words, Japanese firms in Seoul were largely doing business with their home offices in Tokyo. Such transactions had little to do with the Korean national economy, but nevertheless were recorded as a portion of the Korean GNP.

Is the trading business profitable for the Korean economy? Her trade deficit has been increasing except for the year of 1977.

There are three main reasons for the trade deficit. First, South Korea, like Japan, must import most of her raw materials. For instance, more than 90 percent of raw cotton imports come from the United States. Second, her exports are concentrated in two countries, Japan and the U.S. Third, as the world economy slips into recession, competition in international markets becomes more and more severe, and a new supplier like South Korea quickly loses newly-gained markets. In order to hold onto these markets, the Korean government promotes an "export bleeding" policy. For instance, she exported fertilizer at $98 per metric ton, at a loss of $22 per ton since the true cost was $120. On the other hand, the government sold the same commodity to Korean farmers at $240 per metric ton–or at $120 profit per ton. Another example is the case of *Pony,* a Korean automobile. The price of *Pony* is $8,000 in South Korea but the export-price is only $1,000. The trade deficit, meantime, increased year by year.

How is the gross national product (GNP) related to trade? About 72%

of Korean GNP was reflected in export-import trade in 1976, and about 85% in 1978. In other words, an increase in trade means an increase of GNP, or economic "achievement" means an increase of trade. Trade has dominated the national economy. Therefore, whoever dominates the trade in Korea also dominates the national economy.

A serious question is: Was the trading business under the Park regime profitable for the national economy? Under Park's export-oriented policy, actual economic growth had declined.

For instance, an average economic growth over a three-year period, 1959-1961, prior to the Park's regime was 5.4 percent while it was only 4.7 percent during the Third Economic Planning Period from 1972 to 1976.

During the First Economic Planning Period, 1962-66, exports occupied 15.4 percent of GNP. The percentage, however, increased to 58 percent during the Third Economic Planning Period, 1972-1976. Increased GNP has been closely related to increased national exports. There is nothing wrong with the national export situation if increased exportation benefits the national economy. In case of Korea, however, the exportation does not benefit the national economy due to the foreign domination of Korean exports. In other words, not only foreign-invested industries dominate the major portion of the exports of South Korea, but also it creates the continuing imbalance in Korea's trade with Japan. It is caused not by the failure to increase exports to Japan but by the requirements of the Korean economy itself, which demands raw materials and semi-finished products from Japan in order to add some labor and export elsewhere. That is why Korea increases both exports and imports from Japan every year, and the gap also increases in favor of Japan.

Most of foreign-investment enterprises are located in the "Free Industrial Zone" or "Export Industrial Zone" where foreign industries enjoy special favors from the Korean government. Not only do they not pay taxes or customs duties, but they also receive water, power, and other supplies at lower rates, and are protected by the local government from labor strikes and other protests. In other words, Korean government provides special favors to the foreigners in these industrial zones for the purpose of GNP growth. The foreigners are able to import raw materials without customs duties and export manufactured goods without paying a cent of tax to the Korean government.

Meanwhile, they receive all sorts of special favors and protection from the government. These manufactured goods are branded as "made in Korea" when exported, but these goods have nothing to do with the national economy of Korea. The export of these goods increased double and triple during the Third Economic Planning Period. And increase of export meant the increasing these goods from "Free Industrial Zone," and increase of GNP meant the increase of export of these goods. The export growth trend achieved by foreign investment industries. The foreign investment or control enterprises occupied 53.3 percent of the total Korean exports in 1972, 55.6 percent in 1973, and 63.9 percent in 1974. The percentage increased as the government promoted the heavy chemical industries during the Fourth Economic Planning Period which ended in 1981.

How can Korean trade deficits be met? The answer is commercial loans, which carry a high rate of interest and are on short term. In 1974, the Vice-Premier with half a dozen ministers of the Korean cabinet came to New York to negotiate a $500 million short term loan with several banks in New York including Chase Manhattan, First National City, Chemical, and Mellon. This loan was, of course, no solution for the Korean economy. Forty percent of the loan in 1974 was used for debt payment although the purpose of borrowing them was to build new factories. The same thing was repeated in 1975.[10]

Understanding South Korea's desperate condition, Japan was ready to take advantage of her. In 1974, Japanese firms in South Korea reportedly held 65.4 percent of all foreign investment in South Korea. The U.S. held 27.6 percent. And of total 949 foreign invested companies, Japanese accounted for 784.[11]

President Park's promotion of export-oriented industrialization is entirely misguided, because it has not modernized the Korean economy or benefitted the Korean people. On the contrary, this strategy has seriously hurt the indigenous industrial development and primarily benefitted foreign investors.

In 1973, at the time of world oil crisis, President Park supported the export-oriented industries, and totally neglected the domestic-oriented industries. As a result, many textile, lumber, mining, and construction industries were forced to close their factories. For instance, in Kyung-buk Province, 72 percent or 760 textile factories laid off a major portion of the employees, 12.3 percent or 130 factories closed, only 15.6 percent of 166 factories continued their normal operation. In the mining field, 854 enterprises shut down for good, and created 63,000 unemployed.[12]

Can small Korean industries compete with the most advanced foreign industrial powers in South Korea? In the name of free enterprise, President Park deliberately shut down small Korean factories and supported foreign-based export-oriented industries in South Korea. This policy was not the original policy of President Park; it was formulated in Tokyo and Washington.

According to the *Dong-A Daily News* report, the foreign investors have remitted profits double their original investment stake. By early 1976 $26 million each for Skelly and Swift and $20 million for Gulf and International Mineral were remitted.[13] All these U.S. financed plants were 100 percent capitalized by U.S. AID loans. AID loaned the Chinhae plant $24 million with repayment deferred 10 years at one percent interest and then payment at 2 percent for the next 30 years. The corporation had extracted guaranteed profits exceeding $92 million before the U.S. government had begun to recover its loan. Gulf Oil Company's $4 million contribution to Park's election in 1967 and 1971 was a small portion of such profits.

Anticipating a low rate of export growth in the eighties, the Korean government have shifted toward heavy industry exports departing from labor intensive industries. Unless new exports are vigorously developed, Korea cannot capture an increasing share of the world market of manufactured goods. During 1982 the volume of exports grew a mere 5.8%. In terms of value, they increased less than 49%. The sudden surge in demand for ships resulted in much of the export expansion. The demands of ships, electronic goods, and footwear, however, began to decline in following years. The problem which South Korea confronted is not only her light industries placed at a disadvantage in inter national markets, but also competing against products such as consumer electronic goods of the advanced countries. A related question is whether she is capable to challenge them who are the supporters of her export-oriented industries. Furthermore, it is a question of whether a high and rising dependence on exports is desirable.

There are considerable disadvantages in a sudden change from labor intensive industrial patterns to a capital intensive pattern. First of all, the smallness of the economy militated against the realization of scale economies. Second, South Korea has very limited sophistication of the domestic market. Third, her high technology is not sufficiently developed to compete with the advanced countries. Lastly, the advanced countries would protect their markets against the foreign import goods as they are practiced in Japan, the United States, and European countries.

For future market conditions, the following hurdles are mentioned by a World Bank Study on South Korean Economy:

1. the speed of growth in Organization for Economic Cooperation and Development (OECD) countries and the length of business cycles;
2. import elasticities for advanced manufactures;
3. the volatility of product and process technologies in major industrial fields;
4. the future strategy of international corporations that have come to

dominate production and technology of numerous important products;

5. the effects of automation on the future prospects of major subsectors in the industrial economies;

6. the direction of protectionist sentiments and the manner in which they influence imports into OECD countries from the small, East Asian economies.[14]

Korean exports were supported by the high import elasticities prevailing through the seventies. projections in the Fifth 5-Year Economic Plan assume that these situations have remained unchanged. This assumption, however, is very doubtful. The stiffening of import restrictions in the advanced countries during the eighties is undoubtedly to depress market growth for exports from South Korea. At the same time, the fierceness of competition among LDC (Low Developing Countries) exporters have steadily increased the last few years.

Foreign Capital Domination

The second characteristic of the Korean economy is economic control through foreign loans. Through the 1965 treaty with Japan, South Korea received $300 million for property claims, and a $200 million loan over a period of 10 years. In addition, the Japanese pledged $300 million in private loans. This agreement launched South Korea on its phase of loan-based industrialization. In 1966, foreign loans amounted to only $108 million; however, they reached $475 million in 1969, and $628 million in 1973. In the three years following 1973, Korea had to borrow about $4 billion from foreign sources to meet trade deficits. In 1976, the debt increased further by $3.2 billion, bringing the total debt balance to $7.3 billion in 1977, $10 billion in 1978, $27 billion in 1980.[15]

The growth of Korean GNP means only expanding its foreign debt and has nothing to do with the enhancement of Korean economic life.

Most of these loans came to the government-controlled banks[16] and corporations. Korean Industrial Bank received $7,938 million, Bank of Korea $5,507, Citizen's National Bank $1,352, Enterprise Bank $1,351, The Housing Bank $567, and among the corporations, Korea Electric Co. received $2,670 million, The Chungju Fertilizer Co. $146, The Coal Corp. $194, The Agriculture Corp. $181, The Marine Development Corp. $123, and The Korea Steel and Iron Corp. $552, etc.[17] These statistics are based on official reports by the Ministry of Finance in 1972. The current figures are, therefore, expected to be much larger than quoted here.[18]

The debt steadily increased to $32 billion in 1981, $38 billion in 1982, $40.9 billion in 1983, $50 billion in 1984, and reached to $51.4 billion by the end of September 1985. South Korea is one of the biggest debtors in the world in absolute terms. In Brazil, the biggest debtor, the GNP was $1,336 per capita, and the debt balance $711 per capita in 1983. The ratio was 53.2%.But in South Korea the ratio was 53.6% in the same year.[19]

The next question is who lends money? Most of the loans obviously came from the United States and Japan. About two thirds are from them, and about 6.5 percent is from West Germany.

American aid still flows overwhelmingly to those countries in which American officials perceive a strategic interest, not to those countries which might be considered most in need nor to governments that demonstrate genuine commitment to changes in favor of the poor majority. The pattern of loans from the World Bank is no different from American unilateral flows. Evaluation of the Bank's lending patterns show that the officials have no hesitation about lending to "human rights violators." In fact, they are seemingly rewarded. One quarter of all World Bank loans in 1978 went to just four governments (South Korea, the Philippines, Brazil and Indonesia), all widely recognized as systematic violators of human rights. Nor can it be overlooked that many top recipients of American economic aid are also top recipients of American military assistance.

U.S.-funded economic assistance is geared to benefit U.S. corporations. Three quarters of all AID funds are spent in the United States to purchase goods. It is not surprising then that the primary lobbyists for and beneficiaries of foreign aid are multinational corporations.

It is also interesting to note which of the Japanese companies are most active in investment in South Korea. It is not surprising to know that the Mitsui group has about one third of all Japanese investments in South Korea while the Mitsubishi group is second in rank with 21 percent. Ito, Toyomen, Marubeni combined with the Mitsui group amounts to about 80 percent of the total Japanese investments in South Korea. The Mitsui group alone loaned to twenty leading corporations, including The Korea Electric Company and the Korea Fertilizer Company, $135 million, while the Mitsubish group loaned to ten leading corporations, including the largest cement company, Sangyong Corporation, $65 million.[20]

The loans are designed for the establishment and expansion of modern industries. Have Korean industries developed with astronomical strides because of foreign loans? When President Park initiated his industrialization program in 1961, about 60 percent of the GNP belonged to the consumer products including foods, textiles, clothing, etc. Ten years later, in 1972, the ratio had not changed. Foods, textiles, and clothing still dominated and products of machinery has increased only 3 percent from 6 percent to 9 percent. What happened to the foreign loan? Where were they spent? Where did the money disappear?

Another significant aspect of foreign loans concerns the Korean corporations which borrowed to promote their businesses. Most of them were found to be in an "unworthy business" condition. For instance, 40 top Korean corporations which borrowed foreign money had been classified in this category by the government itself and put under the control of banks. Some of them are: The Korea Fertilizer Company, Korea Ship-building Company, Shinjin Automobile, Tonam Textile, Korea Electric and Metal Company, Korea Aluminum Company, Taekwang Paper Mill, Taerim Marine, Taesun Ship-building, Punghan Industry, Korean Plastic, Kongyung Chemical Industry, Korea Chemical, and many others.

Why were such large numbers of "unworthy business" conditions found among those companies which borrowed foreign money? It became clear later that they were set up on the basis of corrupt political ties between Japanese and Korean businessmen and officials, and therefore these Korea "businessmen" had little interest in their business endeavors.

They had already made money before they invested borrowed money into their businesses. On the other hand, Japanese enterprises sold second-hand, low-capacity plants with low productivity for which they had no use from the beginning, and Korean "businessmen" had either neglected to check them or could have cared less. All these illegal, immoral activities contributed to the decay of the Korean economy as time went on.

The Korean government struggled to pay back the principal and interest of the loans. As anticipated, the financial crisis loomed heavily and got worse with time. The international payment position of Korea became increasingly precarious. Meanwhile, the annual trade deficit also grew rapidly. In 1969, Korea had to repay $80 million, but in 1970, the sum was $150 million, and in 1974, 63 per cent of the total foreign loan was spent on repayment alone, rather than in new industrial development as the loan contract stated.

In October 1978, the Export-Import Bank of Korea authorized First National Bank of Chicago and Union des Banques Arabes et Francaises to raise $200 million in a medium term floating rate loan. The Export-Import Bank of Korea was established in July 1976 to promote Korea's economic development through financing of exports, raw-material imports, overseas investment and development of overseas resources. In May of the same year, the Korea

Development Bank and Korea Exchange Bank already borrowed $500 million for 10 years, and another $100 million loan being negotiated for another government agency simultaneously.[21] The payment on foreign debts in 1979 was at $3 billion, and increased to $5 billion in 1981.[22] Adding $3 billion of oil imports, South Korea needed an additional $8 billion loan, of which $1.4 billion is interest, in 1981. The rate of principal and interest payments burden was 20.7% in 1982, surpassing the "dangerous level" of 20%.[23] The amount for 1985 is estimated at $7.9 billion or $1.1 billion more than $6.8 billion of foreign loans.[24]

President Park was compelled to switch his loan-oriented economy to emphasize direct foreign investment. It was not at all coincidental that such a switch took place with the Nixon-Sato Communique of 1969. Through official consultation between President Nixon and Premier Sato, the U.S. made it clear that it was Japan's responsibility to safeguard American interests as well as Japanese interests in South Korea. The content of the U.S.-Japan official statement was political and military, but its hidden intention was unmistakably economic.

With direct foreign investment, foreign managers, not Koreans, now would manage the Korean economy. The development of Korean industrialization, to which President Park committed the nation, was, therefore, transferred to foreign management. This open door policy was officially presented to the Third Japan-ROK Ministerial Conference held on August 26-28, 1969, in Seoul when the Korean delegation proposed the building of the Pohang Steel Mill with the capacity of producing a million ton per year to be financed with Japanese capital. The South Korean government had originally made this proposal to the U.S., but the U.S. rejected it. Reasons for rejection were various, but the key argument made by the U.S. was that the project was unsound economically.

Japanese business firms, particularly the Nippon Steel Corporation, the Japanese Steel giant, which competes with the U.S. Steel Corporation in the world market, supported the Pohang project with enthusiasm. With such enthusiastic support from the Japanese business world, the Japanese government agreed to finance the Pohang project with a sum of $140 million.

In connection with the Pohang project, a leading spokesman of the Japanese steel industry commented:

"The fate of Japanese industry will be decided by the Indian working forces of 500 million, the rich mineral resources of Indonesia, and the prosperity of the Republic of Korea as the anti-communist bulwark for the rest of free Asia." Then, Nagano Shigeo, President of the Fuji Iron and Steel Corporation which later merged with the Nippon Steel Corporation, continued. "The Republic of Korea indeed stands on the forefront of the free Asia."[25]

Why were Nagano Shigeo and other leading Japanese business men so much concerned about the Pohang Steel Mill project? Were they truly concerned about the development of Korean industry? Were they responding to a Korean proposal because Japanese businessmen were anxious to rescue Korean business from its economic and financial dilemma? Were they just obedient to the American request to look after Korean economic problem?

Mainichi Daily News, one of three leading Japanese daily newspapers in Tokyo with five million circulation, commented that the Japanese government's promise to support the Pohang project, despite concerns expressed by the World Bank about Korea's capacity to repay, "can be taken from an expression of its determination to take care of the ROK by all means and at any sacrifices." The newspaper comment continued: "It is recalled in this connection that at the ASPAC Conference in June (1969), an influential (Japanese) cabinet minister said: "A Greater Co-Prosperity Sphere? What's wrong with it? In the past we tried to create it by arms, but today we are building it through our economic might."[26]

Based on this official spokesman of the government, we can declare unhesitatingly that the Pohang Steel Mill project, although officially proposed by Korean delegation, was an important element to build "A Greater Co-Prosperity Sphere" by Japan. In other words, the project was a Japanese project right from the beginning. The project was carefully formulated by the top-level strategic judgment of Japanese business giants such as the Nippon Steel Corporation. The Pohang project marked, indeed, a new epoch in Japan-ROK economic relations. Japan initiated the colonization of South Korea with the support of the American government. The Taft-Katsura Agreement was repeated. Japan again launched "A Greater Co-Prosperity Sphere" in Asia.

"A Greater Co-Prosperity Sphere" of Japan was a precipitating factor in the second World War and was described by Chiang Kai-Shek as "Japanese domination of Asia." This new policy was established under military leadership. During the decade from 1931 to 1941, or from the infamous "Manchurian Incident" to the attack on Pearl Harbor, the balance of power in Japanese politics moved towards the militarists. The leadership of ultra-nationalism was taken over by the Army as the militarists returned to their dominant role in society after the "Manchurian Incident."[27]

Japanese militarists who preferred war and the risk of defeat took charge of Japanese politics. These militarists believed firmly that their mission was "liberating the non-white peoples from white people" and securing "Asia for the Asiatics." But they really meant Asia for the Japanese. Nothing could have prevented their "holy mission," not even the Emperor himself.

The Japanese "new order" meant: 1. Japanese domination of Asia; 2. elimination of the Western influence in Asia; 3. repression of all anti-Japanese activities in Asia; and 4. anticommunism. In order to achieve these goals, they advocated war against China and her allies. These were the purposes of "A Greater Co-Prosperity Sphere," and Japan did, indeed, try to achieve them. As we observe the present aggressive Japanese economic policy in South Korea and Southeast Asia, and are reminded of "A Greater Co-Prosperity Sphere" by an influential cabinet minister, we cannot help but feel concerned about the revival of "A Greater Co-Prosperity Sphere" movement by the present leaders of Japan.

With the new policy of inviting direct foreign investments to South Korea, Japan launched not only the building of the Pohang Steel Mill, but also pressured the Park regime to establish Free Trade Zones. The Masan area, one of the finest ports in South Korea, was selected as the first Free Export Zone and an agency was set up in April, 1970. A group of Japanese businessmen were sent to Masan to investigate the area. Among their demands to the Seoul regime were: rights to build industries freely; privileges for Japanese business firms to deal with the local officials rather than the central government in Seoul; tax exemptions; low-cost industrial rates for power and water; and an abundant supply of low-paid labor.

The Park regime was eager to cooperate with them and adopted new labor laws to control the Korean workers including anti-strike laws. Thus, the Korean government set up Masan Free Trade Zone to accommodate the Japanese businessmen. The Masan project, like the Pohang project, is a necessary product of the export-oriented and loan-oriented Korean industrialization program. No one needs to be reminded that widespread poverty and destitution cannot be "competitive" with the foreign based multi-national corporations, but the name of the game is the "Free Enterprise" system.

South Korea has recently increased its export through the Masan Free Export Zone. The question is whether the products that Japanese firms in Masan export to Japan should be counted as Korean export? The Japanese firm brings its raw materials from Japan to Masan and then sends manufactured goods back to Japan without paying a single penny to South Korea. Major expenses involved in this production are wage payments to Korean workers. Wages to Korean workers employed by foreign firms, 90 percent of which are Japanese in Masan, accounted for about 29 percent of the total expenses in 1975 according to the report by the Masan Free Export Zone authority. Public utility charges, service charges, etc., accounted for 27.6 percent, and a portion of raw materials from South Korea accounted for about 42 percent. Both raw materials and public utilities are, however, provided at lowest possible costs to the foreign firms. The Korean government reports that the Masan Free Export Zone earns foreign exchange, and operates successfully. Nothing could be further from the truth. Professor Sumiya's careful study reveals that South Korea has not benefitted.[28]

If the government of South Korea is really interested in earning foreign exchange from the operation, then they could maximize wages, costs for domestic raw materials, as well as public utilities charges. Government officials, however, say that such policies would simply discourage foreign investors who are attracted to come to South Korea because of the low costs. In other words, the entire operative system is an artificial fixture which contributes little benefit to the Korean economy, particularly the accumulation of national capital in Korea. The economic operation is based on indifference to the surplus value created by Korean workers. True, Masan is politically a part of South Korean sovereignty but economically, it is a Japanese colony. Yet, the Korean government considers the transactions between the Japanese firms in Masan and their home offices in Japan as a portion of Korea's exports and a part of her GNP.

As we have indicated here, the primary purpose of Japan's investment in Masan is to exploit cheap local labor and to benefit from tax and other privileges offered by the Korean government. A total of 233 firms out of the 262 foreign establishments in Masan are small and medium sized electronics, machine building, textile and sundry goods entrepreneurs. The economic giants of Japan came later with the Fourth 5-year program.

The purposes of the Masan Free Export Zone are "the promotion of exports, increase in employment opportunity, and anticipated transfer of technology thereby contributing to growth of the national economy."[29] The idea is to earn foreign exchange and increase employment through combining the capital and technology of advanced Japanese business with cheap Korean labor force and Korean land. However, the South Korean economy became a subcontractor of Japanese business, and gradually was colonized by the Japanese. This has been shown more clearly by the direct foreign investments than by the loan-supported projects in South Korea. The economic situation, however, got worse in South Korea. The U.S. weekly *Time* revealed that South Korea's outstanding foreign loans reached 49% of the working revenues, surpassing the 20% mark and the OECD and other international economic organizations declared South Korea a defaulter.

The most recent official announcement states that "under the new policy" the Chun Doo Hwan government will permit the foreign-equity-investment share to rise to 100 percent for certain projects and abolish almost completely the current regulations regarding withdrawal of foreign investment funds.[30] This policy was one of the basic directions of the Chun regime. The September 16 Economic Policy Measures stated that: "the government will liberalize the economy to accelerate the inflow of foreign capital and technology." Why such a drastic policy change at that time? Again the government announced that it was necessary action due to "the recent economic difficulties in Korea and the new economic measures designated to counter them."[31]

One thing became clear when the economic situation in South Korea deteriorated, and more foreign investments flowed in under the new economic policy measures. Since the early 1960s, the Park regime sought ways to attract foreign investment by establishing production and trade enclaves called "free industrial zones," or "free trade zones," where multi-national corporations can cheaply produce for the world market, pay the lowest possible wages, and enjoy total protection against unions or any form of labor protests. Such enclaves were established in several areas in South Korea. In these cheap-labor havens the internationalization of surplus value can be maximized, and one encounters the highest stage of human exploitation by internationalized capital. Their Korean workers are subjected to particularly poor working conditions, intense exploitation, and strong political repression. The Chun regime expanded its program to attract foreign capital to intensify such human exploitation further by adapting September 16 Economic Policy Measures. Introduction of the new act provided for a favorable transfer of profits and special tax facilities for new foreign capital investments. It was hastily enacted to create a favorable impression with the international financiers and facilitated the quick and easy entry of foreign capital into South Korea. What is the meaning of more foreign capital investments to Korean national economy? Do the foreign capital investments really benefit Korean economic life?

The international situation of the lending became more complex following the second oil shock. Korea's imports of crude oil rose from $2.2 billion on the eve of the second oil shock to $5.6 billion in 1980 (23% of total imports and $6.5 billion in 1981.) First of all, the OPEC countries, which for several years were major net lenders, have been transformed by the weakening demand for oil into large borrowers. Second, borrowing by the U.S. has attracted a significant share of international net savings which finances a substantial part of current net investment.[32] Besides the U.S., whose investment financed through foreign savings may exceed 40% by 1983. France and some of the Scandinavian countries have also been drawing upon the international capital market, with their greater credit worthiness allowing them to nudge aside less affluent borrowers like South Korea. Third, nonvoluntary "lending" by commercial banks to countries faced with debt crises precipitated by high interest costs, has depleted the supply of capital. Fourth, the handful of countries with net savings that others can draw upon–Japan, Germany, Switzerland, Kuwait and UAE–closely monitor access to their capital markets where interest rates are regulated. Fifth, having suffered through the various Latin American crises, neither Japanese banks nor the ministry of France, which supervises their lending operations, are inclined to repeat the experience in South Korea. As a result of this changed international situation, international capital flaws became more conservative. Under such global climate, South Korea, which with $6.8 billion in debt out standing in 1985 is in a more delicate position.

Industrialization at the Cost of Rural Economy

The third characteristic of South Korean economic development is the integration policy of the rural economy with the export-oriented industrialization. Korea has been an agricultural nation for centuries. As a former colony of Japan, she has hardly broken away from her past semi-feudalistic tradition. Her rural economy, which is the backbone of the national economy, is still at the stage of semi-feudalism.[33] Yet, the government forced her rural economy into the export-oriented economy.

The agriculture policy installed by the American Military Government during the three years of occupation from 1945 to 1948 has not been changed to this date. The major American policy was to subsidize or sell the surplus grain of the U.S. to the Korean people. Whatever the intention of this policy, it has created a negative condition to Korean agricultural production. Consequently, the self-sufficient agricultural country has become a nation dependent on foreign grain.

Food imports as a percentage of total imports increased steadily from 9.4 percent in 1960 to 13.0 percent in 1975. In June 1979, the Minister of Agriculture announced that South Korea had contracted to import 43,000 tons of rice from the U.S., 250,000 tons from Japan, and was looking for a supplier for 200,000 tone more-a total of 493,000 tons. At the end of December 1979, the government announced it had decided to import a total of 570,000 tons of rice in 1980.[34]

Self-sufficiency in food grains dropped from 91.4 percent in 1961, 87 percent in 1966, to 74.9 percent in 1976, and about 50% in 1984.[35] About one-third of food grains had to be imported from the U.S. and other countries in 1980-1981, and about 80 percent of the needed wheat is still imported from the U.S. at the present time. Grain imports from America have been increasing steadily: 3,868,000 metric tons in 1977, 3,601,000 in 1978, 6,174,000 in 1979, and the government paid out $613 million in 1977, and about $700 million in 1978 for the grain imports. Besides grain, the government also imported red pepper, garlic, sesame seed oil, and peanuts in large quantities. Naturally, these imported commodities competed against the domestic products.

Between 1962 and 1974, South Korea imported $1.28 billion worth of wheat and $854 million worth of rice. In 1971, at the end of Park's Second 5-year Economic Program, the grain imports increased six times compared with the year 1966, the first year of the program. Korea's food self-sufficiency steadily decreased. Until 1978, Korea was the sixth largest market for U.S. food exporters.[36]

During 1978, however, $1.15 billion worth of agricultural products was imported from the U.S., making Korea the U.S.'s largest foreign customer for agricultural products.[37] No wonder the Carter Administration, with the help of the U.S. Congress, overlooked the serious charges of the "Koreagate" bribery scandal and maintained normalcy between two governments.

Why a shortage of foods in an agricultural country? We find two important reasons. One is that the national policy makers in Seoul are city-capitalists who are closely associated with foreign capitalists. Secondly, the agricultural development has been sacrificed for the sake of the industrial development.

In order to increase agricultural production, the government should encourage land improvement with crop rotation, promote markets for the farm products in the cities, provide quick transportation of farm products, apply scientific method to improve seeds and planting methods, promote new machineries, give loans with low interest rates at the time of spring planting, etc. None of these elementary aids have been given to the farmers. Instead, the government through the Agricultural Cooperatives, which have a 100 percent monopoly in distribution of fertilizer and other chemical products, force the farmers to use expensive chemical fertilizers excessively year after year in order to get rid of the over supply of chemical fertilizers produced in South Korea.

The Korean fertilizer industry is plagued by problems of excess production. At the end of 1976, the nation's combined fertilizer inventory soared to 510,000 element tons. Korea's capacity for fertilizer production is about 3 million tons a year, and the total consumption of fertilizer in 1976 was 1,800,000 tons.[38] As of the end of 1977, the Korean government exported 80,000 tons of urea and ammonium sulphate at a $4 million loss. Her export price was far below the international price. If the Korean government exported 400,000 tons as planned, she would have been about $200 million in the red.[39] Yet, the government continues to expand the fertilizer industry by adding the

Seventh plant with the aid of foreign loan. As with the Third and Fourth plants, all of these contracts with foreign investors are discriminatory in nature. These unwanted fertilizers will become harder and harder for the farmer to afford. As the table in footnote 28 has indicated, the government increased the price of fertilizer 79.2 percent in order to meet the ever accumulating losses in the export of fertilizer.

The economic activities of the foreign dominated fertilizer companies in South Korea. International mineral and chemical owns 50% interest of the Jonghap Chemical Company, while Gulf Oil Corporation has interest in Jinhae Chemical, Skelly Oil Corp. in Yongnam Chemical, and Mitsui of Japan in Hankook Fertilizer.[40]

Another serious problem in connection with the rural economy is the over-consumption of agricultural chemicals. Consumption of insecticide and weedicide increased eight times in seven years from 1968 to 1975 according to the official report of the Ministry of Agriculture in Seoul. Comparing the usage of these agricultural chemicals with Canada and West Germany, the Korean farmers use 20 times more than the Canadian farmer, and 6 times more than the West German farmer."[41]

Such excessive use of the chemicals pollutes not only the environment, but also the farmers themselves. For instance, Mr. Ko Keun-suk and his family at Tamyang County of South Jolla Province have been suffering due to excessive use of the chemicals on their farm. Mrs. Ko and her elder daughter who spread the insecticides and weedicides extensively during the past couple of years became ill, and were confined at home for months. Dr. Yun, a county doctor, declared these women have been inflicted by excessive mercury which he found in the agricultural chemical they used. Choi Jin-su, a laboratory researcher at the National University of Chunnam in Kwangju, found three times the normal quantity of mercury in these victims by employing the dithizone method.[42]

In spite of such harmful effects to the farmers, the government has been promoting these poisonous chemicals to them not to "increase production" as the officials have stated, but to sell over-produced fertilizers and chemicals. The cost of the farm production is another problem. The government has maintained low rice prices by importing U.S. surplus rice over which Tongsun Park had a monopoly control with the support of President Park. Meanwhile, the cost of the production increased an average 16.7 percent per year starting from 1966. Specifically, the price of the farm machines went up an average of 26.2 percent while the chemical products increased an average of 20 percent a year. The total production costs per one bushel of rice was 45,000 Won or about $90, but the government fixed price for the same was only

30,000 Won or $60. Thus, the farmers lost $30 from each bushel of rice they produced.[43-44]

Not all grain importation was due to a shortage of food in the country. For instance, in 1969, rice production in South Korea amounted to over 4 million metric tons, a 28 percent increase over 1968 and 13 percent over 1967. But the regime imported 755,000 metric tons of rice. In 1971, rice production was again almost 4 million metric tons, but the regime again imported 907,000 metric tons valued at about $140 million.[45]

Why has the regime imported rice when the country didn't need it? There were two reasons: first of all, the imported American rice forced the rice price down in the Korean market; secondly, the Park regime imported rice at $150 per ton, and sold it to the Koreans at double the price.[46] It is now a well-known story that the profits from the rice deal were used by Tongsun Park to bribe U.S. Congressmen. Thus, the imported American rice damaged not only the farmers in South Korea, but also created an international bribery scandal.

Consequently, food shortages have become annual occurrences and the price of rice land declines. After a 22 percent drop in the Taejun area in March, 1978 compared with the price in 1977, there were still no buyers in sight."[47] According to the government source, "The Korean agricultural situation is confronted with a critical turning point. It faces a very dangerous situation."[48]

Suffering and a waste of human resources have taken place in the country. In the course of one decade, 1967-1976, the rural population declined from 16 million to about 13 million. Considering natural population increase, an estimated 7 million farmers left their farm land, moved into cities. Seoul's population alone has increased 54 percent from 1969-1976. In 1976, 458,700 farmers left the farm, 476,000 left in 1977, 781,000 in 1978.[49]

The Research Institute of Agricultural Economy reports that 69.5 percent of the Korean farmers are not satisfied with their present situation, and 21.8 percent of them are ready to move out from their farms. Not all of these farmers who want to leave their farms are the poor farmers. Many of them are the middle class farmers. In 1976, 13,000 middle class farm households left the farm, however, the number has increased considerably. In 1978, it increased to 52,000 households.[50]

According to the age group, most of those who are leaving the farm are under 49 years old, especially even younger people. For instance, in 1978, 67.3 percent of the 781,000 who left the farm were under 19 years old. In other words, those who are farming are often 50 years or older.[51]

The absolute decline in the farm population began after the 1965 treaty with Japan when the Park regime emphasized the export oriented industrialization. In other words, the migration of farmers to the periphery of the cities created industrial workers for the foreign investors. As already pointed out, a supply of lowpaid labor was demanded by Japan and guaranteed by the Park regime. There were, however, more workers or ex-farmers seeking employment, thus unemployment rose sharply, and assured the foreign investors their abundance of low-paid labor. This mechanism of underproduction of grain, overproduction of fertilizers, and forced overconsumption of agricultural chemicals has brought about a number of tragic results.

Decline of the rural population resulted with the decline of cultivated acreage. For instance, between 1968-1970, cultivated land declined about 9 percent. In 1973, the farmers who left the farms for the cities increased 13 percent compared with 1972. Most of them, were, of course, the tenant farmers who were one fourth of the farmers in the country. In spite of repeated land reforms, a large portion of the farmers remain landless tenant farmers. They worked hard for the absentee landlords who lived in large cities, and received little satisfaction and comfort on the farm. It has been reported that 83 percent of the farmers' debt is about a hundred thousand Won or about $200 per family, and that the average family will never be able to pay back in their lifetime.

This system is characterized as free and capitalistic. This system of agrarian relations is presumed to be potentially suitable for the dynamic landowners and rich farmers to carry out development given the new technology of hybrid seeds and fertilizers, as they are also endowed with land and capital resources. The benefits of development are supposed to seep through in due course to the rest of the rural society. Expansion of the capitalist sector as time passes absorbs the time and small farms and converts the part of land held by them. Re-distributive land reform is inhibitive to this pattern of development.

Unrestrained expansion of the capitalist sector is credited with a higher rate of capital accumulation in agriculture arising out of its capacity to generate a higher rate of savings. A part of these savings can be invested in the industrial sector, following the Japanese example during the Meiji era, absorbing in the process surplus agricultural labor. Clearly, this perspective does not take into account the present relative endowments of land and labor nor does it assign much weight to social objectives of employment and redistribution of income between different groups and regions of the rural society in South Korea.

It does not take much analysis to understand that the average small farmer cannot afford this kind of development. Nevertheless, he is caught in it. Tenants and small farmers are further compelled to seek more loans from private lenders. As the component of the institutional credit for ploughing is far below the prevailing changes, even the farmers who receive institutional loans are often forced to seek additional loans from private sources. As their repayment capacity is reduced, they become defaulters and thereby disqualified for any further institutional credit. Their process of dispossession and marginalization begins in the traditional fashion. The process has been responsible for an increasing concentration of wealth and land in the hands of a few, the emergence of a class of peasantry with uneconomic holdings, an increase in the proportion of poor peasantry serving mostly under bondage arising out of usury, and also some extra-economic coercion. Bondage is also enforced by leasing tiny bits of land to agricultural laborers.

The intensity of exploitation and impoverishment has increased with the passing of time and eventually sharpened class conflict because the landlords, usurers and traders usually lined up with the foreign powers against the masses of rural Korea.

The export-oriented industrial development required low wages to insure profits for foreign-based industries; for decades the foreign corporate system has impoverished the masses of the Korean people and produced fabulous wealth for the small group of colonialists, neo-colonialists and local compradors. It has operated for the interest of the metropolis. Whether we look at the price policy or the fertilizer policy, the victims are the farmers. Park-Chun's alliance with foreign capital is a clear example of the betrayal of the Korean masses. It is also clear that the local regime cannot survive without the support of foreign capital. The foreign corporate system and foreign aid are both genuine instruments to create the gap, continuously widened, between the rich and poor in South Korea.

Analyzing three characteristics of the Korean economy, it is clear that the Korean economy is not an independent entity, but became a dependent economy of foreign capital, particularly in Japan. The core strategy of this economic development was not initiated by President Park as generally understood, but promoted by the Japanese business and political groups. For instance, in April, 1970, following the Nixon-Sato Communique and the Third Japan-ROK Ministerial Conference in 1969, Yatsugi Kazuo proposed his plan on long-term economic cooperation between Japan and South Korea to the meeting of the Japan-ROK Cooperation Commission in Seoul. The Commission was formed in February, 1969 at Kishi Nobusuke's suggestion, Japan's former Prime Minister and a strong advocate of the close cooperation among Japan, South Korea, and Taiwan, and Kishi's close political and business associates in Japan.[52]

At this important meeting between policy-makers of two countries, Yatsugi Kazuo proposed a striking plan which is known as the Yatsugi Plan or the Mitsuya Plan (three arrow plan). The main points of the Yatsugi Plan are as follows:[53]

1. A unitary Japan-ROK economic cooperation zone should be created to operate in the 1970s so that the two countries can develop a sort of "Asian EEC."

2. In the projected cooperation zone, the South Korean coastal industry zone south of Pohang should be integrated into the Western Japan economic zone including the Japan Sea coastal cities of Tottori Prefecture, Yamagichi Prefecture and northern Kyushu.

3. Japan will relocate to the South Korean industrial zone its steel, aluminum, oil refining, petrochemical, ship building, electronics, plastics and other industries which cannot be   put in Japan because of pollution questions and difficulty of buying enough Japanese load at reasonable prices. In view of the shortage of labor in Japan, Japan will also shift its labor-intensive industries to the territory of the ROK.

4. Japanese business will transcend the stage where it aimed simply to obtain commercial profits from Korea, rising to a new stage where "long-term cooperation through operation of joint-ventures," will be the main form of economic relations. In order to facilitate this form of expansion, Japan will set up a "Public Corporation for the Promotion of Japan-ROK Joint Ventures and Bonded Manufacturing Industry" (Promotion Corp.), and the ROK government should strictly prohibit labor disputes at factories of these Japan-ROK-joint ventures.

5. projected Promotion Corporation, to be set up in Japan, wholly will be financed by private capital and will function as the supplier of raw materials and industrial plants to the ROK. Its counterpart in the ROK (70 percent of whose capital will be provided by the ROK government and the rest by private ROK enterprises) will undertake to process and manufacture on a subcontract basis the materials using plants imported from Japan.

6. The ROK should significantly expand its bonded industrial areas and free trade zones, to fulfill the manufacturing and processing tasks allocated by Japan; flexible domestic measures should be taken within the ROK to facilitate this mode of operation.

Looking at these points, we are reminded of similarities to the past Japanese policy in Korea. In December, 1937, the first year of the Sino-Japanese War, the Japanese government established the "Manchurian Heavy Industry Development Company." The plan was to develop all the rich minerals in Manchuria for the purpose of supporting the Japanese war effort in China, and also in preparation of Pearl Harbor attack.

Ayukawa Zaibatsu invested the initial amount of 250 million Yen while "Manchukuo" invested 225 million Yen under the Kwang Tung Army supervision.

The most amazing thing is that the Yatsugi plan was implemented rapidly with the full cooperation of the Park regime. It was not just an idea of one person, but a blueprint of the Japanese economic giants. The idea of "A Greater Co-Prosperity Sphere" was applied to the Asian scene again, but at this time, the program was being supported by the United States.

Furthermore, the Japan-Korea Economic Cooperation Association announced a plan to form a consolidated JapanKorea-"Korea Industrial Development Corporation" in July, 1976. The KIDC plan had been discussed since the summer of 1972 prior to the "Yushin System" of President Park. What was the main aim of the KIDC? It was established to feed into South Korea's Fourth 5-year Plan (1977-1981) and to be the impelling force in the plan to develop a heavy chemical industry.

The project was capitalized at $1 billion which placed it in the same rank as the Asian Development Bank. Of this 51 per cent was to come from the South Korean side, making it appear on the surface to be a Korean corporation. It was, however, common knowledge that $500 million could not be raised in South Korea, and that eventually the money would come from Japan. The Fourth 5-year Economic Program deepened South Korea's peonage to foreign creditors. Seoul's foreign debt balance, counting only long-term and medium-term loans, was projected to grow from $7.36 billion in 1977 to $13.648 billion in 1981, the last year of the Fourth 5-year Economic Program.[54]

The KIDC project was not a new phenomena in Korea although the plan started with Park's "Yushin" government. A similar plan was proposed by Uemura Kogoro, a close friend of President Park, in 1937. Uemura was supported at that time by Yamakuchi Eiji. Both were war criminals, but they managed to identify again with Japanese neo-colonialism. They were important strategists who advocated a revival of Japanese militarism. Uemura had studied the labor law of Nazi Germany, and imposed an identical rule upon the Japanese workers during the Pacific War, and had initiated a savage labor conscription of Koreans to the Japanese coal mines during the Second World War. Uemura organized "keitanren," the most powerful economic organization in postwar Japan, and became honorary chairman of the body. At the same time, he kept the Chairmanship of Japan-Korea Economic Cooperation Association. In 1974 he referred to "Korea as a part of Japan." He was a characteristic Japanese imperialist, yet President Park maintained close contact with him.

Mitsui and Mitsubishi, two leading zaibatsu groups, and the Nippon Steel Corporation committed vast sums of capital to expand Pohang Steel, to establish one of the largest oil refineries at Sunchun area, and to build a large machinery plant in Changwon as portions of the Fourth 5-year Plan of Park's regime. American business groups, like Japanese groups, were also actively supporting the basic economic policies of South Korea. They, too, were interested in relocation of their productive process and profitable investment of their surplus capital in Third World countries. South Korea provided many favorable conditions which these foreign businessmen look for. They understood that the South Korean economy was seeking their capital investments and their technical aids as well as their trade.

How did American firms take advantage of President Park's "anxious to industrialize" policy in South Korea? Let's take the example of Gulf Oil Corporation's involvement in South Korea's industrialization program. Gulf Oil's initial investment was only $4.8 million and 50 percent ownership of the newly created Korea Oil Company which began its business in April 1964. During its first ten years, Korea Oil grew rapidly, became the largest corporation in South Korea with total annual sales reaching approximately $57 million in 1974. With such successful operation, Gulf Oil decided to increase her direct investment to $29.8 million, and increased her loan to $75 million. Furthermore, Gulf also invested $10 million and loaned $24.6 million to Chinhae Chemical Corporation as well as loaning $43.5 million to Korea Electric Company. Gulf also is part owner of Hankook Ssangsa Company, Ltd., a fuel oil storage and distribution company, and the Sangtung Cement Industrial Company while she owns 100 percent of Korea Gulf Oil. The result has been very profitable for Gulf. By the end of 1977, Gulf remitted to the U.S. over $33.5 million in pro fits from its Korea Oil Company alone, more than any other investor in South Korea.[55]

The economic power of Gulf Oil relative to the South Korean economy can be seen in the fact that its 1974 worldwide revenues of $18.2 billion were almost one and a half times the size of South Korea's $12.9 billion GNP.[56]

As mentioned earlier, Gulf is part owner of the Chinhae Chemical Corporation as a 25 percent stockholder. The company was capitalized at $21 million but Gulf loaned it no less than $24.6 million. There were important reasons for Gulf to loan such a large sum of money to a newly-established fertilizer company. The contract that Gulf received from the South Korean government stipulated that: the plant had to be constructed by U.S. companies; the raw materials for the fertilizer to be produced must come from the U.S.; the South Korean government must guarantee to purchase all production of the plant;[57] and that from 1965 to 1980 Gulf is guaranteed a 20 percent profit per year on its investment and exempted from business tax. The irony of all these business contracts between Gulf and the Park regime is that Chinhae Chemical was 100 percent capitalized through a very favorable U.S. AID loan.[58] In other words, American tax payer's money has been misused to guarantee Gulf's maximum profits in South Korea.

Gulf's profits cannot be separated from the "Yushin" regime. According to the business contracts, the First Vice President who is appointed by Gulf is the Chairman of the Board of Directors, who has complete control over the company. The company's president who is appointed by President Park has little or nothing to say about the operation of the company. Not only does the Park regime endorse such business practices but the regime is the major partner of the Gulf empire in South Korea.

What is serious about such a set-up is not only Gulf's influence on the national economic policy, but its political involvement. First, let us look into the change of economic policy in South Korea since Gulf Oil joined partnership with the Park regime in the operation of Korea Oil Corporation. In 1964, at the time that Korea Oil Corporation opened its business, the nation's energy was supplied primarily with indigenous coal but oil replaced coal once Gulf Oil, Caltex and Union Oil made their appearance in South Korea.[59]

As the imported oil replaced indigenous coal for the major portion of energy supply, it created many problems in the economic system besides human resource problems. For instance, in 1966, the year when Gulf contributed one million dollars to President Park's Democratic Republican Party to be used for the National Assembly elections, the government had ordered all public offices to use imported oil instead of Korean coal as a token of modernization. In 1971, Gulf made a similar payment of $3 million to Park's own re-election campaign. Such generous funds helped not only defeat Kim Dae-Jung, but to change national economic policy. We may even add that Tongsun Park's bribery scandal was closely connected with Gulf's involvement in South Korean politics.[60]

From this date on, all new buildings were required to use oil rather than coal. Korea does not produce a drop of oil, but produces substantial amounts of coal. As a result of such policy implementation, the use of imported oil was natural and necessary. Between 1965 and 1969, the imported oil increased five fold, payment amounted to $97.7 million in 1969 from $23.7 million in 1965. On the other hand, the use of coal declined drastically at all public places including government offices, military facilities, and government-owned industries. As a result, many coal mines were forced to close, many small and medium operators went bankrupt, and thousands of workers

294

lost their jobs. Such economic policy completely ignored the concept of self-reliance which is so important to the development of Third World countries.

In addition to influencing the national policy, Gulf Oil, Caltex, Union Oil, and other American giants were staunch supporters of President Park's authoritarian regime. They had strong reasons to solidify their support of the Park-Chun regimes because the regime guaranteed and protected their maximum profits against all other obstacles like environmental codes. It is also understandable that they would fight any lessening of support for President Park, and President Chun, by the U.S. government.

Notes

1. U.S. Under-Secretary of National Defense Kilpatrick stated in April, 1963 while visiting Japan that Japanese National Defense Forces ought to be able to supervise a part of South Korea in the future. His suggestion soon became a national policy of Japan. Such policy was not a new idea, it had been promoted already by John Foster Dulles. ''In the Spring of 1951 John Foster Dulles, as a special envoy of President Truman, suggested to Premier Yoshida a U.S.-Japan security treaty and strongly demanded the immediate rearming of Japan,'' quoted from ''Japan and China' Domestic and Foreign Influences on Japan's Policy,'' by Shigeharu Matsumoto in A. M. Halperin, ed. *Policies Toward China: Views from Six Continents,* McGraw-Hill for Council on Foreign Relations, New York, 1965, pp. 259-60. Also, ''John Foster Dulles began encouraging Japan to start rebuilding its defense capability,'' A. D. Barnett, *China and Major Powers in East Asia,* The Brookings Institution, 1977, p. 94.

2. Bank of Korea, *Tonqqe Wolbo* (Monthly Statistics), Feb. 1980, Seoul

3. The World Bank, KOREA: Development in a Global Context, Washington, D.C.: *The* International Bank for Reconstruction and Development, 1984, p. 48-49.

4. *op. cit., p.* 27.

5. Yu, Hyuk-in, *Hankuk-e Mokpyo-nin Muosinka ?* (What is Korea's Aim?), Seoul, 1977, p. 91.

6. *Chosun Ilbo Daily* March 10,1978, Seoul.

7. Lee, Yong-shin, ''KOREA: Export-Oriented Industry and Its Secret'' in *The World,* Tokyo: Asia-Pacific Resource Center, Fall, 1979, p. 81.

8. *Wolgan Chungang,* Dec. 1977; Jan. 1978.

9. Kim Tsan-jin, *Oja Doio-non,* (A Discourse on Foreign Capital Investment), quoted by *Minami Chosen-no Keijai, p.* 242

10. *The Dong-A Daily News,* June 16,1975, Seoul.

11. Sunoo, Harold Hakwon, *Repressive State and Resisting Church: The Politics of CIA in South Korea,* New York and Fayette, MO, 1976.

12. *The Dong-A Daily News,* Sept. 24,1974, Seoul.

13. Ibid, February 24, 1977.

14. The World Bank, *op. cit., p.* 54.

15. Nikkan Keizai Kyokai, *Kankoku Dai-4-ji Keizaihatsu 5-ka-nen Keikaku-1977-1981* or The 4th Economic Development Program of the Republic of Korea, Jan. 1977, also see *Ampo,* special issue *Free Trade Zones and Industrialization in Asia,* Tokyo, 1977, p. 20.

16. Economic Planning Board, *Major Statistics of Korean Economy,* Seoul, 1975.

17. *Ibid.*

18. *Shukan Nikkan Sangyo Keizai,* No. 35, Jan. 6, 1977.

19. *Asahi Shimbun,* April 28,1985.

20. Detailed statistics on major Japanese loan supplies in South Korea are available in *Report* on *Japan-ROK Economic Relations* by Study Group on Japan-ROK Relations, Tokyo, circulated by *Am*po, June 1974.

21. *New York Times,* Oct. 23, 1978.

22. *Jung-ang Daily News,* Sept. 26, 1979, Seoul.

23. *Tong-A Daily News, Feb.* 16, 1983, Seoul.

24. *Jung-ang Daily News,* Nov. 4, 1985.

25. *Nihon Keizai Daily News,* Sept. 6, 1969, Tokyo.

26. *Mainichi Daily News,* Sept. 13,1969, Tokyo.

27. *For* details of possible revival of Japanese militarism, see Harold Hakwon Sunoo *Japanese Militarism: Past and Present, Nelson* Hall, Chicago, 1975.

28. Sumiya, Mikio, *Kankokuno Keizai, (or* Economy of South Korea), Iwanami, Tokyo, 1976.

29. *The Establishment Law of the Free Export* Zone, Jan. 1, 1970, Seoul.

30. *Korean Newsletter,* Vol. III, *No.* 6, Oct. 1980, p. 7.

31. *Ibid.*

32. The World Bank, op. *cit., p.* 6.

33. *For* historical background of the agricultural economy, see Harold Hakwon Sunoo, Korea *A Political History in Modern Times,* Ch. 13, 1970, *Seoul.*

34. Korea *Times,* Dec. 30, 1979, *Seoul.*

35. *Shindonga,* Dec. 1977, Seoul, p. 86.

36. *Asia Wall Street Journal* June 7, 1978.

37. *Chosun Ilbo Daily,* Aprii 20, 1979.

38. Kim Chang-soo, "Marginalization, Development and the Korean Worker's Movement" in *Ampo* July-Nov., 1977, p. 25, Tokyo.

39. *The Dong-A Daily News,* Mar. 20, 1978, Seoul.

40. *Dong-A Daily News,* July 4-Sept. 2, 1977, Seoul.

41. *Ibid,* Mar. 27, 1978.

42. *Ibid,* Mar. 28, Apr. 1, 1978.

43. *Seoul Kyungje Shinmun Daily,* April 25, 1979, Seoul.

44. Korean Catholic Farmers Association, *The Survey of Rice Produc*tion, 1978, *Seoul.*

45. Economic Planning Board, *op. cit.*

46. *The Washington Post,* March 25,1977.

   Connell Rice and Sugar Co. of New Jersey, a major American rice exporter, paid Tongsun Park nearly $8 million over 4 years in fees for "assisting" its sales of rice to South Korea, according to U.S. Internal Revenue Service documents. At least $1.5 million of that amount was U.S. government money that financed South Korea's purchase of American rice through the Foods for Peace Programs. The firm's listed sales agent for the Foods and Peace Programs' transaction was Korean Development Fund, Inc. according to U.S. Agriculture Department files. Tongsun Park was the President ana principal stockholder of the Korean Development Fund. U.S. federal regulations prohibit Food for Peace commissions to anyone connected to the importing country. Food for Peace Programs are, of course, subsidized with U.S. tax money.

   Tongsun Park used money from the commissions to entertain as well as bribe U.S. legislators to influence a favorable public image in the U.S. for the Park regime of South Korea.

47. *The Dong-A Daily News,* Mar. 23, 1978.

   The report indicated that the price of rice field per one Pyong in Hongsung county was 3,000 Won in 1970, 3,600 in 1971, 4,000 in 1972, 6,000 in 1978, 6,300 in 1976, but dropped to 4,600 in March, 1978.

48. *Yongnam Ilbo Daily News,* May 19, 1979.

49. *Seoul Kyungje Shinmun Daily,* April 25,1979.

50. *The Agriculture and Forestry Year Book-1978, Seoul.*

51. *Seoul Shinmun Daily News,* May 17,1979.

52. The Japan-ROK Cooperation Commission originated as a semisecret organization. Its primary aim was to promote anticommunist activities, but changed gradually as an economic interest group. At its first meeting, there were about 40 important economic leaders of Japan attending. They included: presidents of the Japanese Chamber of Commerce, Keitanren, Mitsui, Mitsubishi, Sumitomo, Fuji Bank, Bank of Tokyo, etc. Thus, the major Zaibatsu leaders, old as well as new groups, participated in the meeting. Some of them did not actively appear in later activities of the

Commission due to the declaration of Premier Chou En-Lai of China. Premier Chou stated that China would not allow any Japanese business firm which is involved in South Korea and Taiwan.

53. *Report* on *Japan-ROK Economic Relations, p. 19.*

54. *Nikkan Keizai Kyokai, p.* 20.

55. *Korea Times,* Feb. 4,1978, Seoul.

56. McCormack, Gaven and Selden, Mark, *Korea, North and South The* Deepening *Crisis,* 1978, Monthly Review Press.

57. One should be reminded of the fertilizer dumping story as stated elsewhere in this study

58. *AMPO* i, Vol. 9, No. 3, 1977, Tokyo.

59. There *are* three oil giants in *South* Korea. Gulf Oil through Korea Oil Corp. controls 49% of the refining capacity, Caltex through Honam Oil controls 40%, Union Oil of California controls 11%. Caltex has taken out of South Korea $26.8 million compared with Gulf's $33.5m from its operation--the 3rd largest remittance of profits by a foreign investor. (Korea *Times,* Oct. 1,1978.) Caltex has, like Gulf Oil, expanded several times its original plant and is reported to be planning further investment of $600m in the next two years. *(Korea Times,* June 22,1978)

60. Small Business Bank, *Chosa Wolbo,* (Monthly Survey) Sept. 1974, Seoul, p. 3.

15

Results of the Export-Led Development Economy

President Carter in his state visit to Seoul, South Korea on July 1, 1979 said that he was "impressed that the benefits of prosperity are widely shared by the Korean people," adding that he understood that the average rural income currently exceeded the average urban income, calling it an "accomplishment almost unique among developing nations and should be a source of special pride."[1]

Where President Carter received such information is a matter of insignificant speculation, but making such an unconfirmed statement to the public in Seoul makes him more than an uninformed President. If the average rural income exceeded the average urban income as President Carter stated, then why has the urban population recently increased at about 5% a year, well above the rate of population growth – 1.5%? It was so because the farmers left the country to seek better jobs in the cities.

Kim Dae-Jung, South Korea's leading dissident, who won 46% of the popular vote when he ran against Park Chung Hee in the presidential election of 1971, and was kidnapped by Korean CIA agents in 1973 in Tokyo, said that it was "common knowledge" in South Korea that President Carter's statement was inaccurate. Kim added, "A recent World Bank report pointed out that the unbalanced Korean economy was creating unrest.... Even the Korean government acknowledges the problem of uneven distribution of income."[2]

South Korea is well-known as a model for developing countries. Her growth of GNP has been impressive to those who are looking for a profitable investment in the Third World countries. She claims that her GNP has grown at an average rate of about 10% a year since 1962 or at the time when General

Park Chung Hee took over the civilian government by military force.

An American observer commented that "South Korea is an important middle-level power in the world. After Japan, it is in many ways the most important of the non-communist countries in the Asia-Pacific region. Its success at economic growth will demonstrate to both developed and developing countries. South Korea's success will show that growth is possible for those who work at it, and particularly those who work hardest at it." Then, he added that "precisely because of South Korea's success, the United States should consider itself lucky to have such a country on its side."[3] Although this commentator, and many others like him, give credit to hard working Koreans for their "success", the Korean economy is neither prosperous nor successful.

The economic development in South Korea is not to be seen as a national phenomenon, but rather as a transnational one. Without an understanding of the true nature of capitalism in South Korea, we will make the same kind of erroneous evaluation of the situation as President Carter. How did the economic development take a place in South Korea? How did the United States guide her economy during the past 40 years of occupation? What is the meaning of the "success" or "accomplishment" that American policymakers described? If they meant that an average annual increase of 10% a year in GNP is success, they are probably right. But if one is to consider fair distribution of income as important as the growth of production, then their assessment is very wrong.

The necessity for industrialization in South Korea is very evident, and such a program needs to be supported. The question is, however, what is the purpose of the industrialization and who benefits by it? Furthermore, the question is not do we want industrialization, but how do we achieve it? We find that there are three basic problems with industrialization which the government must solve. They are: 1. the problem of capital formation with emphasis on national capital accumulation; 2. the relationship between the economic development and political interference; and 3. the relation ship between the haves and have-nots.

Like all other underdeveloped nations, South Korea is faced with all these problems. The Korean government with the support of both American and Japanese governments has tried to solve them in the most convenient way, namely, borrowing from abroad. The Korean government today is confronted with many critical problems instead of enjoying the fruits of her industrialization which has been called a "miracle" by her sponsors. Let us now briefly examine some of the results of her industrialization, and what is happening to her while the multinational corporations were scoring their remarkable "achievements." Let us, first, explain the economic result.

First, national economy came increasingly under foreign domination. South Korea, like many other newly gained independent nations in Asia and Africa, initiated her industrialization with foreign participation in her economic development. Under such circumstances, an independent economy was illusory. For instance, the dependency of the Korean economy to Japan was revealed by the trade relationship between Korea and Japan. A total of 95% of the iron and steel materials came from Japan, 85% of the petroleum chemical products, 91% of the raw materials for textiles, 74% of the paper, 32% of the rubber, 45% of the copper, 75% of the aluminum, etc. in the 1970s. Furthermore, 100% of the plate glass business was owned and operated by Japanese capital. Chemicals, textiles, the aluminum industry, and the heavy chemical industry, also Japanese controlled, as also are 80% of locomotive wheel production, 70% of electronics, 60% of the steel plate output, 50% of cement production, 57% of refrigerator business, and 40% of the fertilizer industry of South Korea during the Park administration (1960-1979).[4]

Besides the industries, other areas of Korean business, too, were dominated by the Japanese: 85% of the export-oriented plants were built with Japanese money and materials, and more than a half of the foreign banks in South Korea belong to Japan. We have already illustrated Gulf Oil Corp's relationship with Korea Oil Corp. Three major oil companies of South Korea averaged 76% increase of profits in 1976 compared with the year 1975. The Korea Oil Corp's profit increased 86.3% in the same period.[5] All leading Korean companies, like Korea Oil Corp are now dominated by foreign capital. Some cases are more extreme than others. All of the foreign-loan-based industries rip off maximum profits to take home.

Interestingly enough, the seriousness of Japanese infiltration of Korea's economy is also the concern of certain segments of the Japanese as well as the Korean populace. For instance, Mr. Antaku Sunehiko, a member of the Japanese Diet, questioned such practices on February 8. 1975. He pointed out that many Japanese-financed Korean enterprises are known as "unworthy enterprises," and suggested an investigation.[6]

Second, anticipated national capital failed to form. To begin with, the conventional economic argument in favor of foreign investments contemplates more than capital formation; they are supposed to generate a package of capital, managerial skill, and technology; they supplement scarce domestic capital, and therefore contribute to capital formation which in turn generates employment and more output. Do foreign investments in fact supplement scarce domestic capital, and therefore generate employment and more output? Whether foreign investments generate employment and more output hinges on the magnitude of net (foreign and domestic) investments that are created consequent to the entry of foreign investments in an underdeveloped country.

Most multinational corporations in South Korea apparently invested a minimum amount of equity in their operations and used this capital as a means to obtain most of their resources in South Korea. Gulf Oil's operation with Chinhae Chemical Company is such a case. The Gulf Oil Company in this case did not invest a single dollar, but simply capitalized the United States aid loan. Furthermore, the multinationals used branch offices of multinational financial institutions, e.g., Chase-Manhattan Bank, Bank of America, The First National Bank, and several Japanese banks which served these multinationals in Seoul. They gathered Korean savings and loaned them to the multinationals to finance their capital requirements. Just as the Korean industrial firms could not compete with multinational giants, the Korean banks were not in a position to compete with those multinational financial institutions even on their home ground. Under the circumstances, anticipated national capital failed to form in South Korea.

Third, domestic-oriented Korean industries have been sacrificed for the benefit of the export-led industries which are foreign dominated. The objectives and priorities of foreign governments, reflected by foreign businesses, conflict with Korea's economic development. The high level of demand for Korean natural resources, for instance, led to undue emphasis on natural-resource exploitation. This, in turn, imposed major burdens on Korea's future industrial development. Due to production geared to the export oriented industries, most of the domestic-oriented industries, mainly middle-sized firms, became unprofitable.

In 1974, the Department of Commerce in Seoul revealed that 40%, or 4,160 firms out of 10,400 business firms which were classified as medium-sized companies, either declared bankruptcy or operated at reduced capacity. The situation became worse under the Chun regime. Dong Myong Lumber Company which employed 4,000 workers in 1980, reduced to 2,700 in 1981, while Taechang Lumber Company declared bankruptcy in 1985. Ilshin Iron and Steel Company, Daemyong Lumber Company, Dongsan Corporation also declared bankruptcy during the period of 1981-1982. Furthermore, the Myongsong group, a holding company, which controlled 21 companies declared bankruptcy in 1983.[7] During the first three years of the Chun regime, 1980-1983, 150 large-sized companies declared bankruptcy. In 1984, Taehwa Company, one of the major footwear export firms, closed several factories while Daeji Jonghap Technical Company closed business permanently. In 1985, Kookje Group, one of the ten leading Korean multi-national enterprises, declared bankruptcy which affected 820 Korean companies.

Thus, large-sized as well as small, medium-sized enterprises are destitute because of the shortage of funds and are being closed their business one after another. A World Bank Country Study pointed out: ''Increasingly governments are requiring firms to provide a portion of the financing, something that only the largest companies can offer. The many medium-sized Korean operations are, therefore, at a disadvantage unless they are prepared to merge or to collaborate with each other.''[8] Such advice from the World Bank Country Study to remedy the shortcomings of the medium-sized companies did not get a serious attention. Furthermore, the decline of the Korean workers' earnings from the Middle East added more to the increasing problem of the labor forces in South Korea. The declining number of Korean workers engaged overseas (whose wages constitute 15% of the value of contracts) will tend to offset gained elsewhere.

Invisible earnings were very important portion of Korea's export earnings. Invisible earnings have grown from $4.8 million in 1979 to $7.3 billion in 1983, about 30% of merchandise exports, and made a very substantial contribution to the total inflow of foreign exchange. More than two thirds are derived from overseas construction activities and shipping services.[9] The confusion and crisis in the financial community have been deepened by large-scale financial scandals reflecting the shortage of funds and economic convulsion. In face of the shortage of bank funds the government was compelled to issue additional currency, only rekindling the rampant inflation. United States officials estimated that consumer prices in South Korea were going up at a rate of 25% a year despite a harsh credit squeeze imposed by the government. Others put the rate even higher.[10] On the other hand, the foreign investors were making super profits in South Korea. Beside Gulf's $33.5 million remittance, Swift Chemical Company remitted $26 million, Caltex remitted $26 million, and many other American, Japanese, and Western European firms remitted according to the Economic Planning Board in Seoul.[11] The general practice of overpricing imports and underpricing exports coupled with the high reported profits, royalties, and fees remitted to nations other than Korea had a devastating effect on the domestic oriented industries. In other words, multinationals aggravate balance of payments problems through their transfer-pricing practice. When these multinationals buy and sell to their own subsidiaries, they establish prices that have little relation to market prices. Overpricing of imports and underpricing of exports were a good way to extract more profits than the host country allows. Thus, through these practices, the balance of payments of Korea turned gradually from bad to worse.

Through such practices, the foreign capitalists steered the Korean economy from self-reliance. The increasing amount of the foreign debts and the payment problem is compounding as year goes by. Table 6.1 shows a recent amount of the foreign capital.

As the table shows above, excessive reliance on medium-term loans from commercial sources in order to meet the payment would result in a bunching of amortization requirements before Korea has fully recovered from the consequences of the balance-of-payments crisis which continues since 1974. Korea, thus, became completely dependent on foreign capital and exposed her economy to greater risk. Furthermore, the foreign capital contributed to inflation and therefore to greater inequality in income distribution. Since Korean firms could not compete with them, they practiced monopolistic policies and manipulated prices and outputs.

Fourth, another economic result of the Korean industrialization program was the complete failure of agricultural development and the continued sufferings of the farmers as was the case under the Japanese. This perpetuated a deprived social group. The bottom 40% of the population's share of total income fell from 19% in 1965 to 16.9% in 1976. The top 20%'s share increased from 42.3% to 45.3% during the same period, while the bottom 40% of the peasantry had a per capita annual income of less than two hundred dollars, and the percentage of homelessness rose from 18% in 1962 to 25% in 1975. Another reason why the farmers were poor is because of the government price policy.

The Catholic Farmers Association of Korea reported that the production cost of one 80-kilogram sack of rice in 1978 was 45,000 Won. (500 Won equals $1 then) But the government purchase price was set at 30,000 Won. Thus a farmer lost 15,000 Won for every 80-kg. sack he sold. The government's low price for rice was a means of maintaining low wages for workers in export industries whose food costs remained low. The government guaranteed low wages to foreign investors. One wonders how the farmers could survive. Many of them were forced to forfeit their land and became tenant farmers. Land reform law officially forbade tenancy, but the fact is that 28% of the farmers fell into that category. As table 6.2 shows, the losses of farmers became significantly greater every year between 1975 and 1978.[12]

Land is the most important thing to farmers. Who owns the land and how they treat it are the basic issues to farmers. Government land policy helped business rather than the farmers in spite of the land reform law. In Masan, for example, the government used the "Compulsory Land Purchase Law" to confiscate 150,000 pyong (3.3 square kilo meters) of farmland so that Samsung Heavy Industrial Company could build an apartment building for its employees. The land was valued at 35,000 Won per pyong, but the government forced farmers to accept 2,000-8,000 Won per pyong. When the bulldozers came to level the land, the farmers protested and 30 police were mobilized to stop them. Several farmers were injured according to *Donga Ilbo Daily News* on October 19,1977. Such incidents were frequent occurrences. Not only have the industries taken away farmland with the help of the government but they have also polluted the land. For instance, farmland in the vicinities of Ulsan, Yosu-Sunchun, and Changwon industrial zones have been ruined by sewage water and pollution. Is it any wonder, then, that Professor Inanuma of Kyoto University and Professor Sumiya of Tokyo University have concluded, after long and careful research, that the Korean economy under the Park regime was absolutely hopeless.

As we pointed out elsewhere in this study, self-sufficiency in food dropped 54.3% in 1980 and 42.2% in 1985. The ever-deepening agricultural crisis in the country was an offspring of the colonial and semi-colonial policy. The farm land continued to shrink. The area under rice and other grain crops in the ten years ending 1977 decreased 555,000 hectares, or one-quarter of the total, according to data published by the Ministry of Agriculture and Forestry.

The irrigation systems were in a deplorable state. Only 12% of the rivers, big and small, had been harnessed, according to the Ministry of Interior. A total of 70% of the rice fields remain poorly irrigated or rain-dependent, and were vulnerable to a small prank of abnormal weather. The peasants still farmed by primitive methods. Worse still, a large number of young people were drafted into the army or into building of military installations, and left troublesome farming mainly to old folks. The young women were also leaving for the cities having lost all zest for farming. In 1968, the rural population accounted for 51.6% of the total population. But it dropped to 28.9% in 1979.

On top of all these problems, the arable land decreased yearly. In 1979 alone, it decreased by 15,000 hectares. A vast acreage of arable land was requisitioned by the army to expand military bases and military roads. Industrial zones and crop fields were constantly washed away by floods. Consequently, the South Korean people were confronted with a serious food crisis. During the winter of 1980-81, over four million farmers were left without food.[13] To meet the crisis, the Chun regime had to negotiate with the United States and Japan for imported grains.

The South Korean regime imported 8.14 million tons of grain in 1981 to meet the food crisis. Now, the government must import about 60% of the needed grains each year.[14] The food imports were increased from 480,000 m.t. in 1962 to 5.1 million m.t. in 1979, while self-sufficiency dropped from 93.9% in 1965 to 54.3% in 1980, and 42% in 1985.

Fifth, another result of the Korean economic program was the sad condition of the wage earners in South Korea. The mass migration of poor farmers to the cities like Seoul and Pusan created mass unemployment, underemployment, and slum conditions in the cities. From 1969 to 1977, between seven and eight million peasants migrated to the city. In 1981, five thousand farm families left the farm and moved into the cities. In 1963, 63.2% of all employed people were employed in agriculture and fishing. This decreased to 50.5% in 1970, 45.9% in 1975 and was projected to drop to 16.2% by 1986. The Korean Development Institute predicted that by 1991 more than 80% of the Koreans would live in urban areas.[15] There were about 3 million slum dwellers in Seoul alone. These slum dwellers are migrants from the farm into the periphery of the cities. They serve as marginal labor in the urban economy. Most of them are unemployed, underemployed, or work at starvation wages. With such extreme sacrifices of the masses, only about 0.3% of the total population comprises the very rich and powerful group. In October 1977, a New Democratic Party representative caused a stir in the National Assembly by claiming that 0.3% of the population receives 43% of the national income. In 1978, 50 top companies earned 2.6 times more than 1977. The monthly income of Chung Chu-yong, President of the Hyundai group, was an estimated 2.2 billion won (W 800=$1), according to a government source. In other words, one man's income was equivalent to the total income of 22 thousand average workers in the country. Each of ten top financial groups, including the Hyundai group, controls about 100-200 billion won worth of assets. The 200 billion won is about one-tenth of the entire Korean currency.

Today, 30 leading Korean multi-national corporations dominate about 30% of GNP. Most of these corporations, like Kookje group, carry about 400-600% of debts compared with their corporation assets. Yosung, Myonbo, Samamho are no better than Kookje group in their financial situations.[16] In reality, these corporations are illicit enterprises. They can only survive with the government supports.

The rich were getting richer with the government's support, while the poor were exploited. During recent years, defenders of the economic policies of President Park of South Korea used an argument that says that South Korea's income distribution is more equal than Sweden's. Professor Donald Zagoria's article, ''Why We Can't Leave Korea'' in a *New York Times Magazine* stated' ''South Korea today is one of just a few developing countries with an income distribution more equal than Sweden's . . ,[17] To reply to this statement, American Friends Service Committee stated that: ''The statistics used to support this claim are from a World Bank funded study, *Redistribution with Growth*.''[18]

Several things should be noted, the statement continued, ''The figures compared shows that South Korea has less income equality than Niger,

Chad, Surinam, Taiwan or Greece.'' It further stated that the table compares countries with widely differing economic systems. The figures used are for pretax income and therefore don't measure the money people actually have to spend or the social benefits provided through governmental spending. The figures also do not show the pattern of distribution of corporate and property ownership. The statement concluded that the impression given by the argument by Professor Zagoria helps create a myth that the South Korean economy is moving in the direction of more equality, when actually the opposite is happening.[19]

Sixth, beginning with the Fourth 5-Year Plan, the economic development of South Korea promoted heavy chemical industries rather than traditional light and consumer-goods-oriented industries. Why was this emphasis necessary in South Korea? It is true that competition among such major exporting countries as Hong Kong, Singapore, the Republic of China, and Korea will be increasing. For purposes of long-term planning, therefore, it is not realistic to rely on growth in textile and clothing exports of more than 7 or 8 percent a year during the 1980s according to a World Bank Study. The study pointed out that ''unless new exports are vigorously developed, Korea cannot hope to capture an increasing share of the world market of manufactured goods. Because government's rather ambitious plans for shipbuilding have run into the problem of uncertain international demand, electronics and machinery will be particularly crucial in export diversification and growth.''[20] The shipbuilding business declined to three months works out of twelve months in the last few years in South Korea, while protectionist sentiments against the import of manufactured goods have been escalating in the United States and other industrialized countries which are under considerable stress, burdened with excess capacity and having to cope with wide spread unemployment.

Under such circumstances, heavy chemical industries rather than light industries have been promoted in South Korea. Why? Was the promotion necessary? The reason is primarily due to the pressure from Japan. Why was Japan anxious to invest vast amounts of money in heavy chemical industry in general, and the oil industry in particular? Japan had reached its saturation point in environmental standards. The Japanese major firms were unable to locate Japanese sites for their ever-growing expansion programs. South Korea therefore was chosen for additional heavy chemical plants by the Japanese business giants and the Park regime offered full cooperation. The Fourth 5-year Economic Program, which concentrated on the heavy chemical industry, is in principle an expansion of the Pohang Steel Mill project. The oil refinery at Sunchun area has also completed by 1980.

Japan's purpose in locating heavy chemical industries in Korea was to develop war industries. The modernization of the Korean National Army and the expansion of war industries are closely related. Both programs were promoted by the United States after the declaration of the Nixon doctrine. Japan was more than willing to help develop Korean war industry since she can't expand the same industry in Japan due to her constitution. The weapons business was a very lucrative enterprise in South Korea with a ready buyer—the Chun regime—waiting to purchase the products. Actual production of M16 rifles began in 1971, and M1 Carbine production in 1973. Korean factories produced more than two dozen varieties of weapons, which the Korean Army exhibited on June 23, 1977.[21] The Korean government intended to build M.60 tanks as well as Jet bombers under the 5-year planning with $5.1 billion budget, and the United States was willing to loan $3 billion for the project according to Mr. Holbrook, the Deputy Assistant Secretary of the State, who testified to that. effect at the public hearing of the Asia and Pacific Affairs SubCommittee of the U.S. Congress, and the details of the policy implementation were announced by the two governments later.[22] Through presidential decrees, tax-free research institutions have been established including the Korean Science and Technology Research Institute, the Korean Atomic Research Institute, the Korean Chemical Research Institute, and several others.[23]

The Korean Government designated several industrial zones under the Fourth 5-year Economic Planning; Changwon is one of them. Changwon became a center of steel, machine, automobile, and ship building industries, and was ready to produce weapons according to an editorial in *Chosun Ilbo* (April 16, 1977). Besides the Changwon industrial center, Yosu, Onsan, Koje, Pohang, Ulsan, and Pukpyong were also centers of weapon-producing industries. All together, there were 27 known industrial centers in South Korea although not all of them produced weapons or included heavy chemical industries.

The Government of South Korea estimated that about half of the nation's total industrial production will take place in Changwon by 1981. Two hundred twenty (220) companies with about 100,000 workers were scheduled to operate in the early 1980s, and about a half of them were in operation in 1978. The President ordered all of the major Korean corporations to produce certain types of war material, and of course, the government arranged foreign loans and direct investments for them. Japan clearly had absolute control over the projects in Changwon and other industrial zones as planned by the Korean Industrial Development Company.

The Korean Government, however, frequently denied the close cooperation of the Korean Government with the Japanese companies due to the political sensitivity of weapons production. For in stance, Nam Duk-woo, Minister of the Economic Planning stated in his interview with the Japanese newspaper reporters on April 4,1977 that: the Japanese Government will not recognize that Japan and Korea will begin to produce weapons together. From the standpoint of the military secrecy, Korea cannot collaborate with Japan in the project.[24]

The Japanese Government also denied such collaboration. The Japanese consulate-general at Pusan stated that eight industries of Japan were involved with production of auto parts, not with weapons production.[25] Nevertheless, the fact of the matter was that the Changwon Industrial zone was dominated by heavy chemical industries, and these heavy chemical industries were producing weapons. For instance, Taehan Heavy Machinery Company was producing heavy army trucks with Japan's Ito, and Samsung Heavy Industry with Japan's Ishikawajima.

Twenty-one Korean major companies were collaborating with thirty-three Japanese companies producing twenty-two different kinds of weapons in Changwon alone in 1977.[26] Japan's involvement in weapons production in South Korea is not just to meet the demands of the Korean Armed Forces, but to export to the third world market.[27] The United States supported the Japanese involvement in weapons production in South Korea, and became involved herself. General Stillwell commented that the scientists and technicians of the United States and Korea worked together to produce weapons in South Korea.[28]

The Park regime not only enthusiastically supported development of Japanese-dominated heavy chemical industries, but even licensed Korean companies to "import" industrial wastes from Japan. According to Mr. Inouye, a member of the Japanese Diet, Japan "exported" industrial garbages to South Korea under the disguise of "industrial fuel." This international scandal was exposed following severe complaints by Korean Custom officers who detected unusual odors from the cargo at Pusan ports. Why had such "trade" taken place? It was cheaper to "export" wastes to South Korea than to get rid of them in Japan. Both governments of Japan and South Korea had issued licenses for such "trade."[29]

Political Results

It is now a well-established fact that American and Japanese businessmen became the major sources of political funds for the Park regime. Recently the U.S. House (Fraser) Committee Report revealed that American corporations including Gulf, Caltex, Union Oil, and others paid huge sums of money to President Park's political campaign. These millions of dollars may have accounted for Park's victory over Kim Dae-Jung who received 46% of the popular vote in spite of the corrupt involvement of the foreign business community in South Korea.

There are numerous political scandals which are closely associated with economic development in South Korea. Let us take a few examples:

First, in September 1973, several serious political and economic scandals in connection with Korean businesses were exposed at the Appropriation Committee of the Japanese Diet. For instance, the Korean Government authorized the Korean Aluminum Company to borrow $13 million to purchase a plant which was worth only $7 million in Japan. Much of the loan was used for political bribery of Japanese and Korean officials. Several leading Japanese Zaibatsu groups, including Tomen, Hitachi, Show Electric Co., were directly involved in this scandal.[30]

Second, another scandal concerned the purchase of Seoul's subway engines. Japan sold each engine to the Korean Government for 6,400 Yen although the sale price in Japan was only 3,000 Yen. The Korean Government bought 186 engines for Seoul Subway. Several big business firms were again involved in this deal. They were Marubeni, Mitsubishi Shoji, Iwai, and Kokyu Company, each of them the largest in their field of business.[31]

Third, Tongsun Park's bribery scandal is also well-known. The Park brothers inherited their father's Gulf outlets in South Korea. They also owned Pan Ocean Bulk Carriers, a company that has received some questionable payments from Gulf. Gulf and other oil companies arranged to sell oil tankers on extremely favorable terms to politically important people. Gulf learned that President Park favored Tongsun Park and his brother. Gulf arranged for and guaranteed loans for the purchase and then agreed to charter back the vessels for the 20-year life of the ship's mortgages which guaranteed profits for the Parks. In the arrangement for the large tanker, Gulf agreed to pay the company $186,000 a year in various arrangement fees above the cost of operating the tanker.[32]

In 1972, Gulf went to the new Prime Minister, Kim Jong-Pil, and asked him to suggest a purchaser for the vessel Chun Woo. Gulf's own special committee investigating Gulf's political payoffs concluded that "Gulf's decision to offer the new Prime Minister an opportunity to select the purchaser of the Chun Woo had obvious political overtones and was designed to gain some favor with that high official."[33] Between 1971-1975 Gulf paid $2.2 million in kickbacks to the Korean Ministry of National Defense to secure the contracts for very large sales of fuel to the Military. Gulf-owned Korea Oil Corporation's presidents have been past ministers of the National Defense.

Fourth, the political corruption of Park's regime was intimately associated with the ruling political groups of Japan and the U.S., e.g., the Lockheed scandal, the Tongsun Park scandal, the Seoul Subway scandal, and many other similar incidents.

Fifth, starting with Kim Dae-Jung's abduction in 1973, the Korean C.I.A. resorted to terroristic practices. All progressive political movements were suppressed and the unification movement of North and South Korea was sabotaged by the Park-Chun regime. Multinationals contributed to political instability in South Korea. Now the Koreans are asking why can't we achieve economic development without foreign participation?

Social and Environmental Results

First, Pro-rich and Anti-poor Policy which intensified social conflict.

The Park's regime's pro-rich and anti-poor economic-social policy was notorious. The government gave 7 trillion Won to finance big businesses in 1978. This represents 60% of all government institutional financing. One single business received 600 billion Won. In contrast, 1,200,000 farmers received a total of 104 billion Won; in other words, the total government investment in farming was less than 1/5th of that invested in a single company, and 4% of total institutional finance according to the Catholic Farmers Association of Korea.[34]

According to a study by Seoul National University in 1977, 78 percent of all farm households cultivating less than 0.5 hectares were in debt. The average debt per farm household was 138,000 Won or about $276.00.[35] Such a debt amounted to more than one fifth of those farmers' 1976 income.[36]

Meanwhile, wages of Korean workers remained at the bottom of all Southeast Asian countries at a starvation level. For example, the average female worker in Masan earned less than one hundred dollars per month recently, according to the Labor Standards Bureau of ROK. It requires $625 to support a family of five. Generally speaking, the average Korean worker's wage was about one-fifth that of their Japanese counterparts, and one sixteenth that of American workers. In reality, however, Korean workers were much worse off than that. Only 11% of the entire Korean industrial workers earned enough to support a family of four as reported by the Labor Standards Bureau. Seventy-nine percent (79%) of workers, excluding the agriculture sector, received less than $94 a month as of March, 1977 and only 9% earned over $200 a month. Sixty percent (60%) of the two-million manufacturing workers earned less than $62, and only 13% received over $100 a month.[37] Furthermore, 82,400 workers were unemployed as a result of 1,913 firm bankruptcy in 1985 according to the government official report.[38]

The following quotation is from a World Bank study on South Korean wage situation. It stated: "The labor force is projected to grow at nearly 2.7% a year in the 1980s. And despite the creditable record of the Korean economy in distributing the benefits of growth, as many as 3 million Koreans, or 8% of the population, were below the minimum income level in 1975. Significant progress toward basic equity goals can be attained only if employment demand grows at more than 3% a year, which would require GNP growth of at least 9% a year in the 1980s."[39] Contrary to the expectation of the supporters of the South Korean economy like the World Bank, the South Korean economic growth slowdown to the level of zero growth to 2% increase, and the unemployment increases steadily according to the official report.

Second, Unbalanced Population Shift.

Due to pro-rich and anti-poor policy, not only has scarcity of food been an annual occurrence, thus the poor suffer more, but the price of rice lands has also declined--dropping 22% in the Taejun area in March 1978 compared with 1977, but still with no buyer in sight.[40] Waste and suffering have been the lot of human resources in the countryside. In the course of but one decade (1967-1976), rural population declined from 16 million to about 13 million. Taking into account natural population increases, more than 7 million farmers are estimated to have left their farms and moved into the cities. Seoul's population alone increased 54% from 1969 to 1976.[41]

The absolute decline in the farm population began after the 1965 treaty with Japan when the Park regime emphasized export oriented industrialization. Farmers migrated to the peripheries of the cities to swell the industrial reserve army of workers at the beck and call of foreign investors. As already pointed out an abundant supply of low-paid labor was demanded by Japan and guaranteed by the Park regime. There were, however, far more workers or ex-farmers seeking employment than there were jobs so that unemployment rose sharply, thus assuring the foreign investors of the abundance of low-paid labor they craved. The mechanism of underproduction of grains, overproduction of fertilizers, and forced consumption of agricultural chemicals had therefore brought about yet further tragic results.

Decline of the rural population coincided with an increased percentage of land lying fallow.[42] In 1973, the number of farmers leaving for the cities increased 13% compared with 1972. Most of them were, of course, tenants. They worked hard for absentee land lords who live in the large cities, and received little satisfaction or comfort on the farm. It has been reported that 83% of the farmers had debts of about a hundred thousand Won (about $200) per family, a sum the average family cannot hope ever to pay back in the life time of its members.

Third, Environmental Result.

Consistent with its export-orientation which granted huge loans to bail out troubled big business firms while withholding assistance to the small-sized businesses, the Park-Chun regimes neglected completely the problems of environmental pollution. Badly polluted water, land, air, and cities were of no concern to the Park regime. About 1,000 residents from 200 households near the Ulsan industrial complex suffered from skin diseases and eye troubles of unknown origin after late April 1979. Some 150 of them received medical treatment from the Ulsan Municipal Health Center, which was trying to determine the cause of the disease. The disease, developing blisters and red spots on the skin and blurring eyesight, is especially serious among children aged between two and seventeen according to the medical report.[43]

Recent reports indicated that 10 of the 13 plants in the Petrochemical Industrial Complex in Ulsan area were found to have mixed harmful chrome derivatives in cooling water to prevent corrosion of their cooling systems and released the contaminated water freely into the sea. Some 60,000 tons of such water was released into the sea at Ulsan area, including water from the Petrochemical Complex. It became obvious to many who are aware of the "Minamata case" of Japan that the situation in Ulsan, too, could create acute problems to the residents. What was the regime's answer to such environmental problems? President Park commented repeatedly that "environmental problems have to wait until industrialization is accomplished." One of the high public officers in Seoul bluntly stated, "Bring all the industries to Korea if there is any environmental problem in Japan." That's what the Japanese businessmen did in Ulsan and other places in Korea. One reporter used the Han River as an example. The Han River, used by more than ten million people living in Seoul. By the Northern Fork of the Han is the Chinchun Industrial zone. Along the river there are many Saemaul (New Village Movement) factories. On the South Fork of the Han there are many factories in the area from Yoju to Ichon. The reporter stated: "the waste water flows down toward the Paldang area. From Paldang to Manguri Pass there are also countless factories and all that water comes into the Han River. This is the water Seoul citizens are drinking."[44] He added that' "Pusan's situation is almost the same. Water polluted by numerous factories in the Kumi Industrial Zone flows into the Nakdong River. This is Pusan's water supply."[45] More than 38,000 citizens in Nyochon-Dong, Ulsan recently protested to the authorities and demanded measures for preventing pollution damages. They said that they were suffering not only from pollution of all kinds but also that they were not even allowed to sell their farms and houses, and move away from the location. Such mass mobility of the local residents would create a labor shortage for Ulsan Industrial Complex.

The worst situation is that the heavy metal pollution cannot be cleansed from the soil, but is stored up in the soil almost forever. Fertilizer pollution has reached a serious level. The oxen which ate grass growing along the edge of rice paddies have begun dying. More than 0.2% of the farming land has been irreparably damaged by industrial waste, yet the government is planning to build more factories for the foreign investors according to a recent report.[46]

As a result of the unsupervised expansion of Japanese industries in South Korea, the country is now confronted with a serious pollution problem affecting not only the environment near the factory sites in question but also local fishing industries near Masan, Chinhae, Ulsan, and Pusan. The Korean Government has refused to investigate either the pollution problem or the fisherman's financial losses in the areas. Mr. Park was determined to carry the Fourth 5-year economic plan.[47]

Fourth, Total Bankruptcy of the "Yushin" System.

On April 8, 1975, a Japanese delegation at the Japan-Korea Economic Cooperation Conference in Seoul, agreed to help finance Korea's Fourth 5-year plan with a new loan of 23,410,000,000 Yen (or about $100 million). Prime Minister Kim Jong-Pil was in Tokyo to negotiate the loan. Kim discussed the matter with leading Japanese politicians' Kishi, Sato, Miki, Fukuda, Nakasone, Miyazawa, and Funeta. All were leaders of the Liberal-Democratic Party and had been supporting the Park regime.

After many serious meetings with the Japanese leaders, Kim stated at a press conference in Tokyo that: "We must expand our implementation of practical activities of urgent relationship between Korea and Japan." How can the Park regime convince its Japanese counterpart about such determination and reliability on the Korean side? On the eve of April 8th, while negotiations for the $100 million loan were going on simultaneously at the Seoul conference and in Tokyo, the Park regime sentenced 8 persons out of 38 persons convicted to death. The 8 people were hanged on the following day without even notification to their families. Appeal to a higher court was out of the question. Simultaneously, Mr. Park proclaimed Presidential Decree No. 7, and then had troops occupy Korea University, eventually closing down the campus. A month later, on May 13, the notorious President Decree No. 9 was proclaimed, and South Korea became nothing more than a big concentration camp. Who can deny the close relationship between the 8 persons' sacrifice and the $100 million loan? The issue is, therefore, not a matter concerning only a small group of Korean and Japanese politicians, but survival of the entire system itself.

No one can deny that the "Yushin" System was established in 1972 specifically to prolong Park's dictatorship for the duration of his life, or that the establishment of Park's dictatorship at the same time guaranteed maximum profits to the multinational corporations. As long as the Park-Chun regime remained in power and foreign capital accordingly exploited the people of South Korea, the struggle for their rights and democracy was destined to continue and intensify. In 1978, the average monthly wage for all workers was 48,500 Won (about $100), increased from 42,062 Won in 1975,[48] according to the Economic Planning Board of the government, while the estimated minimum living costs for an urban family of five was 85,380 Won.[49] This means 85% of workers fall below the government recommended minimum. The situation has not improved. In 1985, 35.7% of all workers are still seeking jobs day to day, and 64.2% of their monthly income is less than 300,000 Won or less than a half of the estimated minimum living costs for a family of four.[50] Increasing labor disputes demonstrates the problem of low wages. Two-hundred twenty five (225) labor disputes have been reported by the end of October in 1985 alone, according to the Ministry of Agriculture and Forestry. The ministry spokesman indicated that the situation might become worse due to slow export situation.[51]

The Park-Chun regime of South Korea produced economic chaos not an economic "miracle."[52] They brought about political corruption not a "revitalization" program. This resulted in an amoral, unstable society in an uncared-for, neglected environment. Their deliberate suppression of the people in the name of industrialization became the fundamental source of political and social instability. People realized that the nation was approaching the final critical stage of such instability. People also sensed that President Reagan went to Korea to give support to the Chun regime, but even President Reagan was helpless, just as his predecessors were helpless in Iran and Nicaragua. What is the significance of President Reagan's trip to Korea? How long will the Chun regime last in Korea? How long can a foreign government suppress the people's movement for democracy there?

Notes

1. *Japan Times,* July 2, 1979, Tokyo.
2. Ibid.
3. Pepper, Thomas, "South Korea' A New Kind of Ally" in Korean *News-*

letter, April 16,1979, Washington, D.C.

4. Some 40 major Korean corporations are financed and dominated by Japanese capital:

    1. in the textile industry, Hanil, Tongyang, Hankook Nylon Pangil and others-

    2. in the chemical industry, Hankook Fertilizer, Pungnong Fertilizer Taehan Hwasung, etc.

    3. in the cement industry, Ssangnyong, Tongyang, Tsungbuk

    4. in the fishing and marine industry, Korean Marine Development;

    5. in the metal industry, Union Steel, Hankook Aluminum Hankook Steel, etc.;

    6. others, Kia Industry, Chosun Ship-building, Shinjin Auto mobile, Samsung Electronic, Inchun Power and Light, etc.

5. The Hankook Ilbo News, April 3, 1977, Seoul.

6. *The Dong-A Daily News, Feb.* 8,1975

The Japanese Embassy in Seoul studied the condition of Japanese financed Korean enterprises in 1972, and a 276-page long report was available to the members of the Japanese Diet. Mr. Antaku, a member of the Diet, questioned the Minister of Foreign Affairs on the matter. According to the report, 13 large Korean corporations including Korean Fertilizer Co., which is financed by the Mitsui group were listed as "unworthy enterprises." Furthermore, seven of the largest Korean corporations including Korea Electricity Co., Korea Coal Co., Korean Marine Development Co., etc. approximated the "unworthy enterprises" condition.

Besides Korean Fertilizer Co., Taehan Ship-building Co., which has more debts than assets, Shinjin Automobile Co., which is sponsored by both Toyota of Japan and General Motors, Korea Aluminum Co., which is notoriously political in nature and heavily borrowed from the Industry Bank of Korea which is a government owned bank Taewon Paper Co., Taerim Marine Co., Punghan Industry, etc., were all on the list of "unworthy enterprises."

7. The Myongsong group began as a small travel agency, and became a financial giant within three years from 1980-1983. The group is closely associated with the Chun regime. Lee Kyu-dong, the father-in-law of President Chun, and Lee Sunja. the President Chun's wife control the group which controls more than twenty different enterprises. They are engaged in construction, land development, building golf courses and condominiums. They have been engaged in many illegal business activities which have been exposed. This is known as the Myongsong scandal. For details, see "The Myongsong Scandal and Korean Politics" by Yang Il-su, in *Tongil Review,*

Nov. 1983- *The Jeju Daily News*, Nov. 5, 1983.

8. The World Bank, *KOREA: Development in a Global Context*, Washington, D.C.: The World Bank, 1984, p. 58.

9. *op. cit.*, *p*. 57.

10. *The New York Times*, Aug. 23,1979.

11. *Korea Herald*, October 1,1978, Seoul.

12. Nakajima, John, *Korea Communique*, Japan Emergency Christian Conference on Korean Problems, Feb. 28,1979, Tokyo, p. 7.

13. *The Chungang Daily News*, Nov. 3, 1980.

14. *The Seoul Daily News*, Aug. 17, 1983.

15. Korean Development Institute, *Long Term Prospect for Economic and Social Development, 1977-1991*, 1978, Seoul, p. 92.

16. *The Hankook Daily News*, Feb. 24, 1985.

17. *The New York Times Magazine*, Oct. 2,1977.

18. Chenery, et al, *Redistribution With Growth*, New York: Oxford University Press, 1974, p. 8-9.

19. American Friends Service Committee, *South Korea's Income Gap Widens*, Philadelphia, JULY, 1978.

20. Hasan, Parvej and D.C. Rao, *KOREA: Policy Issues for Long Term Development*, Baltimore: The John Hopkins University Press, 1979, p. 79.

21. *The Chosun Ilbo, The Hankook Ilbo*, June 24,1977.

22. *The Chosun Ilbo,*May 18,1977.

23.*The Chungang Ilbo*, Dec. 7, 1976.

24.*The Nippon Keijai Shinbun*, April 5,1977.

25.*The Mainichi Shinbun*, April 16, 1977.

26. *Minami Chosen-noKeijai, p.* 133.

27. *The Sankei*, April 28, 1977.

28. *The Chosun Ilbo*, Oct. 7, 1976.

29. *The Hankook Daily News*, April 3, 1977.

30. Sunoo, Harold Hakwon, "Economic Development and Foreign Control in South Korea" in Journal of *Contemporary Asia*, Dec. 1978.

31. According to Japan's Kyodo News Service, Japanese prosecutorsand tax officials have now concluded that approximately one-third of the amount went to two former Japanese prime ministers.120-130 million Yen, and the other, 10-20 million Yen. No charges will be brought against the two, according to Kyodo, because of the expiration of the statute of limitations. National Tax Administration Agency officials may instead regard the money as "politicaldonations," which are tax free. They may be happy that the moneyhas returned to Japan--the Japanese National Police Agencyestimates that 12.2 billion Yen in cash is illegally exported from

Japan each year, of which 65% goes to South Korea. *Korea Communique,* No. 30, May 31, 1979.

32. Report of the Special Review Committee of the Board of Directorsof Gulf Oil Corporation, Dec. 1975.

33. *Ibid.* Gulf is not only a major supplier to the Korean military, butalso of the U.S. military in South Korea. For example, Gulf sup-plied 62% of the oil requirements of the U.S. Forces in South Koreaduring 1970-72, worth $39 million. A major attraction in SouthKorea for Gulf has been the Korean government's lax environmental standards.

34. *Korea Communique,* No. 28, p. 7.

35. Socio-economic Survey of Korean Farmers, Social Science Institute Seoul National University, 1977.

36. Ministry of Agriculture and Fisheries Statistics, 1977, Seoul.

37. *The Dong-A Daily News,* June 29, 1977.

38. *op. cit.,* Nov. 15, 1985.

39. Hasan and Rao, *op. cit.,* p, 86.

40. *op. cit.,* March 23,1978. The report indicated that the price of rice fields per one pyong in Hongsung County was 3,000 won in 1970, 3,600 in 1971, 4,000 in 1972, 6,000 in 1976, but dropped to 4,600 in March 1978.

41. During 1978, the rural population declined by more than 780,000.About 96% of those leaving the country are under the age of 49. The loss of the young age group has necessitated heavy reliance onwomen and old-aged farmers, and the result has been the decline of production according to *Dong-A Ilbo* 's report on April 24,1979

42. By 1973, the government hadalready designated 17 industrial zones which took away from the farmers and the total area about 22,640,000 pyong. Korea Chamber of Commerce, *A Guide to Industrial Zones in South Korea,* 1973, Seoul, pp. 6-7. These acreageswere sold to foreign investors at low prices in order to attract their investments. One pyong is six feet square.

43. *Korea Communique,* No. 30, May 31, 1979, quoted from *KoreaTimes.*

44. Chung Tae-sung, "Holding the Reins of A Bureaucratic Economy," in *Walgan* (Monthly) *Chungang,* Oct. 1978, Seoul.

45. *Ibid.*

46. *The Dong-A Daily News,* March 22,1979.

47. In connection with the environmental, a more serious issue is perhaps, the Park regime's planning to build 22 nuclear power plants by the year 2,000 in South Korea. Two plants were operating, one of them built by Westinghouse had a similar problem to the disaster at Three Mile Island according to a Westinghouse source, and four more plants were under construction. A country less than one-third the size of California was

building 22 nuclear power plants with support from France and Canada besides the United States.

48. *The Dong-A Daily News,* Oct. 21,1976.

49. *Sekai,* (Monthly World), April 1978, p. 212, Tokyo.

50. *The Dong-A Daily News*, Sept. 2,1985.

51. *op. cit.,* Nov. 6,1985.

52. Sunoo Harold Hakwon, ''The Transnational Development in South Korea in *Unreal Growth: Critical Studies in Asian Development* Vol. I, Ed. Ngo Manh-Lan, Delhi: Hindustan Publishing Corp., 1984.

16

After the Kwangju Uprising

Background

General Chun Doo-Hwan, with guaranteed support of his foreign counselors, arrested Kim Dae-Jung, his political archenemy, and many other democratic leaders, and declared emergency martial law on May 17, 1980. The citizens of Kwangju fought against this "May 17 coup" for ten days, but the special paratroop unit reoccupied the city, killing more than 2,000 citizens. General Chun Doo-Hwan gained infamous reputation of "murderer" from this incident. The nation had never witnessed such a violent national slaughter in her long history.

It is important to note a series of events preceding what is now known as Kangju Uprising or Revolution. On October 26, 1979, President Park Chung Hee, after 19 years of dictatorship, was assassinated by Kim Jai-Kyu,[1] his most trusted Director of the Korean CIA. The uprising of Pusan and Masan during the early autumn of 1979 caused the near-collapse of the military regime which had been aided by the United States.

The democratic forces in South Korea had begun to mobilize their forces to challenge the remainder of the Park's military regime. Major General Chun Doo-Hwan, identified as the logical successor to Park Chung Hee concentrated on building his political power while the university students were reorganizing anti-military democratic forces under the leadership of the students who have returned to the campus after long absences. Many of these students were previously dismissed by the university authority due to pressure from the Park regime. The fact that the anti-Park regime forces returned to the campus and provided the leadership again was significant. It demonstrated the weakness of the military regime after the assassination of Park Chung Hee.

The student movement was not limited to the campus demonstrations, but also began to associate and mobilized the workers. They were more eager to identify with the workers since the Chun Tae-il incident.[2] The workers themselves became more conscious of their problems, and began to demand a just and fair share of income distribution. Four-thousand (4,000) Tongwon coal miners and 1,000 Tongkuk Iron and Steel Company workers had demonstrated and were successful in their strikes.[3] The significant point was that the students had responded to the strikes and supported them to success through solidarity with them. The united demonstrations by the students and the workers in Pusan and Masan prior to the assassination of President Park were good examples of the success by cooperation. In other words, both sides, Chun Doo- Hwan's military group who wished to succeed Park's military tradition and the anti-military forces which wished to bring about a democratic government in South Korea were building forces to prepare for the inevitable confrontation.

On May 1, 1980, 12,000 students assembled at Seoul National University, and demanded the rights of the workers, the poor farmers; dismissal of martial law; stop the revision of the constitutional law; and demanded the resignation of Chun Doo Hwan from political leadership. Furthermore, the students demanded the freedom of political movement, freedom of press, and the building of a democratic government. The Seoul National University student's resolution influenced the entire students of 85 colleges and universities in the country. The impact was not limited to the campus, but spread to the military regime. The military leaders had been ordered to close up the university campuses; meantime, on May 10, the student leaders of 23 universities in Seoul announced that their demonstrations would be peaceful, and that they would remain on the campus as long as the police forces did not interfere with them. The students decided not to confront the military regime. The Government's position was uncertain at this point while Acting President Choe KyuHa left for the Middle East tour in order to avoid the anticipated political crisis.

On May 13, 1980, 2,000 students of Yonsei University demonstrated on the streets; students from six other universities joined later; Seoul citizens joined the students. The numbers of demonstrators reached 200,000. The anti-military democratic movement spread throughout the country. Such mass demonstrations was only witnessed in 1960 when the Syngman Rhee regime was forced to collapse.

On May 16, Major General Chun Doo-Hwan, who was Acting

Director of KCIA, mobilized 6,000 soldiers of the capital garrison. They were specially trained to control riots and demonstrations. General Chun soldiers immediately had under arrest 400 student leaders and other democratic leaders numbering a total of about 1,000. He declared martial law. Neither public meetings nor political activities were allowed: the press was censored; and the universities were closed. Among those arrested included Kim Dae-Jung. There were four major anti-military democratic forces at this time: the university students, the workers, the opposition political party leaders, and the intellectuals including the religious leaders. They were coordinating in their efforts to challenge the military regime. All those leaders were arrested.

Kwangju Uprising

The impact of the early May demonstrations in Seoul affected every citizen in the country and Kwangju was one of them. On May 14, 10,000 students of Chunnam University clashed with the riot police in front of the university gate and the students returned to the main library building. Soon, the students divided into several groups and ran into different sections of Kwangju City, in spite of the tear gas bombs thrown by the police. The students distributed leaflets which condemned the military regime. The students gathered in front of the state capital in order to declare their resolution. Many thousands of citizens gathered to hear the students' declaration and joined them.

On May 15, the student demonstration continued, but there were no police to stop them. Sixteen-thousand students of Chunnam University, Chosun University' Kwangju Teachers College again assembled in front of the Chunnam State Office Building and insisted "relinquish the Martial Law."

On May 16, another student demonstration was held without police interference. A mass meeting was held again in front of the state capital. There were 30,000 students. Chung Tong-Nyon, representing the students, read the prepared statement. The students marched around the street and back to the meeting ground at the state capital. It was eight o'clock at night. They sang the "song of righteousness", the "song of struggle", etc. They had a torch-light march. They had a ritual of burning of effigy of Chun Doo-Hwan. Unlike the demonstrations in Seoul, the demonstrations were peaceful and conducted orderly and even cleaned the streets. They were evidently trying to impress the government officials with their serious behavior and messages. The student wished that the government officials, too, would respond peacefully. The gathering was peacefully disbanded at ten o'clock p.m. Student presidents of 55 colleges and universities in Seoul assembled at Ehwa Women's University during the afternoon in order to plan for future activities.

Why did the government officials not interfere with the student demonstration during these days? Why was the city so peaceful? Two things related with the peaceful events in Kwangju was revealed later. First, Chun Doo-Hwan's special trained capital garrison was transferred to Kwangju from Seoul; second, all the American personnel who were on the teaching faculty at Chunnam University were conspicuously absent from the campus on May 16. In other words, the government was preparing to challenge the student demonstration in Kwangju on a mass scale. During the midnight of the 16th, the leaders of the democratic forces were arrested. Most of the student leaders were hiding out in the mountains since they were informed of the arresting of the student leaders in Seoul on the same day.

On May 18, the police began to put pressure on the student demonstrations, and the soldiers from Seoul began to attack the students and citizens indiscriminately, raising the number of casualties. The demonstration now changed into a civil war situation. The citizens were angry over the merciless killings by the soldiers from Seoul. The students seized weapons from the police warehouse, and 300,000 citizens out of 700,000 city's population participated in battle against the soldiers.[4] The soldiers had to retreat from the city on the 22nd. The students had made the city of Kwangju "a liberated city." It lasted 10 days. The soldiers eventually recaptured the city after severe battle. Depending on the source, the numbers of casualties varied. About two thousand were killed. and many more thousands wounded.

General Chun consolidated the framework of his dictatorial system, dismissed Acting-President Choi Kyu-Ha, and assumed the presidency on September 1,1980. Meanwhile, Chun's military court had passed a death sentence on Kim Dae-Jung, but reduced it to a life sentence under the pressures of international criticism and concern. (In December, 1982, Kim and his family were brought to Washington after long negotiations between Seoul and Washington. In 1984, Kim returned to Seoul).

Why did 300,000 citizens join the student demonstrations in Kwangju? The city of Kwangju has special historical traditions that the citizens are proud of. First of all, Kwangju was the center of the Tonghak Peasant Revolution against the feudalistic government of the Yi Dynasty at the end of the 19th century. Those peasants now residing in the neighborhood of Kwangju are the offsprings of those rebels of the Tonghak movement. Many university students have their roots from these families.[5] Second, the 1927 Kwangju student uprising was another historical event. The Kwangju high school students challenged the Japanese students in order to keep their national pride and dignity. Many offspring of those students who engaged in anti-Japanese struggle are still living in the city. The student's anti-Japanese movement had spread throughout the country.[6] Third, under Park Chung Hee's dictatorial regime, Kwangju, and the entire Jolla region, had been discriminated in social services, and economic aids from the central government. The people of Jolla recognize the central government as "their government," rather than "our government." Major benefits from the central government went to Kyongsang region, including the employment policy, the building modern industries and highways, etc. Such public policies created an animosity among the people of Jolla, particularly the city of Kwangju which is the center of the Jolla region, against the central government. Fourth, the historical tradition, alienation and frustration of the people, and discriminatory public policies aided in creating a more conscientious and concerned attitude among the intellectuals and religious leaders. Thus, these intellectuals and some of the Christian leaders began to advocate more just and fair public policies, and became outspoken against Park Chung Hee's unfair, unjust, and dictatorial national policies.

It is no coincidence that many outspoken national figures, including Kim Dae-jung, Kim Chi Ha, Yang Il-Tong, Yang SungWoo, Song Ki-Sook, and many others pioneered anti-dictatorial
democratic movement in Kwangju. Furthermore, there were many social, cultural, and religious organizations participating on behalf of the fair, just and democratic principles in Kwangju. To name some, Y.M.C.A.; Y.W.C.A; Christian Youth Association; Catholic Youth Association; Christian Farmers Association; Catholic Farmers Association; Catholic Justice and Peace Committee; Kwangju branch of Korea Amnesty International; Council of Democratic Youth; Research Institute of Modern Culture; Noktu Book Store, and others. These were the main reasons which caused the historical uprising against the military dictatorship in May, 1980.

Why did the Chun regime become a dictatorial regime risking more opposition from the people? Why did the regime create a crisis? The Chun regime created an artificial crisis for the purpose of strengthening the government. Why then did the foreign forces support the Chun regime which created a crisis? The foreign investors were hoping to continue their profitable operation in the country under Chun's new regime. Chun's new system was in the midst of an unprecedented structural economic crisis, which was more serious than those of the Park years. There was a four-fold weakness in the Korean economy, namely: negative growth, high inflation, balance of payment deficits, and increased unemployment. The regime confronted the lowest economic growth in recent economic history; e.g., minus 5.7 percent in 1980, against an average 10 percent growth during the 60s and 70s. As far as inflation goes, it was the worst time for the country. The wholesale price index soared 44.6 percent in 1980, while the consumer price index jumped by 29 percent, according to the official reports. The real situation, however, was much worse than these statistics indicated. The Korean Chamber of Commerce and Industry reported that the prices of 30 daily necessities soared by an average of 54 percent; e.g., 49 percent for rice, 89 percent for soybeans, while wheat prices went up 100 percent. Garlic, which is an essential ingredient for Kimchee, jumped 367 percent.

The deficit in the balance of payments, too, was the worst on record. The deficit in the trade balance swelled to $4,700 million, and the total deficit in balance of current accounts amounted to approximately $5,500 million. Consequently, business performances were extremely poor, and an enormous amount of unemployment resulted. Considering the poor agricultural harvest, a decline of 30 percent from the usual harvest in 1980, the economic situation seriously deteriorated in 1980.

Under the impact of this four-fold economic weakness, the political situation became unstable. One strong reason behind the popular uprisings in Pusan and Masan in 1979, which directly caused the assassination of President Park, was economic distress. There were more workers than students among the participants in the uprisings. As bad as it was in 1979, the economic growth rate was 6.4 percent, and the Park regime controlled the inflation by keeping the wholesale and consumer price increases at the level of 18 percent. The Chun regime which failed to maintain the economic level of the Park years, counted upon vigorous suppressive policies.

After the Kwangju Uprising

The Chun regime became a outright dictatorial regime. All opposition forces were eliminated and the country was controlled by fear and violence. Even during the so-called "presidential election," Korea could not escape violence. The Chun Doo-Hwan regime started with violence and ran the government with violence. The United States supported this violent regime openly and unashamedly. Only a logic of violence can endorse such violent policy, and the U.S. Government has endorsed it under the name of security—which isn't there.

In a Washington meeting on February 2, 1981, President Reagan told the visiting South Korean general that "We will preserve our commitment to the security of South Korea. I would like to make it clear that we are not considering any plan for withdrawal of U.S. forces from South Korea." Such an endorsement of the U.S. President has strengthened a worse dictatorial regime than Park's. At least, the Park regime had allowed political opposition, and press opposition even though it was under rigid control. Chun's regime expelled opposition forces from political activities, and banned certain political activities. The so-called "purification committee" was to carry out this task. The Chun regime organized its political party, reorganized the trade unions, streamlined the mass media systems, and controlled the university campuses. These programs were clearly departures from the Park regime.

In order to overcome economic crisis, the Chun regime had to take extraordinary steps to reorganize major Korean industries. The regime was setting up an even sturdier oppressive inequality and economic dependency than that of the "Yushin" System. For instance the regime was coordinating heavy and chemical industries. What would happen under such a policy?

The results would be stronger monopoly and accelerated state capitalism. Meantime, indigenous small and medium-sized industries would be sacrificed. The fragile national economy was on the road to bankruptcy because of the unconditional impact of monopoly capital from advanced countries along with the connivance of some monopoly big money interests. The Chun regime had already announced that "the government will liberalize the economy to accelerate the inflow of foreign capital and technology" and that "greater efficiency will be secured by reorganizing and consolidating certain industries", according to the September 16 economic policy measures of the Seoul regime.[7]

The government stressed that under the declared policy the Korean government would permit the percentage of foreign equity investment to rise to 100 percent. This policy automatically abolished current regulations regarding restricted foreign investments in South Korea. The regime was setting up a monopoly economy, contrary to the interest of the nation, through even stronger measures to the masses.

Under the new policy, the import liberalization ratio will be increased to over 90 percent by 1986. A new policy on direct foreign investment effective from July, 1981 allows an equity share by foreign investors of up to 100 percent in more than 56 industries, reported in *Far Eastern Economic Review*.[8] The new policy, thus, improved credit worthiness. Korea Exchange Bank was able to arrange $700 million syndicated loans immediately after the new policy was implemented. The new policy has been continued during the fifth 5-year plan period which began in 1982.

Not only were they permitted unrestricted investments, but the foreigners were free to purchase land and stocks, and the foreign banks competed with the Korean banks for loan business. Under the circumstances did anyone expect that the fragile Korean enterprises could compete with transnational monopolies? This would only enrich foreign monopoly along with some local monopoly big money interests and would bring on greater dependency, imbalance, and more business failures. These tendencies would cause social polarization and eventually lead to the destruction of the regime. The regime actually undermined its own basis.

A rising inflation rate which went up to more than 40 percent in 1980, declining exports, increased unemployment, and an ever increasing burden of foreign debts are all placed on the backs of the masses. The people are reduced to poverty. In response to the Chun's suppressive policies, the anti-Chun regime movement has been escalated among the students. For instance. Seoul National University students staged an anti-government demonstration on March 19,1981, and were answered with gas fired by riot police. Seventy students were immediately taken to a police station after leaflets were distributed which called the government a "fascist regime."

The demonstration started in the morning when five student leaders, including Mun Yong-sik, a senior in the Department of Korean History, Park Tae-gon, a sophomore in the Department of Korean Literature, and others called a meeting from the roof top of the student hall, using a portable loudspeaker. According to a report, there were about 1,500 students in and around the student hall at that time. Leaflets entitled "Manifesto for Anti-Fascist Struggle" were distributed at this time. The demonstration lasted about an hour, then subsided. Shortly after, a meeting of university deans decided to expel the five student leaders, and alert all faculty members and administration staff to keep an eye on student activities.[9]

The incident received more attention than usual, not because of the demonstration itself, but because of the content of the leaflets. The "Manifesto for Anti-Fascist Struggle" was dedicated to "the souls of the more than 2,000 people who gave their lives for democracy and unification of the country". They were obviously referring to the victims of the Kwangju uprising in May, 1980. The Kwangju uprising clearly became the major grievance which fueled anti-government protests.

The Manifesto analyzed the nature of the regime through comparison to a "fascist" political system. It said that the system preserved the interests of a privileged elite by suppressing freedom and democracy by snatching away man's fundamental right to life with bayonets that destroy the masses who resist them. It identified the Park Chung Hee regime as a diabolical dictatorship, which robbed the people of democracy and threw the masses into the depths of poverty with its destruction of the national economy. It stated further that the regime of General Chun Doo-Hwan was no different from the Park regime. As a matter of fact, the Chun regime was a more wicked fascist, dictatorial regime. The regime crushed the pan-national struggle for democracy prior to its May 17 coup in 1980. The Manifesto declared that "in the eyes of the masses, under the standard of democracy, and before the anger of all the peoples of the world, it has been proven that the Chun Doo-Hwan group are true fascists. After defining the nature of the Chun Doo-Hwan regime, the Manifesto attempted to analyze the "Yushin" System which the Chun regime inherited from the Park regime. The statement pointed out that "the economy build around the rich major monopoly enterprises and based on dependency on foreigners, fueled by starvation wages for workers, low prices for agricultural products, and a high rate of inflation, had already been declared bankrupt at the close of the last decade."

The Manifesto's issue was the ultimate task of struggling for democracy. What should be done? The Manifesto suggested that "there must be a fierce, relentless mass struggle for democratization by all the people against the Chun fascist dictatorial regime." The Chun regime could prolong its life only when it maintained "stability" with the support of the foreign powers. But such "stability" was illusory because the regime had opposed the struggle for democracy. The Manifesto insisted that those who are fighting for democracy must not be deceived by the Chun's propaganda. Those who must fight were the working mass, the workers and peasants, and the progressive, radical intellectuals. The masses must organize to expel from Korea the people's enemies, that is, foreign capitalists and the domestic comprador ruling classes.

One of the protester's slogans was "unite all democratic forces." It was clear that their concept of an anti-regime struggle was based on a broad people's alliance which should be led by the united masses. The student movement must unite with the working masses, but the student group should initiate the struggle since they are the best organized group that has the power to fight at the present time. This united movement between the student group and the working masses would change the nature of the struggle against the dictatorial regime. It would no longer rely on sporadic uprisings as in the past; the movement would be better organized and committed to a total struggle. In order to organize the United Front of the democratic forces, the student movement must strengthen its own power with a clear understanding of the working masses. Truly, the student movement confronted a new situation. It was no longer a problem of how to organize demonstrations on the campuses, but how to plan and mobilize the working masses collectively and systematically. The struggle became strategically and tactically more scientific. It was indeed a significant qualitative transformation in the struggle against the dictatorial regime.

As soon as the Manifesto was distributed, the Chun regime was more apprehensive than ever. The press speculated that "there apparently was a leftist-oriented manipulating force behind the Seoul National University disturbance and that the authorities should do all they could to uproot such dangerous elements."[10] The paper further noted that the Manifesto and slogans contained "militant and leftist style phrases, which had been found in the leaflet scattering incident on the Seoul National university campus..."

Several newspapers in Seoul reported and commented that the Manifesto was written by Communists. Their arguments were basically anti-communist propaganda which failed to recognize the significant development of the United Front movement – initiated by the student group. Regardless of what the government officials said about the Manifesto, it should be interpreted in the light of the conditions of South Korea after Kwangju. Numerous declarations by different university students confirmed this view of the Manifesto.

The following statements were made by different student groups prior to the Manifesto. A September 17,1980 statement by Koryo University students said "Chun Doo-Hwan's military fascist clique is a bastard offspring of Park Chun-hee's "Yushin" dictatorship. Chun ordered the military's bloody massacre in Kwangju. He is a butcher of his own people, directly responsible for the murder of many innocent citizens. Has there been any more brutal and barbaric person in all of our history? The Chun clique committed the unforgivable act of mangling and maiming Korean people with guns and bayonets, made with the blood and sweat of other Koreans, of turning Korean against Korean. The attitude of the U.S. and Japan in this is a flagrant affront to world peace and human rights, and it results from their unspoken yet adamant opposition to allowing the Korean people to govern themselves independently and by majority rule." The statement, then, concluded with a following sentence: "End terror politics and exploitation of the people and open a great new age when power will return to the people and they can govern themselves ! "

Students at Yonsei University, another leading university in Seoul, made a similar statement on September 15,1980: "The anti-people "Yushin" system lasted for 18 long years with the traitorous Park regime, which completely obstructed the realization of democracy and unification." Then, the statement continued, "After Park's death a nation-wide movement demanding democracy arose led by workers, religious people, and students. This movement was stopped for awhile by the tricks of the military, but the heroic ardor displayed by the students who rose up against these stratagems on May 13, showed the ability of our people to take power for themselves. On May 17, the government cynically closed the universities and took away from students a place of truth and discussion, but the struggle against the present anti-people regime continued even stronger."

"Declaration of our willingness to die struggling to protect democracy" was issued by the same student group of Yonsei University on October 30,1980. The Declaration states, "let us stand together and smash this culture of death–the darkness of an oppression that denies the most basic human rights and a pseudo-media that has actively sold out the last vestiges of its conscience." The statement continued, "A just, democratic welfare state is not one based on an artificial consensus fabricated by the government in the midst of a whole culture pervaded by terror and silence." Then it concluded, "let us raise high our flame and dispel this dismal darkness; let us stand firm on this difficult and perilous place in history ! Let us go forward ! We will never turn back!"

Two weeks later,the Yonsei student group again declared in a "Declaration of Democratic Students": "Chun Doo-Hwan has shown for all to see that he is a genocidal murderer and he will go down in history for his immorality. Instead of protecting the nation, he sent paratroops to Kwangju to carry out his private aims. Chun Doo-Hwan has committed too many outrages ! He is worse than a dog or a pig ! "

Agreeing with this analysis of the Chun regime, the Kyunghee University Democratic Students' Federation issued a statement in September, 1980. The statement argued that: "to punish the murderer Chun Doo-Hwan and his clique is the urgent task challenging the future of our people, and the inevitable course of history...the time for that is now to overcome our old feuds and achieve national unification while planting democracy in this land and realizing social justice. While clarifying that the only way to achieve this is by punishing Chun Doo-Hwan and his clique. We want to call upon our 8,000 fellow Kyunghee students and our 40 million compatriots to stand up now."

On October 8,1980, a statement released by the student body of Hankuk Theological Seminary in connection with a memorial service for a fellow student killed in Kwangju was called "Declaration in Blood." The Declaration stated, "Are there no witnesses in our time to testify to the insanely cruel scenes of so many friends being murdered with bullets and bayonets?" The statement continued, "The Park regime lasted 18 years by sacrificing democracy in the name of 'security', but it only resulted in putting the nation itself in jeopardy. And now we have reached the point where 'emergency measures' can't be lifted for even a single moment!...the gravest real threat to our national security are the remnants of Park's dictatorial "Yushin" system....the new regime (of Chun Doo-Hwan) not only illegally moved troops in its December 12,1979 *coup d'etat,* but it shoots down ordinary citizens for demanding democracy.... The Chun regime, which has shown itself to be completely anti-democratic and anti-people, has neither the structure nor the ability to bring reunification and welfare to our land." Then the statement concluded with this urgent plea: "Come! Let us stand up and march, cherishing the memory of Dong-Woon, who was killed during the Kwangju uprising in May, and following the strains of his blood."

As these statements indicate, the student movement in South Korea was transformed. The students understood clearly the nature of the new regime. The acts of atrocious and brutal violence in Kwangju contributed to a change in the nature of the movement. The violence began at Pusan and Masan earlier, but it became so naked and clear at Kwangju, that the people could not miss it. Not only the citizens, students, and workers but the people all over the country witnessed violence. On December 12, 1979, Chun Doo-Hwan, then major-general, arrested martial law commander Chung Seung-Haw group in the "army purge *coup d'etat.*" The general feeling of the population at that time was that either Kim Jong-pil, Kim Young-Sam or Kim Dae-Jung would be the next president if there were a fair election in the country. Chun Doo-Hwan and his group probably didn't dream of taking over the government at this time, but his foreign supporters probably had a different idea. For the purpose of protecting their investments in Korea, they needed political stability at any cost, so the foreign supporters of the Chun group probably encouraged General Chun Doo-Hwan to stop the popular struggle for democratization which was making rapid progress at this time. A nation-wide organized uprising of workers and students was particularly noteworthy.

How did the Chun regime propose to rectify the country's crisis?

Following faithfully the Park's pattern, the Chun regime resorted to nation-wide propaganda based upon false ideology. At his presidential inauguration on March 3,1981, President Chun promised "freedom from the threat of war, from poverty, and from political oppression and the abuse of power." And he added "in order for political repression and abuse of power not to be reproduced in this country, I shall administer the affairs of state in accordance with the law and lead the government in accord with the law." This statement, in reality, was a criticism of his predecessor, Park Chung Hee, whose regime was oppressive. President Chun further commented on his idea of improved government by stressing newness. He said: "the ideal upon which I am determined is the construction of a new era, with the establishment of the democratic welfare state for which all our people are longing." Then, he promised to build a just society through continuing-and-wide-ranging social reforms.

After his promise to build a new and just society, President Chun's propaganda system engaged on nation-wide campaign to indoctrinate the people with a concept of new era, new leadership, and new task of the nation. On September 29,1981, President Chun said again "facing a new era and a new history, and standing at a new point of departure, we bear the heavy responsibility for construction of a new democratic welfare state, through realization of state stability, prosperity and a just society." In order to build "a just society" with a commitment of stabilization and prosperity, President Chun had to carry out two popular demands of the people. True to his commitment, he conducted the presidential election which returned him as the 7-year term president, and promoted a new constitution. As expected, both developments violated both the spirit and substance of democracy.

  Those sympathetic to the new regime may point out a "democratic" or "liberal" tendency demonstrated by repealing the anti-Communist Law, but the fact of the matter is that a stronger anti-Communist law has been included in the new National Security Law. Removing the anti-Communist Law from the statutes helped promote exchanges with non-hostile communist nations like China, a useful move for economic and diplomatic reasons, while the new National Security Law enabled those in power to abuse the law more easily. As a matter of fact, the regime used this law against Kim Dae-Jung, the foremost political opponent of the military dictatorial regime. A Senior Legislative Assembly for Justice Committee member, Kim Yeong-Gyoon, said that repealing the anti-Communist Law was imperative to effectively pursue "our open-door policy to non-hostile communist countries." Then, the Senior Assembly man observed: "it won't matter at all, if the anti-Communist law is incorporated into the upcoming revised National Security Law, because the Social Protection Law and some other laws have been enacted to maintain social order."[11]

  Following the revised law, the police "will be able to subdue future college campus disturbances more freely" because the police, even military troops, will be able to function as regular police in all police functions. The Chun regime's deceptive promises to build a just society with a concept of new era, new history, new leadership, and new justice contrasted with its new repressive laws and their rigid implementations. The regime even set up a "Labor-Management Consultative Council" in order to prevent horizontal relationships developing among the workers and to reinforce management controls over the workers. Why was the Council needed? Because the Chun regime feared the kind of surge in labor militancy that preceded the Kwangju uprising. Is there any wonder why there was no excitement among the people during the balloting for a new constitution. "There was virtually no sign of any excitement", reported the censored press. (The Dong-A Ilbo) . Just as the Yushin constitution was not supported by the people, the Chun's new constitution did not receive the people's support. Furthermore, the Chun regime was not even supported by his own military inner power circle as indicated by the removal of such high military officers as Major-Generals Kim Bok-Dong and the regime soon made many enemies among his own military leadership, as well as among the business and political opposition leaders, during the socio-political purification campaign.

What was the Chun regime's purification campaign? As pointed out earlier in the chapter, the Chun regime arrested the main political figures who would oppose to the regime. That was known as the May 17 *coup d'etat,* a day prior to the Kwangju incident. The purification campaign began then.

According to the new constitution, promulgated in October, 1980, "no citizen shall be restricted in his right to vote, nor be deprived of his right to own property." (Article 6 Section 4 of the Supplementary Provision). Then, the document stated: "in order to renovate the political climate and realize ethical politics, the Legislative Council for National Security may legislate laws regulating political activities of persons conspicuously responsible for political or social corruption or chaos prior to the entry into force of this constitution." (Article 6, Section 4 of the Supplementary Provisions). Those political activities which were restricted under these provisions are becoming a candidate for election as a public official, supporting or opposing any candidate for election, joining any political party or political-social organization, sponsoring a political meeting or speaking at such a meeting, and supporting, assisting or opposing any political party, political organization or person.

What happened to those who violated these provisions? The Law provided that, "Anyone who violates these provisions by taking part in political activities will be sentenced to 5 years' imprisonment and a 10,000,000 won fine." (Article II of the Special Law.) Laws enacted by the Legislative Council for National Security "may not be litigated or disputed. . . " (Article 6, Section 3 of Supplementary Provisions).

It was clearly stated that "no legal objection may be raised against the enactment of this law, nor against the President's confirmation of it, nor against its directions or procedures." There was no question about the clarity of the laws and there were no loopholes in this comprehensive attempt to restrict political activities deemed harmful to President Chun's holding of power. President Chun not only intended to hold power, but also control the daily lives of the people as Hitler did with the German people.

In order to control the daily lives of the people more effectively, President Chun introduced mass media control after the Kwangju incident as part of the social purification program. On November 25, 1980, 44 out of a total of 64 newspapers, radio and news agency companies, 172 periodicals, including some of the nation's most respected intellectual journals, *Voice of the People, The Creation and Criticism,* were closed down. Furthermore, the regime established a new, single *Yonhap* news agency with exclusive control over all domestic news, and prohibited the system of stationing reporters in local areas. In the areas of radio and TV, the government controlled two networks, and the CBS--the Christian Broadcasting Station, which had taken occasionally different views than the government, was allowed to continue, but was restricted to religious broadcasts. During the process of this purification campaign, an estimated 400 or more media persons who were characterized as "not loyal to the state" or believed to possess an "anti-Communist spirit not sufficiently vigorous" were dismissed from their jobs.

The Chun's purification campaign covered all aspects of the daily lives of the people. Purification of education controlled the academic world just as was the case for mass media control. The Legislative Council for National Security proclaimed numerous provisions one after another: the Special Measures Law for Renovation of the Political Climate on November 5, 1980, for the purge of the political opposition; Revision of the Laws Governing Assembly and Demonstration on November 29, to prevent all opposition activity; the Political Parties Law on December 1 to establish parties exclusively sympathetic to the Chun regime; the Social Protection Law on December 5, for preventative punishment of the opposition; a Law Concerning Circulation of Opinion (Basic Law on Opinion) on January 1, 1981, for control of public opinion; and the Presidential Election Law on January 1, 1981 to secure the path to a dictatorial presidency.

During August and September, 1980, a total of 46,117 "perpetrators of social evil" were detained. Some of them supposedly harbored "violent thoughts." Among them 2,243 persons were formally arrested and charged under same pretext. Twenty-nine thousand eight hundred ninety-two persons were taken to military camps where they were forced to undergo "purification education." The Chun's practice of purification of education, or "thought control," is reminiscent of Japanese military control during the World War II. The Chun regime demonstrated its authoritarian nature conclusively. At the same time, the regime promised to build a democratic welfare society. The regime struggled to establish its legitimacy, but the people rejected the regime after the Kwangju incident. It was supported only by the foreign forces particularly the full-scale support of the U.S. and Japanese governments. Why did the U.S. and Japanese governments ignore the people's appeals and support the dictatorial regime of South Korea? The answer is clear. It was profitable to keep the Park-Chun type of government under which their businesses were prosperous. Foreign banks made a 95 percent profit in South Korea in 1977 according to *The Korea Times*. Foreign banks' transactions with the Korean businessmen were guaranteed by the government. That is why the Export-Import Bank approved a $631 million loan to the Chun regime immediately following the Kwangju incident. More than 150 Japanese leaders of the business world went to Seoul to support the Chun regime in spite of his troops' atrocious actions in Kwangju. There were no less than 2,000 U.S. corporations engaged in business in South Korea, and the Japanese firms outnumbered the Americans'. All their businesses were protected by the South Korean government while oppressing the people. There is a law against strikes at foreign originated factories which helps keep wages down. Such a labor policy has naturally attracted the foreign investments, and the U.S. policy to support such policy was consistent for decades.

What hope was there to build a democratic society? Had the democratic spirit disappeared in the land? Had the dictatorial regime won the battle? The students of Seoul National University distributed leaflets on December 11, 1980 challenging the Chun's new law which prohibits any sort of demonstration, which said, "Now history forces us to reflect upon our past struggle most seriously and to establish a new posture that can adjust to the changing situation. Our program is not whether we can fight or not, but how can we fight to get a strong enough grip on our enemy's throat." The statement continued, "First, who is our enemy and what is its true nature? Our clear enemies are the comrador ruling groups who are desperately trying to protect their exploitative system from the resistance of the people around them...." The leaflets stated that "The U.S. seeing an imminent crisis in the growing Korean people's struggle in the 1970s, reorganized the country's ruling system through preventive measures on October 26, 1979, and now props up the new fascist regime. Can we continue forever to think of the U.S. as a friendly country?"

During 40 years U.S. involvement in South Korea following World War II, no prior public statement had questioned the U.S. as a "friend". The students understood that the Chun regime could not attempt their atrocious acts in Kwangju without General Wickham's cooperation. The leaflets said: "It will be a long struggle under difficult conditions—the struggle from now on requires an anti-fascist struggle in which a broad people's alliance fights together until it wipes out the comrador fascist ruling groups. When this struggle is led by the united working masses, it will have positive and definite perspective." Then the statement concluded with this "The most urgent problems facing us, however, are how to most effectively and continuously get our hands around the throat of the enemy and what internal preparations the student movement will require to achieve this. It is the beginning of the struggle that confronts us and it is the deepening of that struggle.''

These students were now seeking to associate with the working people. They moved into factories, rural areas and tried to communicate with them. This was an important movement which had a great impact on the anti-dictatorial struggle. As the Declaration pointed out, the students were organizing to develop their ability to fight effectively against the Chun regime. Learning from the past experiences, like the Pusan and Masan uprisings in 1979, they were organizing carefully and systematically as well as training leaders. A lack of organized leadership was evident even in Kwangju uprising. Statement after statement declared that they were not afraid of death in their struggle. For example, a statement released by the student body of Hankuk Theological Seminary was called ''Declaration in Blood,'' and a statement of Yonsei University students on October 30,1980, was called, ''Declaration of our willingness to die, Struggle to protect democracy.'' Events have proved that they meant what they said. Many more Pusan, Masan, and Kwangju incidents may be expected as long as the Chun regime continues.

After Kwangju, the anti-Chun regime movement changed its substance. The students and workers were more experienced and mature. Sometimes, the deepening of social instability due to structural economic crisis, and the internal conflicts among the ruling groups, will contribute to downfall of regimes like that of Chun in spite of regime's success in eliminating the opposition, and the full-scale support of the Chun regime from the U.S. and Japan.

Chun's regime realized for the first time the declining economy in December 1982, and adjusted to it. The regime, however, continued its export-oriented policy inherited from the Park regime. The economic catastrophe was simply postponed by foreign ''aid'', specially the $4 billion ''aid'' that was negotiated with the Nakasone regime of Japan. Consequently, the Chun regime became more than ever dependent upon Japan and the United States. At the same time in South Korea there is greater anti-American and anti-Japanese activities among the students and workers.

The turning point in anti-American activities among the students were with the seizure of the U.S. Information Service in Seoul by 72 university students representing five major Seoul universities: Seoul, Koryo, Yonsei, Songyungwan, and Sogang, at noon on May 23,1985. The students demanded that the United States apologize for allegedly authorizing President Chun's use of Seoul garrison in May, 1980, to put down the demonstration in the city of Kwangju.

The students expressed their sentiments on huge posters boldly demanding that' United States apologize publicly for its role in the Kwangju Massacre; and that she bear responsibility for the Kwangju Massacre; United States stop support to its military dictatorship, etc. The students made it clear that if Korean police were called by the U.S. Embassy authorities to force them out, they would jump from windows or take poison. Four hundred heavily armed riot police outside of the building waited for them. The tense atmosphere prevailed in and around the U.S. Information Service Center for three days (72 hours).

The students believe that the U.S. commanding officer of the American armed forces in Korea, who also serves as operational commander of the South Korean troops had agreed to move the capital garrison against demonstrators in Kwangju. The American Ambassador to Seoul said: "We have reached a point where it is doubtful whether continuing your current actions can really contribute to the goals which you ask."[12] Ambassador Walker offered to meet with the students after they left the building. However, twenty student leaders were immediately arrested as soon as they stepped out of the building. About 7,000 university students stayed campus demonstrations, chanting anti-government slogans. "The smell of tear gas filled the air at universities around Seoul, where students protested in support of the building takeover." was the way Susan Chiri described the situation in Seoul.[13] The students left the building after 72 hours without receiving an American apology. They issued a statement which read "We realized that there is a great deal of distance between us and them (Americans). We must reconsider the United States as a defender of freedom or a friend of Korea. We are indeed very disappointed with them."[14]

The university students' "Sit-In" at the United States Information Service in Seoul was the turning point in anti-American activities in South Korea. At the same time, the Chun regime moved to curb the students' activities. For four years after seizing power in 1980, President Chun relied on repression to remain in power. Then, early in 1984, he began to tolerate a measure of dissent. After the "Sit-In" incident at the U.S. Information Service in Seoul, a new crackdown began. The chief targets of the new crackdown were, of course, the campuses. There are about 950,000 students among the nation's colleges and universities.

As Chun's crackdown escalated and became more severe, the students' anti-government movement also increased, rather than retreated. For instance, during the month of November, 1985, the students occupied the headquarters of the New Village (Saemaul) Movement, the center of cultural propaganda for the Chun regime under the leadership of President Chun's younger brother, and on November 4, the Office of the American Chamber of

Commerce in Seoul, Branch Office of the Bank of America in Pusan on the 13th; the Office of the Labor Ministry on the 15th; and the Central Political Research Institute of Minjong Party (Chun's ruling party) on the 18th. Such activities spread to Kwangju and Taegu in December. "Hardly a day passes anymore in South Korea without a violent confrontation between students and "Policy"-student opinion has also grown increasingly anti-American" reported Steven Butler.[15] No one seems to deny the seriousness of the students. President of Seoul National University, Lee Hyan Jae, refused to expel the 8 students from his university who were among the 20 leaders who occupied the U.S. Information Service. Consequently, Lee was ousted from his job by the government. It became clear to the public that both the Chun regime and the university students have changed tactics in their confrontations.

According to the Ministry of Education in Seoul, on November 22,1985, 994,632 students of 86 universities, out of 100, participated in anti-government demonstrations during the 18 months starting from March 1, 1984 to August 31, 1985. The numbers of demonstrations counted 3920 times. Meantime, the demonstrators who arrested during the demonstrations numbered 1,449 students.[16]

Chun's national police began to accuse the students of being pro-communist and a new crackdown began. Many concerned individuals and groups began campaigns against torture. On November 4, 1985, the Joint Committee Against Torture and Fabricated Conspiracies held a press conference to reveal the facts about the recent cases of torture. The Committee is composed of 263 members, including Kim Dae-Jung and Kim YoungSam, Co-Chairs of Council for the Promotion of Democracy; Lee Min-U, Chairperson of New Korea Democratic Party; Song GonHo, the former editor of the *Dong-A Daily News;* Rev. Moon IkHwan, Rev. Kye Hun-Jae, and Rev. Park Hyong-gyu, representing Protestant, Catholic, Buddhist bodies, the families of detainees, the united Minjung (people's) Movement for Democracy and Unification (of Korea), the Council for the Promotion of Democracy, and the New Korea Democratic party.

There were then over 500 political prisoners in South Korea, more than at any time during the repressive Park Chung Hee regime, according to the statement released by the Committee. The statement said: we are faced with the truly wretched situation in which such basic human rights for the citizens are cruelly trampled under. The acts of violence were committed by prison officials against Chung Jin-gwan and some 10 other political prisoners incarcerated at Taegu Prison last July (1985), and many similar incidents have continued: the chief editor and staff members of the *Dong-A Daily News* were detained and assaulted; Kim gun-tae, chair of the Youth Federation for

Democracy and other officers were also tortured by interrogators; the where-abouts of some 40 laborers in the Inchon area became unknown after being detained.[17]

In the case of Kim gun-tae, he was subjected to electric torture and water torture, and forced to drink red pepper water, salt water and other similar things; and was bound tightly....He was not allowed to eat. At first, he was tortured for about 5 to 7 hours a day; then the torture time was cut down to 3 hours because he had become weak. He was tortured for 10 days and not allowed to sleep for 20 days.[18]

The Committee's statement indicated: it is simply disgusting that the present regime commits such barbarious outrages against humanity and human civilization while claiming the construction of an advanced nation and at a time when it is hastening to become a signatory to the International Human Rights Covenant. It is all the more shocking with the memory of the May 1980 Kwangju tragedy still fresh in our minds....We urge that it be denounced and immediately stopped in the name of all humanity and civilization because these are inhuman acts and a national disgrace, shaking human dignity and democracy itself to their very roots.[19]

South Korean resistance against the Chun regime and its supporters was growing not only among the students, but also among the Korean workers. Labor unrest was clearly on the rise. Official data shows 445 labor disputes during the first 6 months of 1985, compared with 113 during 1984; 2,200 disputes since July of this year as reported on Sept.8, 1987 by *The Wall Street Journal.* Some of the major strikes have erupted against Daewoo motor Company (a 50:50 joint investment with General Motors) and Daewoo Apparel. The recent unrest stems clearly from discontent with low wage policy and ineffectual unions. Real wage growth has lagged behind improvements in labor productivity since 1980, reflecting Korea's intent to maintain export competitiveness. For example, the 10 day strike at the Buyong Plant of Daewoo Motor Company in April 1985 was sparked by rank-and-file workers dissat-isfied with the timidity of official union leaders in wage talk. The strike was settled with leaders of the dissident workers for a 14.7 percent wage and benefits hike by Daewoo Group Chairman Kim Woo-Joong personally. Thus, good will was created between the workers and the employer. However, the good will lasted a short time because the strike leaders were quickly arrested on national security-related charges. Furthermore, the government estab-lished a national disciplinary commission which began a severe crackdown on opposition and labor activism on July 22,1985. Establishment of the commis-sion could provoke more intense confrontation between the workers and the employers. In addition, with the revival of a strong political opposition, the new Korean Democratic Party, and possible linkages among student, labor and the new Korean Democratic Party activists have heightened official nervousness. Implementation of new torture against the political prisoners, students and workers, is expression of official nervousness. The Seoul regime is.trying to intimidate the dissidents with torture techniques, rather than attempting to rectify their problems.

The main problem of the Chun regime has to do with the economic issue. In 1983, the average operation rate in 26 heavy industry factories manufacturing goods was only 50 percent. The average operation rate of 83 enterprises under the Chang-won Machine Industry Complex was less than 43 percent, according to the Ministry of Commerce and Industry's report to the National Assembly. Along with industry, agriculture was also on a steady decline. The government said that South Korea would be compelled to rely on foreign countries for 60 percent of their total grain needs at the end of the 1980s and over 60 percent after that.[20] Increase of farm production was further hindered by absentee landlords. Nearly half of the farm land in surroundings of the city of Seoul were farmed by the tenants.[21]

What is the solution to the economic dilemma of South Korea? The Seoul regime which had a $52 billion foreign debt, was trying to solve the problem by opening the domestic market to the foreign countries. The United States has decided to induce South Korea to open its market, particularly of tobacco and other farm products. It aims at a profit of 1,800 million dollars annually through export to South Korea of tobacco alone. The U.S. pressure for market opening has met with strong resistance from the people. More than a thousand university students in Seoul waged the anti-U.S. demonstration on November 7,1985 in protest to the U.S. economic pressure upon South Korea. Over 1,500 students of Seoul, Koryo, Yonse, and other universities in Seoul burnt the U.S. goods in effigy at the street meeting.[22]

Meanwhile, more capital of foreign multinational corporations was induced into South Korea. As of December 5,1985, it had amounted to $496 million in 111 cases. This is an increase of 22 percent in case and 28 percent in the amount of money above the figures in the same period of 1984, or about two times respectively compared with 1983. The foreigners' direct investment has increased because the Chun regime has favored such action in order to attract more foreign capital. In 1985, the Chun regime reduced the investment limitation business categories by making the terms of permit for foreigners' investment easier and introduced an ''automatic sanction system'' to considerably simplify investment procedures. Foreign corporations which had already made their way into South Korea under the patronage of the successive regimes wrested $25,000 million profits more than 20 times the money invested by them over the 20 years until the end of 1984 and remitted them home. Owing to the existing economic relationship, South Korean economy could never develop the necessary infrastructure and stand on its own feet although outwardly, it appears to be so buoyant and healthy. The country is now not only handicapped by a foreign debt of about $52 billion as of the end of July 1985 which requires 10 percent of GNP to pay the principal and interest, but also must import more than 8 million tons of grain a year to feed 38 million people. Even if Korean GNP grows by 10 percent every year, it will not be enough to repay the interest and the principal of the foreign debt. Present GNP growth rate is about 5 percent. South Korea must borrow more in order to repay the principal.

During the past five years of the Chun regime, the foreign debt has increased by $30 billion, but few factories were built with that money. The proportion of newly borrowed funds used to repay the foreign debt incurred previously continues to grow every year. It was 50 percent in 1972, 95 percent in 1982, and now has become 100 percent. The Chun regime rely on export business to repay the foreign debt. In order to decrease foreign debt by means of exports, it depends on the excessive dumping of exports. For the first six months of 1985, output expanded by just over 3 percent, the nation's worst performance in 5 years and less than half the rate anticipated by Seoul's economic planners. Exports went down in value by 3.5 percent between January and July, 1985.[23] Furthermore, South Korea has neither developed adequate financial systems nor diversified their markets away from the United States and Japan. For example, more than a third of South Korea's exports (38 percent in 1984) go to the United States. In addition, the labor unrest is increasing because the regime depends on the excessive dumping of exports, and it inevitably will result in low wages for workers and, in order to maintain those low wages farm products will have to be continually supplied at a low price. In other words, the foreign debt will be repaid by maintaining low wages for the workers and the labor movement under control as witnessed in recent actions by the Government against the strikers in April, 1985. The Chun regime has no intention of allowing free trade union movement, and also maintains low prices of farm products. Who benefits by the foreign debt? Who suffers by the foreign debt? The people began to realize what the dictatorial regimes have been saying about raising the living standard. The country's 0.4 percent elites enjoy the export-oriented economic development while the rest of the population suffers.

In order to maintain the status quo, the Chun regime maintains tight controls over the media; about 800 journalists remain banned, censorship regulations are enforced; such sensitive topics as President Chun's political legitimacy are never discussed in the media. Furthermore, the regime also controls all aspects of cultural, social, economic, and political activities. Signs of economic slowdown are abundant recently. Newly constructed blase-and-concrete towers in Yoido's financial district stand roughly half-occupied.[24] These buildings are financed by foreign loans with the government approval. The ship-building business is down one third capacity, and they are bidding for contracts at prices below production costs. In addition, some 500,000 new workers enter the job market annually. Providing jobs for them requires economic growth of at least 5 to 6 percent, according to Seoul economists. The worse situation is among the college graduates in the job market. Only one out of twenty college graduates can find jobs among 349 firms of 30 Korean business groups in 1985, according to the Ministry of Labor's estimation.[25] The situation gets worse as some 60,000 Korean construction workers return from the Middle East since 1984. Very few have found jobs at home when they returned. The struggle, it seems, will increase between the military regime and the anti-regime forces for a long time in South Korea.

Fabrication of the Park regime, now the Chun's, to build a democratic and unified country through the means of economic modernization has been clearly exposed. The anti-regime forces, – combination of the university students, the workers, the intellectuals, the religious leaders, and the unification Democratic Party,–are very conscious of the dilemma of the present regime. Particularly the growing strength of the workers movement illustrates that the workers are not willing to sacrifice by accepting low wages, allowing company-instigated violence and government's continuous repression. During the strikes against the Daewoo Motor and Daewoo Apparel (the Daewoo group is the second largest financial group in the country), there were many sympathy strikes occurred in June, 1985. Another big strike was against Samsung Heavy Industries in Inchon last summer (1985). The following statement represents the present   sentiment of the general public in South Korea: "The problem of foreign debt can be solved only through the formation of a democratic government" issued by the United Minjung (people) Movement for Democracy and Unification in Seoul on October 4,1985. It stated, "The most reasonable way to solve the problem of foreign debt is for the present regime to resign, to form a new democratic government backed by the people and for that newly-formed government to uncover the real aspects and users of foreign debt and what it was used for then, in agreement with the people, solve the problem by mutual agreement with the creditor countries. Otherwise...the lives of the people will become even more painful and eventually, the regime itself will meet a miserable end."[26] Will the seemingly powerful regime accept a realistic solution to the present dilemma?

344

Notes

1. For detailed story about Kim Jai-kyu's motivation of killing president Park, see the court testimony of Kim in *Tongil Review,* Tokyo, June, 1980.
2. For Chun Tae-il incident, read "10th anniversary of Chun Tae-il's death" in *The New Korea,* Toronto, by Hakwon Sunoo, Dec. 13 1980, also Chun Tae-il incident to YH incident by Nakaġawa Nobuo, in *Tongil Review,* Nov 1979.
3. "Background Report on Sabuk Coal Miners' protest" in *Hanyang,* Tokyo, July, 1980.
4. Cho Sung-il, "Koshu shimin hokino iki-to Kyohun" (The meaning and lesson of Kwangju Uprising), *Tongil Review* Aug. 1980.
5. Sunoo, Harold, Chapter seven in *Korea: A Political History in Modern Times.* Seoul: Kunkook University Press, 1970
6. *op. cit.,* p. 242
7. *Korean Newsletter,* Toronto, Oct. 1980.
8. *Far Eastern Economic Review,* Hongkong, Nov. 25,1981.
9. *Korea Times,* Seoul, March 20, 1981.
10. *Ibid.*
11. *Korea Herald,* Seoul, Dec. 28,1980.
12. *New York Times,* May 25,1985.
13. *Ibid.*
14. *Korean Digest,* Nov. 1985, New York p. 22.
15. *The Christian Science Monitor,* Nov. 19,1985.
16. *Sokoku Toichi Shimbo,* (Fatherland Unification Weekly), Tokyo Dec. 5 1985.
17. *Korea/Update,* Washington D.C.: North American Coalition for Human Rights in Korea, Nov. 27,1985, p. 12.
18. *The Christian Science Monitor,* Nov. 19,1985.
19. *Korea/Update,* Nov. 27,1985, p. 12.
20 *Seoul Daily News,* Aug. 17, 1983.
21. *Chosun Daily News,* July 18, 1979.
22. *Reuter dispatch,* Seoul, Nov. 7,1985.
23. *The Christian Science Monitor,* Oct. 18,1985.
24. *Ibid.*
25. *The Dong-A Daily News,* Nov. 13, 1985.
26. *Korea/Update,* Nov. 27,1985, p. 20.

17

The military regime of Chun Doo Hwan, realizing the growing popularity of the democratic forces, is out to destroy it before the world media descends on Seoul for the Olympics. There have been mass arrests of demonstrators and numerous reports of torture, intimidation and false imprisonment. Not only students, but members of the National Assembly have been arrested for statements made in the legislature, the press has been muffled and journalists forcibly silenced. Riot police have disrupted peaceful demonstrations and have violated churches. On June 10, 1987, President Chun Doo Hwan picked, and the ruling Democratic-Justice Party nominated Roh Tae Woo, a retired general, as its presidential candidate. That touched off a nationwide protest. Tens of thousands of students and citizens staged demonstrations and clashed with riot police.

President Chun had already suspended constitutional debate until after the Olympia, and now selected a retired general as his successor in order to continue the military power. Chun and his military associates, however, did not understand the pent-updiscontent of the people finally exploded with the nomination of Roh Tae Woo as their presidential candidate.

In Kwangju City, about 100,000 citizens and students participated in anti-government demonstrations on June 10. The anti-government demonstrations continued daily all over the country. About 44,000 students from 64 universities throughout South Korea participated in anti-government campus demonstrations on June 18. The situation became so serious that President Reagan sent a Personal letter to Chun and Edwin Derwinski, U.S. Under Secretary of State for security assistance, arrived in Seoul for a first-hand look at the situation. Some 2,000 students began shouting, "Oust Americans" and "Oust the Chun regime." Similar demonstrations took place in Pusan, Taegu, Taejon, Kwangju, Inchon, and Chunchon simultaneously.

When about 500 students staged a six-day sit-in inside Seoul's Myongdong Cathedral from June 10, thousands of citizens brought food and other supplies to the students and on June 15, 10,000 citizens joined them and had a candlelight mass. For the first time, these "middle-class" citizens who had been supporting the Chun regime had demonstrated their distrust and hatred of the military regime. Nationwide protest demonstrations spread like a brush fire.

On June 23 alone, more than 20,000 students from 25 universities in Seoul gathered in Yonsei University and staged an oncampus demonstration, and some 30,000 students from 58 universities clashed with riot police across the country the same day. In Pusan, the second largest city of the nation, about 100 clergymen started an indefinite sit-in protest against riot police's outrage against student demonstration on June 24.

On June 26, faculty members of Yonsei University and a number of other universities met in the university chapel to pray for Lee Han-Yol. Lee, a 20-year old sophomore at the university, who was struck by a tear gas canister that police fired into a crowd of students during the campus demonstration. Lee collapsed on the spot and was taken to the university hospital where, with irreparable brain damage, remained in a coma, then died.

American missionaries who have witnessed the peaceful campus demonstration on June 26th have reported their eyewitness story on the event.[1] Dr. Dwight Strawn and his wife, Sonia, United Methodist missionaries in Seoul, reported that when Dr. Strawn went out for his Bible class at the Yonsei University Church, all approaches to the university had been sealed off by riot police. They said: "The silence in the air was foreboding. None of his students were able to get in church through the police barricades." Later, they joined the thousands of students and citizens who began to gather on campus to pay respects. They observed: "As the crowd swelled, we noticed that there were people of all ages, grandmothers and grandfathers as well as students. It was a powerful and dramatic demonstration of support for the cause in which Han-Yol had died.. As an expression of their grief and anger over Han-Yol's death, the assembled multitude began a march through the campus and out toward the street. The march was not led by students, but by a group of older women, and parents of some students were their marching with their sons and daughters." The riot police, however, did not leave those peaceful marchers. Dr.Strawn said: "It was shocking beyond belief to see the police move in again, firing volleys of tear gas, to stop this procession of mourners." Nevertheless, demonstrations continued throughout the week.

The American missionary also attended Han-Yol's funeral. Dr. Strawn reported: "the funeral began at 7:00 a.m. on July 9, on the Yonsei University campus in Seoul. It ended around 11:00 p.m. at the Mangwol Cemetery in Kwangju, about 200 miles south of Korea, which, according to the BBC news from London, drew an estimated crowd of about one million mourners." The riot police could not stop these mourners to march down the streets when one million mourners assembled. Dr. Strawn said: "We went with the multitude of Han-Yol's family, friends and supporters, not only over the tragic death of this one young man, but also because of the oppression and on-going and needless violence which led to his death." Dr. Strawn concluded with these words: "Our ears still ring, after prayers at the funeral by ministers who had just been released from prison, from hearing Han-Yol's mother cry out that her son's death must not be in vain.

While the path ahead is full of pitfalls, the massive popular uprisings in June 1987 have brought a new era in South Korea. The democratic force are not concentrated to three major arenas—the constitutional debate, the political contest for president, and achieving labor rights. Not only the students, labor is already moving ahead in a rapid escalation of demands and actions. More than 4,000 strikes have taken place in 1987.[2] The nation-wide labor strikes have continued for weeks and months after the June popular uprising to protest unfair labor practice in the country. The movement has been long overdue to the oppression by the Chun regime.

On August 18,1987, about 50,000 workers of the nation's biggest Hyundai Companies demanded that: "Free union and higher wages." The maker of "Hyundai" automobile and the Hyundai Shipyard closed indefinitely. Five days later, Daewoo Shipyard workers demonstrated outside the hospital where a fellow worker, Lee Sok-Kyu, 21, died. The young worker had been hit by part of a tear gas grenade during the strike on the Island of Koje. He is the first fatal victim since the labor strike began in South Korea in August, 1987.

Some 33,000 taxi drivers in Seoul, 7,700 drivers in Taegu, and many other cities called a strike in August, and all the major cities' bus drivers massively joined strikes. On the occasion of Lee Sok-Kyu's funeral, student forces joined massively in the service to show their firm solidarity with workers. Faced with this labor unrest, the Chun military regime has mobilized police forces against workers who were staging sit-ins and strikes at the Daewoo Shipbuilding and Heavy Machinery and other places so that tension has been mounting. Despite the police crackdown on striking workers of the Daewoo as well as the Hyundai, the workers were not giving up their demands.

Meanwhile, labor disputes have increased since June. There were 2,555 strikes in August alone, more than in all of the past 10 years. The workers are organizing labor unions which have been prohibited by the military regime counted over one thousand in August alone. The Ministry of Labor said the number of labor unions totaled 1,060 as of September 4,1987. On September 4th when the police raided the Hyundai plant and arrested striking workers, thousands of workers attempted to march into the street to demand the release of their arrested colleagues. On September 7th, about 7,000 workers managed to enter the factory and stage a demonstration, demanding the release of arrested workers.[3]

Behind this sweeping labor strike is the pent-up dissatisfaction to South Korean workers who have sustained South Korea's export-oriented economy at the cost of their sweat and blood. They have been exposed not only to low wages and long hour work, but also to labor accidents and the least organized into trade unions in the world.

The wages of South Korean workers are the lowest among the industrialized nations. For example, average workers in manufacturing industries are paid $1.55 an hour, compared with $2.23 in Singapore, $9.50 in Japan and $13.09 in the United States and their work-week is the longest in the world—54 hours. The labor law bans union shops, and makes it impossible to organize unions so that it has been impossible for them to call a strike for a wage increase or better working conditions. Last year alone more than 23,000 were either killed or crippled in industrial accidents.[4]

For years, these workers have been told that better life is coming after they achieve an economic success which would bring prosperity to the nation. However, the wealth which gained from the economic success was not fairly distributed. Millions of Korean workers still barely scrape by. They work 12 hours a day, six days a week, or more, but do not earn enough to support their decent livelihood. A Korean worker said: "I had always been a model worker. I reported to work 30 minutes early, without pay, to clean around my work area....I opposed the strikes.....On Christmas Eve, 1984, we stayed late, because the company promised they would pay us our October wages—which were two months overdue. At midnight a foreman told us we would not be paid that night...I cried all night in my dormitory, in despair at life and the company."[5] The worker, Chung Dong Keun, worked for an export-oriented company receiving $4.25 for an eight-hour day. He worked every day, including Sundays, 78 hours a week. A group of three workers, including Chung, which later grew to 20, organized a secret union. They received no outside help. One hundred twenty out of 200 workers went on a five-day strike, management agreed to give workers three days off for the New Year holiday, instead of one, and promised to pay back wages. The workers through their hard experiences learned to claim their rights.[6]

What are American approaches toward the Chun regime now? President Reagan has spent several senior government officials one after another in order to urge President Chun Doo Hwan to maintain "dialogue" with the opposition over the nationwide popular protest since June, 1987. With the critical situation in the summer of '87, the Reagan administration has been trying to promote a "spirit of compromise" to deter anti-dictatorship protest and to disintegrate the opposition party and democratic forces. With American supports, the Chun regime began to crackdown the opposition forces on one hand and appease them on the other.

Secretary Shultz on June 16, referring to the breakdown of constitutional debate, said, "It is not quite accurate to say that Chun Doo Hwan was the sole cause of the breakdown on the talks." Why did the American Secretary of State defend the position of Chun Doo Hwan? What sort of impressions were left to the people in South Korea by defending the Chun's regime? A Korean Catholic activist in Kwangju described his participation as an act of nationalism, and said, "Like many young people, he sees the 41,500 American troops here (South Korea) not as protectors but as occupiers," reported in the *New York Times.*[7]

"The basic problem is that Chun Doo Hwan wants a process that would ensure the election of his own nominee," observed former President Jimmy Carter. President Chun has accumulated enough wrong-doing for the past 7 years. It is almost time that the Korean people enjoy the rights of self-determination. "The violent crisis in South Korea goes on..Even the Olympics are threatened. They should be moved unless there are clear signs fairly soon that the government is prepared to calm the atmosphere by seeking reconciliation with its people," observed by the *New York Times.* The Chun regime, however, is not prepared to reconcile with the democratic forces. The Prime Minister Kim Chung-Yul threatened on August 27 that the government was firmly determined to "root out impure leftist forces from our society with all the law-enforcing power we can mobilize from now on," implying a harsh crackdown upon students and workers by using the military force. Kim is a retired general himself. A tense situation continues at this moment and there is a growing evidence of the confrontation between the dictatorial government and the democratic opposition. Will the seemingly powerful regime accept a realistic solution to the present dilemma? Will the American policy-makers in Washington support the Chun regime to the last minute as they did to the Marcos regime? Can the United States secure her national security by embracing immoral tyrants further in South Korea?

It is clearly demonstrated that the struggle of democracy, self-determination, and unification of Korea will continue there regardless of the American or any other foreign forces that might interface with her. The June people's uprising and the current nation-wide labor demonstrations should convince those who had any doubt about the outcome of the long democratic struggle in South Korea.

Notes

1. Letter from Dr. and Mrs. Dwight Strawn.
2. *The Dong-A Daily News,* Seoul, September 2, 1987.
3. *Op. cit.,* September 8,1987.
4. *Yomiuri Daily News,* Tokyo, August 19, 1987.
5. *Far Eastern Economic Review,* Hongkong, August 27, 1987.
6. *Ibid.*
7. *New York Times*, New York, July 12,1987.

18

North Korea : Economic Development

On August 25, 1948, an election was held in North Korea. As a result, the Democratic People's Republic of Korea (DPRK) was born.

Prior to this election, there was a meeting of "All Korea Political Parties and Social Organizations" in Pyongyang. The constitution which was promulgated by the DPRK on September 8, 1948, stated that the Supreme People's Assembly is the supreme sovereign organ of the DPRK, and the legislative right shall be exercised only by the Supreme People's Assembly (Article 33). The statute also pointed out those former pro-Japanese Korean collaborators who have been deprived of their right to vote as a result of judgement pronounced by the court of Justice.

The guiding political power since the inception of the DPRK has been President Kim Il Sung. Under Kim's guidance, North Korea wasted no time in implementing land reform as well as nationalization of the major industries in 1946.

Prior to land reform, only 4% of the farm population owned 58.2% of the cultivated land while 56.7% of the farmers owned only 5.4% of the land in the country.

The declaration of land reform on March 5, 1946 stated that anyone owning more than 5 Chungbo would be confiscated and distributed free of charge to the landless farmers.

As a result of land reform, the big landlords-Japanese and Korean collaborators, have been eliminated, and the small to medium size farmers maintained, and the tenant farmers given land to cultivate.

North Korea has instituted numerous economic plans starting with the

One Year Plan of 1947, each of them expresses the distinctive economic objectives to be achieved during.the period.

The Korean Workers' Party proposed "Peaceful Construction Period" from 1947-1949. The goal was to surpass the output level and efficiency attained during the Japanese occupation. The outgoing Japanese destroyed systematically the existing facilities before they departed Korea. At the same time, the withdrawal of trained Japanese technicians of productive activities created serious economic problems. There were only 12 trained Korean technicians in North Korea at the time of liberation according to Kim Il-Sung's report.

Addressing the second plenary session of the Supreme People's Assembly on January 28, 1949, Kim Il-sung stated that, "The People's Economic Plan for 1948 in the northern half of the People's Democratic Republic of Korea has been triumphantly accomplished. . . the triumphant accomplishment of the People's Economic Plan of 1948 proved how whole heartedly the entire people have demonstrated their patriotic enthusiasm for wealthy and strong development of their fatherland. And it also proves that the entire people have been firmly united around the People's Democratic Republic of Korea and with their maximum devotion and loyalty they have fully put into force all the policies of the government and all the laws of the state."[1]

Kim Il-Sung added that one of the most important factors was that the standard of the people's material and cultural life would be gradually elevated. Clearly there must have been some progress, but how much more compared with the South was not clear.

In announcing the Two-Year-Plan of 1949-50, Kim Doo-Bong, Chairman of the standing committee of the Supreme People's Assembly stated, ". . . the Two-Year-Plan will be successfully accomplished, for it is the only measure which will not only elevate the material and cultural happiness of the people of the North, but of the entire nation."[2]

With this domestic policy in hand, the north Korean regime proceeded to negotiate a Korea-Soviet Agreement for economic and cultural assistance. In March, 1949, Kim Il Sung, as the head of the delegation with Park Heun-Yung, and several other cabinet members left for Moscow. Soviet Premier Stalin welcomed them and extended his hospitality. After the brief formality of exchanging greetings, Foreign Minister, Molotov, representing the Soviet government, initiated the treaty of the Korea-Soviet Economic and Cultural Assistance Agreement. According to this agreement: 1. issues of getting economic, technological, and cultural assistance and help from the Soviet government; 2. to expand trade relations with the Soviet Union and Korea; 3. to establish credits in order to control the price of imported goods in excess of export.[3] On March 17, 1949, the first agreement of the Korea-Soviet Economic and Cultural Assistance was signed. The agreement has been concluded to be valid for ten years on condition that at the end of ten years it be extended at the request of the two countries.

After the Korea War, the main task was to rebuild the devastated national economy. Three-Year Reconstruction Plan of 1954-56 announced. First of all, that the collective farm system be expanded throughout the country. The farmers were ready to participate in the collective system due to their war experiences and their having witnessed the efficiency of the collective production system. The influence of rich farmers and the traditional value of private system disappeared quickly during the war. Entire farm land was managed either by the state of the collective farm except for the small private plots.

There were three steps in the collective farm system in North Korea. First, two or three coops were organized among the poor farmers in the county level. This was the experimental stage. There were 174 coops or only 2% of the total farmers involved in the collective system at the end of the Korea War. However, the number of coops increased to 1091 or 31.8% of the farmers joined the collective system. By this time, the entire population of the poor farmers joined the coops.

Second, the second stage was the mass participation stage. The middle class farmers began to join the collective system. As the result, 80.9% of the farmers joined the coops voluntarily cultivating 78% of the farm land at the end of the 3-year, post-war reconstruction period.

Third, the final stage of the collective farm included the first 5-Year Plan of 1957-61. Those farmers located in remote mountain areas and those on the outskirts of large cities did not join the collective farm. The former groups due to location and later groups due to commercial activities. For instance, 55.8% farmers were members of collective farm in a remote mountain area of Jagang province, and 45% were coop members in the vicinity of Pyongyang city in 1956. However, in two years, all the farmers joined the collective farm system.

According to a report by President Kim Il Sung[4], the basic task of the 5-Year Plan of 1957-61, was to establish a firm foundation for industrialization with emphasis on heavy industry as well as to solve problems of food, shelter, and clothing.

They have built a foundation for industrialization. Industrial development brought with it a marked change in industrial composition. For instance, the machine building industry had reached about one-third of the total industrial capacity. The beginning with the "Chullima Movement", the machine building industry targeted to build a "self-supporting economy" and not rely on foreign support.

The aim of the first 5-Year Plan was to build the foundation for socialistic industry and to complete the collective farm system.[5] Annual growth of 11% of grains was the result due to the completion of the collective farm system. At the same time, rural electrification and irrigation systems were also completed.

Following the successful 5-Year Plan, the 7-Year Plan of 1961-67 was inaugurated. with successful fulfillment of the 7-Year Plan, they predicted a decisive strengthening of material and technical basis for socialism through continued priority development of heavy industry, particularly the machine building industry. However, it's prediction was premature. In contrast to the previous plans, the 7-Year Plan delayed in achieving the goal, and postponed to 1970.

The goal had to change from the enhancement of the people's livelihood to reenforce the national defense due to the "Cuban Crisis" and changing international environment.

A series of policy measures were taken by the regime beginning in 1962 to develop a parallel strategy between defense and non-defense areas necessitated by a threatening from the South, an escalation of the United State involvement in Vietnam, the beginning of the Sino-Soviet conflict. Thus, an increase in defense expenditures was the result.

The national defense budget increased from an average of 4.3% during 1956-66 to an average of 31.2% during 1967-70. this made North Korea one of the world's most highly defense-burdened economies, and economic slowdown was inevitable. In view of the heavy defense burden, low priority to the consumer goods industries is the unavoidable reality in life. President Kim Il Sung summed up the results of the defense construction program:

> "One of the most important accomplishment in our program to strengthen defense capability during the 1961-70 period has been the arming of the entire population, coupled with the transforming of the nation into a fortress. In our country, everyone knows how to use and are carrying rifles. We have built impregnable defense facilities all over the country and have even turned important production facilities into fortress."[6]

The 7-Year Plan completed in 1970 took ten years rather than seven years, increased industrial products which amounted to 74% of GNP compare with 34% in 1956. At the end of 7-Year Plan, North Korea was able to build modern factories of all kinds without outside help. This was possible because of their modern machine building industry grew rapidly. This sector has been growing at a phenomenally high rate of nearly 47% per year during the 3-Year Plan and 5-Year Plan periods.

The policy of allocating priority to heavy industry has resulted in the lagging growth of light industry. Thus, production of consumer goods industry was inevitably sacrificed.

To fulfill the goal of socialism, North Korea needs not only to meet the material the technical requirements, but also cultural and conceptual demands. Not only implement the policy to fair and equality of classless society, but need to eliminate old feudalistic life style which is still visible. For example, discrimination against women inspite of clear statement otherwise in the statute.

At the end of the 7-Year Plan, the first 6-Year Plan was launched immediately. The target of this plan was to accomplish technical advancement in order to liberate the headship of the farmers and the factory workers. Industrial production increased more than double during the period while more than one thousand new modern factories have been built.

The second 7-Year Plan began in 1978 following the first 6-Year Plan. The target for the plan was further enhancement of the people's livelihood through modernization of the national economy. They aim to produce ten million tons of grains while doubling the industrial productions as well as the consumer goods.

The third 7-Year Plan began in 1987. The aim of the plan was to continue the achievement of the second 7-Year Plan aiming to strengthen the technical and material bases to build a socialistic economic system. Special emphasis on development of the basic industries and transportation were noticeable at this time. the success of their ambitious plan is still not known although their previous achievement assure them. Nevertheless, they still have much room for improvement before their management and advance technology can catch up with the advanced industrial societies.

Notes

1. *Minju Chosun* (Democratic Korea), February 3, 1949, Pyongyang.
2. *Ibid.*
3. *Rodong Shinmun* (The Worker's Daily Press), April 20, 1949, Pyongyang.
4. Kim Il Sung, Collection of Kim Il Sung's Works, Vol. I, pp. 223, Pyongyang.
5. Kim Il Sung, "Report to the 3rd General Convention of the Korean Worker's

Party,'' Pyongyang.
6. *Rodong Shinmun*, (the Worker's Daily Press), November 3, 1970, Pyongyang.

19

North Korea : Unification Policy

North Korea's unification policy is based on the concept of the Democratic Confederal Republic of Koryo. The concept was first proposed by President Kim Il Sung on October 10, 1980 in Pyongyang on the occasion of the 6th Congress of the Korean Worker's Party.

Kim Il Sung stated, "our party holds that the country should be reunified by founding a confederal republic through the establishment of a unified national government on condition that the north and the south recognize and tolerate each other's ideas and social systems, a government in which the two sides are represented on an equal footing and under which they exercise regional autonomy respectively with equal rights and duties."

The proposed unified state, the Democratic Confederal Republic of Korea, embracing the entire territory and the people of Korea, has in mind a policy which would concur with the fundamental demands and interest of all the Korean people. The proposal guidelines enumerate a ten-point policy. First, the proposed state should adhere to independence in all state activities and follow an independent policy, Second, Realization of democracy and unity of the people; Third, Economic cooperation between the north and the south; fourth, cooperative development in the fields of science, technology, national culture, art and national education through mutual exchanges; Fifth, Reopen the transportation and communication systems in all pans of the country, Sixth, Systematic improvement of the standard of living and welfare for the entire population; Seventh, a combined national armed forces to defend the country, eighth, Defend and protect the national rights and interests of all overseas Koreans; Ninth, Adherence to foreign relations established prior to unification, and coordination of foreign activities of both regions; promotion of friendly relations with all nations of the world and pursue a peaceful foreign policy. The proposal has already been called as an "immortal" proposal for Korean unification by North Korea. In any event, the proposal has attracted many who are concerned with the unification of Korea

Basic assumption of nationhood, describing an independent, democratic, non aligned as well as a neutral nation, has not changed, but there are a few new concepts in the proposal. for better understanding of the contents, we may categorize them in five groups.

A. First of all, political aspects of the proposal.

The Confederal government must guarantee equally without bias, the interests of the two regions; two systems--Communist system of the North and capitalist system of the South; different political parties, groups, circles; and social classes in the country. It means that North Korea is not advocating class struggle and a proletarian dictatorship in the South as they have in the past.

Furthermore, it has been suggested that the past records of any organization or individuals should not be questioned. In the past, pro-Japanese collaborators were excluded from political participation, but with this proposal, they, too, can participate in political movement compared with the case of Germany, where ex-Nazis have been prohibited from political activities, this seems a more flexible stance. In order to guarantee these political activities, it is proposed that a Supreme National Confederal Assembly be formed with an equal number of representatives from the North and the South and an appropriate number of representatives of Overseas Nationals. A Confederal Standing Committee should be organized by the Supreme National Confederal Assembly. The Supreme National Confederal Assembly and the Confederal Standing Committee, its permanent organ, should be the unified government of the confederal state.

What are the functions of the government of the confederal state besides guaranteeing citizens' political activities? To guide the regional governments in the North and the South, and to discuss, decide on political affairs, national defense problems, foreign affairs and other questions of common concern related to the interests of the country as a whole.

B. Social and cultural aspects of the proposal.

1. The unified government of the confederal state is to guarantee and respect the social systems of the two regions. The proposal states that the freedom of religious belief, speech, the press, assembly and demonstration are guaranteed. Every citizen in the North and the South is free so that one side

cannot exert force to the other side. Kim Il Sung has stated that North Korea doesn't intend to communize the South by force.

2. It suggests a cooperation in culture, education, arts, sciences, and sports. Kim states, Our people have time-honored, resplendent tradition of national culture.- Their stress on national culture, particularly the use of the Korean language, instead of using of Chinese characters, in their press and literature is a well-known practice. More mention has been made about nationalism than communism in the past ten years in their press and literature. The confederal state assures that scientists and technicians in North and South undertake joint scientific research and exchange achievements and experience so as to develop the science and technology of Korea. Furthermore, the confederal state is to promote and cooperate in order to have exchanges between artists and sportsmen of the two regions, and see to it that they jointly discover and nurture the cultural heritage of Korea. It further suggests that the state should pay close attention to the education of the working people and the improvement of their health and adapt adequate measures to this end, so that all working people and their families can receive adequate education and medical treatment.

3. It suggests the reopening of the suspended traffic and communication; the opening of telegraph, telephone, and postal services. In addition, the confederal state would restore the railway and motorroads linking the North and the South and also open ship and air lines to ensure free travel by land, sea and air between the two regions. Further, gradually go over to their joint operation, so that in the future the transport and communications of the entire country be unified.

C. Economic Aspects of the Proposal.

1. It suggests the development of a national economy as opposed to dependency on foreign powers. It also suggests that the confederal state should bring about economic cooperation and exchange between North and South. The proposal emphasizes economic cooperation and exchange between North and South should be realized on the basis of recognizing the different economic systems and diverse economic activities of enterprises in the two regions. Furthermore, it made clear that the confederal state must recognize and protect private property as well as state and cooperative property of the two regions, and refrain from restricting upon the property of capitalism and their business activities so long as they help develop the national economy.

In addition, the proposal states that the confederal state ought to promote the two regions by jointly developing and using mineral, marine and other natural resources, and further the division of labor and trade extensively based on the principles of cooperation and mutual accommodation, while properly coordinating the economic activities of all production units and enterprises in keeping with the interests of different classes and groups. It should, therefore, develop the economies of two regions into an organically interlinked independent national economy through extensive cooperation and exchange between the two regions.

2. Not only the confederal state recognize and protect the business activities of the private entrepreneur of the South, but it will protect the capital investment of the foreign countries in the South. The proposal also states that the confederal state should permit the North and the South to cooperate economical with other countries irrespective of the social system.

3. The confederal state must ensure a stable livelihood for the entire population including the workers, peasants and other working masses. It must promote their welfare systematically. The confederal state must ensure a decent life for all people by guaranteeing adequate conditions of life for them in regard to food, clothing and shelter and by raising the living standard of the poor to those of the middle class: Furthermore, it should provide work for all able-bodied persons, ensure sufficient conditions for work and rest and introduce a wage system, a price policy and an equitable tax system so as to guarantee a stable livelihood for the working people. In order to achieve such a goal, it states that economic cooperation is essential.

D. Military Aspects of the proposal.

1. The proposal suggests that the confederal state abolish the existing Military Demarcation Line in order to remove present military confrontation, and dismantle all military installations in its vicinity.

2. It also suggests that it should cut the military strength of both sides to 100,000,150,000 respectively in order to end the military confrontation and move toward the organization of a single combined national army. The combined national army should undertake the duty of national defense under a unified leadership of the confederal government. All expenditures connected with the maintenance of the combined national army and the defense of the country should be borne jointly by both sides.

3. It also suggests that Korea should be a permanent nuclear-free zone, and prohibit the presence of foreign troops and foreign military base, and ban the production, introduction, and use of nuclear weapons.

On Foreign Affairs

1. It suggests the repealing of all treaties and agreements with other

countries detrimental to national amity including military treaties. However, economic relations not inimical to the common interests of the nation should be continued.

2. It also suggests that the confederal state will have to coordinate the foreign relations of two regions through a single national representative included in the United Nations. It emphasizes the development and pursuance of an independent foreign policy. Historically and in the light of prevailing geo-political reality, Korea has to maintain friendly and cooperative relations with her neighbors. The confederal state should protect the national rights and interests of all Overseas Koreans.

3. The confederal state, above all, should be a neutral country which does not participate in any politico-military alliance or bloc. Since the two sides of the country with different ideology and social systems are to be united into a single confederal state, it is necessary and reasonable in reality for the state to be a neutral state and adhere to the line of neutrality, follow the line of non-alignment, and of a peaceful coexistence. In particular, it should actively develop good neighborly relations with adjacent countries. A unified Korea will not threaten aggression against neighboring countries or any other nations of the world and will not be party to or cooperate in any international act of aggression. President Kim Il Sung's proposal to create the Democratic Confederal Republic of Koryo has been enthusiastically supported by the political parties, social and cultural groups of North Korea ever since its proposal. It has been endorsed by more than 70 countries including the Soviet Union and China as a peaceful solution to the reunification of Korea.[2] Unfortunately, however, the proposal has not been discussed freely among the Koreans in the South, or among the Overseas Koreans. A small scale dialogue, however, has been initiated between the Overseas Korean Christians and the Koreans from the North during the past two years.

Conclusion

What are some of the characteristics and new concepts that appear in Kim's 10-point proposal?

1. First of all, the Democratic Confederal Republic of Korea is proposed as a permanent system, not a provisional scheme as proposed during the '60s, and even the '70s.[3]

2. The DCRK will maintain not only its neutrality, but also remain as a nuclear-free zone, and declares it will not participate in any acts of international aggression. This attitude is that Korea should strengthen solidarity of the Third World countries which is more vital for her than strong unity of

communist countries. The change of emphasis is evident.

3. A reasonable sense of security of both sides is ensured by reduction of armed forces, and eventual combination of them for the purpose of the national security. At the same time, the regional autonomy assures any possible domination of opposite side.

4. Both sides would benefit from reunification since two different politico economic systems: communism of the North and capitalism of the South are assured by the proposal.

5. The proposal emphasizes the nation first, neither political ideology nor economic system should hinder the unity of the nation. It is an unprecedented concept to bring about the divided nation or groups with these concepts. It is a significant challenge to the Korean people.

Where do we find basic ideas and concepts of Kim's recent proposal? We might be able to trace them back to earlier declaration which is known as the July-Fourth North-South Joint Declaration of 1972. Both sides considered, then, that it was the shortest and surest way to national reunification.

President Kim Il Sung stated that: "Our party considers that the most realistic and reasonable way to reunify the country independently, peacefully and on the principle of great national unity is to bring the North and the South together into a confederal state, leaving the ideas and social system existing in the North and the South as they are. This concept is clearly the reflection of the three basic principles laid down in the July-Fourth North-South Joint Declaration of 1972.

In order to unify Korea, according to the July-Fourth South-North Joint Declaration of 1972, it must be free from foreign domination and interference, winning the complete sovereignty of the Korean nation, removing distrust and antagonism between North and South, and achieving national unity. In other words, Korea should be unified independently by the efforts of their own, free from any foreign interference, peacefully through North-South dialogue, and on the principle of unity of all Korean nationals from North and South and Overseas as one nation, irrespective of the difference in their ideas, beliefs, and socio-economic system. The Democratic Confederal Republic of Koryo, it seems, based on these principles laid down in the 1972 statement although some of the new concepts have been added as discussed earlier.

Notes

1. Kim Il Sung, "Total Business Report to the Central Committee of the Korean

Workers' Party at the 6th Congress of the Korean Workers' Party.", Pyong yang: Samhaksa, 1980.

2. Research Institute of International Problems, "Some thoughts on Korean Problems.", in Research Journal of International Problems, Bejing: Research Institute of International Problems, April, 1982.

3. The initial proposal of the confederal system by Kim Il Sung on August 14, 1960, repeated by him on October 23, 1962, mentioned again by Kim on September 17, 1972, after the declaration of the July-Fourth South-North Joint Statement, contains the temporary nature of the confederal system. President Kim proposed, however, the Democratic Confederal Republic of Koryo as a permanent system on Oct. 10, 1980.

20

Unification of Korea

    The two sections of Korea announced an agreement to end hostilities between Seoul and Pyongyang on July 4, 1972, as a step toward reunification of the nation, divided since the end of World War II in 1945. The historic joint communique was signed by both the Republic of Korea and the Democratic People's Republic of Korea.

    The new accord provided for a telephone hot-line between Seoul and Pyongyang to prevent accidental war and a joint political committee to open exchanges in many fields and to promote unification of South and North Korea through peaceful means without outside interference. In an effort to case tensions and foster mutual trust, the agreement added that the two governments agreed not to slander or defame each other or to undertake armed provocations against each other.

    Agreement was reached at meetings in Pyongyang on May 2 through May 5, and in Seoul on May 29 to June 1. Presidents Kim Il-sung of North Korea and Park Chung Hee of South Korea participated in the talks in their respective capitals while Lee Hu-Rak, then director of the South Korean Central Intelligence Agency, went to Pyongyang, and Park Sungchul, second deputy premier, attended the talks in Seoul. The chief negotiator, Kim Young-joo, director of the North Korean Workers' Party's Organization and Guidance Department, and a younger brother of President Kim Il-sung, remained in Pyongyang.

    The communique pointed out three principles for national unification on which the two sides agreed:

    First, unification is to be achieved through independent Korean efforts without subjection to external imposition or interference.

Second, unification is to be achieved through peaceful means, and not through the use of force.

Third, as a homogeneous people, a great national unity shall be sought transcending differences in ideas, ideologies, and systems.

Prior to this historic announcement, the two Korean governments began efforts toward reconciliation in August, 1971, when Red Cross Societies of the South and North agreed to reunite 10 million families separated by the arbitrary formation of the two governments. The meeting on September 20, 1971, at Panmunjum Truce Village was the first direct contact between North and South Korean government officials since 1945.

The announcement of the July 4 statement and the formation of the North-South Co-ordination Commission opened bright prospects for fifty million Korean people. Peace-loving people all over the world welcomed the news. Both the United States and Japan, both of which have economic and political interests in South Korea, expressed warm support. A statement issued in Washington called the agreement: "A salutary impact on the prospect for peace and stability on the Korean peninsula."[1] At the same time, Washington affirmed continuing military support for South Korea and said there would be no reduction in the current forty thousand-man U.S. force in South Korea.

The news of accord has nevertheless disturbed Washington policy makers. One State Department expert confessed that, "Considering the degree of distrust and enmity that existed only a couple of years ago between the two Koreas, this announcement's working is unprecedented."[2] The Japanese Foreign Ministry spokesman praised "The courage and leadership of the two Korean governments" and hoped that they would settle their differences.

Background

How did this historic communique come about? The problems of Korea's unification have been politically acute ever since the country's division. The leaders of both the South and the North have repeatedly promised unification. In discussing the problems, one must remember that South and North Koreans are of the same socio-economic-political heritage. They share many aspirations and goals because of this common heritage.

The reunification of Korea might not have been a problem if the United States, the Soviet Union, and the leaders of Korea had reached some sort of an agreement after World War II. The Soviet Union quickly recognized the People's Republic, but the United States refused to deal with it. Instead, the United States attempted to continue the Japanese colonial administration in office. The response to this was so intense that the United States rescinded the order, but not before the People's Republic was disbanded.

In a speech on October 23, 1962, Kim Il-sung stated: "The occupation of South Korea by the United States imperialists and their aggressive policy are the root cause of all the misfortunes and sufferings of the South Korean people, and the main obstacle to the progress of South Korean society and peaceful unification of the country."[3]

Whether one agrees with Kim Il-sung's statement or not, there is not sufficient evidence to indicate that the United States' policy toward the unification of Korea w as a positive one. The advocacy of the unification of Korea had been sustained by Kim Il-sung through the post-war years.

The principal policy of South Korea was anti-communism, dating from the time the Republic of Korea was established in 1948 under the auspices of the United Nations, and primarily by the United States. With American encouragement and protection, the South's regime, whether Syngman Rhee or Park Chung Hee was its leader, continued faithfully the anti-communism policy which was an integral part of the universal cold war policy--containment of communism by the United States. The tempo of the cold war has been maintained in South Korea better than anywhere else in the world.

In a major policy statement, President Park Chung Hee of the Republic of Korea said that his administration would continue to foil North Korea's attempt to wage aggression by strengthening the nation's ties with Free World allies. He affirmed that the North Korean communists were engaged in a desperate attempt to translate into action their fundamental goal of unification by military means. The Koreans in the South planned to carry out the second five-year economic plan on schedule and to attain a 10 percent or more economic growth during 1970. By doing so, President Park felt that the Republic of Korea would be able to bolster an independent defense system and succeed in solidifying a national framework designed to attain "self-sufficiency and prosperity." He believed that he could unify the divided nation after demonstrating to North Korea the overpowering national strength of South Korea.

President Park said that the government would push ahead with a flexible diplomatic attitude in the United Nations, hoping to create an atmosphere conducive to achieving national territorial unification. In his presidential inaugural address, President Park expressed his wish to see poverty eliminated and the unification of the fatherland achieved.

Taking the oath of office as the sixth president on July 1, 1967, President Park said, "our enemies are poverty, corruption, and Communism. I think they are our three great common enemies." As much as he despises communism, President Park does not propose to solve the problem by means of war.

On South Korea's twentieth birthday, President Park issued a special statement in which he stated that the ultimate national goal would be the reunification of the nation.

> Indeed, it is our prime task to achieve a prosperous, democratic and united nation. We do not want the territorial unification by means of war. But the more we wish the unification through a peaceful and democratic formula, the more we have to strengthen our defense posture and complete our self-reliant defense system.[4]

Park believed the building of a prosperous and free society to be as important as having well-trained troops. This prompted the president to suggest a new concept of the "second economy."

His concept of the "second economy" dealt with the spiritual and philosophical aspects of national modernization. It was to be the basic motivation for the development of material, physical, and technological aspects of the economy if the nation was to attain genuine modernization.

Why suddenly at this time does President Park talk about Korea's unification? It has been clearly demonstrated that the people in the South were getting impatient with Park's promised "modernization." Modernization obviously was not emerging even after the second five-year economic plan with its ever-increasing foreign debts. President Park needed to change the political focus from his failure at modernization to the unification issue, which he knows is in every Korean's heart.

The pressure to pursue national unification was not limited to domestic problems in the South. The international situation changed in favor of reunification talks. The big powers system of alliances has changed a great deal since the end of the Vietnam War. President Nixon's visit to Peking and Moscow reduced the intensity of the cold war. The changed situation enhanced the opportunity for small nations to function independently and promote their own interests. Both South and North Korea probably felt that this was the time for them to become less involved in the politics of the big powers if they wanted to change conditions in Korea.

It now also became clear that the big powers would not support an all-out war effort for unification, nor defend one side against the other, as had happened in 1950. The time was ripe for all parties concerned with a peaceful strategy for unification. In other words, the national unification problem in the seventies was entirely different from the setting in the fifties.

In quest of unification, the South Korean government created, at cabinet level, the office of territorial unification. It has three main departments: Planning, Research, Public Information and Education. "From now on, we must engage in a systematic research on our territorial unification," commented Shinn Tai-hwan, the newly appointed minister. His ministry was to pursue flexible measures for territorial reunification adaptable to the realities in Korea.

The South Korean government has kept to the principle that Korea should be reunified only through free elections by the people of South and North Korea under the supervision of the United Nations. Shinn said, "Therefore, the existing unification principle should be evolved in the direction advantageous to us according to the changing international situation." The minister added that he would guarantee freedom of research and discussion on the problems of unification, and recommended to President Park Chung Hee a thirty-six-member advisory committee for unification research including Paik Nak-jun, Yun Tchi-young, Park Sunchon, Rhee Hyo-sang, Chyung Il-hyung, and Cardinal Kim Su-hwan.[5]

How much serious thought the South Korean regime gave to true territorial unification w as still not clear, in spite of the establishment of the cabinet post for that purpose. For instance, Minister Shinn stated that:

In the foreign policy sector, Korea will adhere to the basic unification policy, under which the government will make efforts to reunify the divided land through the United Nations, during the first half of the 1970s. The government's U.N. strategy will be seasoned....invite representatives of the Republic of Korea and North Korea....the two-Korea theory might gain force.[6]

The minister revealed official intentions concerning national unification, and no one was surprised at the regime's two-Korea policy at the United Nations later in 1973, which received the support of the United States and Japan. Shinn predicted: "Prospects are that the division of Korea will continue through the second half of the 1970s..."[7]

What did the official position of a "two-Korea policy" indicate? Was this policy a flexible unification policy as the Seoul regime claimed? What else could President Park have done when the U.N. office in Geneva on June 1, 1973, granted observer status to North Korea? Could Park have rejected a de facto recognition of the government of North Korea and isolated himself from the world arena? It could have been "senseless competition in the international arena with North Korea," and furthermore, President Park could not alienate his own people who demanded the unification dialogue. Under the circumstances, he suggested the two Korea policy, which the United Nations rejected overwhelmingly. The Korean people would have done likewise had they been given an opportunity.

Dissolving the United Nations Commission for Unification and Rehabilitation of Korea, which was based in Seoul, the U.N. made its position clear to the world that there must be one Korea without outside interference.

Turning our attention to North Korea, the unification movement has developed somewhat differently from that of the South. First of all, the unification policy of Kim Il-sung is not a recent development. It has been enumerated that President Kim has spoken more than 130 times on the subject of national unification since the liberation in 1945.[8]

It is not the quantity, but quality of Kim's statements that should attract our attention. one of the most publicized statements made by Kim Il-sung in regard to national unification was made during the *Daily Yomiuri*'s interview in Pyongyang. A question was asked: The peaceful reunification of Korea will undoubtedly have much bearing on the security and peace of Asia. What are your determination and concrete plans in this respect?

President Kim replied that the general situation of Korea was developing very favorably for the struggle of the Korean people for an independent, peaceful unification of the country. He said:

You asked me about our concrete program for the reunification of the country. Our program for national reunification is not different from the previous one We have invariably maintained that the questions of our country's reunification, an internal affair of our nation, should be solved not by the interference of outside forces but by the efforts of the Korean people themselves, not by means of war, but in a peaceful way.[9]

The significance of the statement is that it includes all the major components of the July 4th Communique which was to follow. Independent, peaceful reunification of the nation without third-party interference was the keystone of the message. The message had also been advanced at a session of the Supreme People's Assembly of the Democratic People's Republic of Korea which was held in April of 1971.

President Kim Il-sung emphasized the importance of the peaceful unification of the country which would in turn enhance peace in Asia as well as in the world. To create a peaceful atmosphere, Kim suggested that the tension in Korea should be reduced. Kim stated, ''It is necessary, first of all, to replace the Korean armistice agreement with a peace agreement between the North and

South. We hold that a peace agreement should be concluded between the North and South and the armed forces of North and South Korea be cut drastically with the condition that the U.S. imperialist aggressor troops are withdrawn from South Korea.''[10]

The issue of the peace agreement between the North and the South was a major issue at a meeting of the North-South co-ordinating committee late in 1972, but South Koreans rejected that proposal. South Koreans feared it would lead to the abolition of the United Nations command in the South and the withdrawal of American military forces.

In addition, North Korea proposed during talks in late 1972 a mutual reduction of troops to the level of 100,000 men, a halt in the introduction of foreign weaponry and making null and void the armistice agreement that ended the Korea War.

In view of increasing American military aid to South Korea, the delivery of a squadron of F-4 Phantoms to the ROK air force at the end of 1969, and intensive militia training of 2 million men, a peaceful proposal to reduce the military force to remove tension in Korea created much confusion to policy makers in the South.[11]

Behind the proposal by North Korea to reduce military forces to remove tension in Korea, there was another serious military matter North Korea probably had in mind. That was the experience of the USS *Pueblo* incident of 1968. The issue had been settled peacefully after eleven months of negotiations.

The USS *Pueblo* was seized by North Korea near Wonsan Harbor, approximately ninety miles north of the DMZ. The *Pueblo* was an American intelligence ship, 179 feet long, 33 feet wide, with a top speed of 12 knots, a crew of eighty-three, armed with three .50 caliber machine guns. It was gathering military data about North Korea. The incident was not the first of its kind by any means. Two American destroyers, the *Maddox* and the *Turner Joy*, in the Tonkin Gulf in 1964 were reported to have been torpedoed by an enemy, and the escalation of war in Vietnam took place. U.S. Senate Foreign Relations Committee Chairman William Fulbright conducted long public hearings which failed to prove whether the vessels had been torpedoed or not. Nevertheless, the Vietnam War was escalated by order of President Johnson.

Why had North Korea seized the *Pueblo?* North Korea claimed that the ship was in its territorial waters, within twelve miles of land. Secretary of Defense Robert McNamara denied North Korea's claims while Secretary of State Dean Rusk was not sure where the ship was really located when seized.

The more important question was not where the ship was located at the time of seizure, but why did the Johnson administration send the intelligence ship into "controversial" areas in a "provocative manner" as Senator Karl E. Mundt put it. The intelligence ship was sent into "controversial" areas in a "provocative manner" in spite of North Korea's warning to stay out of its territorial waters. An American news magazine report stated, "There is evidence of North Korea's intentions about U. S. reconnaissance ships." The report continued:

On January 9th, the North Korean News Agency warned that the U.S. was "infiltrating boats carrying espionage and subversive elements into the coastal waters of our side." A Japanese freighter captain, who returned to Japan from North korea January 19th, reported an increase in North Korea's patrol-boat activity.[12]

U.S. authorities had ignored these warnings as General MacArthur had ignored China's warning prior to sending troops to join North Korea's against the Southern forces in 1950. The fact is that the U.S. Navy had sent into hostile waters a ship which was loaded with electronic gear, supposedly so secret that it was to be destroyed by means of explosives if there was danger of its falling into enemy hands. An editorial pointed out:

The North Koreans were much more circumspect than the Israelis, who mistook the Liberty, another U S. intelligence ship, for an Egyptian warship and shot her up in the Mediterranean, with heavy loss of life. These incidents are an inevitable accompaniment of our insistence on patrolling the water by land, sea, and air, and making our power felt in every nation, large or small.[13]

It was a time of military frustration caused by the Vietnam War. The superpowers faced a dilemma in Vietnam. The United States had to choose either to get out from Vietnam or escalate its involvement. Another U.S. involvement in Korea at that time was an embarrassment. Senator Mundt seemed to reflect the views of many of his colleagues when he asserted that the Johnson administration took great risks sending a spy ship into "controversial" areas in a "provocative manner." Many Americans felt that the Johnson administration provoked North Korea because of American frustrations in Vietnam. Therefore, the *Pueblo* incident was an outcome of the Vietnam crisis. One magazine editorial commented:

The North Koreans were known to have patrol boats with speeds up to 40 knot. (The Pueblo's speed was 12 knots) The *Pueblo* was armed only with a pair of machine guns. She was a sitting duck for anyone who cared to take her. Although we had any number of fighter aircraft in the vicinity, nothing came to her aid. Even if one takes the position that the mission of the *Pueblo* was a necessary one, it looks like a thoroughly botched job, not on the part of the commander and his men, but as directed by the admirals in charge of all this activity.[14]

Another factor which added questions to the seizure of the *Pueblo* incident was the matter of its settlement. Why did the settlement take eleven months? What was the demand of North Korea for release of the crew? An apology from the U.S. authority was demanded. An apology would indicate that the U.S. was wrong in getting caught in an intelligence ship mission and had to acknowledge this error by publicly apologizing to North Korea. One suggestion was that:

> If we can swallow our pride in this situation, such national wisdom might serve to sensitize the national conscience to face the even more difficult task of accepting the fact of our national guilt and folly in the Vietnam crisis.[15]

Moderation in U.S. policy was needed, and it did not come easily. There were some who spoke out more aggressively than the Johnson administration did. For instance, California Governor Ronald Reagan urged a 24-hour ultimatum and then "coming in after it." Secretary Rusk advised both Americans and North Koreans to "cool it." The Johnson-Rusk administration succeeded finally through long negotiations which required twenty-eight secret meetings, and brought the eighty-two American crew-members home safely. Commander Lloyd M. Bucher of the ship said at his first press conference, "I surrendered the ship because there was nothing but a slaughter out there, and I couldn't see allowing any more people to be slaughtered or killed."[16]

The Vietnam War was spreading into Laos, Cambodia, and even Thailand. It could have spread to Korea, Taiwan, and perhaps the Middle East. The Johnson-Rusk policy of containment was at its peak. In view of the time and mood of the policy-makers, the settlement of the *Pueblo* incident was moderate, and indeed, fortunate. One critic of the Johnson Rusk policy in Asia, Walter Lippmann, said, "Until the miscalculations of our present policy are understood, the formation of a constructive policy in the emerging and awakened Asian continent will not be possible."[17] Lippmann understood the Asian situation better than the Washington policy-makers. The U.S. government took a narrow view of what it considered essential to safeguard America's reputation in the world. "A military promise is not the only form of truth," said Norman Cousins. "The national honor may depend far less on creating respect for our muscle than on maintaining our moral stature. The moral integrity of our purposes and policies cannot be contrived; it can only be demonstrated. Making good our threats may be less vital than keeping faith with our history."[18]

President Johnson, taking advantage of the *Pueblo* incident, called up the reserves on a semipermanent basis to reinforce the 500,000 U.S. servicemen already in Vietnam. The *Pueblo* incident proved to be not a lesson for President Johnson's administration, but an opportunity to escalate the war atmosphere at home. The American people, however, were not in the mood to open another land war in Asia. About this time, Great Britain had announced that she would abandon her role as a military power in South Asia from Suez to Singapore. That left the U.S. in the area without the support of a single large power. The withdrawal of Britain from Asia confirmed the total isolation of the U. S. in Asia. That is why critics like Lippmann and Cousins maintained that the U.S. involvement in Indochina, and certainly sending the *Pueblo* to spy in Asian waters, were miscalculations. It was a strategic mistake for the U.S. to engage the bulk of its military power at any one point, like Vietnam or Korea. The response well could have been a breakout of trouble at other points. Fortunately, the American people in demanding an end to military actions were wiser than their political leaders.

In light of the *Pueblo* and the U.S. Navy's FC-121 reconnaissance plane incidents, it became evident that North Korea was taking a positive attitude toward seeking a peace agreement with South Korea.

It is of great significance that North Korea on September 17, 1971, proposed a confederation of North and South Korea as a transitional step to eventual reunification. A North Korean memorandum, distributed by Pyongyang's official news agency, read:

> If the South Korean authorities, fearful of the communization of the whole of South Korea, still consider it impossible to accept free general elections throughout the North and South, confederation..... can be established as a transitional step while retaining the existing differing social systems of the North and South as they are.[19]

Political pressures mounted from the North, and President Park Chung Hee had to accept some of the unification approaches. The first positive statement on unification since 1948 by South Korea came on September 17, 1971, when Park suggested cultural and trade exchanges. He coupled the suggestion with a demand that North Korea publicly renounce the policy of "communizing the whole of Korea by force."

It took a long time to arrive at a joint communique, but it arrived nevertheless on July 4, 1972. Both sides agreed that an independent, peaceful unification without outside interference would be the goal for the nation.

President Park declared that "peace, unification and prosperity – these are the imperative tasks imposed upon us in our time and nation." On the occasion of the twenty-seventh anniversary of national liberation on August 15, 1972, he said:

> The recent South-North Joint Communique means acceptance by the North Koreans of my repeated call for renunciation of force, and signals the opening of a new chapter of national history, as well as signifying a step forward in the great national advance toward peaceful unification.[20]

Regardless of who influenced whom, the July 4th joint communique opened dialogue between the two sides, and merits being labeled an historic event. It was a victory for the national conscience of fifty million Koreans who yearn for a peaceful and independent unification.

Approaches to Possible Unification

Two sides agreeing upon the goal of national unification is one thing, but how to approach it is yet another matter.

If we accept the meaning of unification as an achievement of territorial unification between South and North, and political, economic, social, and cultural integration of two parts of the nation, the term creates unavoidably ambiguous, tautological meanings. Political integration, for instance, closely touches the problem of citizens' loyalties.

Professor Ernest B. Haas comments: "Political integration is a process whereby political actors in several distinct national settings are persuaded to shift their loyalties, expectations, and political activities toward a new center."[21]

In other words, a new center is needed to bring about political integration. Obviously, such an integration process is neither possible nor desirable under the present conditions in Korea. Neither side will allow such a process by government authority.

Unless there is an agreement between the two sectors with regard to a certain degree of commonly shared views on unification, the process cannot be initiated. Views must be shared by the leaders of the two sectors as well as the citizenry. A recent public opinion poll in South Korea indicated an overwhelming desire for unification, but a very small percentage were able to identify any level of the process. For instance, only 14 percent supported visiting privileges between relatives in South and North Korea, while 29 percent favored the immediate exchange of newsmen.[22]

The hesitancy of the majority of the citizens in the South to express more positive views on the political integration process is primarily due to the prevailing anti-communism sentiments of the South.

At the first conference of the Fourth Term of the Supreme People's Council of North Korea on December 16, 1967, Kim Il-sung declared: "We must ideologically and psychologically prepare to mobilize our people to unite to participate in the decisive battle for the unification of the nation when the revolutionary conditions are ripe and the struggle is at a high point."[23]

The basic concept of the revolution has not been changed, but the approach to instigation of revolution in the South has. No longer will North Korea export revolution to the South, for the North now insists upon a peaceful unification. Furthermore, possible federalism of two social systems as they exist should not be threatened in the view of North Korean leaders.

Echoing this official attitude, a recent publication of Pyongyang reveals that whether a citizen is a farmer or a laborer or a writer, he is supposed to be working toward a common political goal—unification of the fatherland.

Under the title "My Working Life of Yesterday and Today," Han Myong-gap writes that "Korea must be unified as soon as possible, so the people of the South can enjoy true happiness in the warm breast of the great father-like leader Premier Kim Il-sung."[24]

A similar statement comes from Ko Tsol-su, an engineer, who claims that he left his native home in the South to join his Northern brothers. He wrote, "If the Southern brothers wish to enjoy true happiness like their Northern brothers under the leadership of a great father-like Premier Kim Il-sung, we must destroy the eternal enemies of our nation—the landlords, and the capitalists, and must achieve the unification of the fatherland."[25]

Whether writing about agricultural production or one's working conditions at a chemical industry plant or one's gratitude for a state hospital, all the writers express two thoughts in common—the unification of the fatherland and an undisputed loyalty to Kim Il-sung.

These examples illustrate the difficulty of finding political opinions common to both sides. It unquestionably requires a more refreshing and creative political approach to unlatch the closed doors.

Besides political views common to the two sectors, there are other factors which could enhance unification. One of the factors is economic. The unification process would proceed more effectively if the economic situations were more advanced. The necessity for structural adaptation will come about when the politico-economic sector recognizes that adaptation is for its own benefit.

Unless the political actors recognize and favor modernization and urbanization, there will be no structural adaptation. In other words, the more modern the thinking of the actors, the better will be the chance for unification; at least, from an economic point of view.

Professor Haas points out that most conducive to achieving integration are economic and welfare tasks, since these are the most productive in terms of facilitating the transfer of loyalties. The professor comments: "Not merely in economic tasks–but the degree of functional specificity of the economic task is causally related to the intensity of integration. The more specific the task, the more likely important progress will be toward an economic community."[26]

It has been well publicized that President Park's determination to bring about South Korea's industrialization is the cardinal principle of his modernization programs and has been accepted as national policy for the past decade. It is, however, doubtful that Park's regime has actually achieved what he has been claiming. All evidence contradicts his "success story" in South Korea–for instance, agricultural conditions, the living conditions of the workers whose wages are still one-fifth of those of Japanese workers, and the bankruptcy of middle-class merchants. The beneficiaries of Park's economic policy are limited to a handful of rich businessmen and a small group of bureaucrats.

Healthy economic competition between the two sides could contribute to the unification of Korea, but it seems that economic progress is limited to North Korea at the present time. Agriculture in the North has been mechanized, modernized, and produces enough grain to meet domestic consumption, while South Korea, formerly the breadbasket of the country, has to import all sorts of grain–rice, wheat, corn–to support its population. For instance, in 1962, a year after the military coup, the export of agricultural products amounted to $23 million, but dropped to $10 million in 1964, and declined steadily due to lack of government promotion. South Korea in 1973 had to import 80 percent of its corn supplies from abroad, primarily from the United States.

One of the characteristics of the Korean economy is small-scale farming. The average Korean farmer cultivates about 1.5 jungbo or one-fiftieth of his American counterpart. Farming on such a small scale, the average farmer can hardly support his family. This is a perplexing problem. With this situation, one might expect the government to try to improve the farm situation by helping farmers to meet their debts and to improve their lot in general by providing better techniques in household management, production and soil management, and to supply them with fertilizers and introduce modern farm equipment. Enlightened policy is clearly needed if the present chaotic condition of the agricultural economy in South Korea is to change. Park's regime has not provided such a policy. North Korea is self-reliant, while South Korea is still very much dependent on foreign countries, even after thirty years of political independence.

The basic mode of Korean industrial production is as backward in nature as agriculture. The low degree of self-sufficiency in industrial production is evidence of its backwardness. The only industry which supplies local demands in the Korean market is the food industry. Next in line would be the chemical industry, meeting about 70 to 75 percent of demand. The average industry supplies about 72 percent of its domestic needs.

Because the chemical industry has a high ratio of meeting production demands, one must not be misled about its advanced development, since the industry merely produces consumer goods by processing imported materials. The increase of export goods is related to the increase of processed goods using imported raw materials.

Korean industry leans heavily on consumer goods rather than on basic products. Consumer goods including textiles, chemicals, and food products come to more than 72 percent in the number of plants, 80 percent in the number of laborers, and 82 percent in production. In other words, Korean industry is primarily light industry.

The government of Korea has undertaken construction with foreign capital in key basic industries, such as electric power, cement, fertilizer and sheet glass, which constitute basic projects. Korea, like many other underdeveloped nations, is trying to build the basic industries as a matter of national pride as much as to meet national needs. Heavy industry has become a symbol of twentieth century national independence. Economically, however, there is danger in this route. Why did the British government desire to purchase F-111 bombers from the U.S. instead of building them at British aircraft factories? British industry is certainly just as capable of building bombers as American industry. The reason for the British purchase is that it is able to buy F-III bombers from the U.S. cheaper than it can build them at home. Should the Korean government build its own fishing boats if it can buy them from Japan at half of the price?

Obviously, not all goods should be purchased from Japan while infant industries at home are crumbling. How should the Korean government then decide to protect and nourish infant industries and what industries should be selected for such treatment? Here, government policy plays an important role.

The Korean economy is too much behind advanced economies of the world. It would be foolish for Korea to try to compete on all levels. Instead, Korea must find those industrial situations where it has an advantage over foreign competition. In this field, we realize the specific character of the medium and small-scale industry of Korea. Generally Korean plants have not converted from tools to automated machinery. They are not modernized. The productive techniques of most industries remain at relatively primitive levels. What Korea needs now is to mechanize its medium and small industries with capital investment by government, rather than having government invest in over-sized heavy industry in efforts to compete with advanced nations or trying to maintain false concepts of national economic independence. This only contributes in many new emerging nations to the halting of economic development.

In 1972, Park's government reported that exports totaled $1.4 billion, an increase of 45.2 percent over the year before. The regime aims for increases each year. The economic growth rate, Park's regime claims, averaged 10 percent annually or the third highest in the world.

Even if we accept these statistics as credible, the meaning of such growth is simply the expansion of exports. It does not help to carry out the development of natural resources; nor does it represent increased industrial skills; nor does it mean an increase in fair employment and further benefits to society. It is only a measure of how workers are exploited by low wages to benefit foreign capitalists. As a result, "The gaining of the foreign currency is not even a match to the minimum of its costs, and it means that South Koreans are exporting their blood to the foreign markets."[27]

The economic growth of South Korea over the past decade has been impressive, but it can hardly be equated with real development, because by and large the size of marginal economic groups has increased and the poverty gap has widened. If this trend continues as it has under present policy, South Korea is headed for a catastrophe. Increases in GNP can be statistically impressive but intrinsically deceptive. Exports of goods can increase while more people are left in greater misery. Given an unjust social framework, increases in the GNP will strengthen the rich and strong and emasculate the weak and poor. This is what is happening in South Korea.

The psychological factor is the third element relevant to the peaceful unification of Korea. In some respects, it is more serious than either political or economic factors in the historical and national sense.

When Premier Willi Stoph of East Germany accepted Chancellor Willy Brandt's offer to meet him in East Germany, and the two leaders discussed the future of the two German sectors, the psychological impact on the people of East and West Germany was tremendous, even though there were no immediate political fruits resulting. In contrast, we find an entirely different situation in Korea. The Korean situation is even more rigid than the Vietnamese situation.

The purpose of the German leaders' meeting was not to talk about reunification. Chancellor Brandt did not propose political and territorial reunification at that time. He sought a limited detente with East Germany, based on mutual renouncing of force. He talked about East Germany as he would with any other government, such as Poland or Czechoslovakia. East Germany, too, opened its doors for talks while presenting a very rigid agenda of its own.

Such communication between the two sections, nevertheless, relaxes tensions and may lead to meaningful dialogue. Professor Karl Deutsch points out:

> Membership in a people essentially consists in wide complementarity of social communications. It consists in the ability to communicate more effectively, and over a wider range of subjects, with the members of one large group than with outsiders.[28]

Along with the propensity to communicate or share messages, an integrated community will evince a propensity to share commodities and to interchange people as well.

Self-reliance in national defense, based on Kim Il-sung's 'Juche' concept, has been the key policy of North Korea.

The policy states that even small communist nations must prepare their own defense rather than rely on the big powers. The Soviet Union's coexistence policy with the United States was considered "revisionistic" by Peking and North Korea, which felt it would indirectly hinder the unification policy of North Korea.

Emphasizing the importance of psychological and ideological warfare, North Korea was exploring four main areas. The first was to encourage anti-government movements in the South. Another approach was aimed against the American presence in Korea. North Korea has been exploiting the theme of "American colonization" in South Korea. One tactic was to parallel American troops stationed in Korea with those in Vietnam. The third area of propaganda was designed to expose the ROK-Japan relationship. The normalization of this relationship has lasted for several years. North Korea looks upon Japanese imperialism as a potential enemy. The fourth area was to unify communist nations under world communism. Therefore, Kim Il-sung advocated military aid to North Vietnam from all communist countries.

The differences between the South and the North in the areas of psychological and ideological matters go beyond the current political attitudes of the two regimes.

Historically the people of the North were penetrated by modern concepts earlier than the people of the South. This was due to the economic structure, strong feudalistic landlordism and fertile land in the South vs. a weak feudalistic system and early Christian influence upon the people of the North, as well as social and cultural heritages which favor the Northerners.

In addition the South has been subjected to ideological orientation of nineteenth-century capitalism as well as misrepresented individualism from the United States' early occupation. As a result South Korea has stagnated under one of the most reactionary political systems anywhere. The first time the concept of modernization was seriously introduced was when the military coup d'etat of May 16, 1961, took place. It is a political irony that a man with a Ph. D. in political science at Princeton under Woodrow Wilson became the bulwark of the reactionary force, only to end his political dream in tragedy. In a practical economic sense, "communistic" North and "capitalistic" South are meaningless labels. The term "communism" is political rather than economic in Korea. More specifically, the term is a politico-psychological one. Communism in North Korea means "have faith in Kim Il-sung" and is almost synonymous with "Kim Il-sung's revolutionary thought" as was the case of "Mao's thought" in China.

Kim Il-sung has commented: "After revolutionary achievement, sharing the good things among us exclusively in the North by closing the door to the South Koreans is the road to suicide." The urgency is psychological .

There are obviously many relevant elements which will affect the unification of divided Korea. The three elements–political, economic, and psychological–dealt with here are seemingly the key factors.

In the absence of some reasonable level of communicative interchange between the two sectors, we might conclude that people in the two sectors are not integrated into a common community. Short of such communication, the transference of individual political loyalties to a newly established political entity cannot take place; therefore, we would not expect to find any significant achievement of unification between two political units.

Professor Deutsch said that mass behavioral patterns are independent of integration, or, in terms of the process, occur prior to the actions or initiatives designed to achieve integration.

There must be relatively significant levels of positive reinforcement before individuals can identify successfully with a new political community. A political community requires the loyalty of its citizens and they must understand how to deal with common social problems through peaceful, nonviolent means.

In other words, a positive approach is to establish a community which must exist prior to the organization of a shared political authority. This would provide the basis for integrating the competing political authorities of the South and the North into a new political system in Korea.

If unification is to be achieved at the national level, there has to be a policy broadly enough constituted to include all political actors and groups. Broadly conceived, the policy of a national organization will be decided by member groups, parties, and organizations that cooperate in common programs.

The security of the community will be established by such integration. Security is the first necessity of modern politics. Individual and national welfare must follow through economic ties. Besides economic security, citizens demand reasonable freedom of movement and thought. Individual dignity and humanistic values should be maintained in an amalgamated community. In short, the new structure should be a modern democratic society. It cannot be overemphasized that only modernized systems and societies can really he unified since only modern society can develop adequate responses to current problems.

Difficult Task Ahead

The achievement of national unification, as we have discussed, is not a simple task. It involves a continuous movement between one's assertions and another's questioning; between thrusting forward and retreating; between being pushed and driven by the forces of the other side. Each section strives to maintain its own advantages, to realize its own goals, and to refuse to change.

Who is delaying the unification process? Who does not want to see Korea unified? Recent developments indicate that President Park's regime has deliberately been blocking the implementation of the July Fourth Joint Communique. He proclaimed martial law in South Korea just a couple of months after the joint communique which promised to bring about an independent, peaceful unification. Park also created an international scandal in having the Korean CIA kidnap Kim Dae-jung, the candidate for president in 1971 of the New Democratic Party.

Two forces that President Park was most afraid of were Kim Dae-jung and the American Congress. So stated Kim Hyung Wook, director of the Korean CIA from 1963 to 1969, testifying on June 22, 1977, before the Subcommittee on International organizations, chaired by Donald M. Fraser of Minnesota. The former director of the KCIA and a close associate of President Park said that President Park did not hesitate to carry out the unconscionable, tyrannical kidnapping of Kim Dae-jung from Tokyo, and throwing him into prison in Korea.[29]

What justification did he have for ordering martial law in the South? President Park claimed that there was a steadily improving economy and he had opened a political dialogue with the North. One senior U.S. official in Washington commented: "There was simply no justification for it." President Park's declaration of martial law has become a pattern of his political operation. Martial law made clear that foreign reporters would be just as affected by the rule as Koreans. one American reporter, *Newsweek's* Tokyo bureau chief, Bernard Krismer, commented on his personal experiences with soldiers in Seoul:

> An armed soldier rushed toward me to grab my camera, but I resisted and soon found myself battling three more soldiers who kicked me, yanked at the camera band around my neck and tore at my suit. I was dragged to a corner police box, where I was refused permission to call the U.S. Embassy. After an hour of this, new troops arrived to drag me by the seat of my pants across the street into the occupied New Democratic Party building.[30]

The reporter was trying to photograph the New Democratic Party, an opposition headquarters, as it was occupied by troops. If they handled an American reporter in such a manner, one can imagine how they handled Korean journalists.

It was the third time since President Park seized power in 1961 that he had proclaimed martial law, and he offered another presidential decree as a New Year's Day present to the nation in 1974. This time he made a thorough job of it. Suspending parts of the constitution which he had revised three times, he dissolved the National Assembly (the majority members were hand-picked by Park himself), and he banned all political activities. Press censorship was imposed, and colleges and universities were closed "for an early winter vacation." To make sure the new decrees were carried out, military troops and tanks patrolled the capital and major cities. President Park revised the con-stitution which he had drafted earlier to run for a third term as president, and

changed it again to allow him to run for two more terms of six years each –
which would keep him in power until 1984.

President Park's actions betrayed his own words. Immediately following the July 4th joint communique, he stated at a ceremony marking the twenty-fourth ROK Constitution Day, July 17, 1972:

> As we look back in the footsteps of our constitutional administration, it comes as a conviction to me that from now on application of the democratic system will have to be developed not on the formal level but on the practical level, in a better organized and more competent way.....

I am convinced that today this significant function on Constitution Day will become another precious moment for us to pledge ourselves to make further efforts, so that the long-cherished desire of the nation for peaceful unification of the fatherland can be realized proudly within our democratic constitutional order.[31]

With such self-confidence President Park did not need martial law. What changed his mind in two months? on August 15, 1970, President Park had issued his "historical August 15 Declaration." In the statement Park proposed to conduct a competition in good faith to find out which system – that of the South or of the North – would enable people to enjoy a better life. If Park was so sure of his system, why did he need the frequent use of martial law in the South? What kind of a state of emergency was there in the South?

In regard to the matter of security and unification, Kim Yong-sik, the foreign minister of the South, commented:

> To our regret, a certain U.N. member state, under the pretext of creating favorable conditions for the success of the dialogue between the South and the North and for the peaceful reunification of Korea, insists on a debate of the Korean question at the forthcoming session of the General Assembly, calling for the dissolution of UNCURK and the withdrawal of the United Nations Forces in Korea, despite that the presence of UNCURK and the U.N. Forces in Korea have repeatedly been reaffirmed with the support of an overwhelming majority of the member states. It is apparent that the hidden intention behind this move is.... to weaken the defense posture of the Republic of Korea, endangering our national security.[32]

Despite the rigid position of the South Korean regime, the United Nation's First Committee at the twenty-eight session in November, 1973, in

New York dissolved the "United Nations Commission for the Unification and Rehabilitation of Korea." It was the first victory for North Korea, which challenged the position of the South at the U.N. on its first historic appearance.

At the same time, Li Jonk-mok, the chief delegate of North Korea, proposed the withdrawal of all foreign troops from Korea, the conclusion of a peace agreement between the North and the South to refrain from attack against each other, and the reduction of armed forces of both North and South to 100,000 men or less, in hopes of reducing tensions.[33]

If the South-North dialogue was the most important endeavor by Koreans themselves to put an end to the division of Korea, as South Korean authorities claimed, then, it was not logical to reject the proposal of the North for a peace treaty.

There was a paradox to the unification movement: it proposed change and yet it exhibited a strong resistance to change. It had to be flexible, yet it was rigid. As a psychologist, Maslow, has said, the essential motivating force behind human action is self-realization. This, in essence, is using one's potential for action of all kinds: freely, creatively, and with great personal satisfaction. The individual is in a position to function at the self-realization level if his love and affectional needs are met. On the other hand, he is unable to function, even at the love and affection level, if his self-esteem needs are not met. As long as his needs remain unsatisfied at a given level, his motives and activities will remain at that level. If we accept the concept that self-realization precludes the satisfaction of more fundamental physical and psychological needs as Professor Maslow states, we realize the importance of the achievement and maintenance of self-realization.

In the achievement of nationhood or unification, there are at least two fundamental tasks which must be accomplished. First of all, there must be a socio-psychological adjustment among the people. This demands an early awareness of the needs of the other section of the divided land. Realizing this awareness requires a wide variety of communication skills. Only by interaction with the other section is one able to recognize the feelings, attitudes, and needs of others as well as the messages expressed by them.

Another necessary task to achieve unification or restoration of nationhood may be described as a promotion of tangible teamwork, or cooperative behavior which could result in satisfaction in attaining a common goal. An example could be an interzone mail service, or the exchange of basic commodities. The parties should not aim too high nor go too fast, as they did during the Soviet-American Conferences in 1946.

In the absence of communication, there is no opportunity to develop cooperation. Successful unification can occur when cooperation is optimized and when positive mutual responsives are maximized in a concerted effort towards the ultimate goal. Until such conditions appear, there can be no positive movement for unification. It is hoped that such conditions can be created internally and externally by nations which are concerned about peace and order in Eastern Asia.

Local loyalties take priority before the concept of a stable nation-state. Such attitudes undermine political cohesion. Sharp ideological differences within a society hamper national security, create disorder and civil war. On the whole, the ideological-psychological beliefs of the two sectors in Korea are of vital significance in determining whether the nation will unify to protect its national interests in the international situation, pursue an expansionist course, or engage in a modernization program. Fundamental ideological differences are the principal obstacles between the North and the South. Cooperation between the two sectors can be furthered considerably by muting ideological differences. Neither North nor South has much to gain by stubborn doctrinaire approaches to a solution. They have much to gain nationally as well as regionally if they follow present trends of international conciliation and flexibility as are the major powers. A small nation like Korea has nothing to lose and everything to gain by a moderate and flexible national policy instead of being the slave to an anachronistic national policy of isolationism from world progress .

Difficulties in pursuing a dialogue between the North and the South exist in spite of the July Fourth Joint Communique. Bright prospects for the nation are not at all certain today. It is darker now than six years ago when the joint statement was issued. Under the present circumstances, it is significant to note the five-point program for unification proposed by President Kim Il-sung on June 23, 1973. The statement made the following points:

1. Remove the state of military confrontation and ease tension between the North and the South;
2. Implement many-sided cooperation between the North and South;
3. Convene a national assembly of representatives of all people of all strata, political parties and social organizations in the North, the South and overseas;
4. Institute a North-South Confederation under the name of the Confederal Republic of Koryo;
5. Enter the United Nations under the name of Confederal Republic of Koryo.

This proposal appealed to many Koreans in and out of Korea. The proposal was mild and practical. It omitted ideology entirely and stressed minimum demands on both sides. When compared with the proposal made by Ulbricht of East Germany, Kim's proposal was minimal.

In August of 1956, Ulbricht laid down the   prerequisites for the reunification of Germany:

> The national interest of our people and fatherland, the cause of peace and reunification demand: 1. The limitation of armed forces in the two parts of Germany..... 2. Removal of all Hitler generals and other revanchists from the state machinery and the armies.... 3. The step-by-step withdrawal of foreign troops from Germany.... 4. The lifting of the ban on the Communist Party of Germany. A ban on all militarist organization and associations.[34]

If Kim Il-sung made such demands, Park Chung Hee, an ex-officer of the Imperial Japanese Army, would not be eligible to negotiate the matter of unification. Kim Il-sung, in fact, had broadened the ground to include all patriots to participate in the unification movement when he called for a national conference from all walks of life in South and North Korea for the purpose of a well-diversified discussion on the subject of reunification.

The unification process is not just a pleasant series of steps forward. Panmunjom is an indication of that. Every step ahead is taken with certain dangers, risks, and threats. But unification is a genuine wish of the people. The leaders must accept the challenge. With each achievement of every significant task, there are new threats and dangers, as well as new advantages and hopes, with which the nation must cope.

There has to be a balance between the positive forces striving for unification, achievement and positive action on the one hand, and the negative forces demanding security, satisfaction with the status quo, and all other forces that represent threats to one's feeling about oneself if one risks movement ahead.

The whole pattern of the achievement of nationhood is marked by rapid spurts ahead and slower periods of doubt and questioning and consolidation of the resources in preparation for the next movement ahead.

At our present state of knowledge, in which we do not yet have adequate practical theories on unification and on other international issues, we need to learn more. However, we do have general principles of international politics, widely accepted by scholars in the field, which tell us that what we consider international political issues such as unification, political crises, and wars, are simply manifestations of international political interaction which can be understood in terms of causal principles about the behavior of men and of groups, including national groups.

Thus, if we have verified principles stating that any group or tribe or its leadership, when challenged by an action threatening its security, will respond in an aggressive fashion, we can apply this general principle of international politics to the Korean circumstances.

Peaceful unification and restoration of nationhood in Korea is possible when the people and their leaders understand these principles of international politics, and move constructively toward unification on political, economic and psychological levels. At least, there should be a minimum agreement on peaceful unification on a political level, some sort of economic agreement on mutual gains, and increased communications and transactions including limited mail services between two sectors.

Only such positive actions by the leaders of both sections, in view of the presence of a sense of nationhood among the people, will advance the unification movement.

We must admit that even most peaceful people like the Koreans cannot be exempt from the general pattern of human behaviors of competitiveness and aggression. In these days of confrontation and protest, pretending to be free of aggressive feelings is a false and risky attitude.

If Koreans are to be totally free to do as they wish and still be able to live together without destroying one another, they must purge themselves of aggressiveness or find a constructive way to handle aggression.

Koreans are in obvious need of a value system based upon a realistic and pragmatic assessment of man's biological and psychological needs. A humanistic value system could provide maximum freedom and autonomy. It could also provide sufficient controls to keep the people from destroying one another.

The task of defining such a value system presents a critical challenge to all who hope to live in a decent and reasonable society. This task should be first on the agenda for a peaceful unification of divided Korea.

The case for reunification was expressed in an open letter "to parliaments and governments of all countries of the world" by the Supreme People's Assembly, Democratic People's Republic of Korea on April 6, 1973 :

The struggle of the Korean people for peaceful reunification took an epochal turn particularly after Comrade Kim Il-sung, President of the Democratic People's Republic of Korea, declared in his historic speech on August 6, 1971, that we had a readiness to discuss at any time the question of national reunification with the present ruling party and all the other political parties, all social organizations and individual personages in South Korea.[35]

The idea of the independent and peaceful unification of Korea won almost unanimous support not only of the Korean people but also of world politicians who assembled at the United Nations in 1973.

A letter dated September 10, 1973, came from the representatives of Algeria and thirty-one other nations in regard to a draft to create favorable conditions to accelerate the independent and peaceful reunification of Korea. It stated:

Recognizing that the termination of the interference of foreign countries in the internal affairs of Korea is the key for easing tensions in Korea, turning the armistice into a durable peace, promoting the dialogue between the North and the South smoothly and thereby achieving the independent, peaceful reunification of the country.

Recognizing that it is in accord with the principles of the Charter of the United Nations....with the principles of the North-South Joint Statement and the principle of national self-determination.....[36]

With this preamble, the draft proposed the following action to be taken at the U.N. General Assembly:

1. to dissolve the ''United Nations Commission for Unification and Rehabilitation of Korea'';

2. to abolish the use of the United Nations flag by the foreign troops stationed in South Korea and dissolve the ''United Nations Command'';

3. to withdraw all foreign troops stationed in South Korea so further steps may be taken in accelerating the independent and peaceful reunification of Korea.

Why was such a draft deemed necessary after thirty-three years of liberation from Japan? Why did South Korea depend so heavily on foreign powers in every aspect of its existence while there had been no foreign soldiers since Chinese troops pulled out twenty-some years ago from the North at the end of the Korean War? Why did United Nations troops remain in South Korea after the armistice in 1953? Many people were puzzled by these questions. Representative Saito of Japan stated his defense of the U.N. troops in South Korea in the following manner:

Should the United Nations Command be dissolved without full consideration of the facts and without regard to the necessity of ensuring the maintenance of peace and security in the area in view of the fact that the present armistice structure has been playing an indispensable role in the maintenance of international peace and security......Should the United Nation's Command be dissolved unilaterally, the stability of the Korean peninsula would be threatened, and this would create conditions which would make it difficult to continue to dialogue.[37]

Japan has been a strong defender of U.N. troops in South Korea ever since its capital investment increased there. It was Japan which supported the two-Korea policy the strongest at the U.N. debate during the 1973 session. For Japan, the security of South Korea is inseparable with the security of Japanese economic interests in Korea. Is the security of South Korea really in the hands of the U.N. Command? A different view was stated during the U.N. debate by Representative Abdulla of the Sudan. He said:

It is common knowledge to us that the name and the flag of this organization have been used to cover up a blatant foreign intervention The police action, the limited war, the useless war or the travesty of a certain president, or whatever might be the phraseology assigned to it by the phrase-makers, was an American affair, fought by the United States and its allies.

The United Nations intervention is a United States intervention General MacArthur said: "My relationship with the United Nations was only nominal. Everything I did was controlled entirely by the Joint Chiefs of Staff.....even my routine reports had to be censored by the U.S. State and Defense Departments I do not recall getting orders in whatever form from the United Nations during the entire war..... No, I would not count on the United Nations for anything."[38]

Does anyone doubt that the Korean War was the "Truman-MacArthur War"? If the purpose of the U.N. Command in South Korea was to bring about the unification of Korea, has it achieved its goal? Or has the U.N. Command's presence contributed to the reduction of tension in the country and created two sides to get closer to peace? Does anyone need to be reminded that South Korea has been under the military dictatorship of Park Chung Hee since 1961? Who can deny the fact the sole purpose of U.N. troops in South Korea is to protect the military dictatorship of Park Chung Hee, just as they had done previously for Syngman Rhee's regime, which the people of the South overthrew in 1960?

As Baroady of Saudi Arabia pointed out at the U.N. General Assembly:

The Korean people are one nation and should never have been divided by the two major powers, which were instrumental in the separation of the Korean people on ideological and strategic grounds. That sentence bears repetition a hundred times.[39]

It is of significance to note that Baroady is a monarchist who spoke in support of the North Koreans, who are communists. He also said:

Where is our conscience? Are we clients of any of the two powers or are we independent sovereign States which should scrutinize every question on its merits and thereby address ourselves to solutions that are based on justice and not on political arrangements.

It has been general practice for the United States to request its allies not only to take sides politically but to join in the crusade of chastising the communists of the North. It was the United States, with the collaboration of the Soviet Union, that divided Korea, maintained two Koreas, and insists on a two-Korea policy today. Should Koreans rely on the United States and Japan to bring about the unification of Korea? Any sensible plan for unification must come from the Koreans themselves. It would only be wishful thinking to rely on the major powers for unification.

A statement originating in Pyongyang on April 6, 1973 said:
We consider that dialogue and negotiations should be conducted extensively on a democratic basis with the participation of political parties, public organizations and personages of all circles of the north and the south by concerted efforts to achieve the independent, peaceful reunification of the fatherland....
The statement continued:
If the U.S. troops are withdrawn from South Korea and the intervention of outside forces in the internal affairs of our country is brought to an end by the joint struggle of the Korean people and the world people, the danger of war will be dispelled in Korea and the dialogue accelerated, the north-south relations radically improved and the question of the country's reunification smoothly solved in a peaceful way on the principle of national self-determination.[40]

There should be no illusion about the rate of progress toward unification. The delegates of the United States, Japan, West Germany and their allies made very clear their views about the future of Korea in separate speeches at the U.N. General Assembly in 1973. The two-Korea policy is their common aim. It is not an accident that these powers promote the two-Korea policy. The Park regime also promotes the two-Korea policy and has been good to their investments in South Korea.

The historic declaration of the July Fourth Joint Communique has been sabotaged, and the unification of Korea remains a dream of fifty million Koreans. The unification movement failed just as the democratization and the modernization programs have failed in South Korea. Democratization and modernization, as well as unification are left to be achieved by the Korean people themselves.

Notes

1. *Denver Post*, July 4, 1972.
2. *Ibid.*
3. *Minju Chosun*, Pyongyang, July 24, 1962.
4. *Korea Herald*, Seoul, August 16, 1968.
5. *Kyunghyang Shinmoon*, May 24, 1969. A year later, Kim Yong-sun, the successor of Shinn Tai-hwan, suggested further that a new policy, replacing the proposed nationwide election under U.N. supervision, might be adopted in view of the changing international situation. In addition, Kim also stated that a new educational policy based on the unification spirit was needed, rather than maintaining the old anticommunist policy in South Korea. See *Hankook Ilbo*, Sept. 3, 1971.
6. Shinn Tai-hwan, "Prospect for territorial Unification 11," in *DRP Bulletin*, Seoul, March, 1 970.
7. *Ibid.*
8. *Dung-dae* (*Lighthouse*), Pyongyang, No. 175, 1973, p. 23.
9. The Daily Yomiuri, Tokyo, Jan. 21, 1972.
10. *Ibid.* President Park Chung Hee proposed for the first time a nonaggression pact with North Korea on Jan. 18, 1974. Pyongyang had made a similar bid several times in the past. See the *New York Times*, Jan. 19, 1974.
11. Kim Sung-eun, Minister of National Defense for six years prior to his appointment as special assistant to President Park early in 1968, praised highly the newly organized militia force, armed with U.S. M-l rifles and carbines which had been shipped from the United States. See the Los Angeles Times, August 8, 1969.
12. *Newsweek*, Feb. 5, 1968, p. 9.
13. *The Nation*, Feb. 5, 1968, p. 162.

14. *Ibid.*
15. *Christian Century,* Feb. 7, 1968.
16. *Associated Press,* Dec. 23, 1969.
17. Walter Lippmann, *Newsweek,* Feb. 12, 1968.
18. Norman Cousins, "In the Wake of the Pueblo," *Saturday Review,* Feb. 17, 1968, p. 24.
19. Associated Press, Sept. 17, 1971.
20. *Japan Times,* August 15, 1972.
21. Ernst B. Haas, *The Uniting of Europe* (Stanford: Stanford University Press, 1964), p. 16.
22. *Hankook Ilbo,* Seoul, Feb. 20, 1970.
23. *Nodong Shinmoon,* Pyongyang, Dec. 17, 1967
24. Han Myong-gap, "My Working Life of Yesterday and Today," in *The Heart of the Fatherland* (Pyongyang, 1969).
25. Ko Tsul-su, *The Heart of the Fatherland.*
26. Haas, *The Uniting of Europe,* p. 101.
27. The Research Institute of Korea Society, "Prospects of Korean Economy" in *The Series of Social Research,* vol. 1, p. 75 (Seoul, 1965).
28. Karl W. Deutsch et al., *Political Community and the North Atlantic Area: International organization in the Light of Historical Experience* (Greenwood, N.Y.: 1957), p. 97.
29. For details on the story of the Kim Dae-jung kidnapping, see Harold Hakwon Sunoo, *Repressive State and Resisting Church: The Politics of KCIA* (New York and Fayette, Mo., Korean-American Cultural Association, 1976).
30. *Newsweek,* Oct. 30, 1972, p. 55.
31. *Korea Herald,* Seoul, July 17, 1972.
32. Japan Times, August 15, 1972.
33. *United Nations General Assembly,* A/C, I/PV, 1957, Nov. 14, 1973, p. 37.
34. Walter Ulbricht, *Whither Germany,* Helga Kargus and Harry Kohler, ed. (Berlin: n.p., 1960), pp. 187-88.
35. "Letter to Parliaments and governments of all countries of the world; Letter to the Congress of the United States," Pyongyang, April 6, 1973.
36. *United Nations General Assembly,* A/9145, Sept. 10, 1973, p. 5.
37. *United Nations General Assembly,* A/C, I/PV, 1958, Nov. 14, 1973, p. 37.
38. Ibid., p. 52.
39. Ibid.
40. "Letter to Parliaments," p. 5.

BIBLIOGRAPHY

I. OFFICIAL, SEMI-OFFICIAL MANUSCRIPTS AND DOCUMENTS.

A. Korean Sources

1. *Ilsongnok* is the memorandum of the kings covering a period of 150 years from the time of King Yongjo (1725-1776). King Yongjo personally began the writing of this political diary during his administration, and later the following kings continued the diary. Some of the memorandum has been written by the ministers. *Ilsongnok* is composed of 2329 volumes, edited at Kyujang-Kak, which was the center of the Confucian studies in the palace. *Ilsongnok* is one of the principal manuscripts used in the study of *Modern Korean History.*

2. *Singjongwon Ilgi* or *The Diary of the Office of the Royal Secretaries in the Palace,* is written by six secretaries who were appointed by the kings, and were assigned specific sections e.g., (I) Civil Office, (2) Revenue, (3) Ceremonies, (4) War, (5) Punishment and (6) Public Works. Each section kept a diary in regards to his own field. This system began during the beginning of the Yi Dynasty and continued until June 29, 1894. During Hideyoshi's invasion, the first half of the manuscript was burned by the invasion army, and was re-written during King Injo's reign (1623-1629). This work is known as *Singjongwon Kasu Ilgi* or *The Revised Diary of the Office of the Royal Secretaries in the Palace. Singjongwon Ilgi* is composed of 3047 volumes. The name of Singjongwon was not always carried since 1894,but sometimes called in order: *Singjonwon, Kungnabu, Pisokam, Pisowon, a Pisokam, and Kyujangkak,*. Under these various names there are an additional 198 volumes. These manuscripts are a principal source for the history of the Yi Dynasty.

3 *Tongmun Hwigo,* was edited originally at the command of Jongjo and Jong T-sang-sun, who were appointed by King Jongjo (1770-1800), who collected the materials on foreign affairs. *Tongmun Hwigo* is the collection of documents and notes of Korean *Foreign Affairs. Tongmun Hwigo* is composed of 129 books in 60 volumes, and divided into four editions: Original Edition, Special Edition, Additional Edition and Appendix Edition. The first modern printed edition appeared in 19361937, and the entire series up to 1894 is 96 volumes. The first edition covers the period 1643-

1786, but after 1786 books have been added as noted above. For the study of the foreign relations of Korea in modern times, *Tongmun Hwigo* is invaluable.

4. *T'ongmun Kwanji* or *Records of the Office of the Interpreters,* was originated by Yishi, a palace scholar, at the time of King T'sung-ryo'l (1275-1308) of the Koryo Dynasty. Many scholars were sent to China, Japan, Mongolia, Yojin, known as the four neighbours, but the Sada (serve China) policy began during the Yi Dynasty. *T'ongmun Kwanji* covers in large the relationship between Korea and China. In 1876, 1882, the government appointed numbers of scholars including authorities on China and Japan, to continue the editorial work. These works in *T'ongmun Kwanji* include historical background, reward for government services, Sada (serve China), Kyorin, (good neighbour policy to Japan), government personnel, past administration, and chronology. *T'ongmun Kwanji* is composed of twelve books in six volumes and is edited by Kim Kyo'ng-mun. (Third Edition 1881, Current Edition, Seoul, 1931,1939, 12 books).

5. *Jingjong Kyorinji* or *Extended Account of Relations with Japan, is* an additional piece of work to *T'ongmun Kwanji* by Kim Kon-so who is the great grandson of the author of *T'ongmun Kwanji.* Kim Kon-so discovered that there was a lack of the detailed study of Korea's relation with Japan in *T'ongmun Kwanji,* and he felt a need for more study in this field. Kyorinji, therefore, is devoted mainly to Japan, covering a period of about 350 years from the 25th year of King Sejong (1419-1450) to the 20tll year of King Jongjo (1777-1800).

It is composed of six books in two volumes published in Seoul, 1862. It is one of the best sources for the study of the foreign relations between Korea and Japan and partially was translated by H. B. Hulbert in the *Korea Review* (Seoul), 3 and 4 (1903-1904).

6. *Ts'o'ljong Sillok* or *The Annals of the King Ts'o'ljong,* Volumes 1-15, is a part of *Yijo Sillok* or *Yi Dynasty Annals* (10 copies of photolithographic printing by Keijo Imperial University-now Seoul National University of original four copies, 1930-1934). *Yi Dynasty Annals* is composed of 864 volumes. A set of *Yi Dynasty Annals* is available at the Library of Congress and also part of them are available at the University of Washington Library. *Yi Dynasty Annals* is selected historical material from *llso'ngnok and Singjo'ngwo'n llgi* primarily by the scholars who were appointed by the kings. Twenty copies of photolithographic printing were for the first time in 1930 1934 in use. Dr. Imanishi's *Richo-jitsuroki-ni tsuite* or *In Regard to the Movement of the Location of Yi Dynasty Annals* are very useful for the information on the annals.

7 *P'yo'ngan Kamyo'ng Kerok* or *The Official Record of the Governor's Office of P'yo'ngan, P'yo'ngan Pyo'ngyo'ng kerok* or *The Official Record of the Military Office of P'yo'ngan, ujo'ngbu Tingnok* or *The Record of the Legistlative Assembly,* Seoul, 1864-1882, are also important materials. *Jungbo munho'n pigo* or *Revised Official Encyclopedia,* 1907, Seoul, 250 books, is also one of the prime sources of the Korean history.

B. Japanese Sources:

1 *Jenrin Kokuhoki,* or *The Important Records of the Good Neighbor Policy* (3 Volumes) by Shuho, a Buddhist priest. From the beginning of the Japanese early relationship with China and Korea. Written in 1466, these volumes are one of the oldest of their kind.
2. *Chosen-shi* or *History of Korea,* is a most useful reference for the study of Korean history. *Chosen-shi* is composed of 38 volumes and was published during 1931-1938 at Seoul. *Chosen-shi* is a set of compilation of abstracts from Korean manuscripts and published sources. There is some biased editing in the series by the Japanese scholars but generally the volumes are well balanced throughout.
3. There are four important personalities in the Korean Japanese during the early stages of negotiations of the Treaty of 1876. They are Kaoru Inouye Iwakura, Okubo and Hirobuni Ito. Their biographies, therefore, are somewhat more important than the ordinary text of history. It seems that their four detailed biographies are invaluable for the students of this specific period.
    a. Inouye Kaoru-Ko Denki Henshu-kai, or The Editorial Association of the Biography of Count Inouye Kaoru, *Segai Inouye-Ko Den.* or *The Biopraphy of Count Inauye,* Segai, Vols. 1-5, Tokyo, 1933.
    b. Iwakura-Ko Kyuseki Hojon-Kai or The Association of the Preservation of the Historical Matters of Count Iwakura, K. Kagawa, Editor. *Iwakura-Ko Jitki,* or *The Facts With and Concerning Count Iwakura,* Vols. 1-3, 1904, Tokyo.
    c. Shoda Magoya, *Okubo Toshimichi-Den* or *The Biopraphy of Okubo Toshfmitus,* Vols. 1-3, 1911, Tokyo.
    d. Hiragawa, A., *Zoku Ito Hirobumi Hiroku* or *The Secret Memorandum of Ito Hirobumi,* 1930, Tokyo. Hisho Ruisan, or *A Collection of Secret Documents* Ito, Hirobumi, 1933-1934, Tokyo.
4 Other important miscellaneous sources:
    a. Mutsu, Munemitsu *Kenken roku, or The Story of Kenken,* 1895, reprinted in 1933 in Iwanami Bunko. *Kenken roku* is a detailed study of the

author's diplomatic life particularly the behind-the-scenes story of the Sino-Japanese treaties. Count Matsu is the Japanese diplomat who dealt with Li Hung- chang on many important diplomatic problems of the Meiji Era.

b. *Chosen Kosai Shimatsu,* or *The Korean Intercourse from Beginning to End,* edited by Okuyoshi, N.

c. *Zenrin Shimatsu,* or *The Good Neighbor Policy from Beginning to End,* Naikaku Bunko, Tokyo.

d. *Chosen Kankei Kosho Hishu* or *Edition on the Study of Korean Relations,* Naikaku Bunko, Tokyo.

e. *Nisshi Nikki,* or *Diary of a Japanese Envoy* (to Korea), 1879.

5 Of recent publications there are the following:

a. Hayashi, Kensuke, *Waga shichi-ju nen-wo kataru,* or *The Story of My Seventy Years,* Tokyo, 1935.

b. Hayashi, Kensuke, *Mutsu Munemitsu-haku* or *Count Mutsu Munemitsu,* Tokyo, 1935

c. *Asahi Shinbun-sha, Nippon Gaiko Hiroku* or *The Secret Record of Japanese Diplomacy,* Tokyo, 1934.

d. Kurino, Shin-ichiro, *Gaiko Omohide Banashi* or *Recollections on Diplomacy,* in *Bungei Shunshi,* Tokyo, January, 1935.

C. Chinese Sources:

1. Ch-ing-ch'ao Hsu Wen-Hsien T'ung-K'ao Four hundred *chuan* compiled by Liu Chin-tsao compiler's preface dated 1921. Movable-type edition of about the same time. 100 *ts'e,* Commercial Press edition, 4 vols: 749-11, 525 pp.

This work was compiled as a supplement to the *Huang Ch'ao Wen Hsien T'ung K'ao;* 300 chuan. Compiled under Imperial auspices, having been ordered in 1747, and follows in chronological order closely in arrangementi deals with the perjod of the Ch'ing Dynasty from 1786 to 1911.

2 *Li Wen-chung Kung Ch'uan-shu* ,edited by Uu Ju, 100 *ts'e* in 16 *han.* Lithographic reprint, 1921. Includcd are Li Hung-chang's memorials, correspondence, and other documents. Printed in 1908 under the title given. It has 165 *chuan,* with an additional *chuan* of biographical information.

3 *Ch'ing-chi Wai-chiao Shih-liao* by Wang Yen-wei and Wang Liang; 120 *chuan,* 1932-1935. This is a collection of documents on foreign relations during the last two regins (1875-1911) of the Ch'ing Dynasty. It was compiled by Wang Yen-mei (1843-1904), edited by Wang Liang, and

printed in 1932-1935. It is composed of 120 *ch'ai.*

4 a. *LiTai Min-Jen Sheng-Tsu Nien-Piso.* compiled by Liano T'ing-ts'an and published in 1933 by the Commercial Press, Shanghai.

    b. *LiTai Ming-Jen Nien-li pi-gu* compiled by Chiang Liang-Fu, and published in 1936 by the Commercial Press, Shanghai.

    A above is a table of the years of birth and death of more than four thousand persons of historical importance, dating from the time of Confucius down to 1900. It is based largely upon the *l-nien Lu-hui Pien.*

5 *T'ung-shang Yo-chang Lui-tsuan,* a collection of the commercial treaties originally compiled by Li Hung-chang. Edited by Hsu Tsung-Liang, Tientsin, 1886. 35 *chuan.*

6 *Ch-ing Kuang-hsu Ch'ao Chung-Jih Chiao-she Shihliao,* Palace Museum, 1932. 44.*ts'e.* (A collection of Siho-Japanese foreign affairs during Kuang-hsu of Ch'ing.)

7 Other important sources are the following:

    a. *Chao-Hsien Kuo-Wang Lai-Shu,* (the letters from the Korean kings) Palace Museum, Peking, 1932.

    b. *Ch'ing-tai T'ing-shi,* (a general history of Ch'ing Dynasty) by Hsieh I-San, Commercial Press, Shanghai, 1935.

    c. *Li Hung-chang*, by Liang Chi-ch'ao, Shanghai, 1901.

    d. *Liu-shin-nien Lai Chung-kuo yu Jih-pen, Sixty Years of Relations Between China and Japan,* by Wang Yun-sheng, vols. 1-7, Tientsin, 1932.

D. English Sources:

Department of State, Washington:
China Instructions. China Despatches. Japan Instructions.
Japan Despatches, Korea Instructions. Korea Despatches.
Navy Department, Washington.
Commodore R. W. Shufeldt, Cruise of the Ticonderoga.
Korean Letter-Book.
Congerssionale Record, Washington. 1866-1885.
Papers relating to the Foreign Relations of the United States transmitted to the U.S. Congress, 1864-1865, with the Annual Message of the President, Washington.
Papers relating to the Commercial Relations of the United States with Foreign Countries, 1870-1885, Washington.
Public Record Office, London.
Foreign Office, Diplomatic Correspondence, Japan Despatches, China

Despatches.

British Parliamentary Papers, 1866-1885, London. Correspondence respecting the Treaty between Japan and Korea, 1876 (C.-1530)

Despatches from her Majesty's Minister in Japan forwarding a Report on
Korea, 1883.(Japan No. 1, 1883)

Memorandum respecting the Trade between Japan and Korea 1877-1882.
(Japan No. 2, 1883)

Treaty of Korea, November 26,1883-1884 (C.-4044)

II. THE TREATIES:

British and Foreign State Papers. Vol. LXXIV. Vol. LXXV.

Carnegie Endowment for International Peace, Korean Treaties and Agreements, Washington, 1921.

China, Imperial Maritime Customs, 111. Miscellaneous Series: No. 19.
Treaties, Regulations etc., Between China and other Powers, 1876-1889,
Shanghai, 1891.

Chung, H. Korean Treaties, N. Y., 1919.

Gaimusho Chosabu Henshu, or *The Research and Investigation Section at The
Department of Foreign Affairs.*

Dai, Nippon Gaiko Munsho, or *The Documents on the Foreign Relation of Great
Japan,* Vol. 5, Tokyo, 1939.

MacMurray, J. V. A. *Treaties and Agreement with and Concerning China,*
1894-1919, New York, 1921.

Rochhill, W. W. Ed. *Treaties and Conventions With or Concerning China and
Korea,* 1894-1904, Washington D. C., 1921.

Ⅲ. PERIODICAL LITERATURE:

Akagi, N., "Chosen-ni Okeru Tenshukyono Ryunyu-To Tenrei-mondai-ni
Tsuite," or "Uber das Einfliessen des Christentums in Korea und die
Ritsufrage" in *Shigaku Zashi,*

Band Li, Nr. 6, Tokyo

Bearnadou, J.B., "Korea and the Koreans," *National Geographic,* 2, 1890, pp.
232-243.

Branat, M. Von, "Drei-und-dreissig Jahre," *Ost-Asien,* Leipzig, 1901.

Chosen Cakuho, Tenri City, nara pref., Japan.

Chosun Ilbo, Seoul.

Chung-Ang Ilbo, Seoul.

Cory, Raplh M., "Gregorio de Cespedes, Korea's First European Visitors,"

Transactions of the Korean Branch of Royal Asiatic Society, Seoul, 1937.

Dennett, T., "Early American Policy in Korea, 1883-1887: The Services of Lt. George E. Foulk," *Political Science Quarterly,* XXXIII, pp. 82-103.

Denny, O.N., "China and Korea," *Congressional Record, 50 Congress, 1st Session, 1888,* pp. 8135-8140.

Habang Ilbo, Seoul, 1946

Hogaku, Ronso, *Kyoto Teikoku Daigaku Hogakukai.* Kyoto, 1906.

Ike, Nobutake, "Truimph of the Peace Party in Japan in 1873," *The Far Eastern Quarterly,* Vol.ll, No. 3, Columbia Press, New York, 1943.

Ka-Pyok, Monthly, Seoul, 1921-1925.

Kim Ki-Jon, *Chosun T'segunSa Pyolgangan,* Vol. 5, No. 3, Seoul, 1930.

Korean Repository, 1892, 1895-1899.

Korean Review, 1901-1905, 1919-1922, Korean Information Bureau, Philadelphia, 1919-1922.

Korean Review, Korean-American Cultural Association, Inc., Seattle, Washington, 1948.

Korean Student Bulletin, published by Korean Student Federation of North America, New York, 1926 1939.

Ky'ong-Ilyang, Daily News, Seoul, 1945.

Lin, T. C., "Li Hung-chang: His Korean Policies, 1870-1885." *Chinese Social and Political Science Review,* 19, 1935, pp. 202-233.

Lowell, Percival, "A Korean Coup d' Etat," *Atlantic,* 58, 1886, pp. 599-618.

New Korea, A Weekly, Los Angeles. 1946-1950.

New York Times, New York.

Pak Tal-Song, "Wiin Nangwan Noryok," or "A Great Man and an Effort." *Pyol-gan-gan,* Vol. 5, No. 3, Seoul, 1930.

Pollard, R.T., "American Relations with Korea," *Chinese Social and Political Science Review,* Vol. XVI, No. 3, October 1932.

Puts'un-Sanin "Hann-mal P'ung-un-e Kol-ts'ul-dil," or "The Personalities in the Last Decade of the Yi Dynasty," *Shin-Tong-A,* Vol. 2, No. 3, Seoul, 1932.

Reskishi, Chiri, or *History and Geography,* a monthly, published by Nippon Rekishi Chiri Gagu-kai, Vol. 1~85, Tokyo, 1900-1940.

Rekishi to Chiri, or *History and Geography,* published by Shigaku Chirigaku Tohokai Henshu once in two months, Vol. 1, No. 1, Vol. 30, No. 6, Tokyo, 1918-1932.

The Ryoksa Hakbo, The Korean Historical Review, Seoul, Korea

Sam Tsolli, a monthly, Seoul, 1938.

Sands, William Franklin, "Korea and the Korean Emperor," *Century Magazine,* Vol. XLVII (New Series) pp. 577-584, 1905.

Sasaki, B. "Nikkan Kakusho To-Kenpo," or" The Japanese-Korean Agreement and the Constitution," *Kyoto Hogakukai,* University of Kyoto, Vol. 4, No. 9, Kyoto, 1906.

Shigaku, quarterly, Mida Shigakukai, Keio University, Vol. 1-19, Tokyo, 1926-1941.

Shigaku, Zashi, or *The Historical Magazine,* monthly, Imperial University, Shirinohensanjo, Vol. 1-51, Tokyo, 1890-1940.

Shirin, or *The Journal of History,* quarterly, published by The Shigaku-Kenkyu-Kai, The Historical Society, The Kyoto Imperial University, Vol. 1-16, Tokyo, 1916-1931.

Sin-Tong-A, a monthly, Seoul, 1932-1934.

Takeda, Katsujo, "Nissen Boeki Shijyono Miura to Wakan," *Shigaku,* Keio University, Vol. No. 3, 1922.

The Voice of Korea, a weekly, Korean Affairs Institute, Washington D.C.

The Times, London.

Tokrip, or *Korean Independence,* Los Angeles.

Tong-a Ilbo, or *The Oriental Daily,* Seoul.

Tong Kwang, a monthly, Seoul, 1931-1933.

Treat, P.J., "China and Korea," *Political Science Quarterly,* 49, 1933, pp. 506-543.

T'sa, Sang-Ts'an, "lmo-gunnan-e-ho-Sang-gi" or "The Memory of the Imo (1882) Military Affair," *Pyol-gan-gan,* Vol. 3, No. 5, Seoul, 1928.

Tsiang, T. F., "Sino-Japanese Diplomatic Relations, 1870-1894," *Chinese Social and Political Science Review,* 17, 1933, pp. 1-106.

Vonliarliarsky, V.M., "Why Russia Went to War with Japan: The Story of Yalu Concession," *Fortnightly Review,* 93, 1910, pp. 816-831, 1030 1044.

Wada, Enjiro, "Kim Ok Kiun Son Sange Juktun-nal, "or "The Day of the Death of Mr. Kim Ok Kiun," *Pyolgan-gan, No. 5,* Seoul, 1927.

OTHER BOOKS BY HAROLD HAKWON SUNOO

Peace and Unification of the South and the North Korea (1991)

Christianity and Juche Idea (1990)

South Korean Economy (1989): *La Corea du Sud: Economic dune dictature et enjeux democratiques* (1988)

China of Confucius: A Critical Interpretation (1985)

America-no Tirema: Asia-no seisaku-to kankoku minshu (in Japanese, 1984)

America's Dilemma in Asia: The Case of South Korea (1979)

Nippon-no Kunkoku Shugi (in Japanese, 1980)

Korean Women, co-ed. (1978)

Koreans in America, Ed. (1977)

Repressive State and Resisting Church: The Politics of CIA in South Korea (1976)

Japanese Militarism (1975)

Whither Korea? co-ed. (1975)

Korea: A Political History in Modern Times (1970)

Modernization and Democracy in Korea (in Korean, 1967)

Vietnam War and Southeast Asia (in Korean, 1965)

Korean Grammar (1952)

Korean Textbook (1944)